LOSING FAITH IN FAITH

From Preacher To Atheist

by Dan Barker

D0915276

FFRF, Inc.
Madison, Wisconsin

© Copyright 1992 by Dan Barker

First paperback printing, September 1992
Second paperback printing, February 1998
Third paperback printing, Summer 2000
Fourth paperback printing, February 2003

First hardback printing, June 2006

ISBN 1-877733-13-X

Printed in the United States of America

Typography and cover design by
KC Graphics, Inc., Madison, Wisconsin

Excerpts from *The Woman's Encyclopedia of Myths and Secrets*
by Barbara G. Walker, © 1983 by Barbara G. Walker. Reprinted
by permission of HarperCollins Publisher.

Published by
Freedom From Religion Foundation, Inc.
PO Box 750
Madison WI 53701-0750
(608) 256-8900
www.ffrf.org
info@ffrf.org

To Norman S. Barker

my
only father

Other books by Dan Barker:

Just Pretend: A Freethought Book For Children
          (FFRF, Inc., Madison Wisconsin, 1988)

Maybe Yes, Maybe No: A Guide For Young Skeptics
          (Prometheus Books, New York, 1990)

Maybe Right, Maybe Wrong: A Guide For Young Thinkers
          (Prometheus Books, New York, 1992)

Edited by Dan Barker:

Paradise Remembered: A Lenape Indian Childhood,
          and other stories by Herbert Barker, Sr.
          (Dan Barker Productions, Madison Wisconsin, 1991)

Also published by FFRF, Inc.

Women Without Superstition: 'No Gods - No Masters'
          Edited by Annie Laurie Gaylor. The collected writings
          of women freethinkers of the 19th & 20th centuries.

Woe to the Women: The Bible Tells Me So, by Annie Laurie Gaylor

The Born Again Skeptic's Guide to the Bible,
          by Ruth Hurmence Green

One Woman's Fight, by Vashti McCollum. Historic Supreme Court
          victory removing religious instruction from public
          schools. Warmly told from the family's perspective.

American Infidel: Robert G. Ingersoll, by Orvin Larsen

World Famous Atheist Cookbook, edited by Anne Nicol Gaylor

See: **http://www.ffrf.org/books/**

Contents

Part 3: Re-examining The "Good Book"

Part 4: Critiquing Christianity

Part 5: Spreading The Best News

Part 6: Separating State And Church

Part 7: Exposing Christian Morality

Part 8: History Or Myth?

Part 9: A Match Not Made In Heaven

Songs

Unless indicated, all bible verses are from the *King James Version*. Although not always the best translation, the *KJV* is most likely to be familiar.

The style of this book is not to capitalize "bible" unless it is a specific bible, such as the *King James Bible*, or when it appears capitalized in a quote by a believer. (After all, popular usage only capitalizes "dictionary" when referring to a particular book, such as Webster's Dictionary.) The same is true with "gospel," which is capitalized only when discussing one of the first four books of the New Testament: Matthew, Mark, Luke, or John. "God" is capitalized only when referring to the biblical deity.

A careful reader might notice that I sometimes say that my ministry lasted "seventeen" years, and at other times I say "nineteen" years. This is because I am not sure if I should count my two years of evangelism during high school. The length of time between my first and last sermons was nineteen years.

A very special acknowledgment goes to Anne Gaylor and Annie Laurie Gaylor for proofreading, editing, and encouraging the completion of this book. A warm thank-you to R. A. for providing invaluable resources, both scholarly and financial, towards the content and printing of this book.

Introduction

IN APRIL, 1984 I received a short, intriguing letter from a man in California, who signed it with a distinctive black autograph. It was unusual, not only to hear from a male praising my book on bible sexism, but because he described a 180-degree about-face:

"I was a minister for a number of years," Dan Barker wrote, "and I used to proudly wave the Bible as the only standard for humanity. I have just emerged from a painful five year process of conversion from Christianity to atheism. Only a few months ago did I announce my change. It is interesting to read the Bible now, with new 'eyesight,' so to speak. I used to read all the ugly parts of the Bible, but for some reason they were 'invisible,' even beautiful. I was taught that God was perfect, loving and righteous—so there could be no question in my mind as to his character. Any apparent contradiction or ugliness could be ignored in the faith of the 'mystery' of God's ways. I'm glad those days are over. Thanks for your book.

"I feel a need to participate in some kind of group that can be an answer to religious thought. Believe me, I know how strong religious thinking is. I spent years in evangelism, missions and Christian music. I wrote two popular Christian musicals which are still being performed around the world. Now that I have left Christianity I still feel the energy to make a kind of contribution to values and intelligence. (Perhaps I am feeling a kind of reverse penance?) I love your style of directness, your guts to tell it like it is; and I want to do the same thing. Please send me any promotional material you may have. Thank you."

I found this letter a confounding, fascinating mystery. Who would credit a fundamentalist minister with rejecting his faith and embracing a *feminist* viewpoint of the bible? But it has become a standing joke between us that I never answered this letter. Since I was not a staff employee of the Freedom From Religion Foundation at that time, I passed the inquiry on to my mother, Anne Gaylor, president and a founder of the group. As soon as he received membership information, Dan Barker joined the Foundation, and the rest, as they say, is history.

A warm correspondence between my mother and Dan commenced. Anne encouraged him to write an article about his deconversion for the Foundation's newspaper, *Freethought Today*. By the middle of May, the Foundation had received Dan's classic article, the title essay which forms the nucleus for this book. My mother wasted no time in securing his acceptance to speak at the Foundation's annual fall convention.

She learned from his requested bio how interesting Dan was, even aside from his dramatic story of deconversion from missionary to atheist: fluent in Spanish; belonging to two I.Q. societies; a cat-fancier who likes to juggle, throw boomerangs, play chess by correspondence, compose puzzles and "read everything I can." His background was interesting in its own right. His father's family is descended from native Americans, making Dan a member of the Delaware Tribe of American Indians. His father, prior to a fundamentalist conversion, had played trombone in Hoagy Carmichael's radio band, and had appeared in movies, including a charming trombone solo, with Judy Garland singing, in "Easter Parade." (It's easy to identify his look-alike father Norman if you ever catch the uncut version on the late show.)

When the producers of the "A.M. Chicago" television show with host Oprah Winfrey called the Foundation offices in 1984, seeking guests who had rejected religion, Anne immediately suggested Dan. It was a natural. The producers of this then-local show were excited by the idea of a fundamentalist preacher-turned-atheist, and decided to fly Dan into Chicago from California. My mother, I, and a former Catholic also were invited to appear. We had never met Dan, and I recall our slight trepidation over inviting him to be a spokesperson for the organization. Was he for real? What if his new-found apostasy turned out to be a passing phase? Would he be intimidated by Christian criticism? After my mother and I were interviewed, Dan was brought in during a commercial. We held our breath, and then, as he began speaking, relaxed in relief and admiration. We had found a "kindred spirit"—if it can be said that there is such a thing in the freethought community—an articulate, well-read, appealing and fearless freethought advocate.

Since Dan's debut, when he dubbed himself a "baby atheist," he has devoted his energies to the freethought movement, through one-to-one conversations, articles, op-ed pieces and letters to the editor, activism, talkshow interviews, debates with ministers and evangelists, speaking engagements before diverse groups and campuses, and through his music. His deconversion makes him an attractive personality for the media, and he has been drafted to appear as the token atheist on such national talkshows as "Donahue," "Good Morning America," and "Sally Jessy Raphael." He joined the staff of the Freedom From Religion Foundation in 1987 as official public relations director, and since then has become our "ambassador of freethought."

The Freedom From Religion Foundation began hearing requests from freethinkers to publish a book by Dan in the mid-eighties, after the regular appearance in *Freethought Today* of his column, "Pagan Pulpit." His original autobiographical articles appear here, augmented with new memoirs. Dan's personal story of conversion from faith to reason is as compelling to the believer as to the unbeliever. Here is a book you can hand that relative who insists on debating religion with you.

Losing Faith In Faith also contains major new works of solid freethought research and commentary, including "Why I am An Atheist" and "Is The Bible Moral?" as well as a valuable exposition on "Jesus: History or Myth?" Also anthologized are many of Dan's professional writings for the Foundation. These selections include pamphlets written by Dan that sell and sell, op-ed pieces published around the nation, and articles expressly written in response to requests from freethinkers or staff begging for some readable material on particular debating points. These make *Losing Faith In Faith* virtually a one-stop resource and reference for any freethinker engaging in debate on the merits of the bible and theological claims. Included by popular demand, is our feminist, freethought wedding ceremony of 1987, one of the most-requested articles we have ever run in *Freethought Today*. The lyrics to Dan's freethought songs are interspersed throughout the book.

Not just another philosophical treatise preaching to the already *de*converted, the material in *Losing Faith In Faith* is tried and tested. These are, after all, the ideas which freed Dan from religion and which have freed some others in his family circle who were as entrenched in religion as he was.

Dan's story offers hope for freethought. It is proof that reason, humanism, feminism, and logic can triumph over indoctrination, authority, and faith. *Losing Faith In Faith's* intellectual vigor, clear thinking, and thorough examination of the claims of religion make it an indispensable contribution to the freethought movement.

Annie Laurie Gaylor, Editor, *Freethought Today*
Freedom From Religion Foundation, Inc.
Madison, Wisconsin
April, 1992

Prologue: "I Changed My Mind"

I N SEPTEMBER OF 1984 I found myself on Oprah Winfrey's "AM Chicago" television show. This was the first time I had *ever* spoken publicly about my atheism. Less than nine months before, I was preaching the gospel to appreciative audiences, and now here I was, about to attack everything I had once professed. I was nervous. I had been on television before, as a Christian musician, but this was entirely different.

Anne and Annie Laurie Gaylor of the Freedom From Religion Foundation (the first atheist friends I had ever knowingly met) handled the first segment of the show, discussing freethought. After the commercial, the camera pointed to me and the lights came up.

"Joining me now," said Oprah, "is a former ordained minister of seventeen years who gave up his religion: Dan Barker. So, tell me your story, Dan, the *ex*-reverend."

"I was one of those guys who would walk up to you on the street and tell you about Jesus Christ," I began, "and would convince you to say the sinner's prayer, would convince you that you were a sinner deserving of damnation, tell you about Jesus's love, read the bible to you and pray with people like yourself. I was an evangelist, and I loved the gospel, the calling of the ministry—and I've changed my mind."

13

"What made you change your mind, Dan?"

"I could give a little levity," I said. "In thirty years of going to church and being a preacher, I never got to sleep in on Sunday mornings." [laughter]

"Well, Dan, for goodness sake! Sleep in on Saturday!" Oprah quipped. "But, what is the real reason? You woke up one morning and you said, what?"

"No, for me it was a five-year struggle. I was always in love with reason, and intelligence, and truth. I thought Christianity had the truth. I really believed it. I dedicated my life to it."

"When did you become a Christian," Oprah interrupted, "when you were a little boy?"

"I was raised in church, but at the age of fifteen I dedicated my life to Jesus Christ. I accepted a calling of God on my life to be a minister, to be an evangelist, and at that age I went out and started sharing. I went to the mountains and jungles of Mexico to share my faith for years. I traveled the United States, standing in parks and on street corners, telling people about Jesus's love. A fifteen-year-old evangelist."

"I know," Oprah said. "I did it in the third grade. I understand."

"And I really haven't changed. I'm still searching for intelligence and reason and values, and I still love the truth. I'm still the same person, the same minister who wants to know what is real and what is true, and I have decided that the evidences for Christianity are not solid evidences. The bible is an unreliable document, and it is a very uninspiring document. My heart cannot accept what my mind rejects."

"And you have decided what? There is no God?"

"I am an atheist."

"You went for seventeen years as a minister to not believing in God! What does that say about you?"

"That I was wrong," I replied.

LOSING FAITH

Part 1

1

Spreading the Good News

WHEN I WAS fifteen I received a "call to the ministry." It happened one evening during a week-long series of "revival" meetings in the mid-1960s at Anaheim Christian Center, in California. This church later became Melodyland Christian Center when they bought the Melodyland entertainment property across the street from Disneyland. This was during the start of the Charismatic Movement, a somewhat "respectable" Pentecostalism within mainline churches, now sporting hundreds of independent congregations and loose associations of independent churches around the world, but back at that time existing primarily as a new, wild, exciting, undefined phenomenon that woke up a lot of dull congregations. The meetings at our "spirit-filled" Charismatic church were intense, bursting with rousing music and emotional sermons. People would speak in tongues and practice faith healing, prophecy (a contemporary divine message), discernment ("diagnosis" of what is wrong with someone, such as "evil spirits"), and other "gifts of the spirit" (*charismata*) listed in the twelfth chapter of First Corinthians which accompany being "baptised in the Holy Spirit."

As I was sitting in these meetings, observing and participating, I felt an intense desire to sing, pray and worship, and I experienced strong inner sensations that I could only describe as "spiritual" at the time. It felt like I was

17

communicating with God and that He was talking to me through His Spirit. I had never had these feelings in any other context, and since they were triggered by the "spirit-filled" environment, I assumed that I was experiencing confirmation of the reality of God. It felt very real, and very good. I had been taught, and I believed, that spiritual sensations are not necessary because it is faith alone that saves you; but it was nice to feel something that wonderful, supplementing my faith.

I listened to sermons about how the end of the world is near, and about how Jesus is returning "any moment" to claim his followers and to judge the earth. I heard preachments from the bible about Jesus's mandate to "Go ye into all the world, and preach the gospel to every creature." I thought God was talking directly to me.

I couldn't articulate it at the time, but as a teenage boy I was probably starting to wonder about my upcoming career decisions. (Girls weren't supposed to wonder about such things.) Whether it is called "spiritual" or "psychological," it must have made sense to be able to settle the question of what I wanted to do with my life, avoiding the struggle that so many other young people experienced. I decided to accept the "call" and become a minister. I wanted the rest of the world to share in the gospel, to be saved, to know Jesus personally, to have meaning in life, and to create a better world. It felt right. Satisfying. I had a purpose in life.

I figured I didn't have to wait until I was ordained to start preaching. I was "born again" and "filled with the spirit." I was "called to preach," and since God is powerful, there was no reason he couldn't start using me right away. There was no time to waste since the world could end at any moment. I started carrying my bible to school, talking to friends about Jesus. I joined up with some evangelistic teams that took weekend missionary trips to poor villages in Mexico, just below the California border, a short drive from the Los Angeles area, where I preached my first sermon alongside the dusty bank of an irrigation canal in a tiny village called Morelia. (It wasn't a real sermon. It was a memorized paragraph in Spanish, but since I was standing in front of a group of people, I figured I was preaching.) During the summer I went on week-long and month-long trips into Mexico and the Southwest, with such groups as YUGO (Youth Unlimited Gospel Outreach), the Frank Gonzales Evangelistic Association, and others. Anticipating that I might become a missionary to Mexico, I devoted myself to mastering Spanish.

My Spanish teacher at Anaheim High School was James Edwards. He is still there, the District head of the foreign language department. I had heard that Mr. Edwards was some kind of agnostic, or unbeliever. This was not long after the 1963 Supreme Court *Schempp* decision that removed prayer and bible reading from the public schools, so we Christians were quite recently wounded and sensitive about the issue of religion on our campus. Anaheim High School was forced to end the tradition of opening each day with a prayer broadcast to each classroom. But I figured that I possessed a calling that originated from a higher level than the Supreme Court, and I proudly took my bible to school, being careful to place it on top of my other books so that everyone would notice.

I often took *two* bibles to school: the *King James Version,* and another in Spanish. When Mr. Edwards would give us some "free time" to read Spanish literature, I would open my *Reina de Valera* Spanish bible and kill three birds with one stone: learn Spanish, worship God, and prepare myself for my missionary career. I noticed that Mr. Edwards noticed.

One day as I was leaving the class, Mr. Edwards called me over to his desk and told me that he wanted to talk with me after school. I told him that I would come back to the classroom right after gymnastics workout. I was pretty sure he wanted to talk about my bible in the classroom, so I prayed all day long, through gymnastics. After showering I steadied my nerve and walked into his classroom. He shut the door and went back to his desk, where I was standing.

"Dan," he said, "I notice that you have been bringing your Bible to class."

"Yes," I said, swallowing hard.

"And I notice that you have been reading your Bible during class time."

"That's right," I answered, ready to do battle with Satan. I was his top student, so I didn't fear any academic lecture.

"Well, then," he continued, hesitating, "maybe you are the one who can help me."

I didn't know what he meant. "Help you, Mr. Edwards?" I asked, anticipating some kind of trick.

"Yes. Maybe you can help me make sense of spiritual things." His whole manner changed, and he started talking like a humbled man, friend to friend, hurting. I had never seen him like this. He told me that he was an agnostic, but that he was starting to realize that there must be something "out there." He had seen and read some things about ESP and other psychic phenomena, and he was discovering that a strictly materialistic view of life was unrealistic and unsatisfying.

"Dan, you seem so confident and happy. Tell me what you believe."

So, I told him that I believed in God, that God was revealed in the Bible, that we were all sinners, that God sent his son Jesus to die for our sins, that we could confess our sins and accept Jesus as our personal savior and be Born Again, becoming "new creatures" without guilt and with a joy and purpose in

19

life. I took advantage of the opportunity, telling him everything I believed. He listened quietly, and as our meeting ended, he thanked me and told me he wanted to hear more.

We met every day or so after that, me talking, him listening. I kept stressing the "reality" of God, and the difference between believers and nonbelievers. We became friends. Sometimes during break between classes he would stop me in the hallway and ask about some verse in the bible. I felt self-conscious, knowing that some of my friends and other students were watching and wondering.

Early one day Mr. Edwards found me in the hallway and excitedly pulled me over. He was grinning. "Dan, I had to tell you. I did it!"

"What happened?" I asked, surprised that the important head of the district language department was treating me like a buddy.

"I accepted Jesus as my personal savior. This morning as I was getting out of my car in the parking lot, it hit me. What you were saying about making a conscious, deliberate decision to accept Jesus made perfect sense. I prayed right there in the parking lot and it happened! My sins are forgiven and I am now a child of God."

After that, he and I became "brothers" in Jesus, spending much time discussing the bible. In spite of the recent court decision about prayer and bible reading in the schools, we started a prayer and bible-study group on campus. We knew it was not allowed, so we called it an "advanced Spanish literature and discussion" group, and the first, and only, piece of "Spanish literature" we discussed was the bible—the *Reina de Valera* translation, which is roughly equivalent to the *King James Version* in style and popularity. (This was a front, folks.) Some other Christian students caught on to what was happening, and this group became a focal point for devout students on campus, including a couple of other high-school evangelists like myself.

James Edwards came to my church a couple of times, and introduced himself as "Dan Barker's son," meaning that I was his spiritual father, which embarrassed me. After I graduated from high school, I would occasionally visit the campus and speak to the expanding Christian group we had started, which was now being held during the lunch hour in the choir room instead of a classroom because it had grown so big. They all wanted to hear about my missionary and evangelistic adventures, and to meet the guy who started it all. I have heard that James Edwards is still holding the illegal religious meeting on campus, twenty-five years later, though he now calls it what it is, a Christian bible study and prayer meeting!

Experiences like this helped to cement my commitment to my "calling from God." I was effective. I was encouraged and appreciated. I felt like I was set apart for a special ministry, and I devoted every day to it. I got involved with several local ministries, including the Peralta Brothers, a family of second-generation Mexicans who sang Spanish gospel music to the Hispanic churches in southern California and northern Mexico, for whom I played piano and with whom I occasionally sang bass, baritone, or tenor. During a trip to Mexico in 1965 I met Manuel Bonilla, a Christian singer, and he asked me to arrange some music for him, and to play the piano on one of his first recordings. When I was sixteen I recorded *"Me Ha Tocado"* ("He Touched Me") for Manuel, and that recording became a best seller in the Spanish-speaking world. It was exciting to hear myself, a high school student, playing piano on Sunday morning Mexican radio stations. Manuel went on to become the leading Spanish Christian recording artist in the world, selling in fifteen countries for many years, using me to arrange and produce most of his recordings.

Right after high school, before going to bible college, I spent a year with a cross-country evangelistic team, singing, playing the piano, preaching, doing house-to-house witnessing and getting doors slammed in my face but winning converts. Playing the accordion standing on picnic tables in the park. Joining hands in a restaurant inviting the rest of the customers to join us as we sang about Jesus. Holding week-long "revival" services in large and small churches across the continent. Driving through freezing blizzards and blinding desert sandstorms. Approaching members of the Hell's Demons motorcycle gang in Phoenix to invite them to hear a sermon about the love of Jesus. Holding "drug awareness" musical rallies in public high schools that were just a front for us to invite the students to an evening evangelistic rally (we didn't know the *first* thing about drug prevention—just a few songs and drug-addict stories). Playing soccer and basketball in countless prisons across Mexico and the United States so that we could witness for Jesus during half-time. Rounding up hundreds of barefoot children in Mexican towns and villages so that we could sing Protestant choruses to them and tell them about *Jesús*. Hiking up and down mountainsides and ravines to remote villages that required an additional interpreter since the Indians there didn't know Spanish. (I tried to learn some Mayo, but all I can remember now is *Dios ta enchianía*—"God bless you.") Inviting ourselves to local TV and radio stations, with some success, so that we could get the gospel to as many people as possible.

I traveled with one evangelistic/missionary team every summer for many years, and they were hectic summers. (I suspect that my present problem with kidney stones originated with that experience—I spent hours and days driving through blistering heat, drinking little, pushing the team, stopping to visit the bathroom only when absolutely necessary.) During the summer of 1967, I dehydrated and spent three days in Guaymas, Mexico on my back being fed glucose through an intravenous needle, eating nothing, sucking on ice cubes. That was the same summer I got mangled by a dirty German Shepherd dog in the town of Zacapu, in the mountains between Mexico City and Guadalajara, when I hopped over the adobe wall behind a church into the next yard to retrieve a volley ball. I didn't get rabies, but I went into some kind of nervous shock and slept for more than two days after being medicated at a local clinic. I know that kind of living is reckless, but at the time I figured it was justified. The world was going to end any day, and it was no great achievement to give my life and body to Jesus, as a "living sacrifice."

In 1968-1972 I attended Azusa Pacific College, an interdenominational state-accredited Christian school, and majored in Religion. Looking back I can see that most of the religion courses I took were simply glorified Sunday-School classes. I took only one class in apologetics—I think it was called "Christian Evidences"—and I don't remember that we delved very deeply into the evidences or arguments for or against Christianity. It wouldn't have mattered much anyway, since I wanted to be out in the streets, preaching the gospel, not stuck in some classroom doing worthless philosophizing. My attitude at the time was that it is not necessary to know how an automobile works in order to drive one; nor is it imperative to become a biblical scholar or theologian in order to save souls from damnation. All of that could be left to the experts who, I believed, had already figured it all out and who could provide the historical, rational, documentary, archeological evidences if anyone ever asked. (No one ever did.) I believed that my education was secondary to my calling. I was pretty successful at winning souls, probably much more successful than my professors, and although I got pretty good grades, I didn't see what difference it made. I coasted through college, spending almost every evening and weekend out somewhere preaching or singing, doing the *real* work of the ministry. I did enjoy the two years of New Testament Greek, which I still find useful. It added a certain credibility to my sermons to be able to throw in an occasional Greek word here and there, though I don't think the listeners cared much.

I was disdainful of ordination. I figured I didn't need some piece of paper bestowed by humans to tell me what I already knew: that I was personally called by God to the ministry of the Gospel. I was even unimpressed with educational degrees. After four full-time years I fell a few units short of graduation and never went back to finish. (In 1988 Azusa Pacific University allowed me to transfer units from the University of Wisconsin, and sent me my degree in "Religion.")

At Azusa Pacific I met a singer named Carol. We were married in 1970, and had Becky (1973), Kristi (1975), Andrea (1977), and Danny (1979).

I was an associate pastor in three churches in California: Arcadia Friends Church, Glengrove Assembly of God (La Puente), and Standard Christian Center (in the town of Standard, in the gold-rush "Mother Lode" foothills north of Yosemite). The pay was not great, but it provided a minimum of financial security for my family. Although I did a lot of preaching to the congregations, filling in for the main pastor, directing the choir, organizing activities for the youth group, I never was the senior pastor, and never wanted to be. I always considered myself first an evangelist. After a few years of working in local churches, directing choirs whose dedication and energy were admirable but whose musicianship was something less than average, counseling people with problems that I hadn't the faintest idea how to approach (except with bible verses and prayer), and working on sermons that I thought were insightful but bounced off the listeners like rain on an umbrella, I found myself getting restless to "hit the road" again. I could only stick it out in each church for about a year and a half before moving on.

I felt bad leaving the Standard Christian Center. We had a good program going there, but I felt it was a dead end for my evangelistic calling. Rather than just leave, with nowhere to go, I decided that I wanted to return to cross-country evangelism, and asked the church if they would consider sending me out as their "missionary" to the world. They reluctantly agreed, but not before the main pastor, Bob Wright, convinced me that for my ministry to be more credible, I would have to become an ordained minister. I yielded to the pressure to become "official," and one Sunday morning the church held an ordination service for me, directed by Pastor Bob, in which I was asked a few questions about my calling, and a few questions about theology, and then was unanimously ordained. They presented me with an ordination certificate, which no one has ever asked to see. (According to state law, an ordination is granted by an individual state-recognized congregation, whether or not that church is part of a denomination. A license is what many denominations grant to an individual minister, with or without ordination.) Looking back, I think I did more "soul winning" before I was ordained.

For the next eight years my wife and I lived "by faith" as touring musical evangelists. Neither of us had a job. All our belongings were in storage for the first year, and we lived "on the road," accepting housing from church members, friends and relatives. When Carol was pregnant with our second child, we booked a national evangelistic itinerary, hopped in our yellow chevy Nova with about $100 cash, and bounced around the country from church to church, not charging for the ministry but accepting freewill "love offerings," trusting that we would get enough money from each service to allow us to make it to the next. I remember many hopeful, desperate, prayerful moments sitting in

23

the car after the service, opening the offering envelope to count the money. We normally got between $50 and $100 per meeting, sometimes nothing at all, rarely more than $150. It was easy to book Sunday meetings; it was difficult to keep busy the rest of the week. When my wife was pregnant with our third child we rented a small house, and she decided to stay home from the long trips, tending to the family, joining me only when I ministered in the Southern California area.

In the summer of 1975, during one of our very first cross-country tours, we heard from our contact in Ohio that the week of meetings had been cancelled. (More likely someone had dropped the ball). I told them that we had no choice, that we had to come to Ohio since our itinerary took us further east the following weeks. If nothing else we would have to sit out the days. When we got to Ohio I managed to book a couple of small last-minute meetings, but otherwise we just sat around in these people's home watching the clock tick. Not able to endure the inactivity, I went down to their basement piano and wrote a musical for children based on an idea that my wife had had when she directed a Sunday-School Christmas program. I figured maybe we could use the musical if we ever went back into local church work.

That fall back in Southern California I did some transcription for a friend who wrote children's songs, and played part of my new musical for her. She liked it and said that she had heard that Manna Music, a Christian publisher, was looking for a new children's musical for Christmas, and she gave them a call. They invited me in, they liked the musical, and in 1976 "Mary Had a Little Lamb" was published and recorded. It was Manna's best seller for a couple of years, and it remained near the top of their list for many years. This gave my ministry a new focus. I followed up with another musical, "His Fleece Was White as Snow," and some additional songs, and suddenly found that I was getting invitations to perform as a national Christian songwriter. The musicals were done by churches and Christian school children, and are still being performed. (I continue to receive royalties.) "Mary Had a Little Lamb" was translated into Spanish and German, and has been performed around the world at Christmas time. (Mary was the mother of Jesus who was the "lamb of God." Get it?)

"His Fleece Was White As Snow" is an Easter musical. It is based on the fact that Jewish law required an offering of an unblemished animal, and that Jesus was supposedly the final, "sinless" Passover sacrifice. Although I have always been happy with the musical and artistic quality of this work, I am now embarrassed by the lyrical content. I actually kill off the star of the show, a cute, unspotted lamb named Snowy!

I was working on a sequel, "Everywhere That Mary Went," based on the few biblical references to Mary, noticing that her appearances always point to her son's ministry—a not-so-subtle rebuke to Catholicism. I'm glad it was never written.

Once I was invited to a church in East Los Angeles to be guest conductor of one of my musicals. Instead of using children, this congregation used the adult choir. They all dressed up like camels, sheep, pigs, and donkeys, and it was quite amusing. But what I remember most about that evening was the huge painted wood sign hanging from the ceiling above the pulpit, saying, "Jesus is Coming Soon!" The sign needed to be cleaned and repainted, and I noticed cobwebs around the edges.

One of my adult octavos, "There is One," was sung by Robert Schuller's "Hour of Power" choir on television. I know this because I received broadcast royalties from ASCAP. As a "street evangelist" renouncing wealth, I didn't think much of Schuller's upper-class Christianity. I was still involved with Manuel Bonilla, and with my new contacts in the recording industry I was able to produce, arrange, and play keyboards on at least a dozen more of his albums, including some innovative Christian children's albums in Spanish that became immensely popular. On subsequent trips to Mexico we would hear the children singing the arrangements exactly as we had recorded them, which they had learned from the radio. One of the songs that Manuel and I co-wrote is a samba entitled, "No Vengo Del Mono," mocking evolution.

No Vengo Del Mono

by Manuel Bonilla and Dan Barker

No vengo del mono, no, no, no!   I don't come from a monkey, no, no, no!
Ni de la naranja, ja, ja, ja!   Nor from an orange, ha, ha, ha!
La cigüeña no me trajo, jo, jo, jo!   The stork didn't bring me, ho, ho, ho!
Pues, ¿Quién me hizo a mí?   Then, who made me?

Fue mi Dios!   It was my God!
Fue mi Dios!   It was my God!
Fue mi Dios quien me hizo a mí.   It was my God who made me.

No tengo gorila de mamá,   I don't have a gorilla for a mama,
Ni tengo chimpancé de mi papá.   Nor a chimpanzee for a papa.
Fue mi Dios quien me hizo a mí.   It was God who made me.
Te hizo a tí, me hizo a mí.   He made you, he made me.

Besides working in evangelism, as a preacher or as an invited Christian songwriter, I made a living by doing record production in the Los Angeles area for various clients, mostly Christian, in addition to Manuel Bonilla. I never did any big-time productions, but I hired some of the best Hollywood musicians for the background music who were willing to work on what might be called "B" projects: a pastor and his wife singing duets, a junior-high-school choir going on tour, songwriters making demos or records for their touring ministry, various Christian vocalists who needed records and cassettes to sell at their meetings, and literally hundreds of children's songs for Christian publishing companies and curriculum houses. I once did a marathon recording session of 128 songs in one week for Gospel Light, a leading publisher of Sunday School and Vacation Bible School (VBS) curriculums. I wrote much of the music and produced all the early recordings for Joy Berry's company, Living Skills Press, which then was connected with the educational division of Word Books, the largest Christian publisher. Word published a collection of some of my religious children's songs in a book called "Ready, Set, Grow!" I worked in more than a dozen studios in the Hollywood/Los Angeles area. I didn't pretend to be the best producer in town, but I was dependable, I was always on schedule, I communicated well with the religious clients, and I was cheap. I figured that this was part of my evangelistic "calling," since it was spreading the word by publishing Christian music.

I also did a lot of piano playing for other Christian artists during my ministry. I played the piano for Pat Boone on one occasion, to a crowd of more than 10,000 in Phoenix. Jimmy Roberts (of the Lawrence Welk Show) used me as his accompanist on a two-week cross-country tour. I played piano for a Christian rock band called "Mobetta" (with lead singer Jim Bolden) for many years, performing mainly at public high-school assemblies. For about ten years I directed a singing group called "The King's Children" in Southern California, ministering in local churches, and also serving a very brief term as musical hosts for the television show hosted by Dr. Gene Scott on Channel 30 in Glendale. It was for the "King's Children" that I wrote my first song: "I'm Tellin' The Whole Wide World About Jesus."

For several years I wrote and produced Gospel Light's summer VBS "mini-musicales." In 1984, when I announced my atheism to everyone, I was right in the middle of writing another Gospel Light VBS mini-musicale, and I told them that I would understand if they decided to find another writer. They were on a deadline, and they were used to working with me, saying that it would be hard at that point to find someone else to pick up and stay on schedule and budget, so I finished writing and producing it! They knew I was an atheist, but I understood their predicament, so I told them to credit me under

During a Sunday morning service at the Christian Center in Standard, California, I was ordained to the ministry. The ceremony involved a question-and-answer test of my knowledge and commitment, as well as a "laying on of hands" by the elders and a vote by the congregation.

27

the pseudonym of "Edwin Daniels" (Edwin is my middle name). I think they were figuring that my atheism was just a temporary phase, a momentary confusion, and that perhaps by the end of the project I would return to my former commitment, maybe as a result of working with them.

I
t was some time in 1979, turning thirty, when I started to have some early questions about Christianity. I was working on a musical for Manna Music (working title, "Penny," about the one lost lamb who was missing from the other ninety-nine), which I never finished because my views were changing while I was trying to write it. I didn't have any problems with Christianity—I loved my Christian life, I believed in what I was doing, and it felt right. I just got to the point where my mind was restless to move beyond the simplicities of fundamentalism. I had been so involved with fundamentalist and evangelical matters that I had been ignoring a part of myself that was beginning to ask for attention. It was as if there were this little knock on my skull, and something was saying, "Hello! Anybody home?" I was starving and didn't know it, like when you are working hard on a project and you forget to eat and you don't know you are hungry until you are *really* hungry. I had been reading the Christian writers (Francis Schaeffer, Josh McDowell, C. S. Lewis, etc.), and really had not read much of anything else besides the bible for years. So, not with any real purpose in mind, I began to satisfy this irksome intellectual hunger. I began to read some science magazines, some philosophy, psychology, daily newspapers (!), and began to catch up on the liberal arts education I should have had years before. This triggered a ravenous appetite to learn and produced a slow but steady migration across the theological spectrum that took about four or five years.

I had no sudden, eye-opening experience. When you are raised like I was, you don't just snap your fingers and say, "Oh, silly me! There's no God."

The first timid steps away from fundamentalism were more traumatic than the huge leaps that came later. When you are raised to believe that every word in the bible is God-inspired and inerrant, you can't lightly change your views on scripture. For example (I'm embarrassed to admit this now, but it was a big deal back then), I used to believe that Adam and Eve were literal, historical persons. The bible said they existed, so they existed. I could have no true spiritual fellowship with anyone who thought otherwise because to doubt God's Word was to doubt God himself. But I got to thinking that there are parts of the bible that are obviously metaphorical. Jesus's story about the

28

Prodigal Son, for example, is just a story. It doesn't matter if the Prodigal Son ever existed as a real person; Jesus told the story to make a certain point. The message contained within the story is what is important, not the literal truth of the story itself. But if Jesus could do this with the Prodigal Son, then why couldn't the early Hebrews have done this with Adam and Eve? The Garden of Eden could have been a Hebrew "parable" to explain God's involvement with the human race regarding origins, good and evil. I wrestled with this for months. My first tiny step away from fundamentalism was not to discard the historicity of Adam and Eve (because, unlike the Prodigal Son, the bible does not specifically say that Adam and Eve is a parable), but to realize that it shouldn't matter to me whether other Christians held it historically. I could still fellowship with these "liberal" Christians. Sounds silly, but that was a big step in the direction of tolerance.

Since I had become an independent evangelist, with no local church to answer to, I perhaps felt freer to experiment intellectually, and to investigate what other Christians believed. From there I continued a gradual swing across the theological continuum, becoming less and less fundamentalist, more of a moderate evangelical. I was accepting invitations to preach and sing in a variety of churches, including many liberal congregations.

After a couple of years I migrated further into a more moderate position where I still held the basic theological beliefs but discarded many lesser doctrines as either nonessential, or untrue. I remember the way I was thinking then: every Christian has a particular hierarchy of doctrines and practices, and most Christians arrange their hierarchy in roughly the same manner, with the existence of God at the top, the deity of Jesus just below that, and so on, down to the bottom of the list where you find things like wearing jewelry or makeup in church. What distinguishes many brands of Christianity is where they draw their line between what is essential and what is not. Extreme fundamentalists draw the line way down at the bottom of the list, making all doctrines equally necessary. Moderates draw the line somewhere up in the middle of the list. Liberals draw the line way up at the top, not caring if the bible is inerrant or if Jesus existed historically, but holding on to the existence of God, however he or she is defined, holding on to the general usefulness of religion, and to rituals, which many people claim to need despite its irrelevance to reality, to give structure or meaning to life.

As I traveled across the spectrum, I kept drawing my line higher and higher. I studied some liberal theologians, such as Tillich and Bultmann. These authors, though perhaps flawed in this or that area, appeared to be intelligent and caring human beings who were using their minds, doing their best to come to an understanding of truth. They were not evil servants of Satan attempting to distract believers from the literal truth of the bible. I came to respect these thinkers and even to admire some of their views, without necessarily embracing the whole package. After a couple more years of evolving theology, I became one of these ominous liberals myself and remembered back to some of the fundamentalist sermons I had preached against such heresies. There is a place in the bible where God says, "I know thy works, that thou art neither cold nor hot: I would thou wert cold or hot. So then because thou art lukewarm, and neither cold nor hot, I will spue thee out of my mouth." *(Revelation 3:15-16)* To the fundamentalist, liberal Christians are worse than atheists. I remembered having despised liberals who have "a form of godliness, but denying the power thereof," and who offer more of a temptation away from devout faith than any atheist could pose. At least with atheists, you know where they stand. Attempting to learn what a liberal Christian believes is like trying to nail jello to a tree. To my amusement, I had become one of those despised liberals.

At that time in my migration I believed in a God, but had no idea how to define God. I was not uncomfortable with Tillich's idea that God is the "ground of all being," or some other vague notion. All the while, however, I was still getting invitations to preach and sing in various churches, many of which were fundamentalist and conservative evangelical. Long before that time I had stopped my direct "soul winning" sermons, and managed to tailor my message to be palatable to just about any church. This was easy since most of the churches that invited me at that time were interested in my published music, so I could simply perform a number of songs with brief inspirational introductions, keeping the "preaching" to a minimum. I was able to adjust each presentation to the expectations of the audience, becoming more or less evangelistic according to the flavor of each individual church. Even then, I felt hypocritical, often hearing myself mouth words about which I was no longer sure, but words that the audience wanted to hear.

In my "secret life" of private reading I was impressed with enlightened writers in science magazines. In particular, an article by Ben Bova about "Creationist's Equal Time" in OMNI Magazine turned the lens around so that I was gazing back at the fundamentalist mindset. The article laid bare the dishonesty of the "equal time for creationism in the science class" argument by asking how many Christians would welcome a chapter about evolution inserted between Genesis and Exodus. I became more and more embarrassed at what I used to believe, and more attracted to rational thinkers.

Finally, at the far end of my theological migration, I threw out all the bath water and discovered there is no baby there. There is no basis for believing that a God exists, except faith, and faith was not satisfactory to me. It was like peeling back the layers of an onion, eliminating the nonessential doctrines to see what was at the core, and I had just kept peeling and peeling until there was nothing there. The line that I was drawing under essential doctrines kept rising until it popped right off the top of the list! To my list of religious metaphors, which included the Prodigal Son and Adam & Eve, I now added God. That made perfect sense.

It was during the summer of 1983 when I told myself that I was an atheist. Nobody else knew this for about six months. Some of my friends, and my wife, were suspecting something, but since I still had a pretty successful ministry, the outward appearance was as if nothing had happened.

Between the summer and Christmas of 1983 I went through an awful period of hypocrisy. I was still preaching, and I hated myself. I was living with the momentum of a lifetime of Christian service, still receiving invitations to minister, still feeding my family with honoraria from preaching and singing engagements in churches and Christian schools. I knew I should have just cut it off cleanly, but I didn't have the courage. In preparation for some vague need for what might lie ahead, I took some classes in computer programming, telling my wife that I enjoyed computers and that perhaps I could supplement our income with this skill. Right away I got a job as a part-time programmer for a company that makes monitoring systems for the petroleum industry. A year later, I worked as a programmer/analyst designing and coding dispatching systems for the railroads, and I got to do a lot of fun, on-site installation and testing for N&W and Burlington Northern in the midwest. This provided me with the perfect transitional job—a way to ease out of evangelism. I was still preaching on the weekends and doing some occasional record production at nights, but in my mind I was giving up the ministry.

In November I accepted an invitation to preach in Mexicali, a Mexican city on the California border. I like that town. Even though I no longer believed what I was preaching, I still enjoyed the travel and the many friends I had south of the border. The night after a service in an adobe mission in the Mexicali Valley south of town, I went to bed on a cot in the Sunday School room that doubled as a guest room for visiting preachers. I didn't sleep much that night. I remember staring up at the ceiling as if I were gazing right up into outer space, contemplating my place in the universe. It was at that moment that I experienced the startling reality that I was alone. Completely and utterly alone. There is no supernatural realm, no God, no Devil, no demons, no angels helping me from the other side. There is just nature, and I am a part of nature, and that is all there is. It was simultaneously a frightening and liberating experience. Maybe first-time skydivers or space-walkers have a similar sensation. I just knew that everything had come to rest, that the struggle was over, that I had truly shed the cocoon, or snakeskin, and I was for the first time in my life that "new creature" of which the bible so ignorantly speaks. I had at last graduated from the childish need to look outside myself to decide who I was as a person. This was no mystical experience, but it was refreshing. I suppose it would be a similar exhilaration to learn that the charges against me had been dropped for a crime of which I had been falsely accused. I was free to put the matter aside and get on with life.

The last time I stood before a congregation as a minister was during the Christmas week of 1983. I had flown up to San Jose for meetings in one church, and after that I drove over to Auburn, northeast of Sacramento, to do a Christmas concert for a young, growing congregation meeting in a public school building. The arrangement was for the Auburn church to provide my plane ticket back to Southern California. They had made a hoopla of the occasion, and as I entered the building I saw that the church was packed with townsfolk.

Before the meeting, I met in a side room with the pastors and other leaders of the church, and we all held hands in a circle and prayed for God's blessing on the concert. They were especially excited because there was a man in the audience who was in church for the very first time. The man's name was Harry, and he was the town atheist. Everybody in town liked Harry. He was a respected businessman who would give you the shirt off his back, but he wasn't a Christian. Harry had recently remarried, and his new wife had become born-again, and she had finally convinced him to attend church with her for the Christmas concert because Harry loved music, and it wouldn't be like sitting through a boring sermon. They were all praying that Harry would be influenced by my ministry that evening, and that Harry would turn his life over to Jesus Christ. They laid hands on me and prayed loudly that God would instill a very special blessing on my ministry.

I was dreading the concert. I was hating myself with every ounce of disdain. As I walked up to the large grand piano that was sitting under the only light in the auditorium, I tried to scan for Harry, though I had no idea what he looked like. They were all seated in the dark, and the effect was that I was singing to a faceless congregation, which meant that I was singing to Harry, in my mind, and to Harry alone. I went through the motions and sang my songs, thinking how utterly stupid they were, and how ridiculous I must be sounding to Harry. Between songs I did my patter, tiny sermonettes that tied things together. It was one of the most difficult things I have ever had to do in my life. It took the most tremendous effort just to get the words out, words that I no longer believed. It can still make me cry to think back on that moment. At a couple of points I just stopped talking, deadly silent, blank as a new sheet of paper. The audience must have thought that the Holy Spirit was moving in my soul. I somehow managed to fall back on showmanship and willed myself to continue. At one point near the end of the concert I almost lost it. I was singing some of my particularly dumb lyrics and almost stopped right in the middle of the song to say, "This is crap." I wanted to turn to the audience and say, "Harry! You are right. I'm sorry. There is no God, and this is mumbo-jumbo nonsense." But I avoided that dramatic possibility and got through the concert somehow. They weren't going to give me my plane ticket until after the meeting.

Afterward, certain people were invited over to the pastor's home for Christmas refreshments. Harry and his wife showed up. I guessed that this was supposed to be my opportunity to "lay it on" to Harry and convert him to Jesus, but I didn't talk to Harry at all that night, except maybe to shake his hand. I was so ashamed of myself, so embarrassed at how we were treating this man, singling him out like he had a social disease. I sat near the Christmas tree and Harry sat across the room in an armchair, and I avoided eye contact. How I was wishing that he and I could just get together and talk. I don't know if I would have liked Harry or not. I don't know if he would have had anything profound to say, or if he would have even cared about my dilemma. But I respected the man immensely. He had the courage to be different in a hostile religious environment. Sometime during the little party the pastor spoke up and said something about how nice it was for all of us to get together to celebrate the birth of the Savior, and Harry immediately said, "Not all of us." He was fearless. He seemed proud to be identified as an atheist, and happy to be an independent thinker.

I never preached another sermon again. I never accepted another invitation to perform a religious concert. To be fair to myself and to everyone else, I knew that I had to cut it off quickly and cleanly. In January I sent a letter to everyone I could think of—ministers, friends, relatives, publishing companies, Christian recording artists, fellow missionaries—and told them that I was no longer a Christian, that I was an atheist or agnostic (I didn't have the distinction clear in my mind then), that I would no longer accept invitations to preach or perform Christian music, and that I hoped we could keep a dialogue open.

The responses to that letter were all across the board: everything from friendly curiosity to outright hatred. But I wasn't at all worried about the reactions; I had done what I had to do. Some responses in fact welcomed my invitation to dialogue, and that is where I began sharpening my skills as a freethought debater, as a new kind of "minister," I guess, spreading the truly good news that there is no Sin, no Hell, no Cosmic Guilt. (Once a preacher, always a preacher?)

My Christian marriage came apart in 1985, due mostly to the tension between viewpoints. I lost a lot of friends, but in retrospect I consider that if the friendships could not tolerate a difference of philosophy, they were not true friends in the first place. Some friendships are based on mutual respect and admiration regardless of views, and others are contingent on things that are external to the relationship, such as belonging to the same church or club. Leaving the club is a sure way to test the friendship.

Then I discovered a whole new batch of friends. Though harder to find, the world is filled with freethinkers who are smart and caring individuals. I moved to Madison, Wisconsin, where the Freedom From Religion Foundation is located, and in 1987 I married Annie Laurie Gaylor, editor of *Freethought Today*.

My parents were fundamentalist Christians, and they now admit that they made some mistakes in raising their three boys. My mother says that their motivation was to do "the right thing." In spite of the religious overkill, I had a very good childhood. Sure, we were indoctrinated with an illegitimate and intolerant world view; but my parents were good people in spite of their faith. They raised me with good principles. One thing they taught me by example is that you should never be ashamed to speak what you think is the truth. My earlier ministry in the pulpit and my current activism for freethought are really one and the same thing. The message has changed, but I haven't. I still consider that I have a "calling." Not a calling from out there somewhere, but a calling from within myself to pursue truth, and not to be afraid or ashamed of what I find.

Blood Brothers

by Dan Barker

When I was four years old,
I had a little friend named Joshua.
Whenever I was alone,
He would come over to play.
Cookies, cartoons, and punch—
He liked all the same things that I liked.
Cheerios and milk for lunch,
Butterflies, balloons, and kites.

Chorus: We were blood brothers, pals forever.
     We were as close as we could be.
     Nobody else could see him,
     But he was real to me.

Whenever I was sad,
I would send Joshua a letter.
He never wrote me back,
But he'd always come right over to play.
I'd never been to his house,
But I knew exactly where he lived.
His Daddy was Oh, so nice
To let us have fun every day.

When I was five years old,
I just got so busy with schoolwork,
Many new friends to get to know—
Joshua moved away.
Sometimes I missed him so—
We had such good times together;
But I know he had to go.
It works out much better that way.

We were blood brothers, pals forever.
He was my very best friend.
Nobody else could see him.
I now know he was just pretend.

Now that some years have passed,
I can look back and smile at my childhood,
At the times when it hurt to grow up,
Like when Joshua moved away.

2

Ripples: From Faith to Reason

EVERYTHING WE DO in life has ripple effects. Sometimes we see the results, and sometimes we don't.

On January 16, 1984, I sent out this letter announcing my new-found atheism to more than fifty colleagues, friends, and family members:

"Dear friend,

"You probably already know that I have gone through some significant changes regarding spiritual things. The past five or six years has been a time of deep re-evaluation for me, and during the last couple of years I have decided that I can no longer honestly call myself a Christian. You can probably imagine that it has been an agonizing process for me. I was raised in a good Christian home, served in missions and evangelism, went to a Christian college, became ordained and ministered in three churches as Assistant Pastor. During those years I was 100 percent convinced of my faith, and now I am just about 100 percent unconvinced.

"The purpose of this letter is not to present my case. Yet, I will point out that my studies have brought me through many important areas, most notably: the authenticity of the Bible, faith vs. reason, church history—and a bunch of other fun subjects like evolution, physics, psychology, self-esteem, philosophy, parapsychology, pseudo-science, mathematics, etc.

"I'm not sure what the purpose of this letter is, except to serve as a point of information to a friend or relative whom I consider to be important in my life, and with whom I could not bear to be dishonest. I have not thrown the baby out with the bath water. I still basically maintain the same Christian values of kindness, love, giving, temperance and respect that I was raised with. Christianity has much good. Yet I feel I can demonstrate an alternate, rational basis for those values outside of a system of faith and authority. Of course, I admit, those values cannot save me from the fires of hell—but it is irrational to hold a fear of something which is non-existent, and to allow that fear to dominate one's philosophy and way of life.

"If the Bible is true I will run to it willingly. If there is a God, I would be silly to deny Him. In fact, the little child in me still sometimes wishes to regain the comforts and reassurances of my former beliefs. I am a human being with the same fears and feelings we all share. The Bible says those who seek will find. You know me. I am constantly seeking. And I have not found. Right now I am somewhere between the agnostic and the atheist, although I spend a great deal of time in both camps.

"There is much more to say, and I would greatly appreciate any input you can offer. I would suggest, though, that before we attempt any meaningful dialogue, we should understand as much as possible about each other's thoughts. If you wish, I will send you any of various papers I am preparing, including: The Bible, Faith vs. Reason, . . .

"Finally, I am not your enemy. Our enemy is the one who doesn't care about these subjects—who thinks that you and I are silly to be concerned with life and values. I intend no disrespect to you, or anyone who is genuinely interested in religion and philosophy. It is the non-thinker who bothers me and with whom meaningful interaction is impossible.

"Dan Barker"

Today I would write a completely different letter, but that's where I was at the time. The "little child" nostalgia lasted about a year, and has been replaced with embarrassment that I ever believed. The distinction between agnostic and atheist has been clarified.

After I put the copies of my letter in the mail, I felt relief. The only thing to do was wait for the reactions.

"Sorry to hear about your recent commitment to be uncommitted to the Lamb of God that you so beautifully had written about and put to music in such a successful way," wrote Assembly of God pastor Mark Griffo, a former co-missionary who had been one of the kids in a church choir I directed, and whom I had encouraged to enter the ministry. "I realize you're not my enemy, as you stated, but Satan is! He's out to rob, kill and destroy life. . . . My heart tears within me trying to figure out the answer you'll give [children] when they ask you, 'Dan, can you write more songs so my future children can know the source of love, Jesus Christ, like you do?' I'm praying for you always and looking forward to your resurrection."

To Mark, I am dead.

Mark's wife Debbie was less charitable: "Meaningful interaction you want? There is nothing meaningful about the beliefs that you have chosen. . . . I am sorry that the Lamb you once wrote about is no longer Lord of your life. To really know the almighty God, Saviour, King, all knowing, all powerful, all loving creator of you and I [sic], is to *never* leave Him. . . . Humble yourself in the sight of the Lord."

David Gustafeson, director of Pacific & Asia Christian University in Hawaii who had been a co-pastor with me at a church in La Puente, wrote: "I was somewhat shocked by your letter . . . I guess I'll just have to pray harder. . . . I believe an acid test is to simply cry out to 'God' (whether you believe or not) and ask Him to radically and ruthlessly correct you if you are wrong. . . . it would be better for God to use 'any means' to show you the truth, than for one to find out he had been misled too late. . . . I have read your papers, and of course they present a good case. I wouldn't expect anything else from someone as brilliant as you. I think the contradictions in the Bible show the beauty of God speaking through frail humanity, and yet keeping the main message of the bible intact." I sent Dave an exhaustive response, and received from him a box of fourteen cassette tapes from a theologian.

I had penned a note at the bottom of my letter to Gospel Light Publications, telling them that I would understand if they decided not to continue working with me. We were in the middle of a project. Wes Haystead wrote: "Thanks for honestly sharing your journey with me. I promise not to start bombarding you with tracts and Josh McDowell books . . . As to our continuing to work together, I vote aye. Provided of course that you can get me three songs for Sunrise Island real quick. Sort of sounds like schedule takes precedence over principles, eh? Actually, I value highly your talent, your sensitivity, your flexibility and your friendship. Therefore I hope we can continue working together until one of us converts the other or you feel the goals of our projects are incompatible with your directions."

I did go ahead and finish writing the Sunrise Island Vacation Bible School mini-musicale for Gospel Light. It was a strange feeling to be working professionally on a project with which I disagreed philosophically, but I justified the hypocrisy by noting that Gospel Light would have had a hard time staying on schedule and on budget if they changed horses in the middle of the stream, and that they were fully aware of my change in views.

Hal Spencer, president of Manna Music, publisher of my musicals and other Christian songs, wrote: "My immediate response is that this can't be true and that you are only going through a doubting time of your life. However, knowing you, I'm afraid that there is more to it than that. . . . I will be asking the Lord to guide me also if there is something that I can say which might influence your feelings." Hal and I met for lunch a couple of months later. Although he is quite knowledgeable about the music industry (his father was Tim Spencer, one of the "Sons of the Pioneers"), he has not given much thought to theology or philosophy. He kept pointing to a leaf in a flower arrangement next to our table, saying, "How did that leaf get here?" After I addressed the problems with the design and first-cause arguments, he turned back to the leaf and said, "But I just can't imagine how that leaf got here without a Creator." We later bumped into each other in the Nashville airport in 1985 when I was debating a minister and he was at a country music awards ceremony, and the chance meeting was so surprising that he said, "See, this proves there is a God!" Though I have not written anything else for Manna Music, my musicals are still selling, and Hal has continued to treat me professionally.

Eli Peralta was my ninth-grade Spanish teacher. He was one of the Peralta Brothers Quartet with whom I had ministered during high school. He wrote: "Thank you for letting us know the status of your life change. Rest assured that the pureness and clarity of your communication is being accepted in a spirit of love and consideration. It is significant that in the days prior to your letter arriving, I was reminiscing about our fellowship and friendship of years gone by and wishing that we could visit sometime. . . . My brothers and I still think of you with many fond memories and fun times we had together. I have informed them regarding your journey from faith to reason, and even though it has made a significant emotional impact on us, I for one feel a deep sense of calm and still consider ourselves friends!"

Jill Johnson, wife of the associate pastor at the Auburn church where I did my final Christian concert, sent me a surprisingly tolerant letter: "I totally support your sincere desire to seek out the truth in love. I feel for you because in a certain sense the decision you've made has got to be a cataclysmic event not only for you and those you love (I keep thinking of your Dad for some reason), but also to so many outside your home sphere. But I believe in honesty and since you believe with all of your being in what you espouse, I'm sure it's a necessity for you to continue following this path. . . . When you 'break the rules' there are always those who will have a desire or a need to punish or judge or condemn . . . and I just hope and pray most people will be gentle with you even though you and they are not in agreement. . . . I am so happy that I was able to hear you in concert and I have no doubt that you will continue to create beauty in spheres other than the Christian one."

Loren McBain, pastor of the First (American) Baptist Church of Ontario, California which my family was attending and where I had briefly served as interim Music Director, wrote: "I'd really like to stay in touch with you if only for lunch once in a while. I'd especially be happy to play chess when you want, the odds now clearly in my favor since God will be on my side!" Perhaps with patience running thin, the same man wrote a less friendly letter ten months later: "You and I both know Dan that you have heard, and you fully understand 'God's rules for living,' and that you are now living by your own rules. . . . I understand them as simple disobedience."

A co-worker, Scoti Domeij, wrote: "Does this mean that we won't be seeing each other at MusiCalifornia [a Christian conference] (Ha! Ha!) . . . I am not offended or the least bit surprised by your journey from faith to reason. Your questioning has surfaced in many different ways when we have been together. I do feel some sadness and wonder what hurt and deep disappointments have precipitated your journey from faith to reason."

Shirley and Verlin Cox had regularly helped me arrange meetings in Indiana. "I must admit to a bit of a shock," Shirley wrote. "At first I wanted to write a 'preachy' letter to you but after much reflection and prayer I realize you know more 'Bible' than I and Verlin will ever know. We haven't been through college the way you have . . . Yes, we are broken hearted that you've rejected our Lord but we have hope and our prayers will continue . . . While in Florida last year we were delighted to see your 'Mary Had a Little Lamb' and churches in Indiana in our area still present it. Oh yes, 'Mary Had' was a puppet show on TV."

I received a letter from Sister Tammy Schinhofen, of whom I have no memory: "About eight years ago you were instrumental in my accepting Jesus as my *personal Savior*. . . . I thank God that I am a jewel placed in your crown. Don't let the enemy take away or tarnish your crown."

One of my best friends was a man who was largely responsible for the promotional success of my musicals, an iconoclastic believer. It is not easy for him, being gay in a fundamentalist community. He wrote: "I don't know if I can say I 'enjoyed' your letter—there must be a better word. I know how you feel. I've surely been there myself (may still be there). What struck me so forcefully was the realization that 'the Christians' react to your questioning as they do, *not* because you have lost *your* faith, but because you have lost *theirs!*"

Many of the letters were sincere, but without content. "I don't have any answers," wrote one friend. "It's not a matter of logic or intelligence," wrote another. "Human intellectual ability and capacities, no matter how great, are not sufficient," wrote a woman faith-healer.

Many of the letters contained *ad hominem* arguments. One co-worker told me that I had "given in to the desires of self life," and a neighbor wrote that I must be "hurt and bitter." Another tried to get me to admit my "deep wounds." A woman preacher announced that "sometime along the way you became angry with God," and a co-pastor told me that "you are on a selfish journey at the expense of your own integrity."

The high-school aged daughter of one of my close Christian friends, living in a missionary compound, wrote: "I can't say I pray for you every day because I don't. . . . Right now in school we are learning Biology from a teacher who only knows about philosophy, medieval history, and English literature. . . . How do you think we got on this planet?" I wrote to her and her mother, who live in a Christian community connected with the University of the Nations, operated by the charismatic evangelistic organization Youth With A Mission in Kona, Hawaii, challenging the school to a debate on the issues. I never heard a thing from them.

About a month after my letter was sent out, I received a call from the Vice President and Dean of Academic Instruction at Azusa Pacific University, Dr. Don Grant. He and the director of alumni affairs met with me for lunch one afternoon to see what had gone wrong with one of their emissaries. Don had been the director of the Dynamics Chorale for which I played piano and sang on scholarship during my years at Azusa Pacific. It was an amicable lunch, but they nevertheless were fishing for some way to get me back in the fold. The conversation was at a more articulate level than most, but when I responded with scholarly and documented arguments that they had never heard, they fell back on the same old *ad hominem* responses, psychological guesswork, and so on. As we were walking back to our cars I thanked them for their time and willingness to discuss the issues, and I made them a challenge. I told them that I would be willing to participate in a debate at Azusa Pacific against any one of their professors on the question of the existence of God. I never heard from them again.

I have never seen Manuel Bonilla again (the Mexican Christian singer), but we did talk on the phone a couple of times. He told me that he just "knew" that the spirit of God was on my life, particularly since I had arranged and recorded an especially inspired version of a religious song on one of his albums in late 1983, playing the piano with conviction behind his singing. I asked Manuel if he would be surprised to know that while I was arranging and playing that song, I was a secret atheist and that my inspiration was musical, not spiritual. He didn't say a word. When I talked with Manuel again in 1985, he was friendly, but told me that he would be willing to offer me some counseling to help me get through my struggles. The only thing I could think of was to say that I was happy, and to thank him for his friendship.

Shortly after my letter was sent out I met for lunch with Bob and Myrna Wright, two very close friends. Bob had been the pastor of the Standard Community Christian Center, and had conducted my ordination ceremony. They told me that they wanted to apologize to me. They said that they were sorry that they had not sensed my inner struggles leading up to my rejection of Christianity. If they had known, perhaps they could have helped me avoid the discouragement and disappointment that led to my change of views. This was a difficult meeting because I loved and respected these people and I knew that they were sincere. I told them that my deconversion had nothing to do with any personal problems, that it had to do with the nature and content of the Christian message itself. I tried to explain that *ad hominem* counseling was beside the point. They didn't get it.

To press my point I decided to create some cognitive dissonance. "What would happen to me," I asked, "if I were to die right now?" They were silent. "Bob, you're an ordained minister. You know your Bible. What happens to unbelievers?"

"Well, the Bible says they go to hell," he responded.

"You know me," I continued. "I'm not a bad person. I'm honest. If I walk out of this restaurant and get killed by a truck, will I go straight to hell?" They didn't want to answer that question, squirming in their seats. "Well, do you believe the Bible?" I pressed.

"Of course," Myrna said.

"Then will I go to hell?"

"Yes," they finally answered, but not without a great deal of discomfort. Perhaps it was not a nice lunch topic, but I wanted to make the brutality of Christianity real to them. I knew it would be hard for them to imagine their God punishing someone like me. I later heard that they were perturbed with me for having coerced them to say I was going to hell. It forced them to acknowledge that, as much as we wanted to be friends, their religion considers me the enemy.

The letters I received and the conversations that followed my "enlightenment" were all across the board. They displayed love, hatred, and everything in between. Many friendships were lost, others transformed, and still others strengthened. Of all of the letters and attempts to get me back in the fold, not a single one had any intellectual impact. Although I was saddened at having discontinued some relationships, I find I do not miss them. I suppose it is much like a divorce; even though there were good times and happy memories, once it's over, it's over.

Few of the letters offered any defense of bible contradictions. No one presented any documentary evidences from the first century. Not a single rational argument for the existence of a god beyond the where-did-we-come-from garden variety. Most of the responses centered on things like humility, shame, attitude, prayer—in short, "spiritual" intimidation.

Dave Gustafeson's challenge to "cry out to God" is nothing less than intellectual dishonesty. One of my friends asked me simply to "pretend that Jesus is real and he will make himself real to you." Have either of them ever "cried out to Buddha" or "pretended that Allah is real" as an acid test of their existence? These people are asking me to lie to myself. Anyway, they should know better. They should know that I had already "cried out to God," that I had frequently prayed and "felt the spirit" within me, that I had many times gone through the motions. They don't seem to realize that I was not seeking inner confirmation—I was seeking objective, external evidence. Besides, even if I did manage to "fake it," would an omniscient god not know this?

The almost universal tone of the letters and conversations was that I was the one with the problem. None acknowledged that my change of mind might be an indictment of Christianity. Some of them formerly had come to me for counseling, but now they no longer want to learn from me. (I don't think they should have to.) They all assumed that the challenge at hand was to get me back. Even the few who did ask to read my papers never commented on them, except superficially.

I don't know if any of these people have changed their views at all, but I do know that none of them will be the same. You can't help but be affected when one of your very own challenges the very core of your beliefs. Although the fallout from my friends and co-workers is hard to determine, the effect on my family was much more dramatic.

W hen my parents got my letter they were shocked. They had been proud of their son's work as an ordained minister, evangelist, and Christian songwriter. Not knowing anything about my gradual change, this announcement came as a total surprise. My mother immediately hopped on a bus, traveling from Phoenix to my home in California, and we had a long, emotional discussion into the early morning hours. She would never be the same, but it wasn't until much later that I learned the long-term effects of her visit.

My mother tells me that she was stunned by the dissonance. Backing off to get some perspective, she never went to church again. In a Wisconsin Magazine article, published by the Milwaukee Journal (July 28, 1991), journalist Bill Lueders quotes my mother, Pat, as she recalled our late-night meeting: "The answers he gave me impressed my heart and mind. . . . I had so much love for my son that I knew in some way he was right." Within weeks she concluded that religion was "just a bunch of baloney," feeling a "tremendously great disappointment in God." She began to do some reading and thinking of her own, and today happily calls herself an unbeliever.

One fact that surprised my mother was that no one in her church ever seemed to care about her departure. She had been a member of the Assembly of God for years, had performed in the choir, had sung solos regularly in services, had taught Sunday School, and had participated in many other functions. The only incident out of the ordinary, after leaving the church, was an embarrassing moment when she was grabbed at the supermarket by an older woman who was shaking, speaking in tongues, and praying to cast the devil out of my mother. Needless to say, this only confirmed my mother's new-found opinion that religion is "baloney."

It took my Dad a little longer. When he got my letter he ran down to the church altar and poured out his heart to God. He enlisted the assistance of church members to pray for me. The pastor laid hands on Dad, asking God for a special blessing during this trial of faith. At first Dad tried to argue with me, in a friendly way, and we racked up many pages of correspondence on the issues. Eventually he backed off, due probably as much to Mom's influence as to mine. He began to read the "other side," and eventually came to respect the reasoning of freethinkers.

The same Wisconsin Magazine article quotes my father Norman Barker discussing how he dealt with his son's change of views: "I tried to straighten him out. It worked the other way around." After Dad stopped believing in God, he was amazed at how quickly his Christian friends turned on him. "I used to think it was a tough thing to be a Christian in this big, bad world. You want to see something interesting, try not being one." He reports, "I'm much happier now." "To be free from superstition and fear and guilt and the sin complex, to be able to think freely and objectively, is a tremendous relief."

One of the immediate benefits to my Dad was in the field of music. Back in the 1950s, when he and Mom became "born again," my Dad abandoned his career as a trombone player in dance bands (he had played for Hoagy

Carmichael's radio orchestra and many other bands, including a stint with U.S.O. during the war, and on some Hollywood movies), throwing away his collection of swing recordings, turning his back on his former "sinful" life, playing his trombone only in church. He had come to view popular music as "worldly" and contrary to spiritual health. When he finally gave up religion in the late 1980s, he had come around full circle, but this didn't happen in one clean break. Before leaving the church, Dad began to play his trombone in local jazz bands in the Phoenix area, reconnecting with the life he had abandoned almost forty years before. He didn't tell anyone at church what he was doing because he knew they would disapprove. One night while Dad was playing in a dance band at a Fourth of July party, there happened to be TV coverage of the event which captured a glimpse of the band in the background. The next day the pastor's wife called my Dad and said, "Did I see you on TV last night?" Ha! The all-seeing eye of God! Dad could not continue this secret double life for long, so he finally made a clean break, abandoning "Onward, Christian Soldiers" in favor of "Don't Get Around Much Any More."

One night, just before he dumped the whole system of belief, Dad drove to church, took his trombone case out of the car and walked toward the building where he could hear the praying, singing, and preaching. When he got to the door it struck him that he did not belong there any more. Hoping that no one would notice, he quickly turned around and went home.

I never suggested to my parents that they should become atheists. They did their own thinking. They decided to investigate all sides of the issues. It is exciting to see what has happened in their lives. I don't think it is possible to pull someone out of religion if they don't want to go. All we can do is provide information and be an example.

One of the ripples radiating out from the example of unbelief was the effect on my younger brother Darrell. At first he was shocked, but then he grew enthused to see an open doubter. Darrell was, after all, a closet skeptic for many years, not knowing exactly what he believed but covering the bases just in case. I like to quip that Darrell never was a very good Christian. When I gave him a book on humanism, he said, "That's what I am! I never knew it until now, but I am a humanist." He was uncomfortable with the word "atheist," and when he asked to accompany me to a meeting of atheists in Los Angeles, he almost changed his mind and sat out in the car. A year or two later Darrell became one of the chapter directors of Atheists United. He went on to complain about violations of state/church separation in Redlands and San Bernardino. He became a plaintiff in a successful lawsuit protesting county ownership and maintenance of a Christian theme park on public property. My folks tell me that Darrell was a solid support for them when they were going through their initial disillusionment with religion. It is helpful to have someone to talk to during times like this, and Darrell called them regularly to compare notes on their new-found analysis of Christianity.

The gradual change in my parents and my brother Darrell was tremendously heartening. I never would have predicted such an outcome. My parents had been fervent evangelists for Jesus for years, and Darrell had been a street preacher with a missionary organization. I should have known that in a relationship that is based on true love and acceptance, there is nothing to fear. The fact that these born-again, door-to-door preachers were open to change gives me hope. It makes me realize that there is something that soars high above religion. There is something in life that is far superior to Jesus, more excellent than dogma. Real love, kindness, and intelligence know no barriers.

My other brother, Tom, is a born-again Christian. He is a good man, hard-working and conscientious. Although we have never been very close, we enjoy seeing each other occasionally, and the subject of religion never comes up. I sometimes refer to Tom as the "white sheep" of the family.

My maternal grandmother "Grams" was an uneducated, loving and generous woman whose views on religion fluctuated according to her medication. She and I were very close. When she received my letter she must have been torn apart with the issue, writing: "I won't give in to the Devil." Later, Grams wrote me again, in a more characteristic mood: "You sure don't have to defend yourself to me. You are a good man, one of the Best I have ever seen, and I am thankful for that. . . . I just stay open minded and try to live a good life. That's all I can do." A few years later Grams told me that she had scared off some Jehovah's Witnesses at her front door, growling, "Get out of here! I'm an atheist!" I don't think she really was an atheist, because at other times she spoke about God and Jesus in her life. But at least she became more broad-minded. To a large degree this was due to the change in my parents.

My paternal grandmother lives in Oklahoma. After Granddad died in 1986, she and I worked on a four-year project together, publishing *Paradise Remembered*, a book of Granddad's collected stories of life as a Delaware (Lenape) Indian boy in Indian Territory before Oklahoma became a state. She has been a member of the Christian Church her entire life, and I know she is uncomfortable with my deconversion. She happened to see one of my appearances on "Oprah Winfrey," and wrote me a postcard saying, "I saw you on TV. That is not *our* Danny." Despite that, we have continued to get along wonderfully.

Two of my uncles have responded in a friendly and civil manner to the obvious change in our views, but Dad's third brother, a committed Christian, is ostracizing us, refusing to answer letters. After I sent him a copy of *Para-*

dise Remembered (his Dad's memories), which has been received with excitement and gratitude by the rest of the family, he sent it back to me without explanation. I can only assume that he is unwilling to associate with his "unclean" relatives.

My four children in California have been very good about the whole controversy. Unless they bring it up, or unless it happens to arise in the course of normal conversation, we do not discuss religion. When they visit Wisconsin, I offer to escort them to the church of their choice, but they have never taken me up on it. Two or three times during her high-school years my daughter Becky sent me a letter urging me to "come back to God," so I know that they have struggled with the issue. But I have repeatedly told them that my love for them is not contingent on what they believe. They can be Christians if they want, as long as they are good people and don't hurt others. They go to church with their mother, who works at a Christian school, and their stepfather, a youth director at a Baptist church. They know what I think. I have never wanted them to be forced into a position of having to choose between parents. They are smart kids, and I have to trust that they have the ability to sift fact from fiction, and right from wrong. I dedicated *Just Pretend: A Freethought Book for Children* to them, which says:

"No one can tell you what to think.

Not your teachers.

Not your parents.

Not your minister, priest, or rabbi.

Not your friends or relatives.

Not this book.

You are the boss of your own mind.

If you have used your own mind to find out what is true, then you should be proud!

Your thoughts are free."

After my Christian marriage ended, I moved into a tiny one-room apartment in Cucamonga. (Yes, there is a Cucamonga.) My brother Darrell had a friend who wrote for The San Bernardino Sun-Times, and they ran a feature story about my de-conversion for which I enlisted the help of the Freedom From Religion Foundation, and in which they gave coverage to *Freethought Today*. It was not long after this that my correspondence with Annie Laurie Gaylor blossomed into a long-distance courtship. I moved to Wisconsin, and in May, 1987 we were married. The freethought-feminist wedding, a "match not made in heaven," took place at Sauk City's historic Freethought Hall. It was conducted by a woman judge wearing purple shoes with her judicial robe, announcing, "You may now kiss the groom." (See Part 9 for complete text of the ceremony.)

One of the "ripple effects" was Sabrina Delata Gaylor, our daughter born in September, 1989, a fourth-generation freethinker on her mother's side of the family, and a full member of the Delaware (Lenape) Tribe of American Indians on my side. Sabrina also has some Chiricahua Apache blood, from my mother's great-grandmother, who was a full-blooded member of the Arizona tribe from which Geronimo came. (Geronimo's clan fought the intrusion of the Spanish missionaries.) Just as some religious parents name their children "Faith," or "Charity," or "Hope," we looked for a name that would reflect reason. "Delata(h)" is the Delaware Indian word for "thought" or "reason."

In 1987 I went to work full-time for the Freedom From Religion Foundation in Madison, Wisconsin. The Foundation is a national organization of freethinkers—atheists, agnostics, secular humanists—working to keep state and church separate and to educate the public about the views of nontheists. Working for the Foundation has been exciting and intellectually satisfying. It has given me an opportunity to continue "spreading the good news," and to utilize (and improve) some of the skills that I gained from preaching. Writing regular articles for the Foundation's newspaper *Freethought Today*, doing radio and TV shows, participating in debates on university campuses and churches, composing freethought music, performing concerts, giving speeches, writing "nontracts" and freethought books for children—all of this has allowed me to continue studying the issues which have interested me my entire life, and to keep speaking out.

During these years with the Foundation, I have noticed that speaking out does make a difference. The Foundation has been able to make contact with thousands of other freethinkers around the continent, and has helped motivate many of them to become more visible with their views. At the end of one of my debates in Iowa, a student came up to me and said, "Go ahead and add my name to your list. I was raised a Catholic in a small farming town and have never been able to acknowledge my doubts until now." Right there, a freethinker was born.

This might sound like a Sunday-evening church testimony, but I have to say that my life has been much better since I got the religious monkey off my back. Invalid friendships have been discarded, the true love of people like my parents has been wonderful and affirming, and the new freethinking friends have more than made up for any initial temporary sense of loss. Dishonesty is too high a cost for maintaining a friendship. In order to get pure gold, you have to melt it and skim off the impurities.

We never know fully how our actions affect others. I have read articles that have had tremendous impact on my thinking, but I never wrote to thank the author. Freethinkers who write letters to the local newspaper sometimes feel discouraged when they receive not a single positive response; but this does not mean someone's life has not been changed. I think all of our actions are like that. What we do produces ripples that radiate out much farther than we may have intended or imagined. In today's religion-crazed world, speaking out as a freethinker can't *help* but have an impact.

I Don't Need Jesus

by Dan Barker

So many solutions
For the "meaning of life."
So many religions—
What confusion and strife!
They spread like a cancer;
They rise and they fall.
But I have an answer
That does away with them all.

Chorus: I don't need Jesus
To give me a smile.
I don't need a holy book
To make my life worthwhile.
Just give me reason,
Fairness, and love.
True human happiness
Does not come from above.

They preach me their sermons,
Though I'm doing just fine.
Can't they live their own lives,
And let me live mine?
They say I'm a sinner,
Who is blind in both eyes.
But I am a winner,
And I can see through those lies.

© *Copyright 1986 by Dan Barker. Song lyrics.*

3

I Just Lost Faith
In Faith

This was my first article for Freethought Today. It ran in the June 1984 issue.

RELIGION IS A POWERFUL thing. Few can resist its charms and few can truly break its embrace. It is the siren who entices the wandering traveler with songs of love and desire and, once successful, turns a mind into stone. It is a Venus fly trap. Its attraction is like that of drugs to an addict who, wishing to be free and happy, becomes trapped and miserable.

But the saddest part of the dependency is the fact that most participants are *willing* victims. They think they are happy. They believe religion has kept its promises and have no desire to search elsewhere. They are deeply in love with their faith and have been blinded by that love—blinded to the point of unquestioning sacrifice.

I know this is true because I was one of Christ's disciples for over nineteen years, and my subsequent self-excision was/is traumatically painful.

51

My Dad was a professional musician during the 1940's. At one of his concerts he met a female vocalist and, as things go, they went (lucky for me). They got married and, when I was a toddler, they both found true religion. Dad threw away his collection of original Glenn Miller recordings (ouch!), turned his back on his former "sinful" life and enrolled in seminary to become a minister. He didn't finish because of the strong demands of raising three boys. But he lived his faith through his family and through lay ministry in local churches.

My folks' spirituality was so strong that they often found it hard to find a church that met their needs. So we church-hopped for many years. I can't remember all the churches, but we were Baptists, Methodists, Nazarenes, Assemblies of God, Pentecostals, fundamentalist, evangelical, "Bible-believing" and charismatic.

For a number of years we formed a family musical team and ministered in many Southern California churches—nothing fantastic—Dad played trombone and preached, Mom sang solos, I played piano, my brothers tooted various instruments and we all joined in singing those famous gospel harmonies. It was a neat experience for us kids. My childhood was filled with love, fun and purpose. I felt truly fortunate to have been born into the "truth" and at the age of fifteen I committed myself to a lifetime of Christian ministry.

My commitment lasted nineteen years. It gave my life a feeling of purpose, destiny and fulfillment. I spent years trekking across Mexico in missionary work—small villages, jungles, deserts, large arenas, radio, television, parks, prisons and street meetings. I spent more years in traveling evangelism across the United States preaching and singing in churches, on street corners, house-to-house witnessing, college campuses and wherever an audience could be found.

I was a "doer of the word and not a hearer only." I went to a Christian college, majored in Religion/Philosophy, became ordained and served in a pastoral capacity in three California churches. I personally led many people to Jesus Christ, and encouraged many young people to consider full-time Christian service.

I served for a while as librarian for Kathryn Kuhlman's Los Angeles choir, observing the "miracles" first-hand. I was even instrumental in a few healings myself.

For a number of years I directed the "King's Children," a local Christian music group that performed quite extensively including a brief term of hosting a local Christian television show.

For fifteen years I worked with Manuel Bonilla, the leading Christian recording artist in the Spanish-speaking world. I was his main producer/arranger, and working with him gave me the opportunity to learn the skills to produce many more Christian albums, including some of my own.

I have written more than a hundred Christian songs which are either published or recorded by various artists, and two of my children's musicals continue to be best sellers around the world. ("Mary Had A Little Lamb," a Christmas musical, and "His Fleece Was White as Snow," for Easter, both published and distributed by Manna Music. You can see the religious symbolism: Christ, the unspotted lamb of god who became the final sacrifice for sin.)

I could go on listing my Christian accomplishments, but I think you can see that I was *very* serious about my faith, and that I am quite capable of analyzing religion from the inside out.

Last Friday evening I directed a bible study in my own home. I opened it to all comers and announced that I would welcome all points of view with the purpose of examining the documents with skepticism rather than faith. The eight people who arrived (to my astonishment) were Christians who had been informed of my present atheistic stance and were curious about my intentions. My closest ally was my brother, a theistic agnostic [Darrell is now an activist freethinker]. One fellow, a theologian, informed me that his purpose in coming was to convert me back to the faith. (He failed.)

It was a fun, lively evening and much information was exchanged, but I noticed something interesting. They were more concerned about *me* and my atheism than they were about the bible. The discussion kept coming around to an analysis of my conversion from the faith. They were intrigued that someone who had been so strongly religious could so radically "stray" and not be ashamed. They kept probing for some deep psychological cause, some hidden disappointment, secret bitterness, temptation or pride. They were like spiritual doctors trying to remove a tumor or blinding cataract.

One fellow suggested I had been blinded by Satan—the Devil being so intimidated by my strong Christian witness that he needed to neutralize the enemy, get me out of commission. That was very flattering, but it misses the point.

The point here is that the merits of an argument do not depend on the character of the speaker. All arguments should be weighed for their own sake, based on their own evidences and logical consistencies.

Before the bible study even commenced one fellow said, "Dan, tell us what caused you to lose your faith." So I told them.

I did not lose my faith, I gave it up purposely. The motivation that drove me into the ministry is the same that drove me out. I have always wanted to *know*. Even as a child I fervently pursued truth. I was rarely content to accept things without examination, and my examinations were intense. I was a thirsty learner, a good student, and a good minister because of that drive. I always took things apart and put them back together again.

Since I was taught and believed Christianity was the answer, the only hope for "man," I dedicated myself to understanding all I possibly could. I devoured every book, every sermon, and the bible. I prayed, fasted and obeyed biblical teaching. I decided that I would lean my whole weight upon the truth of scripture. This attitude, I am sure, gave the impression that I was a notch above, that I could be trusted as a Christian authority and leader. Christians, eager for substantiation, gladly allowed me to assume a place of leadership and I took it as confirmation of my holy calling.

But my mind did not go to sleep. In my thirst for knowledge I did not limit myself to Christian authors but curiously desired to understand the reasoning behind nonChristian thinking. I figured the only way to truly grasp a subject was to look at it from all sides. If I had limited myself to Christian books I would probably still be a Christian today. I read philosophy, theology, science and psychology. I studied evolution and natural history. I read Bertrand Russell, Thomas Paine, Ayn Rand, John Dewey and others. At first I laughed at these worldly thinkers, but I eventually started discovering some disturbing facts—facts that discredited Christianity. I tried to ignore these facts because they did not integrate with my religious world view.

For years I went through an intense inner conflict. On the one hand I was happy with the direction and fulfillment of my Christian life; on the other hand I had intellectual doubts. Faith and reason began a war within me. And it kept escalating. I would cry out to God for answers, and none would come. Like the battered wife who clings to hope, I kept trusting that God would someday come through. He never did.

The only proposed answer was *faith,* and I gradually grew to dislike the smell of that word. I finally realized that faith is a cop-out, a defeat—an admission that the truths of religion are unknowable through evidence and reason. It is only undemonstrable assertions that require the suspension of reason, and weak ideas that require faith. I just lost faith in faith. Biblical contradictions became more and more discrepant, apologist arguments more and more absurd and, when I finally discarded faith, things became more and more clear.

But don't imagine that was an easy process. It was like tearing my whole frame of reality to pieces, ripping to shreds the fabric of meaning and hope, betraying the values of existence. It hurt. And it hurt bad. It was like spitting on my mother, or like throwing one of my children out a window. It was sacrilege. All of my bases for thinking and values had to be restructured. Add to that inner conflict the outer conflict of reputation and you have a destabilizing war. Did I really want to discard the respect I had so carefully built over many years with so many important people?

I can understand why people cling to their faith. Faith is comforting. It provides many "answers" to life's riddles. My Christian life was quite positive and I really see no external/cultural reason why I should have rejected it. I continue to share many of the same Christian values I was taught (though I would no longer call them "Christian"—they are *my* values); and many of my close friends are decent Christian individuals whom I love and respect.

Christians feel deeply that their way of life is the best possible. They feel their attitude toward the rest of the world is one of love. That's how I felt. I couldn't understand why people would be critical of Christianity unless they were inwardly motivated by "worldly" Satanic influences. I pretended to love all individuals while hating the "sin" that was in them, like Christ supposedly did. (We were *taught* that Christ was the most loving example.)

It was a mystery to me how anyone could be blind to the truths of the Gospel. After all, don't we all want love, peace, happiness, hope and meaning in life? Christ was the only answer, I believed, and I figured all nonChristians must be driven by other things, like greed, lust, evil pride, hate and jealousy. I took the media's caricature of the world's situation as evidence of that fact. For me to grow into one of those godless creatures was almost impossible, and I resisted all the way. (I have since discovered that ethics has nothing to do with religion, at least not in positive correlation.)

There was no specific turning point for me. I one day just realized that I was no longer a Christian, and a few months later I mustered the nerve to advertise that fact. That was last January, six months ago. Since then I have been bombarded by all my caring friends and relatives. I appreciate their concern and I sincerely wish to keep a dialogue open.

As an example, while I was typing this article I received a long distance call from a former Christian friend who had heard about my "defection." It is hard to handle calls like that. She was stunned, and I am certain that she is at this very moment in prayer for me, or calling others to join in prayer. I love this person, I respect her and do not wish to cause any undue harm. She told me that she had read an article I wrote to my local paper. (How it got to her area is a mystery.) I understand her concern and sympathize with her since I know exactly what she is thinking.

I was a preacher for many years, and I guess it hasn't all rubbed off. I would wish to influence others who may be struggling like I did—influence them to have the guts to think. To think deliberately and clearly. To take no fact without critical examination and to remain open to honest inquiry, wherever it leads.

What Good Is Your Love?
(To The Christian)
by Dan Barker

Chorus: What good is your love,
If you can't let me be me?
What good is our fellowship,
If we cannot be free?
Don't give me your rules
In the name of "God's love."
Any friendship between us
Will not come from above.

You tell me you love me,
But I can't see a word.
Anxious theology
Is all I have heard.
Why are you afraid
To look in my eyes?
Our common humanity
You cannot disguise.

We don't have forever—
We only have now.
If we're going to be friends at all,
Then let's figure out how.
I offer myself,
For whatever that's worth,
With the hope that together
We'll make true peace on earth.

4

Standing On The Premises

I'LL NEVER forget my first soul-winning experience. One Friday evening in June, near my sixteenth birthday, while I was wondering how I was going to spend the summer vacation of 1965, I received an "urgent" phone call from an evangelistic organization saying my name had been suggested as a possibility to fill a recently vacated spot on a traveling Gospel team.

Early the next morning, traveling from Los Angeles to Texas with ten other young people in one of those long, eight-door "airport" cars, I discovered that I had become the newly appointed captain of one of the outreach groups. My responsibilities were to include a team of three girls (who were older than I), two weeks of preaching in a small San Antonio church, and the direction of a Vacation Bible School for children. They also told me that I would be training the local teenagers in the techniques of soul-winning. I had never done any of these things before, but they assumed I was capable since they had heard I was an "on fire" young Christian. My faith was so strong that I was willing to do anything for Jesus, trusting that he would give me the strength.

I'm sure my nightly sermons were not great, but no one complained. I let the girls handle the day activities for children while I prepared for the soul-winning workshop on Saturday, which worried me considerably since I had never won anyone to Christ before.

When the day arrived we "professional California evangelists" gathered the local teenagers from the church for some preliminary training. I taught them how to share the basic plan of salvation and how to get a person to the point of conversion. When it was time to go out into the park and put it into practice, the kids expressed some hesitation, but I assured them that nothing was too hard for God and besides, they were going to learn some lessons about faith and obedience. They didn't know it was my first time also!

As I moved out into the park, entourage trailing, I remember having conflicting feelings. "What am I doing? What if I fail? I want to go home!" Yet at the same time I was thinking, "This is exciting! This is God's work—and I'm part of it!"

I spotted a young man, perhaps seventeen years old, slowly pedaling a bicycle, and I approached him. "Hi!" I said. "I'm from California and I came here to talk to you about Jesus." He stopped and gave us a funny look.

"Are you a Christian?" I asked.

"No," he said, "I'm a Catholic." He stayed on his bike, spinning the pedal with his foot.

"Great! Then you know about the plan of salvation?"

"No. I'm a Catholic," he repeated.

"Then let me ask you a question. If you died right now, would you go to heaven or hell?"

"I don't know," he answered. "I hope I will go to heaven."

"Well, if you don't know if you're saved, then you're definitely not saved," I said. "The Bible says you can know for certain that you have been redeemed." I continued with the plan of salvation, explaining that we are all sinners worthy of eternal damnation, an idea which he already knew. I described the need to confess sin, repent and accept Jesus into his heart and life, letting the blood of the cross wash away all guilt and shame. Listening politely and shyly, as did the rest of the team, he indicated he understood all I was saying.

"Then, would you like to be born again?" I asked.

"Sure," he said.

"You would?" I asked, trying to swallow my astonishment. It couldn't be this easy. "What do I do now?" I thought. "Well, then, uh .... let's pray," I said.

"Here?" he asked. "In the park?"

"Sure. This park is part of God's sanctuary of creation. He can talk to your heart right here, right now."

We bowed our heads and I prompted the fellow to repeat the "Sinner's Prayer" after me. Actually, I had to make it up, digging the words from my memory of past revival meetings. He prayed with me, out loud. When we were finished I said, "Now, do you know you are saved?"

"I think so," he responded.

"Great. Now be sure to read the Bible and pray every day, go to church and find some Christian friends."

We let him ride off and never saw him again. But the group became quite enthused, spreading out to share the good news of the gospel with the lost souls who had come to spend a nice summer afternoon in the park.

For me it was an exciting moment. I had won a soul to Christ; I had a star in my crown. It was like earning my wings, or getting the first notch on my six-shooter. Of course, I gave all the credit to the Holy Spirit, but I accepted it as an authentication of my calling to the ministry. It was a heady moment. I was a real evangelist, an active participant in God's holy cause, a soldier of the cross. It was like the first taste of blood, and I wanted more.

Since that time I led hundreds of people to Christ through personal evangelism, and thousands more through preaching. I traveled for many years knocking on doors, approaching people in parks, restaurants, prisons and hospitals, on street corners, campuses, beaches, riverbanks, buses and planes. I preached to crowds as large as ten thousand. I hiked through muggy mountains of Mexico, carrying my accordion up and down the valleys and ravines to reach little isolated Indian villages. I ministered on television and radio in the United States and Mexico. I held meetings in homes, churches and large arenas. My witnessing efforts brought me in contact with people from every walk of life: a knot of barefoot children in a Chihuahua ghetto, businessmen at a San Francisco fund-raiser, biker gang members, school principals, drug addicts, skid row derelicts, soccer and basketball teams, a city mayor, prison inmates, hitchhikers, housewives (usually through a screen door), college students, police officers, and countless strangers on the street.

I learned some things about evangelism. Like a salesperson, an evangelist learns techniques of conversation, ways to show genuine concern for the prospect, how to keep the door open for that crucial fraction of a second before it slams in your face (literally), how to seize the moment and close the sale. It was not always easy, but you could count on a certain success rate if you kept it up. It's like the saying, "If you throw enough spaghetti against the wall, some of it is going to stick."

The next person I spoke with after the kid on the bicycle in San Antonio was an atheist! He was barely civil to me. As he walked off I remember feeling not shame, but pity! I felt truly sorry for a man who was going to spend eternity apart from his creator, a man who had obviously swallowed the lie of the Devil, who would ultimately be punished for his arrogance. It motivated me even more! I had to save the lost. I spent a lot of years preaching, and I had a certain success rate.

Why was I successful? Approximately seventy-five percent of those I approached actually listened to me for a while. And about one in twenty prayed with me to accept Jesus Christ as their personal Savior. I encountered very little resistance, very few people who had anything thoughtful to say.

I do remember speaking with a freethinker once who politely and intelligently challenged everything I said. That was unnerving. The tables were turned and I was forced to examine basic issues for which I was unprepared. I was the one who turned and walked off, determined to study more so I would be ready to give God's answers next time.

Why are evangelists effective? There could be different answers to that question:

Freethinker: Evangelists are effective because people don't know how to think.

Christian Convert: Sure I know how to think. It's because Christianity is satisfying. It meets my needs and it answers the basic questions of life.

Evangelist: Evangelists are effective because God's word is powerful. The Holy Spirit can change lives and Jesus's love can heal hearts. Evangelists are merely agents of a divine plan.

I have a friend who owns an ad agency. He gave me this nugget of advertising savvy: "The good advertiser is not the one who makes people think, but the one who makes people think they are thinking." Christianity does not ask people to think. It asks them to accept. It requires a humbling of the mind and a submission of the self. God's mind can not be challenged, and his word, the bible, is absolute law. Those who obey will find true happiness in accordance with divine purpose; those who rebel are sinners who destroy the intimate relationship for which we were designed. Why are these ideas acceptable to so many people? Why do over a third of Americans profess to be born-again Christians. Why was my evangelistic ministry so successful?

I think the answer lies with assumptions. Christians do know how to think; but they don't start deep enough. A thoughtful conclusion is a synthesis of antecedent presuppositions or conclusions. The propitiatory nature of Christ's sacrificial atonement, for example, is very logical. Logical, that is, if you first accept the existence of sin, the fall of humankind, the wrath of God and divine judgment. If you don't buy the premises, then, of course, the conclusion cannot be logical.

Here is another example of a logical conclusion based on faulty premises. "Servants are inferior to their masters. Woman was created from Adam's rib to be a helper to man. Woman is a servant, therefore inferior to man." If you assume the first two premises the resultant conclusion is logically correct.

The reason evangelists are effective is because they capitalize on people's unquestioned assumptions, desires and fears. An assumption is an idea held without prior thinking, taken for granted. We all have them. Some of them are basic (such as "I exist"), but many are learned through parents, culture, school and church. Here are some of the assumptions I used in dealing with people. (You'll note also my assumption that it was acceptable to exclude women from language.)

> Life needs meaning
> Man has a soul and/or a spirit
> Man is basically evil
> The world is in a mess
> Selfishness and pride are evil
> Skepticism is wrong, rebellious and destructive
> Atheists are evil
> There is no happiness without God
> The bible is God's inspired word
> The world was created by a master designer
> Man needs moral guidelines that are absolute
> Suffering is a punishment
> Suffering is a test of virtue
> Emotions and feelings are evidence of another realm

I'm not saying here that these assumptions are wrong or right. The point is that many people accept them without thinking. They are what made my ministry productive. The evangelist merely needs to identify a person's assumptions, or introduce new ones. Then he can build a case for Christianity. He can offer an answer to the basic questions of life, and he can provide a way for a person to resolve inner conflicts. The "peace that passeth understanding" comes as a result of dismissing tensions without understanding why.

No matter that the Christian answers are incorrect—if they are accepted as answers, then they seem to work. Bertrand Russell, in "Dewey's New 'Logic'," recounts an episode:

> "Dr. Dewey and I were once in the town of Changsha during an eclipse of the moon; following immemorial custom, blind men were beating gongs to frighten the heavenly dog, whose attempt to swallow the moon is the cause of eclipses. Throughout thousands of years, this practice of beating gongs has never failed to be successful: every eclipse has come to an end after a sufficient prolongation of the din."

61

Christianity is the same thing: a two-thousand-year-old beating of superstitious gongs which provides sufficient answers for many people.

The reason I was successful with my first conversion attempt is that the person already believed the necessary premises—human beings are sinners, the bible is inspired, etc. The reason my second attempt failed is that the person had denied all the prerequisites—there is a God, life needs purpose, etc. Some evangelists are sometimes effective because some people *want* to be saved.

Christianity can be effectively challenged if people can be made to think at the level of assumptions. It happened to me. When I forced myself to examine basic presuppositions I found the rug pulled out from under my feet. Yes, religion answers some questions, but who said they must be asked in the first place? Or that they are necessarily answerable? Or that there is only one answer?

There are two ways to challenge evangelistic assumptions: 1) deny that the assumptions are valid, or 2) accept the assumptions, but form your own conclusions. As an example, let's approach the assumption that life needs *meaning*. In sermons you will hear statements like these:

"Science has failed to provide a purpose for mankind." (Who said it was trying?)

"Secular philosophies can not answer the basic question, 'What is the meaning of life?' "

"Man can only find fulfillment through a relationship with his designer."

Rather than attacking these assertions at face value, which is often unproductive, it can be more effective to examine the presuppositional underpinnings.

One approach is to deny the assumption. Who said life *must* have meaning? Why can't life just be life? My family has three cats. We enjoy watching them play, eat, sleep, lie in the sun and chase bugs. Do they ask themselves what is the meaning of life? Is their life any less livable because they possess no coherent purpose for existence? Since we humans have larger brains with a greater rational capacity and self consciousness than other animals we somehow assume we must be worthy of a higher purpose. Isn't that arrogance? To ask the question about meaning in life one must first assume the presence of someone to bestow that meaning. This usually amounts to granting the existence of a transcendent reality, a supernatural realm to which we can somehow relate in a "meaningful" manner. If you can live without the need for meaning in life, then you will likewise not need the invented frame of reference, the plan and purpose of a divine will. To many people life is its own meaning, and the word "meaning" becomes meaningless.

A second approach is to accept the assumption but find a different answer. Yes, I would like my life to have meaning. But what is meant by the word "meaning"? The word has something to do with the will and purpose of a mind. The only reason we possess a word like "meaning" is because we are familiar with the functions of the human mind in processes like taking action, making changes, solving problems, expressing desire. Religion is an extension of the human mind in an attempt to authenticate existence. But if a person wants meaning in life, why look elsewhere for a mind? Each person already possesses a mind that is capable of making decisions and providing meaning in life. Why trust a hypothetical divine mind which refuses to reveal its reasons, in fact cannot have reasons? (If God has reasons for what he does, then he is no longer God; he is subject to some higher law or purpose or right-and-wrong.)

What I'm saying is that if God's mind doesn't need external guidelines, then why does mine? A mind is all you need, if meaning is what you want. Since there is no evidence for a transcendent mind, then feel free to find meaning in yourself. In art, music, dance or theater. In philosophy, science, languages or politics. In sports, family, chess or humanitarianism. In nature, antique cars, stamps or psychology. In all of the above. In none of the above.

My present answer to the evangelist is, "My life has meaning and fulfillment already, thank you."

The same approaches can be taken with other evangelistic assumptions. Most soul-winners are unprepared to defend the inspiration and reliability of the bible, without which they have no case. Part of the reason my ministry was so effective is that there is an unwarranted and alarming respect for "God's holy word" in this country. Most people blindly accept it as divine. If they could be made to examine the book they might see that the assumption is unfounded. The bible is filled with contradictions, errors, absurdities, unfairness and ugliness.

Few evangelists realize that there can be strong arguments for ethics and morality outside of religion. And they don't like the fact that many people lead happy and productive lives without God, expecting (desiring) that infidels should suffer the inevitable evil consequences of godless living.

Most of them are unfamiliar and uncomfortable with the findings in the science of evolution, with the fact that humankind does not exhibit evidence of intelligent design. (All species, by the way, do show signs of design, though it is not "intelligent." Design by natural selection is the opposite of chance.) But rational argument and evidence are no threat to the evangelist as long as there are people who continue to accept religious presuppositions, especially the idea of the virtue of submission, obedience and humility—ideas which strangle the mind.

There is another kind of assumption which is particularly subtle and difficult to identify. It is the idea that certain words or concepts refer to real items
apart from the mind, similar to Plato's idealism. I learned a great word a few
months ago as I was reading Stephen Gould's book, *The Mismeasure of Man.*
The word is "reify." It is like "deify" except instead of turning something into
a *god,* it is turning an idea into a *thing.* It is the transformation of a concept
into a concrete.

For example, the word "love" is a label for an idea which may include many
things: respect, concern, passion, admiration, actions of compassion and be-
nevolence. Yet when you think about it, there really is no such *thing* as love.
It is not something you can purchase at a drug store. It is not a substance you
can gain or lose or give away. Love, as I understand it, is a label for those
ideas and actions of mine which are based on a rational appraisal of value to
myself and others whom I value strongly. It is sometimes nonrational, but it
does not control me. I do not possess a certain quantity of it. It is nonexistent,
though I will accept the usage of the word "love" as a convenience for communicating abstract and conventional concepts to others.

Much of religious discussion is made possible by the reification of concepts
like Hope, Meaning, Truth, Evil, Forgiveness, Sin, Pride, Guilt, Love, Humility, and Faith. "Pray for Peace," or "Christ will give you more love," or "Ask
for faith, and God will not withhold it." Many people assume that these words
have a well-defined existence outside of the mind, and they never analyze
them. Heaven is a storehouse of wonderful things that can be obtained with
the right price. Hell is a repository of items you can get for free. (Or maybe it's
the other way around.)

Evangelists are effective because they have access to a stockpile of reified
concepts which, if unquestioned, only strengthen the idea that there is a transcendent realm where these things reside. It is the idea that the mind floats
in a sea of spiritual realities. By the way, I think the God concept is the ultimate reification, reversing creator and creature.

Let me suggest that it is possible for a freethinker to un-evangelize an
evangelist. It happened to me. Evangelists will continue to be effective in this
world as long as the religious premises upon which they stand remain
unchallenged.

*This is the text of a talk given at the annual Freedom From Religion
Foundation convention in Milwaukee, Wisconsin October 13, 1984, my
first freethought speech. It ran in Freethought Today, October/November,
1984.*

5

From Martian
To Earthling

This world is not my home;
I'm just a-passin' through.
My treasures are laid up
Somewhere beyond the blue.
The angels beckon me
From heaven's open door,
And I can't feel at home
In this world any more.
(Popular Christian chorus)

A WORLD VIEW is an interesting thing. We all have one, I suppose. Most freethinkers are naturalistic; most religionists are supernaturalistic. This dichotomy is no more clearly demonstrated than when an atheist tries to converse with a fundamentalist Christian. It is like speaking with someone from outer space, have you noticed? Do you wonder what gears are spinning inside the head of an intelligent person who believes in miracles, demons, talking animals and divinely inspired writings? Where does this spiritual world view come from?

I once believed. Strongly. Now that I am an atheist I can see that my conversion from faith to reason was a radical shift of *mentality*—a change in world view. From Martian to Earthling. I once believed that this present life is a mere temporary sub-reality of a higher spiritual realm, as the above lyrics express.

I preached some of my favorite sermons on this topic. "If any man be in Christ, he is a new creature. All things have passed away, behold, all have become new." *(II Corinthians 5:17)* "Set your affection on things above, not on things of the earth. For ye are dead, and your life is hid with Christ in God." *(Colossians 3:2,3)* "For to be carnally minded is death; but to be spiritually minded is life and peace . . . But ye are not in the flesh, but in the Spirit . . . the body is dead because of sin; but the Spirit is life . . ." *(Romans 8:6-10)* The true Christian considers his or her citizenship to be in heaven, out of this world. They are extraterrestrials!

What we have here is a problem of cross-cultural communication. All attempts to interface must necessarily lose something in the translation. My prior religious world view prohibited me from accurately perceiving freethinkers. I thought all atheists were blind, crazy or twisted; why couldn't they see the truth?

Obtaining a world view is like learning a language: the first one is the easiest. I don't remember struggling to learn English. It came "naturally" through observation and imitation. Learning Spanish, however, was a different matter. It came through a careful, deliberate, methodical and disciplined rational process.

Changing from Christianity to atheism was a similar process, though more difficult since the former had to be completely replaced by the latter. The term "bilingual" cannot fit this analogy.

My religious frame of mind, like my first language, came primarily through observation. I was raised in a Christian universe: evangelistic parents, thousands of sermons, hymns, prayers. It all "made sense" to me. Miracles, a loving/wrathful God, sin and salvation were all substantiated by everyone I knew—so it felt natural. In my mind the Spirit was *real*, very real. He spoke to me, moved my heart, gave direction, joy and peace. I consciously accepted Jesus as Savior and Lord, confessed my unworthiness and was "filled with the Holy Ghost." It felt wonderful. Transforming, integrative, uplifting. My mind floated in the spiritual realm and viewed all of life through the glasses of faith. After I was called to the ministry I possessed a strong sense of purpose, fulfillment, pride and adventure. I truly pitied the atheists who would forever lack this marvelously all-encompassing reality.

Psychologists have tried to examine this phenomenon. Orlo Strunk, Jr., says "religious beliefs are accepted and internalized so that for all practical purposes they become part of the person . . . a case of an individual's theology actually becoming his psychology." *(Religion: A Psychological Interpretation.)* Freud said that religion is the "universal obsessional neurosis of humanity." ("The Future of an Illusion.") "Devotion to an aim, or an idea, or a power transcending man such as God, is an expression of this need for completeness in the process of living." (Erich Fromm, "An Analysis of Some Types of Religious Experience.")

It think that is all true: the religious world view is a powerful psychology. Faith is deeply motivating. And it is heightened by the illusion that it is based on certain facts: the bible, personal testimonies, answers to prayer, apologists' "reasonings," scholarly authority, the life of Jesus, internal feelings of the "presence" of a god. The religious mind-set eagerly perceives these "evidences" as patent realities, while the skeptic views them as superstitious wishful thinking. Which they are.

My experience confirms the fact that it is the religious world view which distorts reality. It does so by imposing supernaturalistic presuppositions on all events and data. The naturalist, on the other hand, is severely limited to the facts, imposing nothing beyond that which is observable, testable and verifiable by anyone. Becoming an atheist has cleared my vision.

I used to think that everything that happened to me had some kind of spiritual significance. If I was looking for a parking space and a car pulled out of a place right near where I wanted to be, then I would say, "Thank you, Jesus, for giving me a place to park." If I had to park far away, then I would say, "Thank you, Jesus, for teaching me patience." I viewed all income as an undeserved gift from heaven. I tried to interpret every news event as fitting into God's plan for the world. If something bad happened, then I would say, "There is the price for evil." If something good happened, then I would say, "There is a sign of God's blessing." *Any* news from the Middle East was a sign that God was focusing attention on the site of the arena for the last days, which was just around the corner. Nothing in my life was accidental. Every occurrence was a lesson to be learned, or a part of divine purpose, or a temptation from the devil. Behind the visible world was a very real spiritual world inhabited by angels, demons, spirits, saints, all fighting, good versus evil, struggling to win my soul and demolish the other side. It made life very interesting, you can imagine.

One day I was driving home through the foothills east of Modesto, California. I was thinking about my ministry and praying that God would teach me how to follow his direction. I really wanted to obey God, to be a faithful servant, and to recognize his "true voice" in my spiritual ear. As I was traveling down the highway I "heard" my mind say, "Turn right." I figured this had to be the voice of God, and if I was ever to learn how to obey I had better do what I was told. I turned right. The little road led off into farmland, and I just kept driving, waiting for another signal. After a while I heard the voice again: "Turn left." So I turned left. This kept up, turning here and there, and I was beginning to feel excited about what God might have in store for me when I got wherever he was leading. Maybe, I thought, there would be some lost, godless person who was desperate to hear the gospel. Or maybe I would find a generous donor to my ministry. I kept driving until I came to a dirt road out in the middle of nowhere, and I heard, "Turn here." I turned and drove about a half mile to a dead end in the middle of a corn field. I stopped my car and turned off the engine, looking around for whatever it was that God had in mind. I really expected someone to come walking out of the corn, or something like that. After about fifteen minutes I began to feel rather stupid. Then a few minutes later I realized that there must have been some other reason why God would bring me out to the end of a dead-end dirt road. It finally dawned on me: God was testing my faithfulness! With a warm feeling all over my body I felt the Spirit say, "I am proud of you, Dan. You are an obedient child. You can go now."

It's not easy to change world views. It is psychologically expensive, but worth the cost in my case, I'm sure you will agree. Faith has its own momentum and belief is comfortable. To restructure reality is traumatic and scary. That is why many intelligent people continue to believe: unbelief is an unknown.

It is like trying to fall out of love. Falling in love is rarely initially the result of a careful rational assessment. Faith produces a psychological dependence on God which is almost impossible to budge. It is the mind-set which refuses to see the faults of a loved one, irrationally defending the indefensible. ("I dare you to say something bad about my Mom!") Most atheistic reasoning falls on deaf ears or is unrecognizably distorted by the Christian. The religionist's love for God is just too strong to be affected by the facts of the case.

Am I saying it is impossible to reason with a Christian? No, it is not impossible; but it is maddeningly challenging. To effect a deconversion, as in my case, requires a train load of patience and perseverance. Such a person is not going to blithely toss a head and say, "Oh, okay, there's no God."

Johnson and Maloney, in their book, *Christian Conversion: A Psychological Perspective*, present an interesting model for conversion to Christianity. They show a person going through a process with three periods of development: growing awareness, consideration and incorporation. The two transitions between the periods are a point of realization and a point of encounter. As I studied this model I realized that this is exactly what happened in my journey *out* of Christianity!

Growing Awareness - **Consideration** - **Incorporation**

▲ ▲

Realization **Encounter**

The period of Growing Awareness was a long gentle process where I gradually became aware that there were other points of view that merited investigation. As an interdenominational evangelist I was introduced to a wide spectrum of Christian theology and eventually came to see my own brand of fundamentalism in perspective. My early thoughts were, "If all these sincere liberals are vulnerable to error, why am I immune?" I came to the point of realization that I had doubts, honest doubts that demanded respectful consideration, though I fully expected to resolve them and keep my faith strong.

The second period, Consideration, was less gentle. It lasted about five years and it just about tore my guts out. I confronted the issues in face-to-face battle, and I kept losing. Biblical reliability, evolution, morality, faith versus reason, prophecy, church history, miracles, answers to prayer, psychology. I did not want to lose my faith, but I became painfully aware that Christianity has no case. I discovered that there is no evidence for Christianity. And I also found out, to my astonishment, that there is no *need* for it.

Can you imagine what these truths did to my world view? Can you sense the desperation, the impulse to run back to the comfortable arms of faith? I loved my Christian life and didn't want to surrender it. Jesus was precious to me, and I saw him slowly die before my eyes, watching flesh and blood turn into vapor. During that five year period I cried, I yelled, I fought, I pounded the doors of heaven. To no avail. Heaven is empty. I finally stopped calling "Father!" and cried "Uncle!"

I came to the point of encounter where I realized I was no longer a Christian. I was a brand new baby atheist—born again! Having emerged from the warm comforts of the womb I winced at the light and shivered at the cold. But I was alive—it was worth the trauma.

The final period, incorporation, is much more enjoyable. At first there was just myself, naked and toddling, with nothing but a strong confidence in reason and trust of my character. I felt alone with my books, hoping there would be some sort of community of freethinkers out there somewhere. Atheists do not have churches on every corner or televangelists on every channel. But I discovered that if you publicize your views you will find kindred spirits. I found the address of the Freedom From Religion Foundation in Annie Laurie Gaylor's book, *Woe to the Women—The Bible Tells Me So,* and immediately wrote a letter. Some of my freethought letters to the local newspapers uncovered some other atheists in my area. We *are* a community of sorts, around the world, ragged and loosely bound, but a community nonetheless. Perhaps we free-thinkers do not all share a common world view, but we do agree in our rejection of the orthodox world view.

Where were the freethinkers when I needed them? Why did no one intercept me as a youth preparing for the ministry? Where was the school counselor, teacher, humanist, atheist, rationalist neighbor that I needed to hear? Freethought is respectable. Freethought is crucial. Freethought needs to be publicized.

Why do intelligent people believe? They believe by default. Unless a rational world view is shown to be an attractive alternative to superstition, the momentum of orthodoxy may never be stopped.

Freethought Today, March, 1985.

6

When All Things Worked Together For Good

I
T WAS THE sound of the organ, more than anything else, that established the mood of the place. With its dramatic sweeps and heady crescendos flooding the huge vaulted building we felt engulfed by the presence of God's Holy Spirit, breathing in, breathing out, laughing and crying for joy and worship. Here and there a woman was standing, arms reaching upward, eyes closed, praying in an unknown tongue. Wheelchairs and crutches littered the aisles. Hopeful candidates pressed to find a seat as close to the front as possible; the balconies were standing-room-only. The Shrine Auditorium, near the Los Angeles Coliseum, was rarely so packed as when Kathryn Kuhlman came for her monthly healing services. I was there for her first regular visit in the mid-sixties and for two years I hardly missed a meeting.

My responsibilities as choir librarian did not inhibit me from sensing the intense hopefulness of the occasion. Before Kathryn walked out on stage the building radiated that unique beauty of an orchestra tuning up before a symphony. I would often watch her as she stood backstage, nervous yet determined, possessing a holy mixture of humility and pride, looking like a goddess in her long flowing gown. The audience was anxious, the Spirit was restless.

The organ crescendo reached a glorious peak as she slowly walked out on

71

stage. Those who could rose to their feet, praising God, weeping, praying. It was electrifying and intensely euphoric. I felt proud to be a witness of such a heavenly visitation.

Kathryn would often deny that she was conducting "healing meetings." She stated that her only responsibility was obedience to God's moving; it was *his* business to heal people, and it didn't have to happen in every meeting. Of course, most of the people had come to receive or witness a miracle, and they would not be disappointed.

Kathryn often seemed uncertain how to start the meeting. She would pray, talk a little, preach somewhat freely, or just stand silently crying, waiting for God to move. He always moved, of course—the audience couldn't stand it, this delay of climax. (It is like the restlessness I felt on Christmas mornings waiting for Dad to finish reading the biblical nativity story before opening the presents.)

In those early months, before the practice of having the local ministers sit on the stage, the choir was placed directly behind Kathryn in folding chairs. I always sat in the front row, right behind her, about eight feet from the miracles, peering past her down into the sea of eager faces who had come to be blessed. The choir would often sing quietly behind the healings, "He touched me, yes, he touched me! And, oh, the joy that floods my soul! Something happened and now I know; he touched me and made me whole!" (One of my friends counted over thirty iterations of that song during one meeting.)

After twenty or thirty preliminary minutes, which included a few choir numbers, the healings would begin. People would be ushered up to Kathryn, one at a time, to receive a "touch from God." She would face the candidate, touching the forehead, and would either ask the problem or directly "discern" the need. Usually the supplicants were "slain in the spirit," meaning they fell backwards to the floor under God's presence, often with arms raised in surrender. I often had to pick up my feet when they fell in my direction.

Kathryn had a "catcher," a short, stocky, red-headed former police officer who would move behind the people and soften the fall. He was often quite busy. People would be dropping all over the stage, even choir members and ushers. He rushed back and forth like a character in a video game, never missing, though it was sometimes quite close.

It didn't matter that most of the "healings" were unimpressive. We were in God's presence—a miracle is a miracle. Sometimes an individual would discard crutches or push Kathryn around the stage in the unneeded wheelchair, things like that. But the healings were usually internal things: "Praise God! The cancer is *completely* gone!"

One very common healing was deafness. Kathryn would tell the person to cover the good ear (!) and ask if she could be heard. "Can you hear me now? Can you hear me now?," louder and louder until the person nodded. Then she would dramatically move away and speak softly to the person, who would jump and say "I can hear you! I can hear you! Praise God!" The place would fall apart, of course, people screaming and hopping. Miracles do that to people. It was an incredible feeling, an ecstasy beyond description. We felt embraced by the presence of a higher strength, participating in a group worship (hysteria), floating on the omnipresent surges of the organ music, joining in song with heavenly voices.

In one service Kathryn replied to the criticism that some of her healings were purely psychosomatic by saying, "But what if they *were* merely psychosomatic, is that not also a miracle?" Doctors, she said, will tell you that the hardest illnesses to cure are the psychosomatic ones. God works in mysterious ways.

I never witnessed any restored body parts or levitations. The bulk of the healings were older women with cancer, arthritis, heart problems, diabetes, "unspoken problems," etc. There was an occasional exorcism (mental illness?) and rebuke.

Most of it, though, as I reflect, was pretty boring. We had come to be blessed and we were not to be cheated, taking the slightest cue to yell and praise God. I think, in retrospect, the organist was the real star of the show, working with Kathryn to manipulate the moods. And we were so pliable.

Experiences like that are extremely confirming to the Christian life. It is said that love is blind. That's probably true, though I think what actually happens is a transformation of faults rather than a denial. We see what we want to see. I was called to the ministry during a meeting of high emotion and intense worship like that. During seventeen years of evangelism I felt I was in direct contact with God's power and that nothing was impossible. "All things work together for good to them that love God, to them who are the called according to *his* purpose." (Saul of Tarsus, *Romans 8:28*) I used that scripture on many occasions to explain the unexplainable. The religious mentality can completely blot out reason and common sense. God becomes more important than truth. No matter what happened I interpreted it to God's glory. To the Christian everything makes sense, there is always an explanation, *always* a way out. Failed healings, for example, simply did not count: God has an explanation.

I often botched up healings in my own ministry. For example, I was called on to pray for someone's healing after I preached to a group of Latin Americans in Arizona. It was a large barn-like building with old wooden folding chairs and unswept floors, poorly lit. My sermon topic was *faith*, and I remember encouraging the listeners to believe that God is powerful enough to perform any miracle.

After the meeting some of the team members brought a woman up to me who wanted to be healed of crippling arthritis. They were all ready to see a miracle. Gulp! They hovered around me and insisted I pray for this woman. Poor thing—she was shaking and crying and praying. Well, why not, I thought—this is God's promise, not mine. So I laid my hands on her shoulder and prayed, asking God, in Jesus's name, to be true to his word and heal this sickness. I then said, "In the name of Jesus, be healed!"

It was very quiet. The woman opened her eyes and looked up at me. Everyone was smiling hopefully. Nothing happened. She kept looking at me. Everyone was looking at me, what was I supposed to do now? I finally found an escape: "Woman, according to thy faith be it unto thee." I know that was a dirty trick, but what would you have done? If she were not healed it was not my fault. She just didn't have enough faith, that's all. I remember the other team members seemed disappointed, but I assured them that God knows what he is doing. The woman left the building, hunching out into the night still sick, but now also rebuked.

I did have better luck on another occasion. I and three friends had organized a missionary trip to a church in Mexico City, just south of the capitol buildings. We formed a male quartet, Steve, Gary, Ralph and I, which sang nightly after which we would take turns preaching. It was our habit to meet at least an hour before the meeting for prayer and organization. These were no ordinary prayer meetings, they were "spirit filled." We prayed, spoke in tongues, sang "in the spirit," laid hands on each other for ministry and sought the mind of God for the evening's service.

One night Gary, the big Teddy Bear of the group, came into the prayer room having lost his voice. He grunted out, "You guys pray for me, I can't sing tonight." We placed him in a chair in the middle of the room and set to praying. After about ten minutes I felt completely caught up in the spirit of God, totally confident of his power, lost to my own concept of self. With authoritative faith I stood up and walked over to Gary. Placing my hand on his bowed head I said, "Gary, in the name of Jesus you are healed!" He immediately sat upright and said, "Praise the Lord!" in a strong voice.

Imagine what that did to our faith! We went into the church, sang our songs, and preached our sermons, though the meeting was not otherwise memorable. (Gary is the same fellow who once threw away his glasses because God had promised to heal his poor eyesight. A few weeks later he stumbled into an optometrist's office and bought another pair.)

"All things work together for good," it doesn't matter how things turn out.

It can all be labeled "good." The rare victories are flaunted, the numerous failures forgotten. Religious hindsight transforms life into one huge "victory."

Believe me, when you deal with a spiritual Christian you are dealing with a powerful psychology. Spirituality snares the mind. Rational arguments are merely *hors d'oeuvres* to the souls starving for miracles. Allegiance to a love relationship with one's Creator supersedes all else. It was easy for me to believe I had seen supernatural workings, they were required, I made myself see what was expected.

It's interesting that when you ask a Christian to demonstrate the effectiveness of prayer (not with anecdotes, but with specific tests), or to prove a miracle, you will receive noncommittal replies: God can not be tempted, prayer is not a toy, truth is invisible to the unbeliever, God's ways are mysterious— all cop-outs. I, like all Christians, learned to be quite creative in my attempts to make "all things work together for good."

Freethought Today, January/February, 1985

7

Ministers
I Have Known

I FINALLY READ *Elmer Gantry*, Sinclair Lewis's classic portrait of a ruthless evangelist, a pathetic product of raw ambition and dishonest superstition. Lewis paints a beautiful and horrible picture of the clerical mind set. And it is a nice touch of irony that when Gantry needed a guaranteed crowd pleaser, his main sermon material was repeatedly borrowed from the writings of Robert Ingersoll! ("Love is the only bow on life's dark cloud. . .")

If you are a freethinker you will relish this book. I was amazed at how well Lewis captured and exposed the subculture of ordinations, congregations and revival meetings. It revived many memories of my own years in evangelism. Too many.

But I must hasten to add that I was not a hypocrite like Elmer Gantry. No. I never stole from Ingersoll. I had never heard of Ingersoll! I considered myself to be truly sincere, and for much of the time, I was.

Lewis is right, of course. There are hucksters in the ministry. But it is my opinion that most preachers are not deliberately dishonest. To be a fraud requires a certain level of intelligence.

Televangelists like Jim Bakker and Jimmy Swaggart may be more intelligent than we think. Let's not pretend that they don't know what they are doing. They're not so dumb: look at all the money, power, and prestige! Of course, this makes their hypocrisy even worse, and their crimes against decency all the more dishonest.

I once did a radio talk show about the Jimmy Swaggart incident involving a prostitute. I was coming down pretty hard against religion in general when the host interrupted me and asked if it were fair to say that Jimmy Swaggart had somehow corrupted Christianity. I said no, Jimmy Swaggart hasn't corrupted Christianity: Christianity corrupted Jimmy Swaggart. If you spend all of your time concentrating on evil, then it can consume you. If you go to massive lengths to deny something as natural as your own sex drive, it can come to control your whole life. We want what we can't have. Jimmy Swaggart, motivated by corrupt views of human nature, has blown his normal sexual desires out of proportion and has created a monster. Just look at that face!

Even though I think most ministers are sincere, I did encounter my share of slime-balls during my years of evangelism. I remember the incident of the sleeping bag. I was eighteen. I woke up one night in a classroom of a large church somewhere deep in Mexico during a missionary tour, and I needed to find the bathroom real quick. (Montezuma's revenge.) Stumbling down the dark hallway, frantically opening doors, I carelessly switched on a light to discover our respected leading evangelist in a sleeping bag with a teenage girl. He sat up surprised, then quickly ducked under cover. (I later learned that this man is notorious for such "personal" evangelism. He is still out there, somewhere, spreading the good news.)

As a teenager I was doing some yardwork at our pastor's home in Anaheim. He was out making arrangements, hosting a visiting evangelist who had erected a huge "healing crusade" circus tent near Disneyland. I took a phone message—it was an angry woman, the evangelist's wife calling long distance, asking if I knew where in heck her husband was. He hadn't called her for weeks, was he in California, would I tell him to call her right away? I rode my bike four miles and found the man at a prayer meeting in the tent. He stuffed the note in his pocket and walked away without saying one word.

But most of the ministers I knew weren't that slimy. It is more fair to call them inept. Like the "world conquerors" I met in Upland. I am not sure why I was impressed with this group of associate pastors at a "family life" church, but I was determined to be admitted to the inner circle and managed to get myself invited to their privileged Tuesday night fellowship. The head pastor had been a linebacker with the Oakland Raiders. Do you know what we did all evening? We played RISK, a table game of world domination! I lost badly and was never invited back. I eventually learned that much of the real church work was accomplished by their wives, who were scripturally barred from any leadership positions or important decision making. (What do women know

77

about military strategy? Christianity is war!)

Later there was a real scandal there. One of the ministers confessed from the pulpit that he had had sexual feelings for a married woman in the congregation—whom he named—who was seeing him for regular counseling sessions. Nothing actually went on, he says, but the fallout just about ruined the church and the two families. (The poor woman—what a betrayal!)

And another man, the very capable youth director, was denied ordination. Do you know why? Because his four-year-old hyperactive son one day ran up to the communion table and unsanctimoniously gulped down some grape juice. How could this man pastor a flock if he could not govern his own family?

After I accepted a post at an Assembly of God church, I was excited to be invited to their annual denominational ministerial fellowship banquet. Do you know what the "fellowship" turned out to be? A loud brag session. One pastor had just added a new educational wing, another had just topped a thousand members, another reached the million dollar mark, built an elaborate sanctuary, and so on. They all seemed to view each other not as brothers, but as competitors. It was one of the most disappointing and enlightening Christmas dinners I had ever eaten.

When I think of ministers I have known, I see a kaleidoscope of images. I was an interdenominational traveling evangelist for many years, and met hundreds of pastors from all denominations. I think of the Quaker pastor who resigned and went into a dark depression, alcoholism and paranoia, perhaps triggered in part by his daughter joining a drug commune. I picture the overweight perspiring Foursquare preachers, waving their hankies, shouting and prancing about the stage, ruling their churches like little kingdoms. Or the staid Methodist cleric who refused to smile at my "Blest Be the Tie that Binds" joke as we were putting on our ties before the meeting. Or the country preacher who *did* laugh at my "Turn the other cheek" joke when he accidentally sat on a cup of coffee.

I think of the skinny Mexican pastor in Nogales whose second wife was pregnant with his twelfth child! His first wife had died at age forty, no one knows why, after giving birth to eleven children. And the televangelist I know who ran off with his secretary and was back on the air in less than two years, preaching about "end time" judgment. (Richard Roberts, son of Oral Roberts, is also now on the air with his second wife. His first wife, Patty, divorced him about the time we started hearing rumors of his philandering at Oral Roberts University.)

I visited a lot of little churches around the country. As an outside evangelist I was "privileged" to hear countless woes of pastors who had no one else to talk to. I listened to tales of financial struggles, bickering deacons, sexual temptations, troublemakers within and without, doctrinal schisms, denominational competitions, and, of course, confessions of doubt and weakness. These ministers are caught in the dilemma of not being able to confide in any of their church members because they need to be a strong example. Neither could they confess to any other local pastors because they wouldn't admit weakness to a rival. Who counsels the counselor? I had nothing profound to tell these men, so I did a lot of listening. (Today I would tell them to leave the ministry and do some honest work.)

And dirty jokes! The filthiest jokes I have *ever* heard have come from the mouths of the clergy. From ministers whom I had otherwise held in high regard. When some preachers finally do manage to communicate with each other as peers, they realize they have nothing to prove to each other, so they take the opportunity to let off some steam. Where else could they tell such racist and sexist stories? Not from the pulpit. (Unless they are quoting the bible.)

I remember the pompous, God-educated pastor who pronounced *indictment* "in-DICKED-ment," and the parson who forced every sermon into a three-point alliterative outline, like "Prepared, Persecuted, and Peach Pie." (The things you learn in seminary!) And there was the arrogant minister who would publicly chastise members by name for being delinquent in tithing or for having "unholy" dating practices. One day he leaned a bit too hard, toppling the pulpit over onto the elegant table of communion wine. That was very messy and very funny. (Grapes of wrath.)

I have a friend who says that if you were to take all the preachers in the world and lay them end to end, it would be a good idea just to leave them there.

They are not all like Elmer Gantry. Most of them are rather uninteresting, actually. But they all suffer from an identity crisis, from the same tragicomic pressures. Most of them sincerely feel they are doing the right thing. But what kind of grip on life can you have working for an invisible boss, speaking with assurance of things which cannot be known? How much integrity can you maintain as a teacher of truth if you are *not allowed* to invite a fair discussion of an opposite point of view? Where is the prestige in representing a god who is so all-powerful that he can't do any work unless people write out (tax-deductible) checks? What honor is there in selling real estate to people who must die before they can take possession? Of course, like Barnum said, there is a sucker born every minute, and as long as there are people gullible enough to donate to religion, stock in heaven will be a bull market. A market for bull. If there were no market for such property, perhaps ministers would move into more productive lines of work. Like the circus.

Freethought Today, April 1987

8

Some
Mistakes

THE NAME OF Bob Ingersoll was first introduced to me in church. It was the summer of 1983, while I was nearing the end of my journey out of faith, just a few weeks before I would admit to myself that I was an atheist. I was still preaching and performing religious concerts, out of habit and financial necessity. I had been invited to perform some music for a Sunday evening missionary convention in a large and wealthy Assembly of God church in San José, California. I sang an original composition about Jonah (the reluctant missionary) and the Whale, and another song from one of my musicals, which this church had performed in the past.

As I took my seat, to enthusiastic applause, I couldn't avoid the conflicting feelings that had been pestering me for months. I knew I would be rejecting religion in the near future; it seemed inevitable. Yet as I looked around me that night I saw the immense power of Christianity: a thousand worshipping faces, huge maps of global missionary endeavors, an immensely impressive and opulent church building, smiling reassuring glances from my friends. The whole thing felt so right, so natural, so encouraging . . . so dreamlike.

The missionary speaker took the pulpit and announced that the bible has been proved to be God's word. He asked us to consider how many other books in history had as much popularity as the bible. How many other writings had inspired such a widespread, continuous and faithful following?

"How many of you have ever heard the name *Bob Ingersoll?*" he asked. No one in that audience, including myself, had ever heard his name. "You see?" he continued, "The critics of the Bible have all washed away to oblivion, but the Bible remains steadfast, immovable."

He then briefly outlined the evils of Bob Ingersoll, the nineteenth-century agnostic orator, followed by an illustration that "proves" the bible is inspired. He said he had visited the public library in Peoria, Illinois, Bob Ingersoll's hometown, and asked the librarian if she had any of his books. According to his sermon, she took a long time searching and came back embarrassed that there was only one old copy of *Some Mistakes of Moses*. When the minister opened the book, he noticed that the last time it had been checked out was in the mid-fifties!

"What is the most popular book in this library?" he asked her.

"Why, the Holy Bible, of course," she replied without hesitation. (I find this hard to believe.)

"You see," he told us, "the Bible is preeminent. Bob Ingersoll died just over eighty years ago and no one even remembers his name, not even in his home-town. Jesus died and rose from the dead two thousand years ago and his name is above all names! Hallelujah!"

The crowd was hysterical with applause for yet another proof of Christianity, while I sat there thinking, "But what did he say? What did Bob Ingersoll *say?*" As the preacher turned his sermon to other proofs of the power of God's Holy Bible around the world, I remained in silent defiance, my mind shouting, "Unfair! What did Bob Ingersoll say? What mistakes did Moses make? Why was Ingersoll wrong?"

It was a few months later when I saw and immediately ordered *The Best of Robert G. Ingersoll*, from a catalog for Crusade Publications. And I loved it. I laughed, I cried, I pondered, I admired. I thought I was the only person who had ever thought these things, and now I had found a friend who had not only thought the same things, but had expressed them much more clearly and forcefully. I remember thinking that if Jesus still lives, then so does Robert Ingersoll. I couldn't help feeling that the "spirit" of Bob Ingersoll was reaching across a century to minister to my groping intellectual needs. (Some lingering remnants of my former way of thinking.)

But it wasn't until this past convention of the Freedom From Religion Foundation in Minneapolis (1985) that I finally obtained a copy of *Some Mistakes of Moses*. I bought it from the Foundation book table just a moment before I went up to take my place on the platform as one of the panelists of ex-clergy atheists, carrying the book with a kind of symbolic sense of completion. No,

81

Robert Ingersoll, you are not forgotten. Freethought is still alive; and the bible's "preeminence" remains as vulnerable now as always.

As I read *Some Mistakes of Moses* I can see why Christian ministers would wish the world to forget it. It hits a nerve. In his own day Ingersoll had to deal with the wounded clergy:

"And here, it may be proper for me to say, that arguments cannot be answered by personal abuse; that there is no logic in slander, and that falsehood, in the long run, defeats itself. People who love their enemies should, at least, tell the truth about their friends. Should it turn out that I am the worst man in the world, the story of the flood will remain just as improbable as before, and the contradictions of the Pentateuch will still demand an explanation."

Ingersoll does a fine job of analyzing the bible. His writing is sometimes scholarly, sometimes informal and humorous, but always insightful. It seems, however, that most of the responses to his work were less than intellectual.

"Why should a believer in God hate an atheist?" he wrote. "Surely the atheist has not injured God, and surely he is human, capable of joy and pain, and entitled to all the rights of man. Would it not be far better to treat this atheist, at least, as well as he treats us?

"Christians tell me that they love their enemies, and yet all I ask is—not that they love their friends even, but that they treat those who differ from them, with simple fairness. We do not wish to be forgiven, but we wish Christians to so act that we will not have to forgive them."

Ingersoll finds the biblical god repugnant: "When I speak of God, I mean that god who prevented man from putting forth his hand and taking also of the fruit of the tree of life that he might live forever; of that god who multiplied the agonies of woman, increased the toil of man, and in his anger drowned a world—of that god whose altars reeked with human blood, who butchered babes, violated maidens, enslaved men and filled the earth with cruelty and crime; of that god who made heaven for the few, hell for the many, and who will gloat forever and ever upon the writhings of the lost and damned."

Five years ago I would not have appreciated Robert Ingersoll. I, predictably, would have denounced him as an angry, misled critic. After all, I was an "ordained" minister, and I had read the the bible and had come to completely different conclusions. So I thought. Actually, though I had read the bible through many times and studied it thoroughly to prepare my sermons, I had never really *read* the bible. I know I had considered those ugly Old Testament horror stories, but they must not have passed through my grid of meaningfulness. I even *supported* the doctrines of hell and sin as necessary aspects of the spiritual world. I would smile at the skeptics, viewing them as the ignorant sinners for whom Christ had died, somehow lacking the required maturity of thought, or attitude of humility which brings the entire bible into complete spiritual harmony. In reality, the skeptic did not share my preconditioned bias toward the bible, was not bound by the requirement that it be true.

I once heard a Mormon official on the radio defending the church against allegations of impropriety which were being brought by a disgruntled former member. "Why should anyone pay attention to this self-appointed critic?" he asked. He said that the only people we should listen to are the "official spokesmen" for the church, those who have dedicated their lives to studying the faith, those who have committed themselves to truly understanding the subtleties and higher meanings of the particular religion.

Would you trust a church-appointed critic? I think the only critics we should pay attention to are the "self-appointed" ones—the Voltaires, Paines, and Bob Ingersolls of the world. Wasn't the New Testament Jesus a "self-appointed" critic of the Scribes and the Pharisees? He didn't toe the party line. Would you trust the "official spokesmen" to give a fair treatment of something to which they have dedicated their lives to defend? Why is it that someone like myself, "officially" ordained to preach, can suddenly be dismissed as a self-appointed critic? (I thought I was supposed to be a "spiritual leader," but I discovered I was nothing more than a crossing guard.)

The bible will remain "preeminent" as long as minds remain unchanged. Most freethinkers, I am sure, have experienced the frustrations of discussing the bible with Christians. Biblical criticism must continue, of course; but more important, we must address the question of epistemology: how do we know what is true? In my case the bible fell to pieces not because of a well-reasoned attack on scripture, but because I embraced a new and better way of thinking, a rational frame of mind, a love for truth. I had to be born again, as a freethinker.

The minister made a mistake that night when he mentioned *Some Mistakes of Moses*. Little did he suspect that in his audience would be an inquiring individual who would someday open Ingersoll's book to read, "Until every soul is freely permitted to investigate every book, and creed, and dogma for itself, the world cannot be free."
Freethought Today, December, 1985.

Promise of Dawn
by Dan Barker and Juanice Charmaine

All I've ever wished for,
All I've ever tried,
Every dream I've longed for has vanished.
All those golden sunsets,
Promising the dawn,
Fade into a night-time
That lingers on.
And every tear I've cried
For every prayer that died*
Can't return that promise of dawn.

Maybe in the shadows
I can find my way—
Maybe reach a brighter tomorrow.
Understand my sorrows,
Reach beyond my fears,
Find a morning rainbow in my tears.
I'll find the time to try.
There's no more time to cry.
Reaching for that promise of dawn.

* Originally "For every love that died"

FINDING FREETHOUGHT

Part 2

Losing Faith in Faith

9

Why I Am
An Atheist

I AM AN ATHEIST because there is no evidence for the existence of God. That should be all that needs to be said about it: no evidence, no belief. However, this simple statement of unbelief always has had profound effects on people.

Many people do feel that there is evidence for a god. Since they cannot imagine *themselves* as nonbelievers, they try to detect some ulterior motive for atheism. Rather than accept the straightforward statement that there is no evidence for a god, allowing the implication that their world view might be wrong, many Christians have claimed to uncover the "true" cause of unbelief. Here are some of the *ad hominem* arguments I have heard:

- "You resent moral guidelines and want to be free to sin."
- "You dislike authority."
- "You just want to be different and stir up trouble."
- "You are arrogant and hate God."
- "Your heart is in the wrong place."
- "You have been hurt by Christians, or offended by certain nonrepresentative immoralities and crimes in the Church."
- "You are cold, empty, and pessimistic."

- "You are an angry person."
- "You are too stupid, limited, or afraid to see what is obvious to everyone else."
- "You are an atheist because you don't know the true meaning of love."

None of these accusations is true. A strong clue that a person is arguing from a position of weakness is when character, rather than content, is attacked. Bertrand Russell pointed out that *ad hominem* is a last-ditch defense of the losing side. My atheism has nothing to do with any of this. Even if it did, how would it add to the evidence for a god?

The argument about not understanding "love" is particularly ironic. I do understand what love is, and that is one of the reasons I can never again be a Christian. Love is not self denial. Love is not blood and suffering. Love is not murdering your son to appease your own vanity. Love is not hatred or wrath, consigning billions of people to eternal torture because they have offended your ego or disobeyed your rules. Love is not obedience, conformity, or submission. It is a counterfeit love that is contingent upon authority, punishment, or reward. True love is respect and admiration, compassion and kindness, freely given by a healthy, unafraid human being.

The argument about "anger" is equally intriguing. There is nothing wrong with anger, if it is not expressed destructively. Paul said believers should get angry *(Ephesians 4:26)*. Jesus got angry *(Mark 3:5)*. Christians get angry often. I am rarely angry, certainly never when I am discussing atheism with believers, but many Christians, projecting their own feelings back on myself, often claim that I am angry when I quote horrible bible verses or level criticisms of Christianity that make *them* angry. What if I were to say, "The reason you are a Christian is because you are an angry person"?

The word "atheist" is not a label, it is merely a description. Since I do not believe in a god, I am by default described as an atheist.

If there *is* evidence for a hypothesis, then I will look at the data like all other information. However, if the claim itself is illogical, or if it is based on something other than honest investigation, it can be dismissed as wishful thinking, misunderstanding, or a lie. Theists do not have a god: they have a belief. Atheism is the lack of theism, the lack of *belief* in god(s). I am an atheist because there is no evidence for the existence of a god.

Some will say such a statement is absurd. Just because a certain atheist is unconvinced is no reason to discard the wealth of evidence accepted by the rest of the world. These believers would ask me to say: "I am an atheist because there is no evidence *that I accept* for the existence of God."

But I can't say that. I have looked at all these so-called evidences, and have tested many of them first-hand, and none of them show a supernatural being. Maybe other people think they do reveal a deity, but I don't. To be consistent, these believers may as well argue that even though few adults believe in Santa Claus, there is nonetheless plenty of evidence for his existence. A real Santa cannot be completely ignored, they might say, because he is revealed somewhere in the millions of youthful testimonials, song lyrics, stories, holiday displays, and a time-tested cultural tradition. Does all this evidence disappear just because we are skeptical? We are free to believe in Santa Claus if we want. The evidence remains, they might say, regardless of our verdict.

Yes, the *facts* remain, but they are not evidence for a real Santa Claus. They are evidence for something else: culture, history, the charming imaginations of children. They are evidence for consumerism and goodwill. But they are not evidence for an actual Santa Claus. We know this because each of the so-called proofs for Santa can be explained in natural terms and understood as part of a myth-making process.

The fact that most children believe in Santa is no argument. Neither is the fact that most adults believe in a god. Most of us have matured into "A-Santa-ists," and some of us have matured into "A-theists." We have grown up and we are satisfied with a natural explanation for the myths.

Of course, even the staunchest skeptic admits that one natural explanation does not completely rule out other possibilities. Perhaps there is a higher level of understanding that allows Santa to exist even though we are unable to prove it yet. The fact that kids have creative imaginations does not necessarily indicate that everything they imagine must be false.

True, but I can still claim that if there are adequate natural explanations that account for all the facts, then there is no driving need to search for higher levels. This is just common sense. Without such a rational limit there would be no end to the fanciful layers that could be added to any hypothesis. (This is usually referred to as "Occam's Razor": the principle of parsimony that suggests that we should normally accept the explanation that requires the fewest assumptions.) The skeptic, slavishly honoring all the possibilities, could be forced to spend a lifetime running around trying to disprove an infinite number of fantastic theories.

For example, maybe Santa is an ambassador from a distant planetary outpost of a galactic kingdom populated with red-and-white creatures who monitor the activities of specially chosen short people (elves and children?), seeking "conducive" humans as psychic vehicles for messages to holy reindeer that levitate when children dream during the winter solstice, most adults being too hardened to believe. Can anyone prove that this scenario is untrue? (You read it here first.) Since I don't have the means or the inclination to disprove such an idea, is this paragraph now allowed to count as evidence for such a theory?

A rational person would give the preceding paragraph an exceedingly low probability (almost zero), knowing nothing else of any psychological or myth-making factors when I wrote it. However, if some natural explanation arises for the existence of the paragraph (such as an admission that I just made it up), then the probability can be safely dropped to zero, and the discussion shifts from the reaches of outer space to the reaches of my inner brain.

Perhaps in a court of law the word *evidence* might be used more loosely. In a trial any object or testimony that might have a relevance to the case may be considered "evidence" before there is a verdict. In science it is the other way around: a fact is admitted as evidence only *after* the connection has been made, unless the exercise is purely hypothetical. (Few believers would claim that their faith is hypothetical.) I may insist something is evidence, but that does not make it so. There must be a connection, and it must be clear.

Theists think the connection is clear. They have traditionally presented a large number of evidences for their faith. These include historical documents, personal testimonies of inner spiritual experience, "revelation" (the idea that a deity has revealed itself through some means, usually written, meaning that the bible is considered evidence), miracle reports, answers to prayer, "changed lives," fulfilled prophecies, and various "rational" arguments including design in nature, cause-and-effect, moral imperatives, the divine wager, the need for perfection (ontological arguments), and appeals to faith, emotion, tradition, and authority. At first glance all of this appears overwhelming. For a skeptic to attack this plethora of widely accepted "proofs" might look like David confronting Goliath! After all, there aren't very many atheists in America (five to ten percent). Most humans accept some kind of god: how can so many believers be so wrong? How can all of these facts be ignored?

They are not ignored. David defeated Goliath. Critical atheists and other liberal thinkers have closely examined these "proofs" for a deity, and have found them wanting. They are all addressed in the following chapters in more detail. I am an atheist because these claims can be shown to have perfectly natural explanations and, as with Santa Claus, the probability for the exist-ence of a supernatural being can be safely dropped to zero. It *must* be dropped to zero, in the name of honesty.

I have often heard Christians say we must "start with God." Isn't that interesting? Would they say we must "start with unicorns," or "start with UFOs?" We can only start where we both agree, and go from there. We both agree that there is a natural universe—no argument there. It is the religious persons who maintain additional "supernatural" or transcendent assertions that go beyond what we both accept. It is unreasonable and unfair for them simply to fold their arms and demand that I disprove their allegations. Any impartial investigator will agree that we should start with what we *do* know, and then proceed from there. We should start with nature. We should start with the nonexistence of God and then the believer should argue *for* God's existence, not demand that atheists argue *against* it. The burden of proof in any argument is on the shoulders of the one who makes the affirmative claim, not the one who doubts it.

Someone once objected to my criticisms as attempts to "explain away" the proofs for a god. I am not trying to explain them away; I am trying to "explain them." The success of this rational approach hinges on something that in theory everyone advocates, but in practice is quite elusive: a complete impartiality on both sides. I am willing to change my mind, but I don't see many believers admitting even the possibility that they might be wrong—that *they* are the ones who might need conversion. They are usually only concerned with winning me to their views. The concept of impartiality, which is adequate for mundane matters, seems always to cave in to the heavier principle of *loyalty* when religious matters are discussed. Since most believers' religious views are something of an extension (or sometimes a *replacement*) of their personality, when you question their beliefs, you are often perceived as directly attacking *them* as persons—their identity within their religious culture, meaning in life, moral basis, their honor, intelligence, judgment, everything they are as individuals. Most of them have invested a lot of time, energy, and money in their faith, and they aren't apt to back off, or "lose face." They would rather earn points within their co-believing community than give any credibility to some Lone Ranger atheist. I don't pretend to be the most impartial observer, but at least I try. Few believers even make the effort.

Of course, none of this proves or disproves either position. Christians may be loyal and partial, but they still may be correct. Atheists might be rational and impartial, but they might be wrong. The believers' lack of impartiality merely underlines the difficulty of dialogue with atheists. One question I often ask of religionists is, "I will happily change my mind if I am proved wrong. Will you?"

Having said all this, what are the natural explanations for theistic evidences and assertions? Other parts of this book deal with most of them in greater detail, but briefly:

- Books like the bible turn out to be not much different from all other mythical/cultural writings, displaying internal contradic-

tions, errors, and absurdities.
- The supposed historical confirmations for Jesus and the bible (such as Josephus, Tacitus, Suetonius) are either forgeries, misinterpretations (innocent or deliberate), or simple archaeological support for uncontested and immaterial facts. (No one doubts that Jews, Moslems, Christians, Hindus, or Buddhists possess documented traditions in historical settings.)
- Personal testimonies and claims of fulfilled prophecy can be naturally accepted as psychological phenomena, exaggerations, lies, or simple mistakes in interpretation—none of them have been proved, and none of them necessarily point to anything outside the mind.
- All of the so-called "rational arguments" are unreasonable. These include first cause, design, ontology, morality, and others. Many of them involve logic which is circular, *ad hoc, a priori, ad hominem,* or *non sequitur.*
- It can be logically proved that "God," by some definitions, cannot, and therefore does not exist. For example, God cannot be both omniscient and omnipotent, or both omnipotent and omnibenevolent.

Bible criticism, though relevant, is not necessary to atheism. (God might be Brahma instead of Yahweh.) Some believers claim that it is unfair to reject Christianity until the bible has been completely studied and correctly interpreted in the context of history and the "total unified message of Scripture." If we doubters just had a better understanding, if we would just hold off a little longer, if we could read it in the original Greek and Hebrew, if we would study under the right teachers, take a course in hermeneutics, earn a Ph.D. in history, theology. . . They demand that we be "qualified" before making a final decision.

But is this a fair request? There are millions of unqualified Christians who have only the slightest familiarity with the bible, yet their decision to believe is considered acceptable. Church pews are packed with biblically illiterate worshippers. If it is necessary to have a degree in theology before making an informed decision, then millions of Christians will have to be ushered out of church.

Even the least educated atheist knows enough about the bible to decide it is not reliable. How many Christians know that much about the Koran? Yet they all feel qualified enough to discard Islam. Is a Baptist rejection of Hinduism based on an exhaustive analysis of the Vedas? Is it fair for a Catholic to dismiss Judaism before memorizing the Talmud? How many Lutherans or Pentecostals can quote even one passage from the Book of Mormon? Let's be fair here: how many atheist books has the average Christian read?

Everyone knows that the bible contains accounts of miracles, and that alone is enough justification for any rational person to conclude that there may be better uses of one's time than studying Scripture. (And, no, this is not an *a priori* dismissal of the supernatural. It is the same criterion Christians use in evaluating other religions. How many Baptists believe that ancient Roman amulets cured diseases?) Most believers are compulsively addicted through repetition to the idea that their bible is the greatest, most important, most inspired book in the world, and therefore the miracle accounts must have some credibility; but the rest of us are under no obligation to feel that way. Many believers have been taught that Scripture is the ultimate measure of truth, never imagining that the bible itself might come under a higher measure of truth, under the scrutiny of reason.

Of course, isn't this the problem? The issue is not so much *what* we think is true, but *how* we go about determining what is true. Epistemology. Logic. To the naturalist, the scientist, the rationalist, knowledge is gained by applying limits. Faith is the opposite; it has no borders. Without limits anything is possible. I could claim, for example, that this book was not written in the normal manner: I just concentrated intently and it materialized before me on the table in an instant of time, complete, typeset, and ready for the printer. Who would believe such an absurd claim? We all know there are limits to what can be true. To the scientist, the historian—to anyone in pursuit of verifiable knowledge—there are specific criteria that apply in a regular and universal manner through time, guiding us in determining what is true or false.

Most religionists, who are normally quite capable of analyzing everyone else's ideas with careful precision, suspend the rational process when they approach their own beliefs. Suddenly, everything is possible, even probable. "The Bible says it, I believe it," some say. We who doubt are accused of an "*a priori* bias" against miracles or a "prejudiced denial" of the supernatural, when we are merely following the process that all humans use to learn anything. If I say that I possess an honest inductive conclusion that all ravens are black, or that people do not resurrect from the dead, based on a careful observation of the world around me, then it is unfair to say that such views are based on an *a priori* dismissal of any and all possibilities.

When ministers who are untrained in science make cosmological pronouncements, why are they granted more credibility than professional physicists or biologists? This certainly is not because they are qualified—it is because, like quacks, they are "believed qualified." Some ministers have specialized knowledge on certain subjects, but otherwise they have no special edge. I know, I used to be one, and I have met more than a thousand ministers personally. There is nothing there. No advantage, no inside track, no superior abilities or sublime knowledge. Ministers are only successful if people want them to be. There are no preachers alive who could succeed without a following, without gullible people willing to call them "Pastor," "Reverend," or "Father."

Yes, there are certain ministers who have clearly earned respect as decent human beings helping other human beings, and their contributions to the betterment of the world should not be ignored. But this could be said about anybody. Ministers have no corner on compassion, no corner on charity. There are thousands of exemplary atheists who do not turn their good deeds into an excuse to pastor (shepherd) other human beings, or to stand up weekly before their "flock" and pontificate.

When I was an ordained minister I was considered an authority on the bible and Christianity. I never pretended to be the greatest theologian or bible scholar in the world (I was a soul winner), but I had been raised in the church, having attended services and Sunday School at least three times a week for my entire childhood and youth, hearing and thinking about the bible from Genesis to Revelation; I received a degree in religion from a Christian University; I took two years of koine Greek, and translated much of the New Testament into English; I passed a theological examination and was ordained as a minister; I preached from every book of the bible during more than nineteen years of evangelism across the continent, pastoring in three churches, and two years of missionary work in Mexico. No one ever objected to the "wisdom" of my sermons, and my ministry was quite fruitful. My credentials were never challenged. Since I was a "man of God," I automatically got respect.

But now that I am an atheist, all of this seems to amount to nothing in the eyes of believers. My opinions are now "foolishness," they say. It appears that Christians are not honest when they ask unbelievers to give the bible a chance. I gave it all the opportunity it could possibly need. Many atheists know far more about the bible than most Christians. Many of us have given Christianity (or Islam, or Judaism) more than a fair shake and have done all the work which, if we were believers, should have earned us the respect granted so easily to others. But the only thing that would impress most believers is an attitude of belief. I was considered a leader, but only as long as I led people where *they* wanted to go (which was heaven). If I were to walk back into one of those churches, would they listen to my preaching now? Would they want

94

to hear what I have learned about the bible? Uncovering this dishonesty, it is no wonder some atheists become cynical about "true believers."

I used to be one of those true believers, and I know that my motives were well-intended. I wasn't trying to deceive deliberately, or to avoid truth. I was a victim myself. Many Christians are fine people who want the best in life. They are trying to do what is right as best as they know how. When I preached the gospel I was not knowingly spreading deception. I was just caught up in an erroneous way of thinking, seeing only what I was allowed to see, forcing facts to fit a preconceived (ill conceived) world view.

In spite of the holy smiles, the Christian world view is not based on love: it is based on fear, wishful thinking, power and pride. In spite of their pretended humility, Christians hope to be favored to live forever, rule with Jesus, punish opposition, and receive personal rewards from an omnipotent Creator. My preaching was like the computer word GIGO: garbage in, garbage out. Can I be blamed, based on my narrow evangelical experience and limited exposure to other viewpoints? Should children be blamed for believing in Santa Claus?

You can only blame someone who *ought* to know better. Hopefully, we all grow up, and it doesn't hurt too much, and we get to the place where we ought to know better. I have grown up; I am an atheist.

What am I supposed to do now, pretend? If a god exists, why is faith necessary? Why force yourself to "be strong" and "completely surrender" to belief? If something is a fact, we don't invoke faith to accept it—it should be true on its own merits.

I am an atheist because I honestly want truth. I don't know everything, but I do know that there is no evidence for the existence of God.

Friendly, Neighborhood Atheist
by Dan Barker

Happy as can be!
I'm your neighborhood atheist*.
Friendly as can be. Hi!
I'm your neighborhood atheist.
I don't have any horns,
If you care to inspect me;
But don't expect me
To think just like you.
I know wrong from right,
And my life has meaning.
Don't worry, I won't bite!
I'm as nice as you.
All of us are made of the stuff of the stars.
Atheists are human beings—we didn't come from Mars.
Atheists are people too!

Caring as can be,
I'm your neighborhood atheist.
Moral as can be,
Your friendly resident atheist.
I'm not afraid of hell—
You cannot intimidate me.
You sure must hate me
To want me to fry.
Rationality
Is my favorite motto.
Your theology
Is just not true.
You keep accusing me of blasphemy all of the time,
But I cannot be convicted of a victimless crime.
Atheists are people too!

© Copyright 1986 by Dan Barker and the Freedom From Religion
Foundation, Inc. Song lyrics.

* I sometimes use the word "humanist" in concert.

10

Inaccurate Conception

I T WAS HOT, and the little adobe church was filled with farmers and a hundred barefoot children. As a teenage evangelist I was interpreting for another missionary who was preaching a "call to arms" sermon in a small village near Guaymas, Mexico.

My Spanish wasn't too good back then, but I was doing fine until he said, "Do not be ashamed of your loving Father." I didn't know the word for *ashamed* but I thought I could guess the word for *embarrassed*, so I said, *"Deben amar a Dios, pero no sean embarazados."* (You should love God, but don't get pregnant.)

I guess that is a classic blunder, because a Mormon friend of mine said it happened to a young woman whom he had encouraged to speak before a congregation in Argentina. *"Estoy muy embarazada,"* (I am very pregnant) she said, and when everyone chuckled she pointed to my friend and said, "Pos, él tiene la culpa!" (Well, it's his fault!)

I once got into real trouble with the word *novia,* which meant *girlfriend* to me, but which meant *fiancée* to the young woman to whom I had inadvertently proposed. There is a little town south of Chihuahua that I need to circumvent, consequently; I won't tell you all the semantic details.

I have noticed that my conversion from fundamentalism to atheism has

97

caused me to learn a new language, almost. Many words have had to be redefined: liberal, morality, religion, love, self, heretic, humanist, beauty, feminist. Take, for example, the word *godless*, which most dictionaries define as *wicked*. I am godless, but I am not wicked, which must mean that dictionaries are not inerrant. (Of course, dictionary editors should not be chastised for reporting a particular usage of a word. It is a religious society which should be blamed for assigning a morally pejorative connotation to an ordinary descriptive adjective.)

I thought I had understood the words *atheism* and *agnosticism* until I embraced them both and discovered they are pregnant with significance. In conversations with Christians I have found that most words need to be carefully defined before we can have any meaningful dialogue.

People are invariably surprised to hear me say I am both an atheist and an agnostic. I usually reply with a question like, "Well, are you a Republican or an American?" The two words serve different concepts and are not mutually exclusive. Agnosticism addresses *knowledge* in general; atheism addresses *belief in a god* specifically.

As such, agnosticism is broader and more useful. It is the refusal to take as a fact any statement for which there is insufficient evidence. It is a philosophy which may be applied to any area of life, whether science, UFO's, politics, or history; though it has most commonly been invoked in a religious context.

The word *agnostic* was coined by Thomas Huxley who attached the privative prefix *a-* (not, without) to the word *gnostic*, which is from the Greek word *gnosis* (knowledge). To promote the concept, Freedom From Religion Foundation member Bill Young organized a lively and informed association, the Society of Evangelical Agnosticism, in Auberry California. [SEA is now dissolved, though Bill is still busy in agnostic/freethought endeavors.]

One common fallacy about agnosticism is that it is a halfway house between theism and atheism. It cannot be, since it performs in a different arena and since the question, "Do you have a belief in a god?" can only be answered with a yes or no. ("Maybe" or "I don't know" are simply delays. They do not answer the question. A person who deliberately avoids the issue in this manner should not be called *agnostic*, but rather something like *indecisive* or *unprepared*. Of course, it is not dishonest to delay answering the question for want of clarification of terms; but the question, when answered, can only prompt a yes or no response.)

Another fallacy is that agnostics claim to know nothing, making them equal to Skeptics (à la Hume) who claim that nothing can be known to exist outside the mind. Although there may be a few who continue to push philosophy to this extreme, most contemporary agnostics do claim to know many things which are supported by evidence; they may possess strong opinions and even take tentative stands on fuzzy issues; but they will not claim as a fact something for which data is lacking, or something which data contradicts. This seems sensible to me.

It turns out that the word *atheism* means much less than I had thought. It is merely the lack of theism. It is not a philosophy of life and it offers no values. It betrays nothing of morality or motives. In my case, *becoming* an atheist was a positive move—the removal of the negative baggage of religious fallacy. But that is rather like having a large debt canceled. It has brought me up to zero, to where my mind is free to think. Being a freethinker is potentially quite positive. (See "What Is A Freethinker?")

Basic atheism is not a belief. It is the lack of belief. There is a difference between believing there is no god and not believing there is a god—both are atheistic, though popular usage has ignored the latter. (George Smith, in *Atheism: The Case Against God,* examines this distinction as the difference between "explicit" [or "critical"] and "implicit" atheism.) Atheism is the *absence of belief* in a god, or gods, whether that absence is due to a critical rejection of theistic assertions, to unfamiliarity with the subject (as with a baby, or with a nontheistic culture), or to noncommittal agnostic/skeptic principles.

If you have a belief in a god you are a theist, otherwise you are an atheist. Atheism and nontheism are the same word, though, of course, they may carry a different stigma in today's society. Smith suggests the term *anti-theist* for the small subset of atheists who positively deny the existence of a god. Of course, most atheists will sometimes speak of "denying" god, or state that "there is no god," informally; it may not be unjustifiable to think of a "lack of belief in god" as a relaxed "belief that there is no god" when repeated attempts to prove theism continually fail. All of us agree that it is permissible to say "there is no Santa Claus" even though such a statement can't be completely proved. However, even the atheists who "deny" the existence of a god (which I sometimes do in casual conversation), will have to back off when pressed against the philosophical wall, and admit that a lack of belief is not a belief.

Give me a definition of a god and I'll tell you whether I am a theist, atheist, or anti-theist. I am definitely anti-Yahweh-ist and anti-Zoroaster-ist since these creatures are self-contradictory and absurd, and since there exist natural explanations for the origins of the myths. If you define "god" as a natural species of superior extraterrestrials orbiting Proxima Centauri then I am an atheist, via agnosticism: I have no present basis for belief in such things, though I am open to evidence. If you want to identify "god" merely as the principle of "love" (or some other semantic twist of fuzzy liberal theology) then I guess you could call me a "theist" by that definition, but I would avoid the word because it would be meaningless and confusing. Naming a natural phenomenon "god" is unnecessary and unsound since it traditionally implies a superior being or transcendent mind. If "god" is just a synonym for some other natural concept, for which we already have a good label, then it can be—should be—thrown away.

Atheism is not a label, it is a description. I am an atheist, not an Atheist. If I ever do use the word Atheist with a capital 'A' it is because I wish to take advantage of the effects such a usage might cause, not because this defines who I am as an individual. (For example, I am a male. If I were to wear a shirt with the phrase "I am a Male," as a label, it would be for some political or emotional reasons designed for public impact.)

There are some who avoid the word *atheist* because of the popular stigma attached to it. In a context where they might be "labeled" and possibly misunderstood, they prefer to be called rationalists, agnostics, or nontheists. (I am not opposed to this. I think there can be some very good reasons for keeping views private, such as family harmony or job security.) Some people just have a distaste for *any* label. On the other hand, there are atheists (like myself) who view the stigma as an advantage, as a chance to be on the cutting edge. Atheists United in Los Angeles makes good use of the word in publicity to combat religious ideologies. If you are discussing religion and you are an atheist, why not say so? Some atheists figure that the word has suffered from bad press and it is time to correct the image. I agree.

Atheism has nothing to offer and nothing to prove. Being an atheist is no guarantee of kindness, morality, fairness, happiness, or even rationality. But this does not mean that atheism is negative. Atheism is a double-negative and can be perceived positively, just as the phrase "non-violence" is a good concept. But any atheist who wishes to make a truly positive statement must look beyond atheism into something like humanism, feminism, ethical culture, philanthropy, education, science.

Since leaving fundamentalism I have noticed a correlation between atheism and humanism. Most atheists seem to be deeply concerned with human values. Why is this? Perhaps it is because any person who has the impulse (the guts) to be identified as an atheist in today's society must be deeply motivated by something. Maybe the motivation is anger at religious immorality, or dissatisfaction with superstitious anti-intellectualism, or fear of the dangers of Christian intolerances, or empathy for the victims of bigotry, or some other such thing. Such impulses likely originate in a mind which is deeply concerned with fairness and compassion, not merely a rational approach to truth. My own rejection of religious morality (if that is not a contradiction in terms) is a by-product of an impulse to discover a truer code of ethical principles (not rules) for me and my species.

The bible says that the *"ungodly* are like chaff which the wind blows away." *(Psalms 1:4)* Religionists consider as chaff all that does not fall within their bounds. That's fine with me. I prefer the winds of freethought to the definitions of orthodoxy.

Freethought Today, January/February, 1986

11

The Great Escape

O N MANY TELEVISION and radio shows on which Foundation staff give sensible arguments against religion or the bible, an audience member or caller will say, "But you have to take it by faith." Losing the rational battle, most believers make a Great Escape into belief.

Faith is a cop-out. If the only way you can accept an assertion is by faith, then you are conceding that it can't be taken on its own merits. It is intellectual bankruptcy. With faith, you don't have to put any work into proving your case. You can "just believe."

Truth does not have to be believed. Scientists do not join hands every Sunday, singing, "Yes, Gravity is real! I will have faith! I will be strong! I believe in my heart that what goes up, up, up must come down, down, down. Amen!" If they did, we would think they were pretty insecure about it.

If faith is valid, then anything goes. Moslems believe in Allah by faith, so they must be right. The Hindus are right. The Greeks and Romans were right. More people claim to have seen or been healed by Elvis Presley than ever claimed to have seen the resurrected Jesus. With faith, *everybody* is right.

Suppose an atheist, refusing to look at any religious claims, were to say, "You must have faith that there is no God. If you believe in your heart that nothing transcends nature and that humanity is the highest judge of morality, then you will know that atheism is true." Wouldn't the Christians snicker?

Hebrews 11:1 says, "Faith is the substance of things hoped for, the evidence of things not seen." In other words, faith is the evidence of non-evidence. *Hebrews 11:6* says, "Without faith it is impossible to please him: for he that cometh to God must believe that he is." Even the bible admits that you can't know if God exists. You have to "believe that he is."

Jesus reportedly said, "If ye have faith as a grain of mustard seed, ye shall say unto this mountain, Remove hence to yonder place; and it shall remove; and nothing shall be impossible." How many faith-peddlers could pass this straightforward test? If Christians are not doing stupendous acts (that could not be done naturally), then how do they know their faith in God is valid at all?

How do they know they are even saved at all? Paul says, "For by grace are ye saved through faith . . . not of works, lest any man should boast." But James says, "Ye see then how that by works a man is justified, and not by faith only." Are believers saved by works, or aren't they?

Religionists sometimes accuse unbelievers of having faith. Every time you flip a light switch you exercise faith, they say. But this is not faith; it is a rational expectation based on experience. If the light fails to turn on, my world view is not shattered. I expect that the light will sometimes fail due to a burnt-out bulb, blown circuit, or other natural cause. This is the opposite of religious faith: the light does not turn on because of my expectation, but rather, my expectation is based on experience. If lights were to begin failing most of the time, I would have to adjust my expectations. (Or adjust my electrical system.)

But religious faith is not adjustable. It remains strong in spite of a lack of evidence, or in spite of contrary evidence. It is irrational.

Freethinkers reject faith as a valid tool of knowledge. Faith is the opposite of reason because reason imposes very strict limits on what can be true, and faith has no limits at all. A Great Escape into faith is no retreat to safety. It is nothing less than surrender.

Freethought Today, April, 1991

12

"What If You're Wrong?"

T HERE ARE TWO kinds of people in the world: those who divide everyone into two groups, and those who don't. Many in the first group say, "There are two ways to look at any issue: my way, and the wrong way."

Blaise Pascal, a seventeenth-century philosopher and mathematician, was one of that rare breed of "theistic agnostics" admitting that we don't know if there is a God, but choosing to believe anyway. His argument ran like this:

1. The existence of God can't be proved.
2. If it is true and you believe, you go to heaven.
3. If it is true and you don't believe, you go to hell.
4. If it is not true and you believe, you have lost nothing.
5. If it is not true and you don't believe, you have gained nothing.
6. Therefore, there is everything to gain and nothing to lose by believing in God.

Pascal's Wager is often expressed: "What if you're wrong?" (As if we unbelievers had never thought of such a question.) "You are risking everything and have no hope," we sometimes hear from concerned believers.

Freethinkers have pointed out that this is not an argument for the existence of a deity; it is simply an argument for belief. It is nothing more than intimidation, the old "Turn or Burn" sermon. Nor is it true that you lose nothing by believing—religion usually requires time, energy and money that could be better spent on more practical things, and often produces guilt, intolerance and fear. Unbelievers gain (if they have never lost it in the first place) peace of mind, open-mindedness, and freedom.

But perhaps the best way to deal with this non-argument is to point out that the wager is not a safe bet in the first place. It is not a fifty-fifty proposition, as the evangelists would have us believe.

There seems to be a tendency to frame a religious argument as an either-or, dichotomous issue—"my position" vs "everything else"—lending equal weight to both sides. The flat-earthers divide everyone into two level camps: those dummies who believe that the earth is a spheroid, and the sages who know it is not. Fundamentalist Moslems view everyone as either Islamic or evil.

What the users of Pascal's Wager do not understand is that there are more than simply two possibilities. Maybe there *is* a God, but he is only going to reward those who have enough guts *not* to believe. All of us atheists and agnostics will end up in paradise, very surprised. This drops the odds to about thirty-three percent. Or maybe there is a God, but he is so unjust that he is gleefully going to damn everyone at the end, regardless of their faith. This lowers it to twenty-five percent. The universalists might be right and we will *all* be saved. Or maybe there is a heaven, but no God, and only rationalists will figure out how to achieve it.

The odds sink below twenty percent with these additions, and we could go further. Perhaps Pascal's Catholic God is the wrong deity. Maybe when Christians die they find themselves in the Islamic hell! Adding a hundred religions to the field lowers the odds to less than one percent, and it is beginning to look like a very bad bet. We all could dream up crazy scenarios: all of reality, for example, is the dream of a cosmic polka-dot chimpanzee, and when our prayers waken it we cease to exist. There is an infinite number of wild possibilities, and even if their relative merits are not equal, the odds drop to zero.

For my money, I'll bet on reason and humanistic kindness. Even if I am wrong I will have enjoyed my life, the existence of which is under little dispute.

Freethought Today, January/February, 1991

13

Without A Doubt

THE LONGER I have been an atheist, the more amazed I am that I ever believed Christian notions. Some of the things I preached, that are believed by millions of Christians, are so silly that it seems to me *now* that I should have been able to see through it back then.

In their most inner thoughts, even the most devout Christians know that there is something illegitimate about belief. Underneath their profession of faith is a sleeping giant of doubt. Preachers constantly admonish believers to keep their faith strong, which betrays an underlying insecurity. Heavy-handed sermons might cause obedient followers to bury normal habits of critical thinking and feelings of uncertainty beneath a mountain of faith, tradition, and fear, but humans in a natural universe can't *help* doubting supernatural claims.

Ignoring doubt, theists recite their doctrines as if they became true by simple repetition. After a while, they become a part of the psyche. They stand as place-holders for thought. They shape the interpretation of reality.

Christians differ from unbelievers in the way they are "primed" to view the world, but this does not mean all Christians hold similar views. The particular doubts of any believer depend on the particular doctrines professed.

I remember once studying the first chapter of Acts with a friend. I was in the middle of my pentecostal phase, and I was hoping that certain bible verses

106

would convince my friend, who was a Quaker, to become "baptized with the Holy Ghost" (a phrase used by Charismatics and pentecostals to indicate receiving the gifts of the Spirit, especially speaking in tongues). I was surprised at how excited she was to be reading the very chapter that was so meaningful to me. Together we read the first eight verses, including:

Acts 1:5, "For John truly baptized with water; but ye shall be baptized with the Holy Ghost not many days hence."

Acts 1:8, "But ye shall receive power, after that the Holy Ghost is come upon you: and ye shall be witnesses unto me . . ."

After reading verse eight, I stopped and asked her what she thought. Her eyes lit up and she said, yes, she was happy to see that we agreed.

"What do you mean?" I asked, curious to know how a non-pentecostal would react to the truth of the Charismatic experience.

"This section is very special to Quakers," she said. "Don't you see it?"

"You mean verse eight?"

"No," she replied. "Verse five!"

For years I had heard verse eight repeated as one of the cardinal scriptures behind pentecostalism. We tongues-speakers took it to mean that modern Christians would receive a very real "power" to do very real things, such as glossolalia, faith healing, prophecy, and other "gifts of the spirit," and that this verse related the very first time such power was given to the church. This was such a strong doctrine to me that I imagined that *Acts 1:8* was a flashing beacon to everyone else who read it. However, my friend zipped right past it.

Because the Quaker tradition was a reaction to Catholic sacraments, she was more interested in verse five. While most Protestant denominations practice fewer sacraments than Catholics, the Quakers (and their modern counterpart, Friends, who are not as strict), observe none. That is, they perform no outward, physical sacraments: no baptism, no communion wine or wafers. Nothing physically symbolic. Their "communion" is inward, spiritual, often attained during a moment of complete silence. Many early Quakers would sit quietly and quake, hence their name. All of her life, my friend had been taught to respect *Acts 1:5* as a cardinal scripture of Quaker doctrine, showing that water baptism is not necessary. She imagined that it was a flashing beacon to *me!* We had both read the same chapter at the same time, and we had seen two entirely different truths.

Knowing that I used to be a true believer, freethinkers often ask me what it was that caused me to give up faith. They are looking for a magic bullet, I think, that does not exist. There is no "zinger" argument that will work with all believers. Every Christian has a particular set of pet doctrines, depending on the texture of their religious upbringing and training, and therefore will have a unique set of doubts. I can enumerate only my own thoughts, and hope that they map—more or less—with those of other believers.

Looking back, I have to admit that my greatest doubt was the efficacy of prayer. Prayer simply does not work. Period. I know that I prayed thousands and thousands of prayers that were a waste of time. That is, I know *now* that they were wasted. But since prayer is such a powerful doctrine of Christianity, I imagined that there was some meaning behind it all.

Prayer is terribly confusing to Christians. Theologians have fabricated such a myriad of unintelligible responses to the failure of prayer that it only makes the problem worse. For example, some say that God answers all prayers with a "Yes," "No," or "Wait." This example of unreasoning might allow someone to say that "prayer is answered" in a semantic sense, but it does little to solve the problem. If the answers to prayer are merely what God wills all along, then why pray?

Some say that prayer is an important exercise because, regardless of the outcome, it puts us in touch with God. But this contradicts the direct teaching of Jesus: "And all things, whatsoever ye shall ask in prayer, believing, ye shall receive" *(Matthew 21:22)*, and "If two of you shall agree on earth as touching any thing that they shall ask, it shall be done for them of my Father which is in heaven." *(Matthew 18:19)* The writer of *I John 5:14-15* said, "And this is the confidence that we have in him, that, if we ask any thing according to his will, he heareth us: And if we know that he hear us, whatsoever we ask, we know that we have the petitions that we desired of him."

Honest Christians know that these verses are false. It does no good to claim that many prayers are unanswered because they are not "according to his will." Even prayers that are clearly in line with the expressed "will of God" are rarely successful. Even if this reasoning were valid, it makes prayer useless as a means of changing nature.

Some Christians interpret failed prayer as an indication that there is something wrong with their spiritual life. They need to "pray harder," or "get right with God" before they can expect to see any results.

Blame the victim.

Most Christians do what I did. I made myself forget the failures, concentrating on the rare moments when it seemed that my prayers truly had been answered. If something wonderful transpired in my life, I would remember back to a general prayer for God's blessing a few days earlier and say, "See! God answers prayer!" If a specific prayer were followed by a specific result, which sometimes happens (if millions of Christians are praying thousands of prayers a year, it would be surprising if this did not sometimes occur), I would smile and accept the outcome as a direct answer to my prayer, not analyzing what was different this time from other times. Was I more "right with God?"

I remember being late for a meeting, not able to find a parking place near the event. Believing that the creator of the universe was intimately concerned with my daily activities, I prayed, "Dear God, please help me find a place to park," and a car backed out of a parking slot right near the door! "Thank you, Jesus," I said, believing that this was a direct answer to my prayer. What I was forgetting were the thousands of similar prayers I had prayed before that moment that simply evaporated into the air. Not thinking critically, I assumed that the "successful" coincidences were proof that God answers prayer while the failures were proof that there was something wrong with *me*. There never could be anything wrong God, in my way of thinking. Today, as an atheist, I continue to experience about the same percentage of lucky events as when I was a believer. Sometimes when something coincidental happens, I will say (as a joke), "See! This proves there is a God!" It proves nothing, of coures, but it gives me a good laugh.

Honest Christians have to admit that there is something dreadfully wrong about the idea of prayer. Now that I am an honest freethinker, I know that there is something dreadfully conceited about it as well. To think that the ruler of the universe will run to my assistance and bend the laws of nature for me is the height of arrogance. This implies that everyone else (such as the opposing football team, driver, student, parent) is *de*-selected, unfavored by God, and that I am special, above it all.

Don't ask Christians if they think prayer is effective. They will think up some kind of answer that makes sense to them only. Don't ask them, *tell* them: "You know that prayer doesn't work. You know you are fooling yourself with magical conceit." No matter how they reply, they will know in their heart of hearts that you are right.

In talking with freethinkers who have had a religious upbringing, I have learned that we all did not arrive at unbelief by the same path. Some struggled with issues that never concerned me: the miracles of the bible, outrageous claims of virgin births, talking animals, floating messiahs, and resurrections.

Another belief that is doubted by many is the claim that Christians are better off than non-Christians. I know that not all believers claim that Christianity will make you a better person in this life, but they all believe that there is *some* difference, *some* advantage over unbelievers. When they see atheists and agnostics who are happy, fulfilled, compassionate, and moral, they can't help wondering if their religion is indispensable.

Most Christians have doubt. Like suppressed anger, suppressed doubt can cause extreme discomfort. In my experience, the best way to conquer doubt is to yield to it.

14

Rule Of Thumb

THE PHRASE, *rule of thumb*, comes from the primitive English common law which forbade a man from striking his wife with a stick wider than his thumb. I think we can put the phrase to a more civilized use by applying it to a nice method of striking down religious arguments with an easy-to-learn technique.

Have you ever been caught off guard? Have you ever been in a debate situation, away from your library, forgetful of the vast freethought arsenal, unprepared for a particular topic? I have—in casual conversations as well as formal debates. I can't always keep all the facts on the tip of my tongue.

Although it is true that the ideal debate strategy is to be completely knowledgeable, it is also true that religious discussions encompass such a wide field that no one could be considered *totally* competent in all areas. A typical dialogue may involve history, philosophy, psychology, morality, biblical criticism, medicine, astronomy, biology, linguistics, economics and politics.

Whenever I have an occasion to jump into such deep waters, which is not infrequently, I do my best to know as much as I can. But I don't worry too much; I have a "Plan B" to fall back on if I need it. It is a critical *rule of thumb* which can be applied to virtually any religious argument, even if I am completely ignorant of the specific subject. It is not always the *best* method, but it works in a pinch.

The principle is this: all arguments can be made to turn back on themselves. All good arguments must be able to survive such a test. In the case of religion it usually causes real embarrassment. The technique is to make religionists defend their beliefs against their own logic—give them enough rope and they'll hang themselves. If you are reeling in a big fish on a thin line you can give it slack and let the fish tire itself out.

An obvious example is the argument from *first cause*: if everything needs a cause, then what caused god? Or the design argument: if complex order requires a designer, then what designed god's complex mind? See how it works? Rather than spending hours attacking the premises and evidences, you can accept the arguments at face value and then make them loop around and strangle themselves.

The argument from morality is a good example. If ethical absolutes originate with God, then on what basis can God be judged moral himself? If the Christian judges God to be "good," isn't that an admission that God is subject to a higher morality, and therefore cannot be God? If *good* is simply equated with *God*, then the religionist admits that morality is indeed relative, and there is no standard for determining that God is moral. Morality becomes meaningless and god becomes a dictator void of principles. Give God enough rope. . .

This rule of thumb is a very handy trick for bible discussions. You may not know much about the bible, but the next time a Christian quotes a scripture, pounce on it. Go look it up. Stop the conversation and act deeply interested in the bible verse. Usually they just want to "hit and run," shaping the argument from biblical authority. Read the whole chapter, before and after the verse. They usually won't like this because it interrupts their planned sermon. In the process, you may help them discover it is taken out of context, which is very common. (See "Out Of Context.") Ask who was the author and how we know that. Ask to whom it was written and when. (Most bible books are anonymous, bearing names assigned by tradition only, and few of their dates are known with any certainty.) Ask to see another translation and how we know this particular version was interpreted accurately. The religionist will agree that if the bible is important then it is crucial to get the *exact* meaning by considering all factors. You will both learn something and will likely take the steam out of the original argument. You may even get the bible to choke on its own words. And how can you be criticized? You are simply taking the religionist's lead, making them do the work of exposing the limits of their own knowledge.

The basic ontological argument (Anselm's version) runs like this: god is a

111

being than which no greater being can be conceived; if god does not exist in actuality, then he can be conceived to be greater than he is; therefore god exists. This is slippery. (Bertrand Russell, who had been very briefly swayed by this reasoning as a young man, later said that all ontological arguments are a case of bad grammar.) You don't need to know Gaunilo's or Kant's refutations to make this argument loop back on itself. Just take it at face value and ask something like this: does god have infinite mass? If he doesn't, then I can conceive him to be greater than he is. If god does have infinite mass, then I can disprove it empirically.

Or suppose someone claims freethought is discredited by the "evil" acts of the former Communist Soviet Union, an overtly atheistic nation. Ask them to explain how it works. Exactly how is a philosophy connected to national policy? Do the evil acts of overtly Christian nations (like Spain during the Inquisition) likewise discredit Christianity? And what about the good actions of the former USSR? Scores of humanitarian hospitals were built by the atheistic Soviets. Does this mean that atheism is therefore a good thing, or that Christian-founded hospitals in America are bad? You don't need to know much history to incinerate this line of reasoning.

If a so-called "creation scientist" is attacking evolution, and you are not an accomplished biologist, what do you do? Ask them to demonstrate *their* science. Tell them that for the sake of argument you will concede the theory of evolution (not because it is false, but because you would argue the numerous details for years); and ask them to now present the scientific evidences for *their* theory. Ask them why they call it a science and what are their methods. You might surprise them into the realization that they in fact have no science. And if they try to discredit evolution because it is just a "theory," ask why the theory of creation science should not be equally discredited. (Does the phrase, "music theory" imply that music does not really exist?)

What do you do when a religionist lists a bunch of authorities and quotes from various authors with whom you "should" be familiar? Whether or not you can produce a list of your own which is longer than theirs, you could ask something like this: is truth determined by vote? If they mention certain authors, stop and ask them to explain why they are important, what they said, why it is relevant. Force them to prove their point. (Give the fish some slack.) This will usually display the depth of the person's familiarity with the author, if any, and will help you to get a handle on the argument. Ask why the author is considered an authority. If the writer is only acclaimed by Christian criteria, then you can show the circular path involved in selectively supporting an idea.

If the believer starts recounting a miracle, ask them to define the word

112

"miracle." If it is an "impossible event," then it defines itself out of existence. If it is a "highly unlikely event," then it is much more likely that there is a simpler natural explanation, or that the tale was inaccurately reported. Ask them if we should believe all reports of miracles, including those from competing religions.

I used to preach that Christians should be ready to "give an answer" to anyone who asks. But we rarely needed to. I was never called to account or made to carry my "reasoning" any further than the pulpit. I thought I was the one doing the fishing, saving heathen freethinkers from a fiery fate.

It might be asked that if this *rule of thumb* is so effective, why couldn't the religionist turn around and use it against the freethinker? The answer is simple. The freethinker is not making any theistic assertions. It is the believer who is making the case. The burden of proof is on the one who is making the claim; the skeptic is not required to say anything. If the religionist tries to make you display your depth of knowledge you can just answer that you are only interested in following *their* lead—make them support their assertions before changing the subject.

If you ever get into a situation where you are stumped, over your head, out of ideas, and can't think of a way to loop the argument around, then there is always the appropriate tactic of backing up and making the person define terms. Go back to any of the religious words used in the discussion and claim (correctly) that no further progress can be made until the linguistic groundwork has been carefully established. I have had the most success with the word "spirit." No one can define it! Make them define the word, or else abandon it. (Other vulnerable words are *omnipotence, faith, peace, sin, revelation, firmament, trinity . . .*)

The word *spirit*, according to the dictionary, comes from *breathe* or *blow*. Of course, religionists are not referring to air molecules, but are using the physical breath of a human being as an analogy of the intangible essence of the person. Spirit means much more to them than just another synonym for air, which would make it a superfluous word for a natural phenomenon. The problem is understanding how anything can be intangible, or nonmaterial. They will usually say that spirit is similar to things like emotion, fear, desire: inner, invisible things which we all accept as immaterial parts of personality. But these things are never observed apart from a physical brain, and can not be said to really "exist" on their own. They are functions of a brain organism. It would be just as silly to say that digestion can somehow exist apart from its being a function of a stomach, or similar organism. Of course, Christians do not claim that spirit is equal to emotion, otherwise the word would be useless. Some liberal Christians may claim that the "spirit of Christ" is meant to be understood in the same manner as "the spirit of the American revolution," in which case it is just a concept without an independent reality. Those who feel that a spirit is a real thing are still left with the problem of explaining what it *is*, regardless of the comparisons or analogies.

A woman once told me that she knows God is real because she regularly sees spirits, dead relatives, and angels walking through her house. I told her that I understood what she meant. I have often had dreams that seemed so real that I thought I was awake. "It's not a dream," she snapped. "Don't you believe that these things are real?"

"Yes, I do," I answered. "Dreams are very real things, and I would never deny that you saw what you saw. I sometimes dream that I am flying, and it seems very real. Do you believe that I was actually flying?"

She didn't answer. If a dream is a very real possibility (I didn't use the word "hallucination"), then isn't that more likely than a real ghost?

This *rule of thumb* may not always be practical in formal debates or radio interviews with time constraints. In such cases scholarly familiarity and prepared responses are essential. Freethinkers are a generally well-informed bunch, and that image should be jealously guarded.

Freethought Today, March 1987

15

Fuzzy, Was He?

IS FAITH THE result of fuzzy thinking? It is often easy to spot religious irrationality, but why is it so hard to correct it? I think it is because believers do their reasoning inside out. Faith is not the result of fuzzy thinking. It is the *cause* of it.

Simply scoffing at religious nonsense is rarely effective; but then neither is a well-reasoned approach, it appears. On April 7, 1987 I participated in a debate at the University of Wisconsin, Madison with Dr. J. Terence Morrison (of InterVarsity Christian Fellowship) on "Jesus of Nazareth: Messiah or Myth?" My position was that the New Testament Jesus character, whether or not he actually existed (and I think he probably never lived), is myth, like any other myth. (See "Jesus: History or Myth?") My opponent, of course, argued that Jesus is completely historical and that the current evangelical theologies are based on solid fact.

Morrison demonstrated a general familiarity with some of the strong points of the apologists' arguments: the existence and dating of the New Testament documents, and the growth of the early church. His secondary points were also well-stated: his testimony of meeting Jesus personally, and the claim that we shouldn't feel like we have to *prove* everything. The debate was lively on those points.

However, he was unprepared to discuss the (lack of) historical confirmation outside the New Testament, saying he was a chemist, not a historian. This was an unforgivable defect in his presentation. How can you have a historical discussion without looking at history? (Morrison's ignorance, of course, does not cause the whole temple to topple. There are other Christian apologists who are quite capable of discussing Josephus, Tacitus, Suetonius, and other early historians, though there is nothing to be gained for their side. Perhaps Morrison knew this and avoided the trap.) But his fatal flaw, on the subject of miracles, was that he either innocently or deliberately failed to grasp the importance of a strict natural regularity as a criterion for critical history.

A miracle is defined as a violation, or overriding, of natural law. It assumes a solid line between the natural world and a supernatural world (which is sometimes punctured when the gods want to get our attention). A miracle, therefore, is *defined* by natural impossibility.

David Hume showed that history cannot be used to prove a miracle. Historical data can only be interpreted if we assume that the same natural laws apply through time. In reconstructing the past we must use as criteria all of our knowledge of what is possible or impossible, probable or improbable. A miracle, by definition, is outside the sphere.

This does not mean (*a priori*) that miracles have not happened, of course. It just means that history is impotent to prove them. Morrison agreed that history is the weakest science, a science of approximations. And history is the bedrock of Christian apologetics! It seems comical to invest infinite interest in a weak approximation.

Morrison did not appreciate the dilemma. On the one hand, he needs a strict natural regularity, else the miracles count for nothing. If people routinely return from their graves, then Jesus's resurrection would be no sign of anything supernatural.

But on the other hand, Morrison gave arguments that indicate he would like to weaken, or even remove, the natural/supernatural barrier. At one point he appealed to the audience to provide testimony of modern miracles. Doesn't he see that this cripples his case? Miracles cannot afford to be numerous.

Besides, when we scratch the surface of modern miracle reports we routinely uncover exaggerations, frauds, or "innocent" religious misinterpretations of perfectly natural healings. Healings happen all the time, at different rates, and although they are not always fully understood, they reside squarely within our natural world. You never see proof of restored body parts, floating mountains, or sticks turning into snakes.

Of course, events which were previously deemed impossible might in fact be likely in the light of new knowledge, so skeptics and historians should be willing to revise the criteria if necessary. Natural laws are merely descriptions, after all. But this would not help the case for miracles; it would simply demote them to natural events, destroying their ability to point to a transcendent realm.

Morrison claimed that he could devise scientific ways to duplicate all of the biblical miracles, making them more believable: the word *miracle* should just be translated as "wonder." Again, don't Christians see how this erases the line? It turns god into an advanced extraterrestrial with high-tech visual effects.

He claimed that the Gospel miracles should be exempt, after all, from scientific testing since, like the resurrection, they are not repeatable events. This is a revealing admission that Christians want skeptics to keep "hands off" their precious articles of faith. Repeatability is not the only scientific test for truth.

Morrison's main argument was his worst. He claimed that modern science has demolished the certainties of reality. Quantum mechanics has turned the universe into a less concrete, more "mystical" place. Old Newtonian positivistic concepts like *reason* are now passé. There is room for faith in the new scientific worldMorrison concluded.

Of course, the discussion over the new science is very green. Philosophers are just beginning to tackle the implications, with diverse opinions; but this is all beside the point. There is either a transcendent realm or there is not. Yanking miracle stories into a natural world view, new or old, gets us no closer to a supernatural deity.

These Christian arguments make the natural/supernatural barrier fuzzy. If such reasoning is correct *we can do no history!* Everything is up for grabs and we may as well believe any myth that tickles our fancy. Without strict tools of critical historical judgment, all documents are worthless.

Morrison, like most religionists, demonstrated that he is capable of critical thinking when he analyzes the beliefs of other religions. Even though he accepts bodily ascension into heaven (a flat-earth idea, if you think about it), he nevertheless rejected the report made by the historian Suetonius, ratified by the Roman senate, that Augustus Caesar did just such a thing when he died. Morrison said that Suetonius therefore could not be considered a reliable historian, though he had earlier admitted that Christian apologists do trust his supposed testimony of Christ! This was the one, clear contradiction produced by our debate.

My claim is that the miracle stories, among other things, make the New Testament reports unhistorical. I did not invoke the *a priori* argument that miracles cannot happen—I said that critical historians observe and conclude, by admittedly inductive reasoning, that such events as are told in the New Testament *do not* happen. People do not vanish into thin air and then rematerialize through solid doors. Nor do they magically wither fig trees, command weather changes, walk on water or cause fish instantly to multiply. It is therefore much more likely that the biblical miracle reports are due to honest error, deceit, or zealous theological interpretation of perfectly natural events.

Yet Morrison still feels that my skepticism is an *a priori* subjective dismissal of facts, based on a fear that god might want to "crimp" my lifestyle. Although he claims we should not treat the bible any differently from other historical documents, he admits that his own reading of the "inspired" scriptures is influenced by *his* subjective experience of personally meeting Jesus in prayer. And he agrees with Paul *(I Corinthians 2:12-14)* that he has an edge over me, a "natural man," when he studies the bible.

If Morrison's personal prayer experience is permitted to influence historical criteria, then so is mine! It is my testimony that inner religious experiences, though very powerful, are merely delusions. Perhaps it would "crimp" the Christian lifestyle to admit such a possibility.

So we see more evidence that Christian "reasoning" is produced by faith, not vice versa. If a person truly wishes to believe something, little evidence is required. If there really were a historical Jesus of Nazareth, he wasn't that fuzzy, was he?

Freethought Today, May, 1987

16

An Open-minded Discussion

ONE MINISTER OFFERED that the reason I am unable to see the truth revealed by the precious facts of Scripture is that I am depending on my own reason rather than trusting the Creator of the universe, by faith.

"The human mind is limited," he said, "and it is arrogant for you to try to pull yourself up by your bootstraps and proclaim what can't possibly be proved: that there is no God. You are lost if you use your own mind and intelligence."

"Well, whose mind do you suggest I use? Yours?" I asked. "Are you suggesting that I should never evaluate any data? Are you telling me to turn off the analysis and just swallow what some authority feeds me? Would you willingly do the same thing if approached by the flat-earthers or the Zoroastrians, or the Rev. Jim Jones?"

"You are not being open," he responded. "You have already closed your mind to Jesus." He said this in spite of the fact that he knew that I had once been a minister and have demonstrated that I am able to bend.

"But I will change my mind," I said, "if you give me some evidence. Are *you* willing to change your mind about Jesus if the facts warrant?"

"No," he replied quickly, "because I know Jesus personally. I can't possibly deny what I know to be true."

"But those are just words. They point to an intangible image in your mind,

119

to something that no one else can verify. What if it could be pointed out that there is no possible way for anyone, yourself included, to distinguish between your 'knowledge' of Jesus and the mystical delusions of shamans? What if it could be shown that your inner experience is just normal psychological creativity? Then would you be willing to admit you might be wrong? Can you admit at least the *possibility* that you are participating in a near-universal human tendency to embrace fantasy?"

"I can't do that," he answered.

"Then I think I have proved that I am open-minded and you are not," I said.

"Oh, no. I am definitely open," he added. "I am open to the truth of the Bible, and that is all that matters."

"Well, so am I. I am open to the possibility that the bible might be true. I am willing to read it, to study it, to read any books you recommend on the bible, and to listen to any of your explanations and arguments. How does that make me close-minded?"

"Because your attitude is wrong. You look at the bible and you don't see its beauty and importance. Since the bible is true, and since you haven't accepted its truth, then there is something wrong with you."

"What is wrong with examining the bible in the context of the entire human experience, learning how it compares with other myths, and how it differs?"

"See! You called it a myth," he said. "That is a prejudice that you bring to the bible before you even start reading it. You can't possibly know its truth if you are treating it like any other superstitious book."

"When you read Virgil's *Aeneid,* do you keep your mind open to the possibility that the Cyclops was a real creature?"

"No one has ever claimed that the Cyclops was real, but millions of people claim that Jesus is alive and real. Since you have never met Jesus, you are hardly in a position to criticize us or to know what the Bible is all about."

"Just like you, I used to believe that I had met Jesus personally, but I now know that such an argument is purely subjective. It would be like saying that the only people who are qualified to make a decision about the existence of leprechauns are those who have met a leprechaun personally. Have *you* met a leprechaun personally?"

"No, but I have met Jesus personally."

"You haven't met any leprechauns, but I bet you have an opinion about their existence."

"Leprechauns are irrelevant. We're talking about Jesus."

"Let's put it this way. Do you agree with me that the human race has exhibited an immense propensity to believe errors?"

"What do you mean?"

"There are millions of people who devoutly worship Allah, millions who fear primitive superstitions, millions who think the Angel Moroni spoke to Joseph Smith, and I am not so sure that no one ever believed in the existence of the Cyclops. All of these people are not right, are they?"

"They have been deceived!"

"Then you agree with me that there is something about human nature that makes most of us susceptible to error."

"Yes, I would have to agree with that," he conceded.

"Then what makes *you* exempt?"

He was silent for a moment, then answered, "Well, somebody has to be right. I believe that I am right. I believe that I have good reason for my faith."

"So do the Moslems."

"But none of those other religions have anything like the bible, or anything like the unique message of salvation through Jesus," he triumphed.

"You have not done your homework. Any serious student of Christianity, who does not ignore the context of myth and human experience, would never make such a claim."

"It would be a waste of my time to study those other myths and religions when I already know that I have the truth."

"And if an atheist said that it would be a 'waste of time' to study the bible, what would you think?"

"That would not be open-minded," he concluded, without a flicker of embarrassment.

17

Refuting God

T HEISTS CLAIM THAT THERE is a god; atheists do not. Religionists often challenge atheists to prove that there is no god; but this misses the point. Atheists claim god is *unproved*, not *disproved*. In any argument, the burden of proof is on the one making the claim.

If a person claims to have invented an antigravity device, it is not incumbent on others to prove that no such thing exists. The believer must make a case. Everyone else is justified in refusing to believe until evidence is produced and substantiated.

Some atheists feel the argument is pointless until the term "god" is made understandable. Words like "spirit" and "supernatural" have no referent in reality, and ideas like "all-knowing" and "omnipotent" are self-contradictory. Why discuss a meaningless concept?

Nevertheless, there are many lines of theistic reasoning and volumes have been written on each. The following sections briefly summarize the arguments and the refutations. Atheism is the default position which remains when all theistic claims are dismissed.

Design

*"Where did it all come from? How can you explain the complex order of
the universe? I can't believe the beauty of nature just happened by
accident. Design requires a designer."*

This argument merely assumes what it wishes to prove. Any attempt to
"explain" anything requires a higher context within which it can be understood. To ask for the explanation of the "natural universe" is simply to demand a "higher universe."

The universe is "all there is." It is not a *thing*. A god would certainly be a
part of "all there is," and if the universe requires an explanation, then god
requires a god, *ad infinitum*.

The mind of a god would be at least as complex and orderly as the rest of
nature and would be subject to the same question: Who made god? If a god
can be thought eternal, then so can the universe.

There is design *in* the universe, but to speak of design *of* the universe is
just theistic semantics. The perceived design in nature is not necessarily intelligent. *Life* is the result of the mindless "design" of natural selection. *Order*
in the cosmos comes from the "design" of natural regularity. There is no need
for a higher explanation.

The design argument is based on ignorance, not facts. Failure to solve a
natural riddle does not mean there is no answer. For millennia humans have
created mythical answers to "mysteries" such as thunder and fertility. But
the more we learn, the fewer gods we need. God belief is just answering a
mystery with a mystery, and therefore answers nothing.

*"The universe is governed by natural laws. Laws require a lawgiver.
There must be a Divine Governor."*

A natural law is a *description*, not a *prescription*. The universe is not "governed" by anything. Natural laws are merely human conceptions of the way
things normally react, not behavioral mandates, as with societal laws. If the
design argument is valid, the mind of a god would be equally "governed" by
some principle of order, requiring a higher lawgiver.

*"It is improbable that the complexity of life occurred by accident; and the
second law of thermodynamics, which states that all systems tend to
disorder, makes evolution impossible. There must have been a Creator."*

These pseudo-scientific objections are based on error. No biologist claims organisms suddenly appear in one step of "accidental" mutation. Evolution is the gradual accumulation of tiny changes over millions of generations of environmental suitability. Humans, for example, did not *have* to evolve—any one of billions of viable possibilities could have adapted, making it quite likely that something would survive the ruthlessness of natural selection.

Using probability, *after the fact*, would be like a lottery winner saying, "It is highly unlikely that I could have won this lottery, therefore I must not have won."

Creationists often misquote the second law of thermodynamics, which states that disorder increases in a closed system. The earth is currently part of an *open* system, getting energy from the sun. Driven by the input in solar energy (and other forms of energy, such as chemical), complexity routinely increases, as with the growth of an embryo or crystal. Ultimately, of course, the sun will cool and life on earth will disappear.

Personal Experience

"Millions of people personally know God through an inner spiritual experience."

Most theists claim their particular god can be known through meditation or prayer, but such experiences point to nothing outside the mind. Mysticism can be explained psychologically; it is not necessary to complicate our understanding of the universe with fanciful assumptions. We *do* know that many humans habitually invent myths, hear voices, hallucinate and talk with imaginary friends. We *do not* know there is a god.

There are millions of god-believers; but this is a statement about humanity, not about god. Truth is not something which is attained by vote. Religions arose to deal with death, weakness, dreams, and fear of the unknown. They are powerful mechanisms for giving meaning to life and personal/cultural identity. But religions differ radically, and appeals to inner experience only worsen the conflict.

"Atheists lack spiritual insight and can hardly criticize the theistic experience of God. That would be like a blind person denying the existence of color."

Many theists claim that god is known by a special "spiritual" sensitivity.

124

But is faith a "sixth sense" which perceives another world? Skeptics deny such a thing exists.

The blindness analogy is inapt because blind people do not deny the sense of sight, or that color exists. The blind and the sighted live in the same world, and both can grasp the natural principles involved. The path of light can be traced through a normal eye to the brain. Frequencies can be explained and the spectrum can be experienced independently of vision. The existence of color need not be taken by faith.

The theist, however, gives no independent means of testing "spiritual" insight, so it must be doubted. The skeptic does not deny the reality of subjective religious experience, but knows it can be psychologically explained without reference to a supposed transcendent realm.

The implication that theists are the only "complete" human beings is unfounded and arrogant.

Morality

"We all have a feeling of right and wrong, a conscience which puts us under a higher law. This universal moral urge points outside of humanity. It is consistent that God, a nonphysical being, would relate to us by such sublime means."

Here is another argument based on ignorance. Ethical systems are based on the worth humans have assigned to *life:* "good" is that which enhances life, and "evil" is that which threatens it. We do not need a deity to tell us it is wrong to kill, lie or steal. Humans have always had the potential to use their minds to determine what is kind and reasonable.

There is no "universal moral urge" and not all ethical systems agree. Polygamy, human sacrifice, cannibalism (Eucharist), wife beating, self mutilation, war, circumcision, castration and incest are perfectly "moral" actions in certain cultures. Is god confused?

To call god a "nonphysical being" is contradictory. A *being* must exist as some form of mass in space and time. Values reside within physical brains, so if morality points to "god," then we are it: the god concept is just a projection of human ideals.

"If there is no absolute moral standard then there is no ultimate right or wrong. Without God there is no ethical basis and social order would disintegrate. Our laws are based on scripture."

125

This is an argument for *belief* in a god, not for the existence of a god. The demand for "absolute" morality comes only from insecure religionists. (Voltaire quipped: "If god did not exist, it would be necessary to invent him.") Mature people are comfortable with the relativism of humanism since it provides a consistent, rational and flexible framework for ethical *human* behavior—without a deity.

American laws are based on a secular constitution, not the bible. Any scriptures that might support a good law do so only because they have met the test of human values, which long predate the ineffective Ten Commandments.

There is no evidence that theists are more moral than atheists. In fact, the contrary seems to be true, as evidenced by centuries of religious violence. Most atheists are happy, productive, moral people.

Even if this argument is true, it is of little practical value. Devout, bible-believing Christians cannot agree on what the scriptures say about many crucial moral issues. Believers regularly take opposing positions on such matters as capital punishment, abortion, pacifism, birth control, physician-assisted suicide, animal rights, the environment, the separation of church and state, gay rights, and women's rights. It might be concluded from this that there is either a multiplicity of gods handing out conflicting moral advice, or a single god who is hopelessly confused.

First Cause

"Everything had a cause, and every cause is the effect of a previous cause. Something must have started it all. God is the first cause, the unmoved mover, the creator and sustainer of the universe."

The major premise of this argument, "everything had a cause," is contradicted by the conclusion that "God did not have a cause." You can't have it both ways. If *everything* had to have a cause, then there could not be a first cause. If it is possible to think of a god as uncaused, then it is possible to think the same of the universe.

Some theists, observing that all "effects" need a cause, assert that god is a cause but not an effect. But no one has ever observed an uncaused cause and simply inventing one merely assumes what the argument wishes to prove.

Pascal's Wager

"God can't be proved. But if God exists, the believer gains everything (heaven) and the unbeliever loses everything (hell). If God doesn't exist, the believer loses nothing and the unbeliever gains nothing. There is therefore everything to gain and nothing to lose by believing in God."

This argument, first formulated by French philosopher Blaise Pascal, is sheer intimidation. It is not a case for a god's existence: it is an argument for belief, based on irrational fear. With this kind of reasoning we should simply pick the religion with the worst hell.

It is not true that the believer loses nothing. We diminish this life by preferring the myth of an afterlife, and we sacrifice honesty to the maintenance of a lie. Religion demands time, energy and money, draining valuable human resources from the improvement of *this* world. Religious conformity, a tool of tyrants, is a threat to freedom.

Nor is it true that the unbeliever gains nothing. Rejecting religion can be a positive liberating experience, gaining perspective and freedom of inquiry. Freethinkers have always been in the forefront of social and moral progress.

What kind of person would eternally torment an honest doubter? If their god is so unjust, then theists are in as much danger as atheists. Perhaps god will get a perverted thrill from changing his mind and damning everyone, believers and unbelievers alike. Or, inverting the gamble, perhaps god will only save those who have enough courage *not* to believe!

Pascal was a Catholic and assumed that the existence of god meant the Christian God. However, the Islamic Allah might be the true god, which turns Pascal's wager into a riskier gamble than intended.

In any case, a belief in a deity based on fear is not a belief that produces admiration. It does not follow that such a being deserves to be worshipped.

Ontological Argument

"God is a being than which no greater being can be conceived. If god does not exist in actuality, then he can be conceived to be greater than he is. Therefore, God exists."

There are dozens of varieties of the ontological argument, but St. Anselm was the first to articulate it in this manner. The flaw in this reasoning is to treat existence as an attribute. Existence is a *given*. Nothing can be great or perfect that does not first exist, so the argument is backwards.

A good way to expose this reasoning is to replace "being" and "God" with some other words. ("Paradise Isle is an island . . .") You could prove the existence of a perfect "void," which would mean nothing exists!

The argument squashes itself, because god can be conceived to have infinite mass, which is disproved empirically. And it is comparing apples and oranges to assume that existence in conception can somehow be related to existence in actuality. Even if the comparison holds, why is existence in actuality "greater" (whatever that means) than existence in conception? Perhaps it is the other way around.

No wonder Bertrand Russell said all ontological arguments are a case of bad grammar!

Revelation

"The Bible is historically reliable. There is no reason to doubt the trustworthy testimonies that would hold up in court. God exists because He has revealed Himself through scriptures."

The bible reflects the culture of its time. Though much of its setting is historical, much is not. For example, there is no contemporary support for the Jesus story outside the Gospels, which were anonymously written thirty to eighty years after the supposed crucifixion (depending on which scholar you consult). Many accounts, like the creation stories, conflict with science. The stories of the bible are just that: stories.

The bible is contradictory. A glaring example is the discrepancy between the genealogies of Jesus given by Matthew and Luke. The story of the resurrection of Jesus, told by at least five different writers, is hopelessly irreconcilable. Scholars have noted hundreds of biblical errors which have not been satisfactorily addressed by apologists.

The bible, like other religious writings, can be accounted for in purely natural terms. There is no reason to demand it be either entirely true or false. Christianity is filled with parallels from pagan myths, and its emergence as a second century messiah cult stems from its Jewish sectarian origins. The Gospel authors admit they are writing religious propaganda *(John 20:31)* which is a clue that it should be taken with a grain of salt.

Thomas Paine, in *The Age Of Reason,* pointed out that scripture cannot be revelation. Revelation (if it exists) is a divine message communicated *directly* to some person. As soon as that person reports it, it becomes second-hand hearsay. No one is obliged to believe it, especially if it is fantastic. It is much more likely that reports of the miraculous are due to honest error, deceit or zealous theological interpretations of perfectly natural events.

Outrageous claims require outrageous proof. A criterion of critical history is the assumption of natural regularity over time. This precludes miracles, which by definition "override" natural law. If we allow for miracles, then all documents, including the bible, become worthless as history.

Science

"There are many scientists who believe in God. If many of the world's most intelligent people are theists, then belief in God must be sensible."

This is just an appeal to authority, which atheists could do equally well, or better. Academicians, as a group, are much less religious than the general population. Though it is easy to find scientists who believe, none of them can scientifically demonstrate their faith. Belief is usually a cultural or personal matter separate from occupation and no one, not even a scientist, is immune from the irrational seductions of religion.

"The new science of quantum physics is showing that reality is uncertain and less concrete. There is now room for miracles. A theistic world view is not inconsistent with science."

This is nonsense. A miracle is supposed to be a suspension of natural law which points to a transcendent realm. If the new science makes miracles naturally possible (a self-contradictory concept), then there is no supernatural realm, and no god.

In quantum physics, the term "uncertainty" does not apply to reality, but to our *knowledge* of reality.

Theism implies a supernatural realm. Science limits itself to the natural world. So theism can *never* be consistent with science, by definition.

Faith

"Belief in God is not intellectual. Reason is limited. The truth of God is only known by a leap of faith, which transcends but does not contradict reason."

This is no argument. Admitting that something is nonintellectual removes it from the realm of discussion. Yes, reason *is* limited: it is limited to the facts. If you ignore the facts you are left with nothing but hypotheses or wishful thinking.

Faith is the acceptance of the truth of a statement in spite of insufficient or contradictory evidence, which has never been consistent with reason. Faith, by its very invocation, is a transparent admission that religious claims cannot stand on their own two feet.

Sartre said that to believe is to know you believe; to know you believe is to not believe.

Even if theism were a consistent hypothesis (which it is not), it would still need to be proved. This is why most theists downplay *proof* and *reason* and emphasize *faith,* sometimes ludicrously claiming that science requires faith or that atheism is a religion.

Psychic Powers

"There is strong evidence of psychic powers, reincarnation and such. You have to admit there is something out there!"

Most scientists disagree that there is strong evidence for "parascientific" claims. When carefully examined with rigid controls, they are generally exposed as misinterpretations or outright fraud.

Even if they were legitimate, mysterious phenomena could have perfectly natural explanations. In such cases, skeptics prefer to withhold judgment rather than jump to superstitious conclusions.

Conclusion

It should be noted that even if these theistic arguments were valid, they would not establish the creator as personal, singular, perfect or currently alive (except for "revelation," which is free to create any kind of god desired). Nor do any of the arguments address the presence of chaos, ugliness and pain in the world, which make an omnipotent deity responsible for evil.

Many theists, when they realize their philosophical arguments have failed, will resort to stereotypical character attacks. All atheists are labeled unhappy, immoral, angry, arrogant, demonic, unfeeling wretches who have no reason to live. This is untrue and unfair. But even if it were true, that would not make theism correct.

Since by careful examination all theistic arguments are faulty, atheism remains the only rational position.

Definitions

Religion: System of thought or practice which claims to transcend our natural world and which demands conformity to a creed, bible or savior.

God: A being who created and/or governs the universe. It is usually defined with personal aspects like intelligence, will, wisdom, love and hatred; and with superhuman aspects like omnipotence, omniscience, immortality, omnibenevolence and omnipresence. It is most often pictured interacting with humanity, but is sometimes held to be an impersonal "force" or nature itself.

Theism: Belief in god(s).

Atheism: Absence of belief in god(s).

Agnosticism: Refusal to accept the truth of a proposition for which there is insufficient evidence or logical justification. Most agnostics suspend belief in god.

Freethought: The practice of forming opinions about religion on the basis of reason, without reference to authority, tradition or established belief.

Rationalism: The idea that all beliefs should be subject to the proven methods of rational inquiry. Special treatments like *faith* or *authority,* which are not allowed in other disciplines, are not acceptable for analyzing religion.

Truth: The degree to which a statement corresponds with reality and logic.

Reality: That which is directly perceivable through our natural senses, or indirectly ascertained through the proper use of reason.

Reason: A tool of critical thought which limits the truth of a proposition by the tests of **verification** (what evidence or repeatable observations confirm it?), **falsifiability** (what, in theory, would disprove it, and have all such attempts failed?), **parsimony** (is it the simplest explanation, requiring the fewest assumptions?) and **logic** (is it free of contradictions and *non sequiturs*?).

Humanism: Secular humanism is a rationalistic natural outlook which makes humanity the measure of values.

All of these words have suffered from multiple definitions. The definition of *religion,* of course, can vary with the religionist. Most atheists consider themselves to be concurrently freethinkers, rationalists and agnostics since they are not mutually exclusive labels. *Agnosticism* is here defined by Huxley's original intention, though current popular usage wrongly views it as a halfway house between theism and atheism. Any person who cannot say, "I have a belief in a god," for *whatever* reason, is an atheist.

131

For Further Reading:

The Age of Reason, Thomas Paine.

An Anthology of Atheism and Rationalism, edited by Gordon Stein, Prometheus Books, New York, 1980.

A Second Anthology of Atheism and Rationalism, edited by Gordon Stein, Ph.D., Prometheus Books, New York, 1987.

Atheism: The Case Against God, George Smith, Prometheus Books, New York, 1979.

Atheism: A Philosophical Justification, Michael Martin, Temple University Press, Philadelphia, 1991.

Bertrand Russell on God and Religion, edited by Al Seckel, Prometheus Books, New York, 1986.

Critiques of God, edited by Peter Angeles, Prometheus Books, New York, 1976.

Ten Common Myths About Atheists, Annie Laurie Gaylor, Freedom From Religion Foundation, Madison, Wisconsin (booklet), 1987.

This chapter originally was printed as a booklet, sold and distributed to members of the Freedom From Religion Foundation. Its purpose was to provide a handy, nutshell response to common theistic arguments. Most of the arguments have been developed in greater detail elsewhere in this book.

18

What Is A Freethinker?

A FREETHINKER IS a person who forms opinions about religion on the basis of reason, independently of tradition, authority, or established belief. Freethinkers include atheists, agnostics, secular humanists and rationalists.

No one can be a freethinker who demands conformity to a bible, creed, or messiah. To the freethinker revelation is invalid and orthodoxy is no guarantee of truth.

What Is A Freethinker's Basis For Knowledge?

Freethinkers are naturalistic. *Truth* is the degree to which a statement corresponds with reality. Reality is limited to that which is directly perceivable through our natural senses or indirectly ascertained through the proper use of reason.

The scientific method is the only trustworthy means of obtaining knowledge. For a statement to be considered true it must be *testable* (what repeatable experiments or methods confirm it?), *falsifiable* (what, in theory, would disconfirm it, and have all attempts to disprove it failed?), *parsimonious* (is it the simplest explanation, requiring the fewest assumptions?), and *logical* (is it free of contradictions or *non sequiturs*?).

Arguments based on faith, authority or *ad hominem* character attacks are unacceptable.

Do Freethinkers Have A Basis For Morality?

Freethinkers accept human life as the primary basis for morality. That which enhances humanity is "good"—that which threatens it is "evil." There are no cosmic absolutes. Given our existence in the universe, life must be the basis for values. Hence, most freethinkers are humanists. This usually embraces a respect for the welfare of our entire planet, including the other animals.

An ethical choice is rarely a simple "right and wrong" decision. Most moral questions involve a conflict of values, requiring a careful use of reason. Obedient conformity to the dictates of *another* mind is supremely immoral and very dangerous.

Do Freethinkers Have Meaning In Life?

Freethinkers know that *meaning* must originate in a mind. Since the universe is mindless and the cosmos does not care, *you* must care, if you wish to have purpose. Individuals are free to choose, within the limits of humanistic morality.

Some freethinkers have found meaning in compassion for needless suffering, social progress, the beauty of humanity (art, music, literature), personal happiness, pleasure, joy and love, and the advancement of knowledge.

Doesn't The Complexity Of Life Require A Designer?

The complexity of life requires an *explanation*. Darwin's theory of evolution, with cumulative nonrandom natural selection "designing" for billions of years, has provided the explanation. A *Divine Designer* is no answer because the complexity of such a creature would be subject to the same scrutiny itself.

Freethinkers recognize that there is much chaos, ugliness and pain in the universe for which any explanation of origins must also account.

Why Are Freethinkers Opposed To Religion?

Freethinkers are convinced that religious claims are false—they have not withstood the tests of evidence and reason. Not only is there nothing to be gained by believing an untruth, but there is everything to lose when we sacrifice the indispensable tool of reason on the altar of superstition.

Most freethinkers consider religion to be not only untrue, but harmful. It has been used to justify war, slavery, sexism, racism, mutilations, intolerance, and oppression of minorities.

Hasn't Religion Done Tremendous Good In The World?

Some religionists are good people—but they would be good anyway. Religion cannot take credit for actions which are just as easily accomplished by freethinkers.

In fact, most modern social and moral progress has been made by people *free* from religion—including Clara Barton, Margaret Sanger, Albert Einstein, Andrew Carnegie, Thomas Edison, Marie Curie, Elizabeth Cady Stanton, Susan B. Anthony, H. L. Mencken, Charles Darwin, Sigmund Freud, Robert Burns, Percy Shelley, Johannes Brahms and many others whom we honor today for their contributions to humanity.

Most religions have consistently resisted progress—including the abolition of slavery; women's right to vote and to choose contraception and abortion; medical developments such as the use of anesthesia; scientific understanding of the heliocentric solar system and evolution, and the use of lightning rods; and the American principle of state/church separation.

Do Freethinkers Have A Particular Political Persuasion?

No, freethought is a philosophical, not a political, position.

Freethought today embraces adherents of virtually all political persuasions, including capitalists, libertarians, socialists, communists, Republicans, Democrats, liberals and conservatives. There is no connection, for example, between atheism and communism. Some freethinkers, such as Adam Smith and Ayn Rand, were staunch capitalists; and there have been communistic groups which were deeply religious, such as the early Christian church.

Is Atheism/Humanism A Religion?

Atheism is not a belief. It is the "lack of belief" in god(s). Lack of faith requires no faith. Atheism is indeed based on a commitment to rationality, but that hardly qualifies it as a religion.

Freethinkers apply the term *religion* to belief systems which include a supernatural realm, deity, faith in "holy" writings and conformity to an absolute creed.

Secular humanism has no god, bible or savior. It is based on natural rational principles. It is flexible and relativistic—it is not a religion.

Isn't A Plurality Of Ideas Unsettling To Humanity?

Yes. That is the only way we will have progress. A multiplicity of individuals thinking, free from restraints of orthodoxy, allows ideas to be tested, discarded or adopted. The totalitarianism of religious absolutes chokes progress.

Why Should I Be Proud To Be A Freethinker?

Freethought is reasonable. Freethought allows you to do your own thinking. Freethinkers see no pride in the blind maintenance of ancient superstitions or self-effacing prostration before divine tyrants known only through primitive "revelations." Freethought is respectable. Freethought is truly free.

This piece was printed by the Freedom From Religion Foundation as a brochure introducing freethought.

The World is My Country
by Dan Barker

The world is my country,
To do good is my religion.
No prophet or priest,
No bible for me.
My mind is my own church.

We are all one human family
Wanting love, fairness, and freedom.
This simple creed
Is all that we need
To enjoy peace on earth.

Sunday Morning Blues

by Dan Barker

It's Sunday morning and I'm lying in bed—
Church bells are echoing around in my head,
But I won't get up.
'Cause my religion is to worship at the Temple of the Inner Springs.

Preacher, don't you try to tell me what's best,
'Cause I know that Sunday is the "Day of Rest."
And I won't get up.
'Cause my religion is to worship at theTemple of the Inner Springs.
(Bedside Baptist)

I will pray to no Lord my soul to keep.
What the world really needs is a good night's sleep!
So, I won't get up.
My religion is to worship at theTemple of the Inner Springs.
(Church of the Holy Comforter)

If I should die before I wake,
Don't bury me in church, for heaven's sake.
I won't get up.
'Cause my religion is to worship at the Temple of the Inner Springs.
(Mattress Methodist)

What could I learn in Sunday School?
Here on my pillow is the best Golden Rule:
That I won't get up.
My religion is to worship at the Temple of the Inner Springs.
(Pillow Presbyterian)

If I get awakened by another church bell,
I will tell that preacher he can go to . . .
Well, I won't get up.
My religion is to worship at the Temple of the Inner Springs.

19

Dear Theologian

D EAR THEOLOGIAN,

I have a few questions, and I thought you would be the right person to ask. It gets tough sometimes, sitting up here in heaven with no one to talk to. I mean *really* talk to. I can always converse with the angels, of course, but since they don't have free will, and since I created every thought in their submissive minds, they are not very stimulating conversationalists.

Of course, I can talk with my son Jesus and with the "third person" of our holy trinity, the Holy Spirit, but since we are all the same, there is nothing we can learn from each other. There are no well-placed repartees in the Godhead. We all know what the others know. We can't exactly play chess. Jesus sometimes calls me "Father," and that feels good, but since he and I are the same age and have the same powers, it doesn't mean much.

You are educated. You have examined philosophy and world religions, and you have a degree which makes you qualified to carry on a discussion with someone at my level—not that I can't talk with anyone, even with the uneducated believers who fill the churches and flatter me with endless petitions, but you know how it is. Sometimes we all crave interaction with a respected colleague. You have read the scholars. You have written papers and published books about me, and you know me better than anyone else.

It might surprise you to think that I have some questions. No, not rhetorical questions aimed at teaching spiritual lessons, but some real, honest-to-God inquiries. This should not shock you because, after all, I created you in my image. Your inquisitiveness is an inheritance from me. You would say that love, for example, is a reflection of my nature within yourself, wouldn't you? Since questioning is healthy, it also comes from me.

Somebody once said that we should prove all things, and hold fast that which is good. My first question is this:

Where did I come from?

I find myself sitting up here in heaven, and I look around and notice that there is nothing else besides myself and the objects that I have created. I don't see any other creatures competing with me, nor do I notice anything above myself that might have created me, unless it is playing hide-and-seek. In any event, as far as I know (and I supposedly know everything), there is nothing else but me in-three-persons and my creations. I have always existed, you say. I did not create myself, because if I did, then I would be greater than myself.

So where did I come from?

I know how you approach that question regarding your own existence. You notice that nature, especially the human mind, displays evidence of intricate design. You have never observed such design apart from a designer. You argue that human beings must have had a creator, and you will find no disagreement from me.

Then, what about me? Like you, I observe that my mind is complex and intricate. It is much more complex than your mind, otherwise I couldn't have created your mind. My personality displays evidence of organization and purpose. Sometimes I surprise myself at how wise I am. If you think your existence is evidence of a designer, then what do you think about my existence? Am I not wonderful? Do I not function in an orderly manner? My mind is not a random jumble of disconnected thoughts; it displays what you would call evidence of design. If you need a designer, then why don't I?

You might think such a question is blasphemy, but to me there is no such crime. I can ask any question I want, and I think this is a fair one. If you say that everything needs a designer and then say that not everything (Me) needs a designer, aren't you contradicting yourself? By excluding me from the argument, aren't you bringing your conclusion into your argument? Isn't that circular reasoning? I am not saying I disagree with your conclusion; how could I? I'm just wondering why it is proper for you to infer a designer while it is not

139

proper for me.

If you are saying that I don't need to ask where I came from because I am perfect and omniscient while humans are fallible, then you don't need the design argument at all, do you? You have already assumed that I exist. You can make such an assumption, of course, and I would not deny you the freedom. Such *a priori* and circular reasoning might be helpful or comforting to you, but it does me little good. It doesn't help me figure out where I came from.

You say that I am eternally existent, and I suppose I would have no objection if I knew what it meant. It is hard for me to conceive of eternal existence. I just can't remember back that far. It would take me an eternity to remember back to eternity, leaving me no time to do anything else, so it is impossible for me to confirm if I existed forever. And even if it is true, why is eternal greater than temporal? Is a long sermon greater than a short sermon? What does "greater" mean? Are fat people greater than thin people, or old greater than young?

You think it is important that I have always existed. I'll take your word for it, for now. My question is not with the duration of my existence, but with the origin of my existence. I don't see how being eternal solves the problem. I still want to know where I came from.

I can only imagine one possible answer, and I would appreciate your reaction. I know that I exist. I know that I could not have created myself. I also know that there is no higher God who could have created me. Since I can't look above myself, then perhaps I should look below myself for a creator. Perhaps—this is speculative, so bear with me—perhaps you created me.

Don't be shocked. I mean to flatter you. Since I contain evidence of design, and since I see no other place where such design could originate, I am forced to look for a designer, or designers, in nature itself. You are a part of nature. You are intelligent—that is what your readers say. Why should I not find the answer to my question in you? Help me out on this.

Of course, if you made me, then I could not have made you, I think. The reason that I think I made you is because you made me to think I made you. You have often said that a Creator can put thoughts in your mind. Isn't it possible that you have put thoughts in my mind, and now here we are, both of us, wondering where we each came from?

Some of you have said that the answer to this whole question is just a mystery that only God understands. Well, thanks a lot. The buck stops here. On the one hand you use logic to try to prove my existence, but on the other hand, when logic hits a dead end, you abandon it and invoke "faith" and "mystery." Those words might be useful to you as place-holders for facts or truth, but they don't translate to anything meaningful as far as I am concerned. You can pretend that "mystery" signifies something terribly important, but to me it simply means you don't know.

Some of you assert that I did not "come" from anywhere. I just exist. However, I have also heard you say that nothing comes from nothing. You can't have it both ways. I either exist or I don't. What was it that caused me to exist, as opposed to not existing at all? If I don't need a cause, then why do you? Since I am not happy to say that this is a mystery, I must accept the only explanation that makes sense. You created me.

Is that such a terrible idea? I know that you think many other gods were created by humans: Zeus, Thor, Mercury, Elvis. You recognize that such deities originate in human desire, need, or fear. If the blessed beliefs of those billions of individuals can be dismissed as products of culture, then why can't yours? The Persians created Mithra, the Jews created Yahweh, and you created me. If I am wrong about this, please straighten me out.

My second question is this:

What's it all about?

Maybe I made myself, maybe some other god made me, maybe you made me—let's put that aside for now. I'm here now. *Why* am I here? Many of you look up to me for purpose in life, and I have often stated that your purpose in life is to please me. (Read *Revelation 4:11*) If your purpose is to please me, what is my purpose? To please myself? Is that all there is to life?

If I exist for my own pleasure, then this is selfish. It makes it look as if I created you merely to have some living toys to play with. Isn't there some principle that I can look up to? Something to admire, adore, and worship? Am I consigned for eternity to sit here and amuse myself with the worship of others? Or to worship myself? What's the point?

I have read your writings on the meaning of life, and don't misunderstand me, they make sense in the theological context of human religious goals, even if they don't have much practicality in the real world. Many of you feel that your purpose in life is to achieve perfection. Since you humans fall way short of perfection, by your own admission (and I agree), then self improvement provides you with a quest. It gives you something to do. Someday you hope to be as perfect as you think I am. But since I am already perfect, by definition, then I don't need such a purpose. I'm just sort of hanging out, I guess.

Yet I still wonder why I'm here. It feels good to exist. It feels great to be perfect. But it gives me nothing to do. I created the universe with all kinds of natural laws that govern everything from quarks to galactic clusters, and it runs okay on its own. I had to make these laws, otherwise I would be involved with a lot of repetitive busy work, such as pulling light rays through space, yanking falling objects down to the earth, sticking atoms together to build molecules, and a trillion other boring tasks more worthy of a slave than a master. You have discovered most of those laws, and might be on the verge of putting the whole picture together, and once you have done that you will know what I know: that there is nothing in the universe for me to do. It's boring up here.

I could create more universes and more laws, but what's the point? I've already *done* universes. Creation is like sneezing or writing short stories; it just comes out of me. I could go on an orgy of creation. Create, create, create. After a while a person can get sick of the same thing, like when you eat a whole box of chocolates and discover that the last piece doesn't taste as good as the first. Once you have had ten children, do you need twenty? (I'm asking you, not the pope.) If more is better, then I am obligated to continue until I have fathered an infinite number of children, and an endless number of universes. If I must compel myself, then I am a slave.

Many of you assert that it is inappropriate to seek purpose within yourself, that it must come from outside. I feel the same way. I can't merely assign purpose to myself. If I did, then I would have to look for my reasons. I would have to come up with an account of why I chose one purpose over another, and if such reasons came from within myself I would be caught in a loop of self-justified rationalizations. Since I have no Higher Power of my own, then I have no purpose. Nothing to live for. It is all meaningless.

Sure, I can bestow meaning on *you*—pleasing me, achieving perfection, whatever—and perhaps that is all that concerns you; but doesn't it bother you, just a little, that the source of meaning for your life has no source of its own? And if this is true, then isn't it also true that ultimately you have no meaning for yourself either? If it makes you happy to demand an external reference point on which to hang your meaningfulness, why would you deny the same to me? I also want to be happy, and I want to find that happiness in something other than myself. Is that a sin?

On the other hand, if you think I have the right and the freedom to find happiness in myself and in the things I created, then why should you not have the same right? You, whom I created in my image?

I know that some of you have proposed a solution to this problem. You call it "love." You think I am lonely up here, and that I created humans to satisfy my longing for a relationship with something that is not myself. Of course, this will never work because it is impossible for me to create something that is not part of myself, but let's say that I try anyway. Let's say that I create this mechanism called "free will," which imparts to humans a choice. If I give you the freedom (though this is stretching the word because there is nothing outside of my power) not to love me, then if some of you, a few of you, even *one* of you chooses to love me, I have gained something I might not have had. I have gained a relationship with someone who could have chosen otherwise. This is called love, you say.

This is a great idea, on paper. In real life, however, it turns out that millions, billions of people have chosen not to love me, and that I have to do something with these infidels. I can't just un-create them. If I simply destroy all the unbelievers, I may as well have created only believers in the first place. Since I am omniscient, I would know in advance which of my creations would have a tendency to choose me, and this would produce no conflict with free will since those who would not have chosen me would have been eliminated simply by not having been created in the first place. (I could call it Supernatural Selection.) This seems much more compassionate than hell.

You can't have a love relationship with someone who is not your equal. If you humans don't have a guaranteed eternal soul, like myself, then you are worthless as companions. If I can't respect your right to exist independently, and your right to choose something other than me, then I couldn't love those of you who do choose me. I would have to find a place for all those billions of eternal souls who reject me, whatever their reasons might be. Let's call it "hell," a place that is not-God, not-me. I would have to create this inferno, otherwise neither I nor the unbelievers could escape each other. Let's ignore the technicalities of how I could manage to create hell, and then separate it from myself, apart from whom nothing else exists. (It's not as though I could create something and then simply throw it away—there is no cosmic trash heap.) The point is that since I am supposedly perfect, this place of exile must be something that is the opposite. It must be ultimate evil, pain, darkness, and torment.

If I created hell, then I don't like myself.

If I did create a hell, then it certainly would not be smart to advertise that fact. How would I know if people were claiming to love me for my own sake, or simply to avoid punishment? How can I expect someone to love me who is afraid of me in the first place? The threat of eternal torment might scare some people into obedience, but it does nothing to inspire love. If you treated *me* with threats and intimidations, I would have to reconsider my admiration for your character.

How would you feel if you had brought some children into the world knowing that they were going to be tormented eternally in a place you built for them? Could you live with yourself? Wouldn't it have been better not to have brought them into the world in the first place?

I know that some of you feel that hell is just a metaphor. Do you feel the same way about heaven?

Anyway, this whole love argument is wrong. Since I am perfect, I don't lack anything. I can't be lonely. I don't need to be loved. I don't even *want* to be loved because to want is to lack. To submit to the potential of giving and receiving love is to admit that I can be hurt by those who choose not to love me. If you can hurt me, I am not perfect. If I can't be hurt, I can't love. If I ignore or erase those who do not love me, sending them off to hell or oblivion, then my love is not sincere. If all I am doing is throwing the dice of "free will" and simply reaping the harvest of those who choose to love me, then I am a selfish monster. If you played such games with people's lives, I would call you insensitive, conceited, insecure, selfish and manipulative.

I know you have tried to get me off the hook. You explain that Yours Truly is not responsible for the sufferings of unbelievers because rejection of God is their choice, not mine. They had a corrupt human nature, you explain. Well, who gave them their human nature? If certain humans decide to do wrong, where do they get the impulse? If you think it came from Satan, who created Satan? And why would some humans be susceptible to Satan in the first place? Who created that susceptibility? If Satan was created perfect, and then fell, where did the flaw of perdition come from? If I am perfect, then how in God's name did I end up creating something that would not choose perfection? Someone once said that a good tree cannot bring forth evil fruit.

Here is the title for your next theological tome: *Was Eve Perfect?* If she was, she would not have taken the fruit. If she wasn't, I created imperfection.

Maybe you think all of this gives me a purpose—putting Humpty Dumpty back together—but it actually gives me a headache. (If you won't permit me a simple headache, then how can you allow me the pain of lost love?) I could not live with myself if I thought my actions were causing harm to others. Well, I shouldn't say that. Since I think you created me, I suppose I should let you tell me what I could live with. If you think it is consistent with my character to tolerate love and vengeance concurrently, then I have no choice. If you are my creator, then I could spout tenderness out of one side of my mouth and brutality out of the other. I could dance with my lover on the bones of my errant children, and pretend to enjoy it. I would be very human indeed.

I have a thousand more questions, but I hope you will allow me one more:

How do I decide what is right and wrong?

I don't know how I got here, but I'm here. Let's just say that my purpose is to make good people out of my creations. Let's say that I am to help you learn how to be perfect like me, and that the best way is for you to act just like me, or like I want you to act. You goal is to become little mirrors of myself. Won't that be splendid? I'll give you rules or principles, and you try to follow them. This may or may not be meaningful, but it will keep us both busy. I suppose that from your point of view this would be terribly meaningful, since you think I have the power to reward and punish.

I know that some of you Protestant theologians think that I give rewards not for good deeds, but simply for believing in my son Jesus who paid the punishment for your bad deeds. Well, Jesus spent only about thirty-six hours of an eternal life sentence in hell and is now back up here in ultimate coziness with me. Talk about a wrist-slap! He was not paroled for good behavior—he was simply released. (He had connections.) If my righteous judgment demanded absolute satisfaction, then Jesus should have paid the price *in full,* don't you think?

Beyond that, it is entirely incomprehensible to me why you think I would accept the blood of one individual for the crime of another. Is that fair? Is that justice? If you commit a felony, does the law allow your brother to serve the jail sentence for you? If someone burglarized your home, would you think justice was served if a friend bought you new furniture? Do you really think that I am such a bloodthirsty dictator that I will be content with the death of *anyone* for the crime of another? And are you so disrespectful of justice that you would happily accept a stand-in for your crimes? What about personal responsibility? It is tough to open my arms to welcome believers into heaven who have avoided the rap for their own actions. Something is way out of kilter here.

But let's ignore these objections. Let's assume that Jesus and I worked it all out and that evil will be punished and good rewarded. How do I know the difference? You are insisting that I not consult any rule book. You are asking me to be the Final Authority. I must simply decide, and you must trust my decision. Am I free to decide whatever I want?

Suppose I decide that I would like you to honor me with a day of my own. I like the number seven, I don't know why, maybe because it is the first useless number. (You never sing any hymns to me in 7/4 time.) Let's divide the calendar into groups of seven days and call them weeks. For harmony, I'll divide each lunar phase into roughly seven days. The last day of the week—or maybe the first day, I don't care—I'll set aside for myself. Let's call it the Sabbath. This all feels good, so I suppose it is the right thing to do. I'll make a law ordering you to observe the Sabbath, and if you do it then I will pronounce you good people. In fact, I'll make it one of my Big Ten Commandments, and I'll order your execution if you disobey. This all makes perfect sense, I don't

145

know why.

Help me out here. How am I supposed to choose what is moral? Since I can't consult any authority, the thing to do, it appears, is to pick randomly. Actions will become right or wrong simply because I declare them to be so. If I whimsically say that you should not make any graven or molten images of "anything that is in heaven above, or that is in the earth beneath, or that is in the water under the earth," then that is that. If I decide that murder is right and compassion is wrong, you will have to accept it.

Is that all there is to it? I just decide, willy-nilly, what is right and what is wrong? Or worse, I decide based on whatever makes me feel good? I have read in some of your literature that you denounce such self-centered attitudes.

Some of you say that since I am perfect, I can't make any mistakes. Whatever I choose to be right or wrong will be in accordance with my nature, and since I am perfect, then my choices will be perfect. In any event, my choices will certainly be better than your choices, you feel. But what does "perfect" mean? If my nature is "perfect" (whatever it means), then I am living up to a standard. If I am living up to a standard, then I am not God. If perfection means something all by itself, apart from me, then I am constrained to follow its path. If, on the other hand, perfection is defined simply as conformity to my nature, then it doesn't mean anything. My nature can be what it wants, and perfection will be defined accordingly. Do you see the problem here? If "perfection" equals "God," then it is just a synonym for myself, and we can do away with the word. We could do away with either word, take your pick.

If I am perfect, then there are certain things that I cannot do. If I am not free to feel envy, lust, or malice, for example, then I am not omnipotent. I cannot be more powerful than you if you can feel and do things that I cannot.

Additionally, if you feel that God is perfect, by nature, what does "nature" mean? The word is used to describe the way things are or act in nature, and since you think I am above nature, you must mean something else, something like "character," or "attributes." To have a nature or character means to be one way and not another. It means that there are limits. Why am I one way and not another? How did it get decided that my nature would be what it is? If my "nature" is clearly defined, then I am limited. I am not God. If my nature has no limits, as some of you suggest, then I have no nature at all, and to say that God has such-and-such a nature is meaningless. In fact, if I have no limits, then I have no identity; and if I have no identity, then I do not exist.

Who am I?

This brings me back to the conundrum: if I don't know who I am, then how can I decide what is right? Do I just poke around in myself until I come up with something?

146

There is one course I could pursue, and some of you have suggested this for yourselves. I could base my pronouncements on what is best for you humans. You people have physical bodies that bump around in a physical world. I could determine those actions that are healthy and beneficial for material beings in a material environment. I could make morality something *material*: something that is relative to human life, not to my whims. I could declare (by conclusion, not by edict) that harming human life is bad, and that helping or enhancing human life is good. This would be like providing an operation manual for something I designed and manufactured. It would require me to know all about human nature and the environment in which you humans live, and to communicate these ideas to you.

This makes a lot of sense, but it changes my task from one of *determining* morality to one of *communicating* morality. If morality is discovered in nature, then you don't need me, except maybe to prod you along. I saw to it that you have capable minds with the ability to reason and do science. There is nothing mysterious about studying how humans interact with nature and with each other, and you should be able to come up with your own set of rules. Some of you tried this millennia before Moses. Even if your rules contradict mine, I couldn't claim any higher authority than you. At least you would be able to give *reasons* for your rules, which I can only do by submitting to science myself.

If morality is defined by how human beings exist in nature, then you don't need me at all. I am off the hook! From what I have read, most of you have your feet on the ground with no help from me. I could hand down some stone tablets containing what I think is right and wrong, but it would still be up to you to see if they work in the real world. I think we all agree that grounded reason is better than the whim of an ungrounded deity.

This is a wonderful approach, but what bothers me is that while this may help you know what is moral in your environment, it doesn't help me much. I don't have an environment. I'm out here flapping in the breeze. I envy you.

Nor does the humanistic approach help those of you who want morality to be rooted in something absolute, outside of yourselves. It must be frightening for you who need an anchor to realize that there is no bottom to the ocean. Well, it's frightening for me also. I don't have an anchor of my own. That's why I'm asking for your help.

Thank you for reading my letter, and for letting me impose on your busy schedule. Please answer at your convenience. I have all the time in the world.

Sincerely,

Yours Truly

20

Omni-Aqueous

RELIGIOUS DOCTRINES ARE most vulnerable when expressed in absolute terms. "All," "always," and "never" beg for scrutiny. This includes the cardinal Christian doctrines about the nature of God: omniscience, omnipotence, omnipresence, and omnibenevolence.

According to Christianity, God is "all-knowing." Although this doctrine is fundamental, it is rarely defined or examined. It is simply a given. Critical thinking, however, proves that omniscience—knowing everything in the past, present, and future— is impossible. The concept loops back on itself and creates an infinite hurdle that not even a deity can leap.

To "know" is to contain a true image or idea within a mind. A being that knows *everything* must also know itself. Therefore, the mind of an omniscient being must contain an image of itself within itself. This is impossible.

Suppose you wanted to make a perfect map of the earth. This map would be so precise that it would include not only the oceans, continents, cities, roads, and landmarks, but blades of grass, roof shingles, and bubbles behind a whale surfacing in the Pacific—*everything*. Such a map would have to be updated regularly. The map would have to be very large to admit a useful resolution. Let's say that it would be a few square miles, placed out in the desert, where it does not obscure too much of the surface that it has to represent.

148

To be perfect and up-to-date, such a map would have to include itself. Since it represents everything on the earth, on the map would be a tiny drawing of the map itself; and to be perfect, the tiny drawing would include the little details on the map, including a tiny drawing of the tiny drawing, and so on. It becomes clear that such a map is impossible. The necessary degree of resolution would require that it be at least as large as the earth itself, obscuring the earth totally, and at that point it would make no sense to have a copy of what we can look at directly. We could do away with the map and simply claim that reality is its own map.

If we try to avoid the difficulty by placing the map out in the solar system, then we could frame the problem as an attempt to map the galaxy, or the entire universe, with the same problem. We can't take the map outside the universe, because the universe is defined as "all there is."

Imagine that the map is computerized, to be updated more efficiently. Visualize a huge, automated representation of the universe, somewhere out in the universe. Since the computer is part of the universe, it must contain a representation of itself. To be perfect, it would need to keep track of itself keeping track of itself. This would add to its size. It would take so much time and energy tracking itself tracking itself tracking itself that it would get caught in an infinite loop, draining its resources and accomplishing no useful work. (Some computer viruses work like this.)

In order for God to know everything, he has to know everything about himself. He has to know what he is going to think next. He has to anticipate that he is going to need to know what he is going to think next. Like the computer virus, an omniscient God gets caught in an infinite loop and cannot have a single thought. It doesn't matter what method God uses to store and retrieve data in his super mind, he has to have *some* kind of internal representation. If theists argue that the intelligence of God is something altogether different from human or computer intelligence, then they are admitting that the idea of omniscience is meaningless. If "all-knowing" does not compare with "knowing," then the phrase lacks relevance to human understanding, and we may as well say "God is mmpfghrmpf" instead of "God is omniscient."

The Christian God cannot be both omniscient and omnibenevolent. If God were omniscient, then he knew, when he created Adam, that Adam would sin. He *knew* human beings would suffer. Regardless of whether the existence of evil can be theologically explicated, an all-knowing Creator deliberately placed humans in its path. This is at least criminal negligence, if not malice. Those who invoke "free will" forget that we all act according to a human nature that was supposedly created by God himself. You can argue all around the bushes on this point, but you can't get away from the fact that

Adam did not create his own nature. At the moment of creation, an omniscient deity would have been picturing the suffering and damnation of most of his creation. This is mean-spirited. God should have had an abortion.

What do believers mean when they say their god is all powerful? (Let's ignore the fact that the biblical God is weaker than chariots of iron, according to *Judges 1:19.*) "Power" can be taken two ways: ability or authority. The word "omnipotent" contains "potent," relating more to force than to command, although Christians claim that their God possesses both strength and leadership. To have power is to have the ability accomplish a certain task. Power is a physical force, at least, and if God, at minimum, is not materially mighty, then he is not God. An omnipotent God must be able to counteract the greatest possible force that could exist in the universe. Imagine a black hole created by all the mass of the universe collapsing in one place. God must possess a physical energy at least as great as this.

The universe encompasses all the mass/energy available anywhere. If God possesses energy that interacts with the material world, then, by definition, he is part of the natural universe. Whatever God's source of energy might be, it exists *somewhere,* adding to the size of the universe. An omnipotent God would make the cosmos infinitely massive, a fact that is contradicted by the expansion of the universe (or, if God is outside the known universe, by the uniformity of such expansion), or by the fact that we are not all instantly compressed by the gravity of infinite matter or incinerated with heat.

Some argue that God works from a "spiritual" dimension, and therefore does not add to the material world. Somehow, God can manipulate the existing mass/energy in the universe without adding to it, and without collapsing into an infinite black hole himself. But if "omnipotence" is meaningful, it has to indicate something to us humans who do not transcend nature. Whenever God supposedly proves his power to us earthly creatures, it is manifested as a physical act in the tangible world: an earthquake, flood, moving star, plague of locust, voice, burning bush, and so on. If God is "directing" nature from outside, he is still required to do so in a way that causes ordinary matter to react. If "all-powerful" does not relate to "powerful," as we humans understand the word, then the phrase is incoherent. We may as well say, "God is rrrghphrrth" instead of "God is omnipotent."

Those who would claim that God does not have to be infinitely powerful to counteract the largest possible force in the universe are forgetting that God supposedly *created* the universe out of himself. The argument of limited omnipotence (sufficient power to do anything that would ever need to be done) implies that God has a restriction on how large a universe he could create. Could he have created a universe infinitely more massive than the current one? If not, he is not omnipotent. The old riddle is not entirely inapt: could God create a stone so large that he couldn't lift it? Either way, God emerges short of omnipotence. Avoiding the question by claiming that God would never want to do such a thing implies that God's power has bounds, and that he is a slave to his own character.

Why should God need power, anyway? Power is what you utilize when you have a problem, a hurdle to jump, a need in your life. If God is able to manipulate matter and energy with some spiritual magic, then what good is power? To admit that God uses power is to concede that God has problems, needs, and physical challenges. Why drown the human race with a flood? Why not just make them disappear?

Omnipotence gives God a moral problem. Since God has the desire and the power to eliminate evil, why doesn't he? If God truly is omniscient and omnipotent, then he is not omnibenevolent. He cannot possibly be all three at once. How could he have created an angel named Lucifer who possessed some quirk in his character that would cause him to go wrong? If this were deliberate, then God is an accessory to evil. If it were accidental, then God is not omnipotent.

Omnipotence contradicts omniscience. To be omniscient means that all future facts are known. This means that the set of knowable facts is fixed and unchangeable. If facts cannot be changed, then this limits the power of God. If God knows what will happen tomorrow, then he is impotent to change it. If he changes it anyway, then he was not omniscient.

Omnipresence has similar problems. To be "present" means to be at a physical location. Technology extends our senses with machines, allowing viewers, for example, to be "present" at a televised event, but even this requires a physical connection: camera, microphone, sensor, receiver, speaker. God is not "present" at every location in the universe, not in any ordinary sense. To say that God is present in a "spiritual" sense is meaningless until "spirit" is defined. Since spirit is normally described as something "immaterial," or "transcendent" (which merely identify what it is *not,* not what it *is*), this means that being present spiritually is not to be present at all. We may as well say "God is sshhffhgtyrh" rather than "God is omnipresent."

John 7:38 reports: "He that believeth on me, as the scripture hath said, out of his belly shall flow rivers of living water." I take this to mean that those who believe in an omnipresent, all-knowing, all-good, and all-powerful god are omni-aqueous: all-wet.

You Can't Win With Original Sin

by Dan Barker

You can't win!
You can't win with Original Sin.
It doesn't even matter how intelligent or kind you may have been.
You just can't win.
It was all over before it began—
You were doomed in the fall of man.
You can't win.

I was dead—
I was dead before my life had begun.
I was dead,
Because of something my great-great-great grandparents had done.
Adam and Eve didn't do any wrong—
They were set up by God all along.
They couldn't win.

I've been told
I must believe on Jesus Christ to be saved;
But first,
I must admit that I am totally depraved.
Before you go pointing that finger of blame,
Just remember that Eve Was Framed!
She couldn't win.

The kind of God
Who's so insecure that he needs to send me to hell
Is the kind of God
Who'd probably get a kick out of damning all the Christians as well!
It was all over before it began—
I was doomed in the fall of man.
But as a skeptic I must insist,
Adam and Eve didn't really exist,
And neither does God, then, for that matter,
And until the day that old myth is shattered,
We can't win.
No, we just can't win.

© Copyright 1984 by Dan Barker. Song lyrics.

RE-EXAMINING THE "GOOD BOOK"

Part 3

Losing Faith in Faith

21

Out of Context

ON A BOB Larson radio show Dr. Norman Geisler (of Falwell's Liberty University) quoted *Psalm 14:1* to me: "The fool hath said in his heart, There is no God." I countered with *Matthew 5:22* where Jesus said, "Whosoever shall say, Thou fool, shall be in danger of hellfire." Geisler quickly responded, "You're taking that out of context!"

Context, the true savior of fundamentalists, is a handy, knee-jerk defense against troublesome bible verses. Whenever Foundation staff quotes some horrible scripture on the TV or radio, such as, "Samaria ... hath rebelled against her God: they shall fall by the sword: their infants shall be dashed in pieces, and their women with child shall be ripped up" *(Hosea 13:16),* believers say, "But that's not what it really means!"

Context is important, of course, but when fundamentalists invoke it, it is not normally to discern the true historical meaning of a bible passage. "Context," to them, is a fuzzy way to make something not mean what it actually says.

I sometimes point out that Jesus encouraged castration: "There be eunuchs, which have made themselves eunuchs for the kingdom of heaven's sake. He that is able to receive it, let him receive it." *(Matthew 19:12)* Believers are quick to chide me for not grasping the distinction between prose and poetry.

This is not about castration, they claim; it is about celibacy. Tell that to Origen, the third-century church father who took this verse literally and "made himself a eunuch."

Believers sometimes show an uncanny ability to recognize metaphor, especially where a text runs contrary to their theology; but why can't they extend this literary critical talent to the rest of the book? They agree that Jesus's parable about the Prodigal Son is a metaphor. It doesn't matter if the Prodigal Son actually existed; the underlying message of the story, not the historical verification, is what is important. But the same could be said about Adam and Eve. It could be said about God, for that matter. They are Hebrew metaphors which contain an underlying message that attempts to explain our origin. The whole thing is one huge figure of speech.

When Christians throw the "out of context" defense at you, here are some ways to check whether they know what they are talking about, or whether they are just throwing up a convenient smoke screen. Ask them some specific questions about the bible verse under consideration.

1. Who wrote it, and how do you know? The authorship of much of the bible is under serious debate. The four Gospels (Matthew, Mark, Luke, and John) are all anonymous. No one knows who wrote them, and the names were attached much later. In spite of this, most Christians will quote the bible, saying, "Matthew says . . ." or "John states . . ." as if it were written by eyewitness reporters.

2. Why was it written, and to whom? If a first-century love letter said, "Helen, you are the most beautiful woman in the world," you might take this superlative with a grain of salt. Propaganda, rhetoric, and polemics are the same: they tend to exaggerate. The author of John (whoever he was) admits that he is writing propaganda: "But these are written, that ye might believe that Jesus is the Christ . . . and that ye might have life through his name." *(John 20:31)* This is hardly an objective agenda.

3. When was it written? A prophecy is not a prophecy if it was written after the fact. The supposed prediction of the destruction of the temple in 70 AD was written no earlier than 90 AD. *(John 2:19)*

4. Is the translation accurate? In some cases, Christian scholars have tampered with the meaning. *Isaiah 7:14*, a putative prophecy of the virgin birth of Jesus, should read "young woman," not "virgin," as most Christians (including the writer of *Matthew 1:22-23*) insist. Some translations have corrected this fraud. (The *New Revised Standard Version*, favored by scholars, has "Look, the young woman is with child and shall bear a son.") We can't all be Greek and Hebrew scholars, but we can all use the simple technique of comparing different translations to ascertain the meaning. Anyone who refuses to do this is ignoring context.

5. Does the same author offer any clues to the meaning? When Isaiah quotes the Lord as saying, "I create evil [*ra*]" *(Isaiah 45:7)*, does it really mean "evil," or is it simply "calamity" as some apologists assert? (Though that wouldn't seem to solve much.) Looking through the rest of the book of Isaiah we find that the Hebrew word *ra* indeed means "evil" in a moral sense: "For before the child [from the "young woman" in *7:14*] shall know to refuse the evil [*ra*], and choose the good . . ." *(7:16)*, and "I will punish the world for their evil [*ra*]." *(13:11)* These, and other, verses show that *ra* is the opposite of good and deserves punishment. It can also be helpful to check with other biblical authors to confirm the general usage, such as when the writer of Genesis mentioned the "tree of knowledge of good and evil [*ra*]." To say that "God created evil" is not to take things out of context at all. (All you need to do this yourself is an inexpensive English concordance, such as *Strong's* or *Young's* that indicates the original Hebrew and Greek for each word.)

6. Are there any literary allusions or parallels involved? Jesus reportedly said, "Therefore, all things whatsoever ye would that men should do to you, do ye even so to them: for this is the law and the prophets," but this Golden Rule is not unique to him. Hillel, a Jewish scholar who died about 10 AD, said, "What is hateful to you, do not to your fellow-men. That is the entire Law; all the rest is commentary." The gospel writer simply borrowed the idea from Hillel, who may have got it from the Brahmans ("This is the sum of duty: Do naught unto others which would cause you pain if done to you."— 300 BC), who may have taken it from Confucius ("Surely it is the maxim of loving-kindness: Do not unto others that you would not have them do unto you."—500 BC), or from the Zoroastrians (who go back to 1500 BC: "That nature alone is good which refrains from doing unto another whatsoever is not good for itself.")

7. What is the text's relevance to the immediate and general topic? Christians claim that *Micah 5:2* is a prophecy of the birthplace of Jesus: "But thou, Bethlehem Ephratah, though thou be little among the thousands of Judah, yet out of thee shall he come forth unto me that is to be ruler of Israel . . ." Yet the context is the struggle with the Assyrians in 700 BC, not the Romans; and Bethlehem is most likely a person here, not a city. (*I Chronicles 4:4* mentions "the sons of Hur, the firstborn of Ephratah, the father of Bethlehem.") Besides, in the context of history, when was Jesus ever the "ruler of Israel"? Is he now?

8. What was the social, political, religious, and philosophical climate? The first century was a time of intense myth-making, all over the world, and especially in the Mediterranean area. Superstitions were being born, modified, swapped, stolen, and discarded at the time the New Testament was written. The idea of a virgin-born savior was very big two thousand years ago, and the Jesus story is cut from the same fabric as other ancient mythologies. Why do so many Christians ignore *this* context?

Context involves many other considerations, of course, but rarely do the average pew-sitters go even this far. If they don't know the who, when, or why of a passage, how can they smugly claim that it is taken "out of context?"

When fundamentalists talk about "context," they don't usually mean the literary or historical context of the text; they really only mean the context of their own particular theology. A bible verse makes sense to them as it relates to what their pastor, church, denomination, or personal ideas dictate what the "whole ball of wax" is all about. Since the Jesus in their mind is kind and loving, he could not have meant that we should truly "hate" our parents:

"If any man come to me, and hate [*miseo*] not his father, and mother, and wife, and children, and brethren, and sisters, yea, and his own life also, he cannot be my disciple." *(Luke 14:26)*

Most Christians feel obligated to soften the face meaning of the word "hate" to something like "love less than me," even though the Greek word *miseo* means "hate." (The prefixes on "misanthropy" and "misogyny" are from *miseo*.) You can cite a hundred references to show that the biblical God is a bloodthirsty tyrant, but if they can dig up two or three verses that say "God is love," they will claim that *you* are taking things out of context!

When it comes to interpreting the bible, it is surprising how much certainty is professed by fundamentalists. These people speak the same language and share a common culture, yet they often misunderstand each other (not to mention that they often fail to comprehend us freethinkers). What makes them think they can so easily interpret Paul the Apostle, who wrote millennia ago in a different language from a foreign and extinct culture?

Even if they are right, even if liberal scholars are indeed blind to the "true" context, why would an intelligent God write a book that is so easily misunderstood?

Jesus said, "And that servant, which knew his lord's will, and prepared not himself, neither did according to his will, shall be beaten with many stripes." *(Luke 12:47)* Can the Christian slaveholders during the Civil War be faulted for thinking that this verse encourages the ownership and abuse of slaves?

Paul said, "Wives, submit yourselves unto your own husbands, as unto the Lord. For the husband is the head of the wife." *(Ephesians 5:22-23)* Can Christian husbands be blamed for thinking that this verse allows them to lord over their wives?

Leviticus 24:16 says, "And he that blasphemeth the name of the Lord, he shall be surely put to death, and all the congregation shall certainly stone him." Why shouldn't a fundamentalist Christian believe that the Ayatollah was morally right to sentence author Salman Rushdie to death?

Proverbs says, "Withhold not correction from the child: for if thou beatest him with the rod, he shall not die." *(Proverbs 23:13)* and "The blueness of a wound cleanseth away evil." *(Proverbs 20:30)* Can Christian parents be faulted for beating their kids?

An omniscient deity should have known what Origen had in mind when he was inspired by *Matthew 19:12* to pick up that knife.

Freethought Today, November, 1990

22

Square Circles

FUNDAMENTALISTS CAN BE among some of the most creative people in the world. It requires a strong imagination and profound wisdom to be able to juggle deep spiritual mysteries, Greek and Hebrew, theological interpretations, cosmic associations, and principles of faith.

Christian intelligence is very special. It's not easy to have the "mind of Christ," but with a little faith and a lot of practice anyone can achieve this higher level of spirituality and discernment. And one of the more practical benefits of this superior comprehension is the ability to explain the "supposed" contradictions of the bible. Scriptural discrepancies just vanish under the light of godly understanding.

For example, I was recently speaking with a Christian relative about the biblical claim that God, who is light, and dwells in light also dwells in darkness. (See "Bible Contradictions" for references.) She saw no problem with these incompatible statements and proceeded to explain that a room is dark until the light is turned on, so it makes sense to say that the light dwells in darkness. Silly me—I thought I had found a contradiction!

Thomas Paine should have known better than to criticize the authors of Matthew and Luke for giving Jesus contradictory genealogies. There's an easy explanation. The Lukan line is not through Joseph, as it says in Luke 3:23, but through Mary! Commentator Finis Jenning Dake says, "As women are never reckoned in genealogies, Joseph, the legal son of Heli naturally took the place of Mary . . . " Ignoring the fact that this is another example of biblical sexism, Dake overlooks the female names that appear in Matthew's list! *(Matthew 1:5)* He also makes the convenient—though unsupported—assumption that Heli must have been Mary's father. I have had it patiently explained to me that the author of Matthew, writing mainly to Jews, would be more concerned with the paternal line; but the author of Luke (we have no idea who were the actual writers of Matthew and Luke), writing mainly to the Greek world, would be naturally more concerned with the maternal line. Naturally. So, even though the text names Joseph, it really means Mary. Get it? We skeptics must be blind to truth—if we continue to call this a contradiction, then God help our rebellious souls.

Christians also have this amazing ability to discern deeper meanings. They know exactly what God meant when the text is confusing to others. I'm not that smart. I figure that God would mean what he says. When I read, "No man hath seen God at any time," I take it to mean that no man hath seen God at any time. How can this be misunderstood? No one has ever looked at God. Ever. But when Jacob said, "I have seen God face to face," I take that to mean that he looked at God. I have had it neatly explained to me that the phrase actually means "No man hath seen God at any time *in all his fullness and glory.*" Of course! Why couldn't I see that? God must have meant something else, else it would be contradictory. It requires a disciplined Christian genius to see exactly where certain words should be inserted into God's inspired text.

(This is a brave and risky tactic, since the writer of Revelation says, right at the very end of the bible: "For I testify unto every man that heareth of the prophecy of this book, If any man shall add unto these things, God shall add unto him the plagues that are written in this book . . ." *Revelation 22:18*)

In *Genesis 2:17* God tells Adam "thou shalt surely die" in "the day that thou eatest" of the fruit. Yet Adam ate the forbidden food and lived to be 930 years old! *(Genesis 5:5)* But don't be too quick to flag this as contradictory. The word "die" actually means "die spiritually" in this context. When Adam took his nasty nibble he died *inside*, though his body was able to live another eight hundred years. Doesn't that make sense? He was a zombie, but he planted crops, made love to Eve, and raised a family. I don't know how Christians develop the skills to be able to discern where certain words should be redefined; but, of course, they have spiritual insight. (It is interesting how fundamentalists, who are usually so rigid in interpreting words literally, are the quickest to mangle definitions for the sake of theological convenience.)

Apparently, God is sometimes allowed to exaggerate. And the apologists always seem to know exactly when and where he does this. For example, when God said that Noah was "righteous" and that Job was "perfect and blameless," he didn't mean to imply that they had never committed any sins because Paul tells us that "no one is righteous" and "all have sinned." Obviously, then, God must feel that you can commit a few sins and still be blameless; and when he says "perfect" he means "almost perfect." It makes perfect sense, almost. (Of course, we could consider the possibility that God was right and that Paul didn't know what he was talking about. But that would mean that we would have to throw out much of the New Testament, and once you start throwing things out . . .)

According to the gospels of Mark, Luke, and John, Jesus's tomb was already open when the women arrived on Easter morning. But the writer of Matthew said it was closed when they arrived; it was opened in their presence. One of my theologian friends says this is not contradictory at all. It was not meant to be understood chronologically (though he can't explain exactly how he knows this). *Matthew 28:2-4* should really be understood as having happened in chapter 27 so that it will agree with the other writers. Why didn't I see that? I guess I just lack the knowledge and confidence to be able to shuffle God's holy word around.

After this same theologian had deftly fielded about twenty of my naive claims of biblical contradictions I asked him, "Then what *would* you accept as a contradiction, if not these examples? By what criteria do you judge other writings? What would the bible have to say, hypothetically, in order for it to be discrepant?" He was quiet for a moment before answering. I was eagerly appreciative of the fact that he was going to dispense some honest and thoughtful wisdom.

"I would accept it as contradictory if the Bible said that Jesus died on both Tuesday and Friday," he finally answered.

"You would?" I asked. "Then I have one for you." I directed him to the fact that Jesus was crucified at the third hour *(Mark 15:25)* yet he was standing before Pilate at the sixth hour *(John 19:14)* when he should have been hanging on the cross. However, my friend did not disappoint me. He explained, with a patient smile, that this apparent inconsistency is the result of our uncertainty as to how the first-century Jews kept track of time. It is possible that Jesus was before Pilate at the sixth hour of the day, but he was crucified at the third hour since sunrise. We should not apply a twentieth-century hypercritical attitude to the writings of ancient Jews. There is likely something we do not yet know about how they reckoned time, so we shouldn't pronounce it contradictory because of *our* lack of knowledge.

All of these defenses leave us "hypercritical" skeptics in a useless position.

We are wasting our time. The mighty fortress of scripture is impregnable, it seems. It is folly to scrutinize the inscrutable.

The scientific principle of falsifiability asserts that all true statements must be able to be phrased as a double negative. In other words, there must be something that can be said about the statement which, if true, would make the statement false. For example, horse skeletons in the Cambrian fossil strata would immediately falsify over a hundred years of evolutionary thought. The honest scientist says, "Here's what would prove me wrong. Go for it." As yet, no horses have been found sleeping with the ancient trilobites.

In fact, one of the best ways to prove something is true is to try to prove it false. If all discrediting attempts fail, then it stands with more certainty. If the bible is not falsifiable in principle, then it cannot be said to be true. It must be testable or it is worthless. But fundamentalists have little use for scientific principles; they have "spiritual insight." They just *know* that the bible is true, and that's that.

To demonstrate my point I will often ask a Christian to produce a statement for me that is contradictory, just so we will know what we are talking about when we use the word "contradiction." I challenge them to state a discrepancy that I cannot explain away. They quickly see that, without criteria, it is impossible. For example, "This circle is a square" seems contradictory. But I have learned from Christians many ways to interpret a phrase to make sense. It could mean a circle of squares, or a square of circles. Or, in the original language the word "square" was used to refer to any bounded geometric object. Or, the circle is functioning in the place of a square temporarily. Or, yesterday there was a circle here, today it is a square. Or, the circle is "square," meaning odd or corny—it might be an ellipse, yeah, that's what it is. Or, the word "circle" is actually used in the general sense of "circling around" or encompassing, which is what a square can do. Or, this circle was cut from a square—the word "is" really means "is from." Or, the word "square" doesn't really belong in this sentence; it goes chronologically with a previous sentence. Or, the term "square" is symbolic, like "the four corners of the earth." Or the word "circle" is meant loosely, as in "circle of friends"—a square cirlce is an old-fashioned group of acquaintances. Or, it's a deep mystery that only God comprehends, and we will understand it all someday in heaven. (Heaven would be boring if there weren't things like this to look forward to.)

See what I mean? We skeptics could learn a lot from the creative religious mind set. If only we weren't so hypercritical.

Freethought Today, April/May, 1985

23

Bible Contradictions

P AUL SAID, "God is not *the author* of confusion," *(I Corinthians 14:33),* yet never has a book produced more confusion than the bible! There are hundreds of denominations and sects, all using the "inspired Scriptures" to prove their conflicting doctrines.

Why do trained theologians differ? Why do educated translators disagree over Greek and Hebrew meanings? Why all the confusion? Shouldn't a document that was "divinely inspired" by an omniscient and omnipotent deity be as clear as possible?

"If the trumpet give an uncertain sound," Paul wrote in *I Corinthians 14:8,* "who shall prepare himself to the battle? So likewise ye, except ye utter by the tongue words easy to be understood, how shall it be known what is spoken? for ye shall speak into the air." Exactly! Paul should have practiced what he preached. For almost two millennia, the bible has been producing a most "uncertain sound."

The problem is not with human limitations, as some claim. The problem is the bible itself. People who are free of theological bias notice that the bible contains hundreds of discrepancies. Should it surprise us when such a literary and moral mish-mash, taken seriously, causes so much discord? Here is a brief sampling of biblical contradictions.

164

Should we kill?

Exodus 20:13 "Thou shalt not kill."

Leviticus 24:17 "And he that killeth any man shall surely be put to death."

vs.

Exodus 32:27 "Thus sayeth the Lord God of Israel, Put every man his sword
by his side, . . . and slay every man his brother, . . . companion, . . .
neighbor."

I Samuel 6:19 " . . . and the people lamented because the Lord had smitten
many of the people with a great slaughter."

I Samuel 15:2,3,7,8 "Thus saith the Lord . . . Now go and smite Amalek, and
utterly destroy all that they have, and spare them not; but slay
both man and woman, infant and suckling, ox and sheep, camel
and ass. . . . And Saul smote the Amalekites . . . and utterly destroyed all the people with the edge of the sword."

Numbers 15:36 "And all the congregation brought him without the camp, and
stoned him with stones, and he died; as the Lord commanded
Moses."

Hosea 13:16 "they shall fall by the sword: their infants shall be dashed in
pieces, and their women with children shall be ripped up."

*For a discussion of the defense that the Commandments prohibit only murder,
see "Murder, He Wrote."*

Should we tell lies?

Exodus 20:16 "Thou shalt not bear false witness."

Proverbs 12:22 "Lying lips are an abomination to the Lord."

vs.

I Kings 22:23 "The Lord hath put a lying spirit in the mouth of all these thy
prophets, and the Lord hath spoken evil concerning thee."

II Thessalonians 2:11 "And for this cause God shall send them strong delusion, that they should believe a lie."

Also, compare *Joshua 2:4-6* with *James 2:25.*

Should we steal?

Exodus 20:15 "Thou shalt not steal."

Leviticus 19:13 "Thou shalt not defraud thy neighbor, neither rob him."

vs.

Exodus 3:22 "And ye shall spoil the Egyptians."

Exodus 12:35-36 "And they spoiled [plundered, *NRSV*] the Egyptians."

Luke 19:29-34 "[Jesus] sent two of his disciples, Saying, Go ye into the village
. . . ye shall find a colt tied, whereon yet never man sat: loose him,
and bring him hither. And if any man ask you, Why do ye loose

him? thus shall ye say unto him, Because the Lord hath need of him. . . . And as they were loosing the colt, the owners thereof said unto them, Why loose ye the colt? And they said, The Lord hath need of him."

I was taught as a child that when you take something without asking for it, that is stealing.

Shall we keep the sabbath?

Exodus 20:8 "Remember the sabbath day to keep it holy."

Exodus 31:15 "Whosoever doeth any work in the sabbath day, he shall surely be put to death."

Numbers 15:32,36 "And while the children of Israel were in the wilderness, they found a man that gathered sticks upon the sabbath day. . . . And all the congregation brought him without the camp, and stoned him with stones, and he died; as the Lord commanded Moses."

vs.

Isaiah 1:13 "The new moons and sabbaths, the calling of assemblies, I cannot away with; it is iniquity."

John 5:16 "And therefore did the Jews persecute Jesus and sought to slay him, because he had done these things on the sabbath day."

Colossians 2:16 "Let no man therefore judge you in meat, or in drink, or in respect of an holy-day, or of the new moon, or of the sabbath days."

Shall we make graven images?

Exodus 20:4 "Thou shalt not make unto thee any graven image, or any likeness of anything that is in heaven . . . earth . . . water."

Leviticus 26:1 "Ye shall make ye no idols nor graven image, neither rear you up a standing image, neither shall ye set up any image of stone."

Deuteronomy 27:15 "Cursed be the man that maketh any graven or molten image."

vs.

Exodus 25:18 "And thou shalt make two cherubims of gold, of beaten work shalt thou make them."

I Kings 7:15,16,23,25 "For he [Solomon] cast two pillars of brass . . . and two chapiters of molten brass . . . And he made a molten sea . . . it stood upon twelve oxen . . . [and so on]"

Are we saved through works?

Ephesians 2:8,9 "For by grace are ye saved through faith . . . not of works."

Romans 3:20,28 "Therefore by the deeds of the law there shall no flesh be justified in his sight."

Galatians 2:16 "Knowing that a man is not justified by the works of the law, but by the faith of Jesus Christ."

vs.

James 2:24 "Ye see then how that by works a man is justified, and not by faith only."

Matthew 19:16-21 "And, behold, one came and said unto him, Good Master, what good thing shall I do, that I may have eternal life? And he [Jesus] said unto him . . . keep the commandments. . . . The young man saith unto him, All these things have I kept from my youth up: what lack I yet? Jesus said unto him, If thou wilt be perfect, go and sell that thou hast, and give to the poor, and thou shalt have treasure in heaven."

The common defense here is that "we are saved by faith and *works." But Paul said "not of works."*

Should good works be seen?

Matthew 5:16 "Let your light so shine before men that they may see your good works."

I Peter 2:12 "Having your conversation honest among the Gentiles: that . . . they may by your good works, which they shall behold, glorify God in the day of visitation."

vs.

Matthew 6:1-4 "Take heed that ye do not your alms before men, to be seen of them . . . that thine alms may be in secret."

Matthew 23:3,5 "Do not ye after their [Pharisees'] works. . . . all their works they do for to be seen of men."

Should we own slaves?

Leviticus 25:45-46 "Moreover of the children of the strangers that do sojourn among you, of them shall ye buy, . . . and they shall be your possession . . . they shall be your bondmen forever."

Genesis 9:25 "And he [Noah] said, Cursed be Canaan; a servant of servants shall he be unto his brethren."

Exodus 21:2,7 "If thou buy an Hebrew servant, six years he shall serve: and in the seventh he shall go out free for nothing. . . . And if a man sell his daughter to be a maidservant, she shall not go out as the manservants do."

Joel 3:8 "And I will sell your sons and your daughters into the hand of the children of Judah, and they shall sell them to the Sabeans, to a people far off: for the Lord hath spoken it."

Luke 12:47,48 [Jesus speaking] "And that servant, which knew his lord's will,

and prepared not himself, neither did according to his will, shall be
beaten with many stripes. But he that knew not, and did commit
things worthy of stripes, shall be beaten with few stripes."

Colossians 3:22 "Servants, obey in all things your masters."

vs.

Isaiah 58:6 "Undo the heavy burdens . . . let the oppressed go free, . . . break
every yoke."

Matthew 23:10 "Neither be ye called Masters: for one is your Master, even
Christ."

*Pro-slavery bible verses were cited by many churches in the South during
the Civil War, and were used by some theologians in the Dutch
Reformed Church to justify apartheid in South Africa. There are
more pro-slavery verses than cited here.*

Does God change his mind?

Malachi 3:6 "For I am the Lord; I change not."

Numbers 23:19 "God is not a man, that he should lie; neither the son of man,
that he should repent."

Ezekiel 24:14 "I the Lord have spoken it: it shall come to pass, and I will do it;
I will not go back, neither will I spare, neither will I repent."

James 1:17 " . . . the Father of lights, with whom is no variableness, neither
shadow of turning."

vs.

Exodus 32:14 "And the Lord repented of the evil which he thought to do unto
his people."

Genesis 6:6,7 "And it repented the Lord that he had made man on the earth
. . . And the Lord said, I will destroy man whom I have created from
the face of the earth . . . for it repenteth me that I have made him."

Jonah 3:10 ". . . and God repented of the evil, that he had said that he would
do unto them; and he did it not."

See also *II Kings 20:1-7, Numbers 16:20-35, Numbers 16:44-50.*

See *Genesis 18:23-33,* where Abraham gets God to change his mind about the
minimum number of righteous people in Sodom required to avoid
destruction, bargaining down from fifty to ten. (An omniscient God
must have known that he was playing with Abraham's hopes for
mercy—he destroyed the city anyway.)

Are we punished for our parents' sins?

Exodus 20:5 "For I the Lord thy God am a jealous God, visiting the iniquity of
the fathers upon the children unto the third and fourth generation." (Repeated in *Deuteronomy 5:9*)

Exodus 34:6-7 " . . . The Lord God, merciful and gracious, . . . that will by no means clear the guilty; visiting the iniquity of the fathers upon the children, and upon the children's children, unto the third and to the fourth generation."

I Corinthians 15:22 "For as in Adam all die, . . ."

vs.

Ezekiel 18:20 "The son shall not bear the iniquity of the father."

Deuteronomy 24:16 "The fathers shall not be put to death for the children, neither shall the children be put to death for the fathers: every man shall be put to death for his own sin."

Is God good or evil?

Psalm 145:9 "The Lord is good to all."

Deuteronomy 32:4 "a God of truth and without iniquity, just and right is he."

vs.

Isaiah 45:7 "I make peace and create evil. I the Lord do all these things." *See "Out of Context" for more on Isaiah 45:7.*

Lamentations 3:38 "Out of the mouth of the most High proceedeth not evil and good?"

Jeremiah 18:11 "Thus saith the Lord; Behold, I frame evil against you, and devise a device against you."

Ezekiel 20:25,26 "I gave them also statutes that were not good, and judgments whereby they should not live. And I polluted them in their own gifts, in that they caused to pass through the fire all that openeth the womb, that I might make them desolate, to the end that they might know that I am the Lord."

Does God tempt people?

James 1:13 "Let no man say . . . I am tempted of God: for God cannot be tempted with evil, neither tempteth he any man."

vs.

Genesis 22:1 "And it came to pass after these things, that God did tempt Abraham."

Is God peaceable?

Romans 15:33 "The God of peace."

Isaiah 2:4 ". . . and they shall beat their swords into plowshares, and their spears into pruninghooks: nation shall not lift up sword against nation, neither shall they learn war any more."

vs.

Exodus 15:3 "The Lord is a man of war."

169

Joel 3:9-10 "Prepare war, wake up the mighty men, let all the men of war draw near; let them come up: Beat your plowshares into swords, and your pruninghooks into spears: let the weak say, I am strong."

Was Jesus peaceable?

John 14:27 "Peace I leave with you, my peace I give unto you."

Acts 10:36 "The word which God sent unto the children of Israel, preaching peace by Jesus Christ."

Luke 2:14 " . . . on earth peace, good will toward men."

vs.

Matthew 10:34 "Think not that I am come to send peace on earth: I came not to send peace, but a sword. For I am come to set a man at variance against his father, and the daughter against her mother, and the daughter in law against her mother in law. And a man's foes shall be they of his own household."

Luke 22:36 "Then said he unto them, . . . he that hath no sword, let him sell his garment, and buy one."

Was Jesus trustworthy?

John 8:14 "Though I bear record of myself, yet my record is true."

vs.

John 5:31 "If I bear witness of myself, my witness is not true."

"Record" and "witness" in the above verses are the same Greek word, μαρτυρι'α, *(martyria).*

Shall we call people names?

Matthew 5:22 "Whosoever shall say Thou fool, shall be in danger of hellfire." [Jesus speaking]

vs.

Matthew 23:17 "Ye fools and blind." [Jesus speaking]

Psalm 14:1 "The fool hath said in his heart, There is no God."

Has anyone seen God?

John 1:18 "No man hath seen God at any time."

Exodus 33:20 "Thou canst not see my face: for there shall no man see me, and live."

John 6:46 "Not that any man hath seen the Father, save he which is of God [Jesus], he hath seen the Father."

I John 4:12 "No man hath seen God at any time."

vs.

Genesis 32:30 "For I have seen God face to face."

Exodus 33:11 "And the Lord spake unto Moses face to face, as a man speaketh unto his friend."

Isaiah 6:1 "In the year that king Uzziah died I saw also the Lord sitting upon a throne, high and lifted up, and his train filled the temple."

Job 42:5 "I have heard of thee by the hearing of the ear: but now mine eye seeth thee."

How many Gods are there?

Deuteronomy 6:4 "The Lord our God is one Lord."

vs.

Genesis 1:26 "And God said, Let us make man in our image."

Genesis 3:22 "And the Lord God said, Behold, the man has become as one of us, to know good and evil."

I John 5:7 "And there are three that bear witness in heaven, the Father, the Word, and the Holy Ghost: and these three are one."

It does no good to claim that "Let us" is the magisterial "we." Such usage implies inclusivity of all authorities under a king's leadership. Invoking the Trinity solves nothing because such an idea is more contradictory than the problem it attempts to solve.

Are we all sinners?

Romans 3:23 "For all have sinned, and come short of the glory of God."

Romans 3:10 "As it is written, There is none righteous, no, not one."

Psalm 14:3 "There is none that doeth good, no, not one."

vs.

Job 1:1 "There was a man . . . who name was Job; and that man was perfect and upright."

Genesis 7:1 "And the Lord said unto Noah, Come thou and all thy house into the ark; for thee have I seen righteous before me in this generation."

Luke 1:6 "And they were both righteous before God, walking in all the commandments and ordinances of the Lord blameless."

How old was Ahaziah?

II Kings 8:26 "Two and twenty years old was Ahaziah when he began to reign."

vs.

II Chronicles 22:2 "Forty and two years old was Ahaziah when he began to reign."

Should we swear an oath?

Numbers 30:2 "If a man vow a vow unto the Lord, or swear an oath . . . he shall do according to all that proceedeth out of his mouth."

Genesis 21:22-24,31 " . . . swear unto me here by God that thou wilt not deal falsely with me . . . And Abraham said, I will swear. . . . Wherefore he called that place Beersheba ["well of the oath"]; because there they sware both of them."

Hebrews 6:13-17 "For when God made promise to Abraham, because he could swear by no greater, he sware by himself . . . for men verily swear by the greater: and an oath for confirmation is to them an end of all strife. Wherein God, willing more abundantly to shew unto the heirs of promise the immutability of his counsel, confirmed it by an oath."

See also *Genesis 22:15-19, Genesis 31:53,* and *Judges 11:30-39.*

vs.

Matthew 5:34-37 "But I say unto you, swear not at all; neither by heaven . . . nor by the earth . . . . Neither shalt thou swear by thy head . . . . But let your communication be, Yea, yea; Nay, nay: for whatsoever is more than these cometh of evil."

James 5:12 ". . . swear not, neither by heaven, neither by the earth, neither by any other oath: but let your yea be yea; and your nay, nay; lest ye fall into condemnation."

When was Jesus crucified?

Mark 15:25 "And it was the third hour, and they crucified him."

vs.

John 19:14-15 "And about the sixth hour: and he saith unto the Jews, Behold your King! But they cried out . . . crucify him."

It is an ad hoc *defense to claim that there are two methods of reckoning time here. It has never been shown that this is the case.*

Shall we obey the law?

I Peter 2:13 "Submit yourself to every ordinance of man . . . to the king, as supreme; Or unto governors."

Matthew 22:21 "Render therefore unto Caesar the things which are Caesar's."
See also *Romans 13:1,7* and *Titus 3:1.*

vs.

Acts 5:29 "We ought to obey God rather then men."

How many animals on the ark?

Genesis 6:19 "And of every living thing of all flesh, two of every sort shalt thou bring into the ark."

Genesis 7:8-9 "Of clean beasts, and of beasts that are not clean, and of fowls, and of every thing that creepeth upon the earth, There went in two and two unto Noah into the ark, the male and the female, as God had commanded Noah."

Genesis 7:15 "And they went in unto Noah into the ark, two and two of all flesh, wherein is the breath of life."

vs.

Genesis 7:2 "Of every clean beast thou shalt take to thee by sevens, the male and his female: and of beasts that are not clean by two, the male and his female."

Were women and men created equal?

Genesis 1:27 "So God created man in his own image, in the image of God created he him; male and female created he them."

vs.

Genesis 2:18,23 "And the Lord God said, It is not good that the man should be alone; I will make him an help meet for him. . . . And Adam said, This is now bone of my bones, and flesh of my flesh: she shall be called Woman, because she was taken out of Man."

Were trees created before humans?

Genesis 1:12-31 "And the earth brought forth grass, and herb yielding seed after his kind, and the tree yielding fruit, whose seed was in itself, after his kind: . . . And the evening and the morning were the third day. . . . And God said, Let us make man in our image . . . And the evening and the morning were the sixth day."

vs.

Genesis 2:5-9 "And every plant of the field before it was in the earth, and every herb of the field before it grew: for the Lord God had not caused it to rain upon the earth, and there was not a man to till the ground. . . And the Lord God formed man of the dust of the ground . . . And the Lord God planted a garden eastward in Eden; and there he put the man whom he had formed. And out of the ground made the Lord God to grow every tree that is pleasant to the sight, and good for food."

Did Michal have children?

II Samuel 6:23 "Therefore Michal the daughter of Saul had no child unto the day of her death."

vs.

II Samuel 21:8 "But the king took the two sons of Rizpah . . . and the five sons of Michal the daughter of Saul."

How many stalls did Solomon have?

I Kings 4:26 "And Solomon had forty thousand stalls of horses for his chariots, and twelve thousand horsemen."

vs.

II Chronicles 9:25 "And Solomon had four thousand stalls for horses and chariots, and twelve thousand horsemen."

Did Paul's men hear a voice?

Acts 9:7 "And the men which journeyed with him stood speechless, hearing a voice, but seeing no man."

vs.

Acts 22:9 "And they that were with me saw indeed the light, and were afraid; but they heard not the voice of him that spake to me."

In both verses "hear" is ακου'ω *(akouo) and "voice" is* φονη' *(phoné). The fact that* φονη' *is in two different cases is irrelevant since case flexibility is common throughout the New Testament. For example, Matthew 26:65 and Mark 14:64 tell the same story using different declensions for "blasphemy," which is not considered contradictory.*

Is God omnipotent?

Jeremiah 32:27 "Behold, I am the Lord, the God of all flesh: is there anything too hard for me?"

Matthew 19:26 "But Jesus beheld them, and said unto them, With men this is impossible; but with God all things are possible."

vs.

Judges 1:19 "And the Lord was with Judah; and he drave out the inhabitants of the mountain; but could not drive out the inhabitants of the valley, because they had chariots of iron."

Does God live in light?

I Timothy 6:15-16 " . . . the King of kings, and Lord of lords; Who only hath immortality, dwelling in the light which no man can approach . . ."

James 1:17 " . . . the Father of lights, with whom is no variableness, neither shadow of turning."

John 12:35 "Then Jesus saith unto them, . . . he that walketh in darkness knoweth not wither he goeth."

Job 18:18 "He [the wicked] shall be driven from light into darkness, and chased out of the world."

Daniel 2:22 "He [God] knoweth what is in the darkness, and the light dwelleth with him."

See also *Psalm 143:3, II Corinthians 6:14,* and *Hebrews 12:18-22.*

vs.

I Kings 8:12 "Then spake Solomon, The Lord said that he would dwell in the thick darkness." (Repeated in *II Chronicles 6:1*)

II Samuel 22:12 "And he made darkness pavilions round about him, dark waters, and thick clouds of the skies."

Psalm 18:11 "He made darkness his secret place; his pavilion round about him were dark waters and thick clouds of the skies."

Psalm 97:1-2 "The Lord reigneth; let the earth rejoice . . . clouds and darkness are round about him."

Does God accept human sacrifice?

Deuteronomy 12:31 "Thou shalt not do so unto the Lord thy God: for every abomination to the Lord, which he hateth, have they done unto their gods; for even their sons and their daughters they have burnt in the fire to their gods."

vs.

Genesis 22:2 "And he said, Take now thy son, thine only son Isaac, whom thou lovest, and get thee into the land of Moriah; and offer him there for a burnt offering upon one of the mountains which I will tell thee of."

Exodus 22:29 "For thou shalt not delay to offer the first of thy ripe fruits, and of thy liquors; the firstborn of thy sons shalt thou give unto me."

Judges 11:30-39 "And Jephthah vowed a vow unto the Lord, and said, If thou shalt without fail deliver the children of Ammon into mine hand, Then it shall be, that whatsoever cometh forth of the doors of my house to meet me, when I return in peace from the children of Ammon, shall surely be the Lord's, and I will offer it up for a burnt offering. So Jephthah passed over unto the children of Ammon . . . and the Lord delivered them into his hands. . . . And Jephthah came to Mizpeh unto his house, and, behold, his daughter came out to meet him with timbrels and with dances: . . . And it came to pass at the end of two months, that she returned unto her father, who did with her according to his vow which he had vowed."

II Samuel 21:8-14 "But the king [David] took the two sons of Rizpah . . . and the five sons of Michal . . . and he delivered them into the hands of the Gibeonites, and they hanged them in the hill before the Lord: and they fell all seven together, and were put to death in the days of harvest . . . And after that God was intreated for the land."

Hebrews 10:10-12 " . . . we are sanctified through the offering of the body of Jesus Christ . . . But this man, after he had offered one sacrifice for sins forever, sat down on the right hand of God."

I Corinthians 5:7 " . . . For even Christ our passover is sacrificed for us."

Who was Joseph's father?

Matthew 1:16 "And Jacob begat Joseph the husband of Mary, of whom was born Jesus."

vs.

Luke 3:23 "And Jesus himself began to be about thirty years of age, being (as was supposed) the son of Joseph, which was the son of Heli."

This chapter was first printed as a "nontract," a freethinkers' version of a (non-proselytizing) tract. Since it was first published, I have received numerous replies from Christians who think that these contradictions are either trivial or easily explained. Yet not a single "explanation" has been convincing. Most of them do little homework, inventing off-the-cuff defenses of what the bible "could have meant," or devising creative explanations that actually make the problem worse. For example, one Christian, agreeing with Eusebius, explained that "Thou shalt not bear false witness" does not prohibit lies, and that God actually wants us to tell falsehoods if it will further the kingdom of heaven.

Many of the defensive attempts are arguments from silence. Some apologists assert that since the writer of John does not say that there were not more women who visited the tomb with Mary, then it is wrong to accuse him of contradicting the other evangelists who say it was a group of women. But this is a non-argument. With this kind of thinking, I could claim that the people who accompanied Mary to the tomb included Mother Teresa, Elvis Presley, and Paul Bunyan. Since the writer of John does not specifically exclude these people, then there is no way to prove that this is not true—if such fragile logic is valid.

All of the above contradictions have been carefully studied, and when necessary the original languages have been consulted. Although it is always scholarly to consider the original languages, why should that be necessary with the "word of God?" An omnipotent, omniscient deity should have made his all-important message unmistakably clear to everyone, everywhere, at all times. No one should have to learn an extinct language to get God's message, especially an ancient language about which there is much scholarly disagreement. If the English translation is flawed or imprecise, then God failed to get his point across to English speakers. A true fundamentalist should consider the English version of the bible to be just as inerrant as the original because if we admit that human error was possible in the translation, then it was equally possible in the original writing. (Some fundamentalists do assert that the *King James Version* is perfect. One preacher reportedly said, "If the *King James Version* was good enough for the Apostle Paul, then it's good enough for me.") If a contradiction exists in English, then the bible is contradictory.

The above list of thirty-three contradictions is a very small portion of the *thousands* of biblical discrepancies that have been catalogued by scholars. See "Leave No Stone Unturned" for seventeen additional contradictions specific to the resurrection of Jesus. One monthly publication, "Biblical Errancy," is devoted entirely to this topic. (published by Dennis McKinsey, 3158 Sherwood Park Drive, Springfield OH, 45505.) Even if a defender of the bible were to eliminate all of the above (and no one has come close), we are still only scratching the surface. The bible is a flawed book.

24

Leave No Stone Unturned

I HAVE AN EASTER challenge for Christians. My challenge is simply this: tell me what happened on Easter. I am not asking for proof. My straightforward request is merely that Christians tell me exactly *what* happened on the day that their most important doctrine was born.

Believers should eagerly take up this challenge, since without the resurrection, there is no Christianity. Paul wrote, "And if Christ be not risen, then is our preaching vain, and your faith is also vain. Yea, and we are found false witnesses of God; because we have testified of God that he raised up Christ: whom he raised not up, if so be that the dead rise not." *(I Corinthians 15:14-15)*

The conditions of the challenge are simple and reasonable. In each of the four Gospels, begin at Easter morning and read to the end of the book: *Matthew 28, Mark 16, Luke 24,* and *John 20-21.* Also read *Acts 1:3-12* and Paul's tiny version of the story in *I Corinthians 15:3-8.* These 165 verses can be read in a few moments. Then, without omitting a single detail from these separate accounts, write a simple, chronological narrative of the events between the resurrection and the ascension: what happened first, second, and so on; who said what, when; and where these things happened.

Since the gospels do not always give precise times of day, it is permissible

178

to make educated guesses. The narrative does not have to pretend to present a perfect picture—it only needs to give at least one plausible account of all of the facts. Additional explanation of the narrative may be set apart in parentheses. *The important condition to the challenge, however, is that not one single biblical detail be omitted.* Fair enough?

I have tried this challenge myself. I failed. An Assembly of God minister whom I was debating a couple of years ago on a Florida radio show loudly proclaimed over the air that he would send me the narrative in a few days. I am still waiting. After my debate at the University of Wisconsin, "Jesus of Nazareth: Messiah or Myth," a Lutheran graduate student told me he accepted the challenge and would be contacting me in about a week. I have never heard from him. Both of these people, and others, agreed that the request was reasonable and crucial. Maybe they are slow readers.

Many bible stories are given only once or twice, and are therefore hard to confirm. The author of Matthew, for example, was the only one to mention that at the crucifixion dead people emerged from the graves of Jerusalem, walking around showing themselves to everyone—an amazing event that could hardly escape the notice of the other Gospel writers, or any other historians of the period. But though the silence of others might weaken the likelihood of a story, it does not disprove it. Disconfirmation comes with contradictions.

Thomas Paine tackled this matter two hundred years ago in *The Age of Reason,* stumbling across dozens of New Testament discrepancies:

"I lay it down as a position which cannot be controverted," he wrote, "first, that the *agreement* of all the parts of a story does not prove that story to be true, because the parts may agree and the whole may be false; secondly, that the *disagreement* of the parts of a story proves *the whole cannot be true.*" Since Easter is told by five different writers, it gives one of the best chances to confirm or disconfirm the account. Christians should welcome the opportunity.

One of the first problems I found is in *Matthew 28:2,* after two women arrived at the tomb: "And, behold, there was a great earthquake: for the angel of the Lord descended from heaven, and came and rolled back the stone from the door, and sat upon it." (Let's ignore the fact that no other writer mentioned this "great earthquake.") This story says that the stone was rolled away after the women arrived, in their presence.

Yet Mark's Gospel says it happened *before* the women arrived: "And they said among themselves, Who shall roll away the stone from the door of the sepulchre? And when they looked, they saw that the stone was rolled away: for it was very great."

Luke writes: "And they found the stone rolled away from the sepulchre." John agrees. No earthquake, no rolling stone. It is a three-to-one vote: Matthew loses. (Or else the other three are wrong.) The event cannot have happened both before and after they arrived.

Some bible defenders assert that *Matthew 28:2* was intended to be understood in the past perfect, showing what had happened before the women arrived. But the entire passage is in the aorist (past) tense, and it reads, in context, like a simple chronological account. *Matthew 28:2* begins, "And, behold," not "For, behold." If this verse can be so easily shuffled around, then what is to keep us from putting the flood before the ark, or the crucifixion before the nativity?

Another glaring problem is the fact that in Matthew the first post-resurrection appearance of Jesus to the disciples happened on a mountain in Galilee (not in Jerusalem, as most Christians believe), as predicted by the angel sitting on the newly moved rock: "And go quickly, and tell his disciples that he is risen from the dead; and, behold, he goeth before you into Galilee; there shall ye see him." This must have been of supreme importance, since this was *the* message of God via the angel(s) at the tomb. Jesus had even predicted this himself sixty hours earlier, during the Last Supper *(Matthew 26:32)*.

After receiving this angelic message, "Then the eleven disciples went away into Galilee, into a mountain where Jesus had appointed them. And when they saw him, they worshipped him: but some doubted." *(Matthew 28:16-17)* Reading this at face value, and in context, it is clear that Matthew intends this to have been the *first* appearance. Otherwise, if Jesus had been seen before this time, why did some doubt?

Mark agrees with Matthew's account of the angel's Galilee message, but gives a different story about the first appearance. Luke and John give different angel messages and then radically contradict Matthew. Luke shows the first appearance on the road to Emmaus and then in a room in Jerusalem. John says it happened later than evening in a room, minus Thomas. These angel messages, locations, and travels during the day are impossible to reconcile.

Believers sometimes use the analogy of the five blind men examining an elephant, all coming away with a different definition: tree trunk (leg), rope (tail), hose (trunk), wall (side), and fabric (ear). People who use this argument forget that each of the blind men was *wrong:* an elephant is not a rope or a tree. You can put the five parts together to arrive at a noncontradictory aggregate of the entire animal. This hasn't been done with the resurrection.

Another analogy sometimes used by apologists is comparing the resurrection contradictions to differing accounts given by witnesses of an auto accident. If one witness said the vehicle was green and the other said it was blue, that could be accounted for by different angles, lighting, perception, or definitions of words. The important thing, they claim, is that they do agree on the basic story—there *was* an accident, there *was* a resurrection.

I am not a fundamentalist inerrantist. I'm not demanding that the evangelists must have been expert, infallible witnesses. (None of them claims to have been at the tomb itself, anyway.) But what if one person said the auto accident happened in Chicago and the other said it happened in Milwaukee? At least one of these witnesses has serious problems with the truth.

Luke says the post-resurrection appearance happened in Jerusalem, but Matthew says it happened in Galilee, *sixty to one hundred miles away!* Could they all have traveled 150 miles that day, by foot, trudging up to Galilee for the first appearance, then back to Jerusalem for the evening meal? There is no mention of any horses, but twelve well-conditioned thoroughbreds racing at breakneck speed, as the crow flies, would need about five hours for the trip, without a rest. And during this madcap scenario, could Jesus have found time for a leisurely stroll to Emmaus, accepting, "toward evening," an invitation to dinner? Something is very wrong here.

This is just the tip of the iceberg. Of course, none of these contradictions prove that the resurrection did *not* happen, but they do throw considerable doubt on the reliability of the supposed witnesses. Some of them were wrong. Maybe they were all wrong.

This challenge could be harder. I could ask why reports of supernatural beings, vanishing and materializing out of thin air, long-dead corpses coming back to life, and people levitating should be given serious consideration at all. Thomas Paine was one of the first to point out that outrageous claims require outrageous proof.

Protestants and Catholics seem to have no trouble applying healthy skepticism to the miracles of Islam, or to the "historical" visit between Joseph Smith and the angel Moroni. Why should Christians treat their own outrageous claims any differently? Why should someone who was not there be any more eager to believe than doubting Thomas, who lived during that time, or the other disciples who said that the women's news from the tomb "seemed to them as idle tales, and they believed them not" *(Luke 24:11)*?

Paine also points out that everything in the bible is *hearsay*. For example, the message at the tomb (if it happened at all) took this path, at minimum, before it got to our eyes: God, angel(s), Mary, disciples, Gospel writers, copyists, translators. (The Gospels are all anonymous and we have no original versions.)

But first things first: Christians, either tell me exactly what happened on Easter Sunday, or let's leave the Jesus myth buried next to Eastre (Ishtar, Astarte), the pagan Goddess of Spring after whom your holiday was named.

Here are some of the discrepancies among the resurrection accounts:

What time did the women visit the tomb?

Matthew: "as it began to dawn" *(28:1)*
Mark: "very early in the morning . . . at the rising of the sun" *(16:2, KJV)*; "when the sun had risen" *(NRSV)*; "just after sunrise" *(NIV)*
Luke: "very early in the morning" *(24:1, KJV)*
                "at early dawn" *(NRSV)*
John: "when it was yet dark" *(20:1)*

Who were the women?

Matthew: Mary Magdalene and the other Mary *(28:1)*
Mark: Mary Magdalene, the mother of James, and Salome *(16:1)*
Luke: Mary Magdalene, Joanna, Mary the mother of James, and other women *(24:10)*
John: Mary Magdalene *(20:1)*

What was their purpose?

Matthew: to see the tomb *(28:1)*
Mark: had already seen the tomb *(15:47)*, brought spices *(16:1)*
Luke: had already seen the tomb *(23:55)*, brought spices *(24:1)*
John: the body had already been spiced before they arrived *(19:39,40)*

Was the tomb open when they arrived?

Matthew: No *(28:2)*
Mark: Yes *(16:4)*
Luke: Yes *(24:2)*
John: Yes *(20:1)*

Who was at the tomb when they arrived?

Matthew: One angel *(28:2-7)*
Mark: One young man *(16:5)*
Luke: Two men *(24:4)*
John: Two angels *(20:12)*

Where were these messengers situated?

Matthew: Angel sitting on the stone *(28:2)*
Mark: Young man sitting inside, on the right *(16:5)*
Luke: Two men standing inside *(24:4)*
John: Two angels sitting on each end of the bed *(20:12)*

What did the messenger(s) say?

Matthew: "Fear not ye: for I know that ye seek Jesus, which was crucified. He is not here for he is risen, as he said. Come, see the place where the Lord lay. And go quickly, and tell his disciples that he is risen from the dead: and, behold, he goeth before you into Galilee; there shall ye see him: lo, I have told you." *(28:5-7)*

Mark: "Be not afrighted: Ye seek Jesus of Nazareth, which was crucified: he is risen; he is not here: behold the place where they laid him. But go your way, tell his disciples and Peter that he goeth before you into Galilee: there shall ye see him, as he said unto you." *(16:6-7)*

Luke: "Why seek ye the living among the dead? He is not here, but is risen: remember how he spake unto you when he was yet in Galilee, Saying, The Son of man must be delivered into the hands of sinful men, and be crucified, and the third day rise again." *(24:5-7)*

John: "Woman, why weepest thou?" *(20:13)*

Did the women tell what happened?

Matthew: Yes *(28:8)*

Mark: No. "Neither said they any thing to any man." *(16:8)*

Luke: Yes. "And they returned from the tomb and told all these things to the eleven, and to all the rest." *(24:9, 22-24)*

John: Yes *(20:18)*

When Mary returned from the tomb, did she know Jesus had been resurrected?

Matthew: Yes *(28:7-8)*

Mark: Yes *(16:10,11)*

Luke: Yes *(24:6-9,23)*

John: No *(20:2)*

When did Mary first see Jesus?

Matthew: Before she returned to the disciples *(28:9)*

Mark: Before she returned to the disciples *(16:9,10)*

John: After she returned to the disciples *(20:2,14)*

Could Jesus be touched after the resurrection?

Matthew: Yes *(28:9)*

John: No *(20:17)*, Yes *(20:27)*

After the women, to whom did Jesus first appear?
Matthew: Eleven disciples *(28:16)*
Mark: Two disciples in the country, later to eleven *(16:12,14)*
Luke: Two disciples in Emmaus, later to eleven *(24:13,36)*
John: Ten disciples (Judas and Thomas were absent) *(20:19, 24)*
Paul: First to Cephas (Peter), then to the twelve. (Twelve? Judas
                was dead). *(I Corinthians 15:5)*

Where did Jesus first appear to the disciples?
Matthew: On a mountain in Galilee (60-100 miles away) *(28:16-17)*
Mark: To two in the country, to eleven "as they sat at meat" *(16:12,14)*
Luke: In Emmaus (about seven miles away) at evening, to the rest
                in a room in Jerusalem later that night. *(24:31, 36)*
John: In a room, at evening *(20:19)*

Did the disciples believe the two men?
Mark: No *(16:13)*
Luke: Yes (*24:34*—it is the group speaking here, not the two)

What happened at the appearance?
Matthew: Disciples worshipped, some doubted, "Go preach." *(28:17-20)*
Mark: Jesus reprimanded them, said "Go preach" *(16:14-19)*
Luke: Christ incognito, vanishing act, materialized out of thin air,
                reprimand, supper *(24:13-51)*
John: Passed through solid door, disciples happy, Jesus blesses
                them, no reprimand *(21:19-23)*

Did Jesus stay on earth for a while?
Mark: No *(16:19)* Compare *16:14* with *John 20:19* to show that this
                was all done on Sunday
Luke: No *(24:50-52)* It all happened on Sunday
John: Yes, at least eight days *(20:26, 21:1-22)*
Acts: Yes, at least forty days *(1:3)*

Where did the ascension take place?
Matthew: No ascension. Book ends on mountain in Galilee
Mark: In or near Jerusalem, after supper *(16:19)*
Luke: In Bethany, very close to Jerusalem, after supper *(24:50-51)*
John: No ascension
Paul: No ascension
Acts: Ascended from Mount of Olives *(1:9-12)*
Freethought Today, March, 1990

25

Prophecy

DID YOU KNOW that the French prophet Nostradamus accurately predicted the founding of the United States more than four centuries ago? He wrote:

> *"From the aquatic triplicity will be born*
> *One who makes Thursday his holiday."* (Century I.50)

He also foretold the fate of the Kennedys when he wrote:

> *"To maintain the great troubled cloak*
> *The reds march to clear it.*
> *A family almost ruined by death,*
> *The red reds strike down the red one."* (Century VIII.19)

Amazing! How did Nostradamus obtain such clear-sighted prescience? Scholars who are skilled at interpreting such passages assure us that they are authentic evidence of the gift of prophecy.

The word *prophecy*, originally, means *preaching*, though most religionists emphasize its predictive nature. (Otherwise it would be worth little as evidence for the existence of a god or psychic power.) Many *foretellings* were initially *forth-tellings* which in time evolved (through unnatural selection) into predictions. For example, the very first "Christian" prophecy is found at the beginning of the Jewish creation story when the god Elohim cursed the serpent for tempting Eve:

> *"And I will put enmity between thee and the woman,*
> *And between thy seed and her seed:*
> *It shall bruise thy head,*
> *And thou shalt bruise his heel."* (Genesis 3:15)

To me, this looks like women and snakes are to hate each other. Yet Christians magnificently interpret this to mean that the virgin Mary's "seed" will someday do battle with evil. Of course.

The opening two chapters of the New Testament contain no less than five claims to fulfilled prophecy. The anonymous author of the book of Matthew (we'll call him Matthew) digs through the Old Testament and "discovers" that it was prophesied that:

1. Jesus would be born of a virgin.
2. Jesus would be born in Bethlehem.
3. Jesus would flee to Egypt as a baby.
4. Herod would try to murder Jesus by killing all the babies.
5. Jesus would live in Nazareth.

As Matthew's story unfolds he notices an amazing correlation between the predictions and the actual events. The rest of his book is peppered with additional "fulfillments" making it clear that foretelling is a fundamental aspect of Christian faith.

If Matthew's claims are true, then Jesus is indeed very special. It would be very unlikely that so many predictions would all be accidentally satisfied in one person. But are these true prophecies, and if they are, are they true fulfillments of prophecy? Let's look at them, one by one.

Matthew quotes Isaiah in his first attempt to prove the divinity of Jesus through prophecy: "Now all this was done, that it might be fulfilled which was spoken of the Lord by the prophet, saying, Behold, a virgin shall be with child, and shall bring forth a son, and they shall call his name Emmanuel . . ." *(Matthew 1:22-23)* Let's see what the prophet Isaiah actually said: "Therefore the Lord himself shall give you a sign; Behold, a virgin shall conceive, and bear a son, and shall call his name Immanuel." *(Isaiah 7:14)*

At face value it seems Matthew had done his homework. But a closer examination shows he had done no such thing. He made the same mistake most preachers make today: he forced the interpretation of an ancient scripture to fit his own particular theology.

The seventh chapter of Isaiah is not discussing a future Messiah, much less a baby named Jesus. The context of the passage is a civil war between Israel and Judah. Isaiah was saying the baby would be a "sign," a confirmation that a planned siege of Jerusalem would fail.

This applies to Isaiah's current events, not to some future Christian sect. If Matthew had read further he would have seen it was ludicrous to force the meaning to his day: "For before the child shall know to refuse the evil, and choose the good, the land that thou abhorrest shall be forsaken of both her kings." *(Isaiah 7:16)* The next nine verses continue the prophecy, including a promise that "in that day" the land will become "briers and thorns," which of course happened in neither Isaiah's nor Matthew's "day."

Isaiah 7:14 is clearly a local prophecy. In fact, Isaiah himself tries to make it come true in the next chapter: "And I went unto the prophetess; and she conceived, and bare a son. Then said the Lord to me, Call his name Maher-shalal-hashbaz. For before the child shall have knowledge to cry, My father, and my mother, . . . the spoil of Samaria shall be taken away before the king of Assyria." *(Isaiah 8:3-4)* This did not happen—Isaiah's fornication was for naught. It is pure dishonesty for Matthew to try to force this failed prophecy to fit his own day, his own sectarian theology.

A deeper problem with this prophecy, though, is the word "virgin." The writer of Matthew was likely working from the Greek Septuagint translation of the Hebrew writings which has the word *parthenos*, which does mean "virgin." But the original Hebrew word here is *almah*, which means "young woman" or "maiden." It is the feminine of *elem*, which means "young man" (not "young virgin man," if there were such a concept). The Hebrew word for virgin is *bethulah* (which often appears in the Old Testament as a spoil of Jehovah's holy wars). The Greek translators goofed, innocently or deliberately, and Matthew simply relayed the mistranslation, innocently or deliberately. Either way, the writer of Matthew was a sloppy scholar.

The Jews, who ought to know better than Christians how to read their own prophets, have correctly translated *almah* as "young woman" in *Isaiah 7:14.* Some of the more scholarly English translations, such as the *New Revised Standard Version,* have corrected the error, but the Authorized (*King James*) Version maintains the fallacy. It is only Christians who insist that it mean virgin, because it serves their purposes. Anybody who was *anybody* in those days, like Julius Caesar, had to be born of a virgin, and the Jewish Christian sect, trying to elevate their "Messiah" to special status, took liber-

187

ties with Hebrew thought and tried to make him a god. If Matthew were thinking, he may have realized that Isaiah may have avoided the use of the word *bethulah* because he knew something about the woman with whom he was about to have sex in the next scene. If Isaiah had meant virgin, he would have said so.

A final embarrassment is that neither Jesus nor Maher-shalal-hashbaz were called "Emmanuel."

So, in the first prophecy of the first chapter of the New Testament, Matthew destroys any credibility as a reliable historian; yet Christians will continue to assert that Jesus was born of a virgin as a fulfillment of prophecy. It's inconceivable!

What about the "little town of Bethlehem"? Is this a valid example of fulfilled prophecy? Matthew tells us that Herod asked the Magi where Jesus would be born, "And they said unto him, In Bethlehem of Judea: for thus it is written by the prophet, And thou, Bethlehem, in the land of Juda, art not the least among the princes of Juda: for out of thee shall come a Governor, that shall rule my people Israel." *(Matthew 2:5-6)*

The original prophecy is slightly different: "But thou, Bethlehem Ephratah, though thou be little among the thousands of Judah, yet out of thee shall he come forth unto me that is to be ruler in Israel . . ." *(Micah 5:2)* Notice that this does not say, "Jesus, the Messiah, will be born in the city of Bethlehem." Matthew had to do a lot of twisting to make this one fit his theology.

The first problem is that Micah is addressing a local situation only. The prophecy continues, "And this man shall be the peace, when the Assyrians shall come into our land . . ." *(Micah 5:5)* and goes on to list an orgy of vengeances. Micah's struggle was with the Assyrians, Matthew's was with the Romans. Jesus was never governor of Israel, nor did he overthrow the Romans or the Assyrians.

But a deeper problem is the fact that Micah is likely not referring to the *city* of Bethlehem at all. Bethlehem was a person: "These are the sons of Hur, the firstborn of Ephratah, the father of Bethlehem." *(I Chronicles 4:4)* It is true that many, including the Jews, have interpreted this passage of Micah to be a prophecy of David's city producing a Savior. It is also true that "Bethlehem Ephratah" can mean either "Bethlehem, of the region of Ephratah," or "Bethlehem, son of Ephratah." However, the verse says, "though thou be little among the *thousands* of Judah . . ." There were not thousands of Judean cities which were larger than Bethlehem. This most clearly means "thousands of *people*" not "thousands of *cities*." Those who insist that this is the city of Bethlehem need to explain why it cannot be taken to be the person of Bethlehem, without circularly referring to Matthew's interpretation. Matthew was not inerrant.

Matthew must have been aware of this problem since he changed "thousands of Juda" to "land of Juda" and added "princes." It is also suspicious that he deleted the name Ephratah from the quotation, a further indication that he was uncomfortable with his manipulations. He had already given his famous genealogy (through Joseph, the nonfather of Jesus!) which did not (could not) include Ephratah or Bethlehem, who were not of the royal line. Since King David had been born in Bethlehem, Matthew simply forced the facts to make it the most believable birthplace for *his* version of the Messiah, David's supposed heir.

A prediction should be a prediction. If Isaiah had said, "At 8:20 p.m. on December 25th, 5 B.C., an uninseminated girl named Mary will give birth to a male child named Jesus at 666 Stable Street, Bethlehem, Judea," and if reliable historical records confirmed the date of the prediction and the date of the fulfillment—now that would be a prophecy! Instead, we have an unknown Christian propagandist telling us a story that happens to coincide with his sectarian views, butchering quotations and pillaging history in order to lift his Messiah to the status of other gods in the area.

You know, if someone of Matthew's genius were alive today, he could have a heyday with the writings of Nostradamus. Imagine the new religion that could be started with that!

"I'm surprised at you, Mr. Barker! You really should know better," said a sweet, motherly caller during a recent talk show on an Orlando radio station. "You spent seventeen years in the ministry—how can you ignore all the fulfilled prophecies?" she continued.

"Such as?" I asked.

"Oh, come now! You, of all people, should know of the amazing Bible predictions that have come true."

"Give me an example," I insisted, expecting the usual assertion of the virgin birth or Bethlehem.

"Well, there's—you know—the whole Bible is filled with many precise prophecies. I can't remember them all, but there's just too many to have all come true by accident."

"For instance?" I pressed.

She was silent for a few seconds. "Well, the earthquakes and wars, and the children being disobedient to parents," she triumphed. This woman has been taught that we are currently living in the "end times," a belief that has been popular since Jesus. The catastrophes that she mentioned are from Christ's description of the end of the world in *Matthew 24 and 25,* and the disobedience is from *II Timothy 3:3* or *Romans 1:30.*

"Socrates used to complain about *his* unruly generation of children; there has rarely been a period of history when nations have not been at war; and the earth has been quaking for millions of years," I suggested.

"Oh, come on!" she replied, in a tone of voice which was losing some of its sweetness. "It's never been *this* bad!"

Indeed. Just how do we deal with the pervasive mistaken notion that the bible contains an incredible array of divine predictions and confirmed fulfillments? The only way is to sit down and look at them, one by one—something Christians rarely do.

Christians, if they want to be consistent, and if they desire to convince us unbelievers, should welcome a close examination of their holy scriptures. Perhaps the reason they avoid close scrutiny is that such inquiries only show that the claims of fulfilled predictions are either gross exaggerations or downright lies. The refutation of prophecies can be arranged into five general categories: vagueness, forced fulfillments, post-dated predictions, non-prophecies and chance fulfillments.

Some predictions are so vague or general that any number of situations might be made to fit. "For nation shall rise against nation, and kingdom against kingdom; and there shall be famines, and pestilences, and earthquakes, in divers places." *(Matthew 24:7)* There have been twenty different centuries since Matthew that could have qualified as fulfillment of that situation. Christians for two thousand years have consistently considered that the world is ending. The world is "always ending." The imprecision of this "prophecy" makes it impossible to nail down. In the same way, if I were to predict that a Democratic politician will die before the year 2,000 you would not be able to prove me wrong.

Forced fulfillments occur when an author manipulates the story to conform to a "supposed" prediction. Isaiah and Matthew both tried (and failed) to force the "virgin birth" prophecy of *Isaiah 7:14,* and Matthew forced Jesus to be born in Bethlehem. I once heard Jan Crouch (wife and co-host of Paul Crouch, president of Trinity Broadcasting Network) say on TV that their new satellite, nicknamed "Angel," was the literal fulfillment of *Revelation 14:6:* "And I saw another angel fly in the midst of heaven, having the everlasting gospel to preach unto them that dwell on the earth, and to every nation, and kindred, and tongue, and people." I'm sure many viewers actually believed her!

An example of a post-dated prediction is Christ's prophecy of the destruction of Jerusalem. *(Luke 21:20-24)* Since the book of Luke was written *after* Jerusalem was demolished by Rome in 70 C.E., it can hardly be considered prophetic.

A famous non-prophecy is found in *Matthew 2:14-15:* "When he arose, he took the young child and his mother by night, and departed into Egypt: And was there until the death of Herod: that it might be fulfilled which was spoken of the Lord by the prophet, saying, Out of Egypt have I called my Son." Matthew, the only writer who mentioned Jesus's Egyptian vacation, gets his "prophecy" from *Hosea 11:1:* "When Israel was a child, then I loved him, and called my son out of Egypt." This is no prophecy. Anyone (except Matthew) can see it is referring to the exodus during Moses's time. It is a past event which is magically made into a future event, for no reason other than sectarian expedience. Maybe this kind of thing is a "proof" to those who already believe, but they should certainly be able to understand why the rest of us raise our eyebrows.

Matthew did the same thing with Herod's supposed slaughter of the children (for which there is no historical confirmation): "Then was fulfilled that which was spoken by Jeremy the prophet, saying, In Rama was there a voice heard, lamentation, and weeping, and great mourning, Rachel weeping for her children, and would not be comforted, because they are not." *(Matthew 2:17-18)* It is not necessary to read the original quote *(Jeremiah 31:15)* to see that this is no prophecy. Whom is he trying to fool?

The next New Testament fulfillment is similar: "And he came and dwelt in a city called Nazareth: that it might be fulfilled which was spoken by the prophets, He shall be called a Nazarene." *(Matthew 2:23)* The only possible Old Testament reference is of the birth of Samson in *Judges 13:5:* "For, lo, thou shalt conceive, and bear a son; and no razor shall come on his head: for the child shall be a Nazarite unto God from the womb: and he shall begin to deliver Israel out of the hand of the Philistines." There are obvious problems here. *Judges 13* refers to Samson and the Philistines, not Jesus and the Romans. It's not confirmed that there was even a city of Nazareth before the second century C.E. (The current city of Nazerat, in northern Israel, can not be dated back that far.) A Nazarite is a long-haired cult member, not a city. (If *Judges 13:5* is not what Matthew was referring to, then it must have been some unwritten or lost prophecy, in which case it is even more useless as evidence.)

Looking over Matthew's first five fanciful claims of fulfilled prophecy, we get the impression that he is frisking the Old Testament for any mention of a child that could be construed to document Christ's importance. (Bible scholars will say it is not that simple to ascertain motive and method, but it certainly looks as if that is what he has done.) Look at all of them: they all deal with some kind of special child or son. The commentaries of the Dead Sea Scrolls prove that first-century sects were famous for digging through scriptures and reinterpreting ancient writings in the light of their own "modern" understanding. It's incredible that such bald-faced manufacturing should be so widely believed. But, of course, it happens in all religions.

Occasionally events can be found which seem to correspond with an earnest prophetic attempt. In 1555 Nostradamus wrote:

> *"The oldest sister of the British isle*
> *Will be born 15 years after her brother."* (Century IV.96)

It's not difficult for some to imagine the United States as brother (1776) and France as sister (1791).

Likewise, in *Ezekiel 26:11-12*, it's easy to conjure Alexander's siege of Tyre two hundred years before the fact: ". . . he [Nebuchadnezzar] shall slay thy people by the sword, . . . And they shall break down thy walls, and destroy thy pleasant houses: and they shall lay thy stones and thy timber and thy dust in the midst of the water." Although Ezekiel names Nebuchadnezzar as Tyre's destroyer, some interpret his change from "he" to "they" as a switch to more distant events (Alexander). Otherwise the prophecy would have been (is) a complete embarrassment. In fact, this is an example of a *failed* biblical prophecy: Nebuchadnezzar was not successful, as predicted. Tyre remained standing for centuries after Nebuchadnezzar's death. If the bible has any failed prophecies, then can any of it be believed? If we allow Alexander to take the place of Nebuchadnezzar (and there is no reason to do so) then this prediction might be salvaged, in part. The city of Tyre *was* eventually destroyed, though not to the degree predicted in Ezekiel.

The best reply to the tiny number of barely plausible successes is to point out that if Ezekiel is a true prophet, then so are Nostradamus and Jeanne Dixon. They all share a small random rate of vague accuracy. I could do the same by making a few hundred predictions myself—some are bound to come close.

It's ironic that many Christians, like the bewildered caller on the radio, would consider us critical freethinkers to be the literal fulfillment of Jesus's prophecy, "If they have persecuted me, they will also persecute you." *(John 15:20)*

Or is it ironic?

This is a combination of two Freethought Today articles, "Prophecy 101" (April, 1986), and "Prophecy 201" (May, 1986)

Eleven months after sending out my letter of deconversion, I was in Gopher Baroque studio (Westminster, California) recording freethought music, including "You Can't Win With Original Sin" and "Blood Brothers."

This man is obviously one of my ancestors. John and Angeline (Moreno) Sopher, my mother's maternal grandparents, wedding day, March 18, 1905, Arizona. John's mother, Isabel Camacho, was a Chiricahua Apache (Geronimo's tribe) who had lived on the reservation near the Mexican border.

My parents, Norman and Patricia (Swenson) Barker, on their wedding day, October 19, 1947. They had met in a dance band (lucky for me), and were still performing "worldly music."

Sunday morning, all dressed for church, Hawthorne, California, 1952. I and Tommy in front of Mom, Dad, and Darrell. About this time my folks found religion in a big way. Dad entered Pacific Christian Bible College, preparing for the ministry. Mom says that on my first day of Sunday School, I screamed, kicked, and hollered; she sat with me for three or four weeks until I got used to it.

I was 16 when I played "His Eye Is On The Sparrow," my mother's favorite Christian song, before the entire student body at the Anaheim Public High School talent show. Always the evangelist.

Rev. Daniel E. Barker in prayer, bible in hand, while performing the wedding of Eric (my mother's cousin) and Patsy Sopher, October, 1978. My mother, who sang at the ceremony, is praying in the background.

Two of my Christian musicals for children, Manna Music's best sellers during the late 1970s. I still receive royalties from my Christian songs.

1975 publicity shot

Soulful 1976 publicity shot

Family Tree.
With my kids,
Wisconsin
vacation, 1987.
From the top:
Becky, Andrea,
Kristi, and
Danny.

"Baby Atheist," speaking at
the 1984 FFRF convention

Conversing with minister Paul Ratzlaff at
the Morristown NJ Unitarian Society, 1986.
Speaking and singing for freethinkers and
humanists is a lot more fun than church.

Making my much-censored atheist commercial, 1985

On the "Donahue Show," 1988

On "Sally Jessy Raphael" 1987

Marrying Annie Laurie Gaylor at Freethought Hall, Sauk City, Wisconsin, May 30, 1987. Presiding in robes and purple shoes was Dane County Judge Moria Krueger. "Witnessing" was a statue of Thomas Paine, left on stage. The text of our freethought/feminist ceremony is on page 381.

When this photo of Annie Laurie and me appeared in the Huntsville Times in 1991, a Christian woman wrote that she could see "phantom horns" on our heads, noting that Alabama experienced a record heat wave that day. One of the songs I sang at the Unitarian Church that weekend was, "I'm Your Friendly Neighborhood Atheist," which contains the phrase, "I don't have any horns, if you care to inspect me; but don't expect me to think just like you."

Freethought Hall. National office of the Freedom From Religion Foundation in downtown Madison, Wisconsin. *Photos on this page by Brent Nicastro.*

The Meaning of Life. Sabrina and I enjoy our favorite food, corn on the cob. Who needs heaven? Sabrina Delata Gaylor was born in September, 1989. "Delata(h)" is the Lenape Indian word for "thought."

26

Cross Examination

T HE FREEDOM FROM Religion Foundation used to be located on the eighth floor of a building facing the Wisconsin State Capitol. People who walked into our offices were treated to a wonderful view of the largest capitol dome (by volume) in the United States, situated on a spacious, manicured concourse, with a glimpse of Lake Monona through the treetops.

The panorama would have been perfect except for one thing. Across the street from the Capitol is a lofty golden cross, perched on the towering steeple of 130-year-old Grace Episcopal Church, staring at us as we worked for freethought. Our line of sight was directly between the two buildings, which was fitting for a group that keeps an eye on the separation of church and state.

Crosses are all over the place. There is probably not a city on the continent that does not have a cross in plain view. An organization in West Virginia called "Cast Thy Bread" (of course) erects huge Calvary scenes along roadsides. In 1986 they had "just over 320 clusters now installed" and were sending crews into five more states.

An attorney here in Madison "jokingly" makes the sign of the cross when he sees me, warding off the evil atheist. The cross is deeply meaningful to some, but to others the T-shaped symbol is merely a social punctuation mark. It is more "in" than the American flag. People wear cross earrings and necklaces as if they were beautiful!

A cross is not beautiful. It is an emblem of humiliation, agony, and death, no matter how you look at it. It represents a public execution, like a gallows, guillotine, or gas chamber. Approaching a cross is like walking into a firing squad. Try to picture a steeple supporting an electric chair; or imagine people wearing noose jewelry!

"Easter was always a time of horror for me," said Ruth Green in the Foundation film, "A Second Look At Religion." "I wanted to retire from the world. I shuddered at any mention of torture or crucifixion. I feel that this Christian torture symbol, the cross, is being imposed more and more upon our landscape."

Suppose someone saved your life by blocking a terrorist's attack, but died from the bullets. Would you hang little gold machine guns on your ears? Would you want to be confronted with the grisly details, day after day? Instead of dwelling on the brutality, wouldn't a healthy person rather take action to prevent such atrocities from happening again, forgetting the horror to live a normal life?

Yet the most popular Christian hymn says:

> *In the old rugged cross,*
> *Stained with blood so divine,*
> *A wondrous beauty I see;*
> *For 'twas on that old cross*
> *Jesus suffered and died*
> *To pardon and sanctify me.*
> *So I'll cherish that old rugged cross . . .*

Referring to the blood running from Jesus's pierced side (reported by John only, perhaps in confusion over the exact manner of death), another favorite hymn drones:

> *Jesus keep me near the cross,*
> *There a precious fountain*
> *Free to all, a healing stream*
> *Flows from Calvary's mountain.*
> *In the cross, in the cross*
> *Be my glory ever . . .*

A sow's ear, to me, is a sow's ear. But look at what believers have done in these lyrics:

In the cross of Christ I glory,
Towering o'er the wrecks of time;
All the light of sacred story
Gathers round its head sublime

When the sun of bliss is beaming
Light and love upon my way,
From the cross the radiance streaming
Adds more luster to the day.

Swaggart and Bakker took that "luster" business a little too seriously, but however you look at it, the cross is offensive. Ten thousand psalms might deaden the senses of the average pew sitter, but they can't turn lead into gold. (Note that even in these lyrics, the real message of Easter—spring, light, the sun, the vernal equinox—is not completely disguised.)

The gold-plated cross which glowered at our offices sits on a forty-foot spire resting on a six-story steeple. Even as a minister I had known that there is no spire in the bible: spires are phallic architectural structures borrowed from paganism.

But I just learned something about the cross that absolutely astonishes me, something that makes me embarrassed that I ever believed. Most free-thinkers know that Christianity is borrowed mainly from earlier religions. There is nothing unique about it. Other myths have their virgin births, saviors, and resurrections. The Babylonians, Egyptians, Aztecs, and others, had cross symbols. But what I never knew before—and it is still hard to believe—is that *there is no cross in Christianity*. No cross at all!

The enduring emblem of atonement is an impostor. There is no cross *anywhere* in the bible.

Christian apologists, when pressed, often resort to the "true meaning of the original language," but this is one case where they are better off ignoring the Greek. The words which have been translated "cross" and "crucify" in the New Testament are σταυρο'ς (pronounced "stau-ross" or "stav-ross") and σταυρο'ω ("stav-ro-oh"). All translators, even fundamentalists, agree that a σταυρο'ς is not a cross.

Liddell & Scott's *A Greek-English Lexicon* defines σταυρο'ς as "*upright pale or stake.* Of piles driven in to serve as a foundation. A pale for impaling a corpse." Thayer's Greek-English Lexicon, a "King James" reference much used by believers, agrees, and says the English word "staff" derives from σταυρο'ς (citing *Skeat*, Etym. Dict.).

W. E. Vine's *Expository Dictionary of New Testament Words*, another

Christian resource, reports that σταυρος "denotes, primarily, an upright pale or stake. On such malefactors were nailed for execution. Both the noun and the verb . . . are originally to be distinguished from the ecclesiastical form of a two beamed cross. The shape of the latter had its origin in ancient Chaldea, and was used as the symbol of the god Tammuz (being in the shape of the mystic Tau, the initial of his name) . . . By the middle of the 3rd cent. . . . pagans were received into the churches . . . and were permitted largely to retain their pagan signs and symbols. Hence the Tau, or T, in its most frequent forms, with the cross-piece lowered, was adopted to stand for the cross of Christ."

The verb σταυρο'ω means "to affix to a stake." Herbert Cutner, in *Jesus: God, Man, or Myth* (The Truth Seeker, 1950), says, "A *stauros* was a mere stake, and horrible to contemplate; it was used in the cruelest fashion to execute criminals and other persons . . . It was sometimes pointed and thrust through the victim's body to pin him to earth; or he was placed on top of the stake with its point upwards so that it gradually pierced his body; or he was tied upon it and left exposed till death intervened; and there were other methods too. There is not a scrap of evidence that a *stauros* was ever in the form of a cross or even of a T shape." If Jesus had been executed, mythically or historically, it would not have been with outstretched arms on a cruciform structure.

Cutner reports that scholars have been aware of the error but have been unable to resist the traditional mistranslation. In the eighteenth century some Anglican bishops recommended eliminating the cross symbol altogether, but they were ignored.

There is no cross in early Christian art before the middle of the fifth century, where it (probably) appears on a coin in a painting. The first clear crucifix appears in the late seventh century. Before then Jesus was almost always depicted as a fish or a shepherd, never on a cross. Constantine's supposed fourth-century vision of a cross in the sky was not of the instrument of execution: it was the Greek letter X (chi) with a P (rho) through it, the well-known "monogram" of Christ, from the first two letters of Χριστο'ς, the Greek for Christ. (This is where we get the X in "Merry Xmas.")

Any bible that contains the word "cross" or "crucify" is dishonest. Christians who flaunt the cross are not only unwittingly advertising a pagan religion, especially if it sits on a spire, but they are also breaking the second commandment: "Thou shalt not make unto thee any graven image . . ." (Now I know why many Christians are so cross!)

Most Christians, if confronted with these facts, will claim that the cross has a "spiritual" meaning beyond its physical appearance. They might point to *Matthew 16:24,* when the New Testament Jesus character said long before his death, "If any man will come after me, let him ... take up his cross [σταυρο'ς] and follow me." (Freethinking scholars realize that this anachronistic phrase is historical nonsense. It could not have had any meaning to the disciples *before* the cruci-fiction.) To the believer, the cross represents self denial, and salvation from sin. But there is no such thing as "sin."

Or maybe there is. The threatening cross that brazenly stared into our windows—*that* is a sin.

Freethought Today, March, 1989

The Chi-Rho symbol, representing the monogram of Christ.

27

Murder, He Wrote

T HE FREEDOM FROM Religion Foundation has a series of inexpensive "nontracts" which are very popular with members. They have been used to counter proselytizers and to introduce inquiring friends to the reasonableness of freethought. They are called "nontracts" because "tract" can connote propaganda. Most freethinkers are happy to live and let live, and only respond when confronted by believers; although one unbeliever became so exasperated over a local church that he sneaked into the sanctuary and inserted "Dear Believer" into every hymnbook.

The nontracts have been passed out all over the continent, and guess who gets the fallout. The Foundation office regularly receives letters from the recipients and has even picked up a few supporters. One fellow read "Ten Common Myths About Atheists" on a laundromat bulletin board and promptly joined. Usually, however, we hear from believers who want to correct our heresy.

"Bible Contradictions" provokes the longest letters. We get these tortured point-by-point defenses of the "inerrant word of God" from fundamentalist preachers and other Christians who think the discrepancies can be explained. What they lack in logic they make up for in volume.

The first contradiction in the nontract deals with the Ten Commandments, contrasting *Exodus 20:13*, "Thou shalt not kill," *with Exodus 32:27*, "slay every man his brother." The bible is filled with killings and mass murders committed, commanded, or condoned by deity, and if this is not a contradiction, then all squares are round.

Yet most believers think they can square up this discrepancy with circular reasoning, or with creative *ad hoc* arguments. The most common claim offered in defense of this contradiction is that, supposedly, *Exodus 20:13* really says "Thou shalt not *murder*." To murder is to kill unlawfully, maliciously, or premeditatedly. If the Commandments forbid only "murder," then it can be argued that other forms of killing are allowed, or even encouraged. God can ordain capital punishment, or command a holocaust of heathens without breaking his own law.

Of course, it is a useless tautology to define murder as an "unlawful" killing in this context. Since the Ten Commandments supposedly *are* the law, they would be merely saying, "It is unlawful to kill unlawfully." This type of circular thinking excuses anyone who kills "in the name of the Lord, the source of law." It is not only illogical, but immoral to claim that there is a law above the law which justifies bloodshed.

Many Christians claim that the genocide of idolaters is permitted because "God knows best." But every murderer feels some kind of justification for the crime. Why is God special? Why should a deity get away with atrocities that would send you or me straight to prison?

Malice is a desire to cause harm, so if murder means anything, it means a deliberate taking of life. Except for euthanasia—a nonmalicious and (usually) requested termination of waning life—few would doubt that killing a person is harmful, no matter who commits it.

Do the Ten Commandments really say, "Thou shalt not murder?" The Hebrew word for "kill" in *Exodus 20:13* is *ratsach*. (The word for "slay" in the contradictory command in *Exodus 32:27* is *haraq*.) Depending on which version you use, there are about ten Hebrew words which are translated "kill." The five most common, in Hebrew order (with translation in order of *King James* frequency) are:

muth:	(825) die, slay, put to death, kill
nakah:	(502) smite, kill, slay, beat, wound, murder
haraq:	(172) slay, kill, murder, destroy
zabach:	(140) sacrifice, kill
ratsach:	(47) slay [23], murder [17], kill [6], be put to death [1]

Modern preachers must be smarter than Hebrew translators if they claim that *ratsach* means "murder" exclusively. *Muth, nakah, haraq, zabach,* and *ratsach* appear to be spilled all over the bible in an imprecise and overlapping jumble of contexts, in much the same way modern writers will swap synonyms.

Referring to the "cities of refuge" set up by Moses to shelter killers, *Deuteronomy 4:42* says, "that the slayer [*ratsach*] might flee thither, which should kill [*ratsach*] his neighbor unawares, and hated him not in times past." This is hardly murder—it is neither premeditated nor malicious. It is an accidental killing, classed at most as manslaughter in our society.

Numbers 35:6-34 gives perhaps the best glimpse of how the words were used interchangeably. "Then ye shall appoint you cities for refuge from the avenger; that the slayer [*ratsach*] may flee thither, which killeth [*nakah*] any person at unawares." *(35:11)* "He that smote [*nakah*] him shall surely be put to death [*muth*]; for he is a murderer [*ratsach*]." *(35:21)*

Again showing that *ratsach* can be accidental: "But if he thrust him suddenly without enmity, or have cast upon him any thing without laying of wait, or with any stone . . . seeing him not . . . and was not his enemy, neither sought his harm: Then the congregation shall judge between the slayer [*ratsach*] and the revenger of blood according to these judgments." *(35:22-24)*

Verse 27 shows that *ratsach* can be considered a justified killing: "[if] the revenger of blood kill [*ratsach*] the slayer [*ratsach*]; he shall not be guilty of blood." Verses 30 and 31 show how the words are interchanged, and also indicate that *ratsach* was used for capital punishment: "Whoso killeth [*nakah*] any person, the murderer [*ratsach*] shall be put to death [*ratsach*] by the mouth of witnesses . . . Moreover ye shall take no satisfaction for the life of a murderer [*ratsach*], which is guilty of death: but he shall surely be put to death [*muth*]."

If this doesn't remove all doubt then consider *Proverbs 22:13:* "The slothful man saith, There is a lion without, I shall be slain [*ratsach*] in the streets." Can animals be guilty of murder?

As a desperate final straw, naive apologists might point to *Matthew 19:18 (KJV)* where Jesus recites the Commandment, "Thou shalt do no murder [φονεύ′ω]." But of the twelve times *phoneuo* appears in the bible, this is the only place where it is translated "murder." It is translated "kill" everywhere else; and the Revised Version uses "kill" in *Matthew 19:18*. The writer of Matthew was quoting the Septuagint, a Greek translation of the Hebrew scriptures, and this is an example of the difficulty of handling three slippery languages at once. It is hardly a persuasive argument in favor of "Thou shalt not murder," and most likely reflects a translator bias.

Considering the biblical evidence, "Thou shalt not kill" is a better translation than "Thou shalt not murder." However, as a very slight argument in favor of inerrantists, even though the biblical deity overindulged in *nakah*, *haraq*, and *muth*, there is no instance where God did any *ratsach* himself. It was ordered and approved by God, but not directly committed. But since *ratsach* is used relatively sparsely, it makes sense to assume that the writers of the bible just never got around to assigning that particular word to the godly massacres.

But all of this is irrelevant when we find verses repeating "Thou shalt not kill" in other Hebrew words. *Leviticus 24:17* says, "And he that killeth [*nakah*] any man shall surely be put to death [*muth*]." *Exodus 21:12,* just twenty-one verses after the Ten Commandments, says, "He that smiteth [*nakah*] a man, so that he die, shall be surely put to death." According to Scripture it doesn't matter what word you use: killing is against the law.

Joshua *nakah*'ed the people of Ai *(Joshua 8:21),* and David *nakah*'ed Goliath *(I Samuel 19:5).* This was considered justifiable killing in spite of the fact that *nakah* was expressly forbidden. What does this do to the "*ratsach* = murder" defense? If Joshua and David are not criminals, then the bible is again proved contradictory.

Some might argue that no matter how the Ten Commandments are translated, we still need them as a basis for law and order. But do we really? If Moses had not existed would it have never occurred to us that murder is immoral? Without "The Law" would we all be wandering around like little gods, stealing, raping, and spilling blood whenever our vanity was offended? The first four Commandments have nothing to do with ethics (see page 343), and any value in the remainder is based on rational humanistic principles which long predated the Jewish religion. It is wrong to kill, *even* according to the bible; and since the biblical god and his followers were murderers, the bible is contradictory.

When the Israelite warriors marched through a village, slaughtering and plundering in the name of the Lord, ripping up animals, children, men, and women, saving the virgins alive for themselves *(Numbers 31:15-18),* did they say to the pregnant woman with a sword in her belly, "By the way, I want you to know that I am not *murdering* you. I am lawfully killing you in God's name"? Would such a fine semantic distinction make much difference to the victims of righteousness?

Freethought Today, April, 1989

28

In The Family Way?

This is adapted from my participation in a debate, "Is the Bible Anti-abortion?" in Birmingham, Alabama, April 5, 1990. Dr. Delos McKown of Auburn University and I teamed up against two local preachers. Delos analyzed the Old Testament, and my focus was on the New Testament.

I was talking with a Catholic attorney recently who said, "Dan, this abortion issue is so emotional that no one is ever going to change their mind."

"I did," I answered.

"Well, I was raised to respect the sanctity of life," he said, "and I will always vote with my church."

"And that's why I changed my mind—I respect the sanctity of the woman's life."

He looked at me for a moment, and in hushed tones said, "But you know what? I don't know what I would do if my fourteen-year-old daughter got pregnant."

"You would get her a quick, quiet abortion and worry about the morality later," I offered. With a guilty grin, he nodded his head in agreement. "You have the money and you have the contacts," I continued, "but if you keep voting wrong you may not have the option." He didn't know what to say, the big hypocrite.

I used to believe that the bible is antiabortion, back when I thought it mattered what the bible said. For the record, I do not believe the bible any more, and I support a woman's right to choose an abortion; but neither of these positions is relevant to what the bible actually says on the matter. There are a few atheists who are antiabortion, and there are millions of bible-believing Christians who are pro-choice.

Religious groups that have issued some form of pro-choice position include the American Baptist Church (though they have back-pedaled to a neutral position), American Lutheran Church, Central Conference of American Rabbis, Disciples of Christ, Church of the Brethren, Episcopal Church, Reformed Church in America, Reorganized Church of Jesus Christ of Latter Day Saints, United Church of Christ, United Methodist, United Presbyterian Church, the YWCA, and Religious Coalition for Abortion Rights, to name just a few. These groups respect the bible, yet they are not antiabortion. If the bible is antiabortion, then these established religious organizations are all renegades.

Hosea 13:16 shows the Old Testament's respect for life. The Lord thunders: "They shall fall by the sword; their infants shall be dashed in pieces, and their women with child shall be ripped up."

What does the New Testament say about abortion? It says nothing. Jesus and Paul give all sorts of minute details about living, yet they are silent about the topic which is so crucial to modern antiabortionists.

Paul tells women to "adorn themselves in modest apparel, with shamefacedness and sobriety; not with broided hair, or gold, or pearls, or costly array." *(I Timothy 2:9)* He takes the time to tell women what to wear, but says nothing about dealing with a problem pregnancy. Have you seen how women are adorned in church these days? Plenty of "costly array" and naughty gold wedding rings. If today's women can't obey Paul's simple dress code, why would they heed his nosy advice about abortion, had he ever made any?

Baptist theologian Paul D. Simmons, in "The Fetus as Person: A Biblical Perspective," writes: "The absence of specific prohibitions in Scripture could mean either: (1) no Hebrew or Christian ever terminated a problem pregnancy, or (2) abortion was a private, personal and religious matter, not subject to civil regulation. The latter seems the more plausible explanation."

This biblical silence, however, does not deter the faithful. They continue to base their views on the command to "Be fruitful, and multiply, and replenish the earth." I have news for these people: the earth has been replenished! And replenished.

Some believers claim that since the bible is "pro-family," it is therefore antiabortion. But the word "family" appears only once in the *(KJV)* New Testament. The word on which it is based, *patria*, appears only three times in the Greek, but is always used in the sense of the general "family" of humankind, never referring to the close-knit nuclear unit of Mom, Dad and kids.

Jesus reportedly said, "If any man come to me, and hate not his father, and mother, and wife, and children, and brethren, and sister, yea, and his own life also, he cannot be my disciple." *(Luke 14:26)* This is hardly pro-family! This Prince of Peace also said, "Think not that I am come to send peace on earth: I came not to send peace, but a sword. For I am come to set a man at variance against his father, and the daughter against her mother, and the daughter in law against her mother in law. And a man's foes shall be they of his own household." *(Matthew 10:34-36)*

Regarding marriage Jesus said, "they which shall be accounted worthy to obtain that world, and the resurrection from the dead, neither marry, nor are given in marriage." *(Luke 20:35)* Jesus never married or fathered children; but if he followed his own advice he would not have been *able*: " . . . there be some eunuchs, which have made themselves eunuchs for the kingdom of heaven's sake. He that is able to receive it, let him receive it." *(Matthew 19:12)* The son of God should have been strong enough to castrate himself, especially since he never intended to become a father or have sex.

Seventeen verses later he said, "And every one that hath forsaken houses, or brethren, or sisters, or father, or mother, or wife, or children, or lands, for my name's sake, shall receive an hundredfold, and shall inherit everlasting life." In order to be a true follower of Jesus, one must be *anti*-family!

Paul never married either. He said, "It is good for a man not to touch a woman." *(I Corinthians 7:1)* He did tolerate marriage, however, as the lesser evil, "to avoid fornication." Not one word about the family or having children.

Why didn't Jesus or Paul take advantage of their authority to clear up the abortion issue? Jesus was always saying, "Ye have heard it said . . . but I say unto you . . ." He could have said, "The Old Testament Law was silent on this crucial matter, but I say to you, abortion is wrong." But he didn't.

Although the bible is neither antiabortion nor pro-family, it does provide modern antiabortionists with a biblical basis for the *real* motivation behind their views: the bible is not pro-life, but it is anti-woman. A patriarchal system cannot stand women who are free.

Paul said, "the head of the woman is the man," and ordered women (not men) to cover their heads. *(I Corinthians 11:3-5)* He said, "Let your women keep silence in the churches; for it is not permitted unto them to speak; but they are commanded to be under obedience, as also saith the law. And if they will learn anything let them ask their husbands at home: for it is a shame for women to speak in the church." *(I Corinthians 14:34-35)*

The rationale behind Paul's sexism is the fact that "Adam was first formed, then Eve. And Adam was not deceived, but the woman being deceived was in the transgression." *(I Timothy 2:13-14)* There are many places where Paul tells women to submit to their husbands, but never once is a husband told to submit to his wife. *(Ephesians 5:22-23; Ephesians 5:33; Colossians 3:18)*

The New Testament presents women as defiled and less valued than men. *Luke 2:23* says, "Every male that openeth the womb shall be called holy to the Lord." Daughters don't count, apparently. Talking about heaven, *Revelation 14:3-4* says, ". . . and no man could learn that song but the hundred and forty and four thousand, which were redeemed from the earth. These are they which were not defiled with women; for they are virgins . . ." Maybe this was why Jesus thought castration was so important—to keep from being "defiled" with women. No women were allowed to be among the twelve disciples. (The pope has argued that this is the reason why the clergy must be male. But then why do we have a Catholic-Polish pope? The disciples were all Jews!)

Ruth Green in *The Born Again Skeptic's Guide to the Bible* wrote, "It's what Jesus *doesn't* say that is more a key to his attitude toward women than what he says or does. For instance, he doesn't say that Eve was wrongly blamed, . . . that the Mosaic law is cruelly demeaning of women, . . . that women need not submit to their husbands in everything, . . . that wives may ever divorce their husbands or marry again if their husbands divorce them for 'fornication,' . . . that there are no witches and in any case they should not be burnt to death, . . . that a hapless girl thought not to be a virgin when she is wed should not be stoned or burnt to death (and her despoiler go free) . . . It must be concluded that Jesus was the usual male chauvinist of his day."

And this is the real drive behind the antiabortionists: misogyny. I don't believe that any one of them cares a hoot for a fetus.

They care about this issue because it gives them a chance to flex their righteous muscles. It is a simplistic, open-and-shut matter to them, requiring little thought. They need this kind of thing to give them an opportunity to march around pretending to be morally concerned. If their marching tramples women's rights, feelings, and bodies, well, that is just fine. According to the bible women don't deserve fair treatment.

Although the bible is not antiabortion, it is antichoice. If there is one thing the bible (and fundamentalist men) can't tolerate, it is a woman who takes control.

Freethought Today, May, 1990

29

Dear Believer

This piece originally was published as a nontract. At the request of some members of the Freedom From Religion Foundation, it was deliberately written to be less gentle than other nontracts, in order to have something to counter the street preachers and obnoxious door-to-door evangelists. It was presented to the state of Indiana as an "equal-time" piece, at their request, to be placed alongside Gideon Bibles in state-owned hotel rooms, but was then censored by the governor as "blasphemous." It was later reprinted in Harper's Magazine.

D

EAR BELIEVER:

You ask me to consider Christianity as the answer for my life. I have done that. I consider it untrue, repugnant, and harmful.

You expect me to believe Jesus was born of a virgin impregnated by a ghost? Do you believe all the crazy tales of ancient religions? Julius Caesar was reportedly born of a virgin; Roman historian Seutonius said Augustus bodily rose to heaven when he died; and Buddha was supposedly born speaking. You don't believe all that, do you? Why do you expect me to swallow the fables of Christianity?

I find it incredible that you ask me to believe that the earth was created in six literal days; that women come from a man's rib; that a snake, a donkey, and a burning bush spoke human language; that the entire world was flooded, covering the mountains to drown evil; that all animal species, millions of them, rode on one boat; that language variations stem from the tower of Babel; that Moses had a magic wand; that the Nile turned to blood; that a stick turned into a snake; that witches, wizards, and sorcerers really exist; that food rained from the sky for forty years; that people were cured by the sight of a brass serpent; that the sun stood still to help Joshua win a battle, and it went *backward* for King Hezekiah; that men survived unaided in a fiery furnace; that a detached hand floated in the air and wrote on a wall; that men followed a star which directed them to a particular house; that Jesus walked on water unaided; that fish and bread magically multiplied to feed the hungry; that water instantly turned into wine; that mental illness is caused by demons; that a "devil" with wings exists who causes evil; that people were healed by stepping into a pool agitated by angels; that disembodied voices spoke from the sky; that Jesus vanished and later materialized from thin air; that people were healed by Peter's shadow; that angels broke people out of jail; that a fiery lake of eternal torment awaits unbelievers under the earth . . . while there is life-after-death in a city which is 1,500 miles cubed, with mansions and food, *for Christians only.*

If you believe these stories, then you are the one with the problem, not me. These myths violate natural law, contradict science, and fail to correspond with reality or logic. If you can't see that, then you can't separate truth from fantasy. It doesn't matter how many people accept the delusions inflicted by "holy" men; a widely-held lie is still a lie. If you are so gullible, then you are like the child who believes the older brother who says there is a monster in the hallway. But there is nothing to be afraid of; go turn on the light and look for yourself.

If Christianity were simply untrue I would not be too concerned. Santa is untrue, but it is a harmless myth which people outgrow. But Christianity, besides being false, is also abhorrent. It amazes me that you claim to love the god of the bible, a hateful, arrogant, sexist, cruel being who can't tolerate criticism. I would not want to live in the same neighborhood with such a creature!

The biblical god is a macho male warrior. Though he said "Thou shalt not kill," he ordered death for all opposition *(Exodus 32:27),* wholesale drowning and mass exterminations; punished offspring to the fourth generation *(Exodus 20:5);* ordered babies to be smashed and pregnant women to be ripped up

215

(Hosea 13:16); demanded animal and human blood to appease his angry vanity; is partial to one race of people; judged women inferior to men; is a sadist who created a hell to torture unbelievers; created evil *(Isaiah 45:7);* discriminated against the handicapped *(Leviticus 21:16-23);* ordered virgins to be kept as spoils of war *(Numbers 31:15-18, Deuteronomy 21:11-14);* threatened to curse people by spreading dung on their faces *(Malachi 2:3);* sent bears to devour forty-two children who teased a prophet *(II Kings 2:23-24);* punished people with snakes, dogs, dragons, drunkenness, swords, arrows, axes, fire, famine, and infanticide; and said fathers should eat their sons *(Ezekiel 5:10).* Is that nice? Would *you* want to live next door to such a person?

And Jesus is a chip off the old block. He said, "I and my father are one," and he upheld "every jot and tittle" of the Old Testament law. *(Matthew 5:18)* He preached the same old judgment: vengeance and death, wrath and distress, hell and torture for all nonconformists. He believed in demons, angels and spirits. He never denounced the subjugation of slaves or women. Women were excluded as disciples, and as guests at his heavenly table. Except for hell he introduced nothing new to ethics or philosophy. He was disrespectful to his mother and brothers; he said we should hate our parents and desert our families. *Matthew 10:35-36, Luke 14:26* (So much for "Christian family life.") He denounced anger, but was often angry himself. *Matthew 5:22, Mark 3:5* He called people "fools" *(Matthew 23:17,19),* "serpents," and "whited sepulchres," though he warned that such language puts you in danger of hellfire. *Matthew 5:22* He said, "Think not that I am come to send peace on earth. I came not to send peace, but a sword." *Matthew 10:34* (So much for "Peace on Earth.") He irrationally cursed and withered a fig tree for being barren out of season. *Matthew 21:19* He mandated burning unbelievers. *John 15:6* (The Church has complied with relish.) He stole a horse. *Luke 19:30-33* He told people to cut off hands, feet, eyes and sexual organs. *Matthew 5:29-30, 19:12* You want me to accept Jesus, but I think I'll pick my own friends, thank you.

One of Jesus's many contradictions was saying good works should be seen, and not seen. *Matthew 5:16, 6:1-4* One of his mistakes was saying that the mustard plant has the smallest seed. *Matthew 13:31-32* The writers of Matthew and Luke could not even get his genealogy straight, contradicting the Old Testament, and giving Jesus two discrepant lines through Joseph, his non-father! *(Matthew 1:1-16 versus Luke 3:23-34)*

I also find Christianity to be morally repugnant. The concepts of original sin, depravity, substitutionary forgiveness, intolerance, eternal punishment, and humble worship are all beneath the dignity of intelligent human beings and conflict with the values of kindness and reason. They are barbaric ideas for primitive cultures cowering in fear and ignorance.

Finally, Christianity is harmful. More people have been killed in the name of a god than for any other reason. The Church has a shameful, bloody history of Crusades, Inquisitions, witch-burnings, heresy trials, American colonial intolerance, disrespect of indigenous traditions (such as American Indians), support of slavery, and oppression of women. Modern "fruits" of religion include the Jonestown massacre, the callous fraud of "faith healers," the sex scandals of televangelists, and fighting in Northern Ireland. Religion also poses a danger to mental health, damaging self respect, personal responsibility, and clarity of thought.

Do you see why I do not respect the biblical message? It is an insulting bag of nonsense. You have every right to torment yourself with such insanity—but *leave me out of it.* I have better things to do with my life.

Just Say NO to Religion
by Dan Barker

Chorus: Just say NO to religion.
                No more myth and superstition!
                Just say NO!

When they try to get you hooked on their psychedelic book,
(What do you say?) Just say NO!
Religion is a fiction; it is like a drug addiction.
Just say NO!

("Just Say NO" after each line):

When the door-to-door preachers try to wake you from your slumber,
When the television preachers want your credit card number,

When the ministers try to tell you that they have the only way,
When they try to make you feel you shouldn't question what they say,

If you're tired of those evangelists who tell you to confess,
When they ask for all your money, then they say that *you've* been
        blessed,

Since the bible is bologna and you cannot swallow Jonah,
When they say their fishy story is the source of hope and glory,

When they ask you to believe something quite imaginary,
If the "Spirit" wants to use you as another Virgin Mary,

When you hear the allegation that this is a Christian nation,
Do you think it's very funny that they desecrate our money?

When they say that unbelievers are immoral or depraved,
Are we all degenerate sinners who should cry out to be saved?

© *Copyright 1988 by Dan Barker and the Freedom From Religion*
Foundation, Inc. Song lyrics.
This song is aimed at those religions that are supernaturalistic and
irrational. It intends no disrespect for Unitarians, or for those who might
consider humanism to be a religion. Credit for the "Just Say NO To
Religion" slogan goes to Deanna Frank, former director of the Denver
chapter of the Freedom From Religion Foundation, and to its members.

CRITIQUING CHRISTIANITY

Part 4

Losing Faith in Faith

30

Washed
In The Blood

WE ALL KNOW that a prolonged exposure to something negative can produce a desensitization. Children who watch thousands of murders on television can grow to ignore violence, to accept it as inevitable, or even desirable. Degrading pornography can lose its shock value when regularly viewed. Violence, besides being *learned* by prolonged exposure, can also become *invisible*. We get numbed, after a while.

Something like this happened to me. I grew up in a Christian family, spending thousands of hours in a pew listening to the bible and singing hymns. For many years I preached and gave religious concerts, spouting words, words, words. There is an old hymn which says:

> *Sing them over again to me,*
> *Wonderful words of life;*
> *Let me more of their beauty see,*
> *Wonderful words of life.*

Beauty indeed! As a Christian I thought I was luxuriating in words of truth; but as a freethinker I now look back and see that, like a pig, I was wallowing in mud. It took a while to become UN-desensitized, or resensitized.

Here are some lyrics we often happily sang in church:

> *There is a fountain filled with blood*
> *Drawn from Immanuel's veins;*
> *And sinners plunged beneath that flood*
> *Lose all their guilty stains.*
>
> *E'er since by faith I saw the stream*
> *Thy flowing wounds supply,*
> *Redeeming love has been my theme*
> *And shall be till I die.*

These words used to fly right by me, and I missed the ugliness. But now, visualizing the song, all I see is waste: a gruesome basin sloshing with sticky redness, believers gleefully diving in to be "washed" in blood. Even if it is purely symbolic, why would I want to sing such a thing?

How do you react emotionally when you hear the word *blood*? I don't know about you, but I tend to be squeamish. However, blood is a precious and powerful symbol to Christians. We all agree that blood is necessary for human (animal) life. To someone needing a transfusion it is indeed a precious commodity. Blood *in our veins*, where it belongs, represents life itself.

But Christians are obsessed with blood *out of our veins*—blood where it does not belong: death. Looking through a hymnbook recently, I was shocked at how many Christian songs deal with blood. Blood that is shedding, streaming, flooding, dripping, staining, ebbing, flowing, washing, sprinkling, and generally splattering all over. When blood is not in its proper place, it is obscene.

"There is a fountain filled with blood." How much blood would it take to fill a fountain? Jesus, if he ever lived, would have shed about five quarts when he died. A small baptistery needs about five hundred gallons, so to fill a little fountain would require the death and "Dracula-ization" of about four hundred adults! A typical fountain at the city square might use ten times that amount. Pretty gruesome image, when you think about it.

Since becoming an atheist, I have noticed that sometimes freethinkers try to shock believers by quoting ugly bible verses or by singing some obscene hymn lyrics, not realizing that these words which seem so disgusting to us are actually perceived as beautiful by the Christians!

> *Oh, that old rugged cross,*
> *So despised by the world,*

Has a wondrous attraction for me;
In the old rugged cross,
Stained with blood so divine,
A wondrous beauty I see.

To a person who has been brainwashed (or blood-washed), a man dying on a cross might be called a "wondrous beauty," but in reality it is cruelty, death, suffering, pain and waste. It is ugly. It is not beautiful, even to Christians, else their song lyrics wouldn't elaborate on the irony of it.

Some of the ancients believed that a transfusion could be accomplished by simply drinking blood. The rite of communion, supposedly instituted at Jesus's Last Supper, comes from that primitive idea. If modern Christians are truly concerned with the life-giving properties of blood, why don't they substitute the syringe for the wine glass? The Eucharist, in its present violent form, is raw cannibalism.

Christians agree that death is ultimately undesirable. Even Jesus could not bear to stay dead. (Did he really die, then? If you continue to live, especially if you were busy "on the other side," as Jesus was, haven't you actually had a "near death" experience?) Since Christians fear death as much as everyone else, why do they glorify it? Can't they see the ugliness of such ideas?

It's hard (and embarrassing) to remember how I felt back then. I know that it is not enough for freethinkers simply to quote the horrors and expect Christians to shrink back in disgust. They won't get the point. If you cite some of the bible's dark words, they will just smile at you. They have become desensitized to the violence and obscenity in their religion. How else could they gaily sing:

Draw me nearer, nearer blessed Lord
To thy precious bleeding side.

Or:

Would you be free from your passion and pride?
There's power in the blood.
Come for a cleansing to Calvary's tide;
There's wonderful power in the blood.

Or:

Come to this fountain so rich and sweet;
Plunge in today and be made complete;
Glory to His name!

Or:

O how sweet to trust in Jesus,
Just to trust His cleansing blood;

> *Just in simple faith to plunge me*
> *'Neath the healing, cleansing flood!*

And who but the numbed will miss the grotesqueness (and humor) of these words?

> *He pointed to the nail-prints,*
> *For me His blood was shed,*
> *A mocking crown so thorny*
> *Was placed upon His head:*
> *I wonder what He saw in me,*
> *To suffer such deep agony.*

Why do Christians like to grovel in death? What is so attractive about suffering, pain, and ugliness? Why is it wonderful to view Jehovah as a blood-thirsty executioner, coldly murdering his own son to appease his anger? And what kind of "beautiful" justice is there in letting one person suffer for the wrongdoings of another? Christians are obviously numbed.

The way they sing these hymns, you would think that they find some kind of sadistic glee in blood-letting and flesh-eating. They have changed pain into glory, self-denial into virtue, militarism into peace.

> *Onward, Christian soldiers,*
> *Marching as to War,*
> *With the cross of Jesus*
> *Going on before.*
> *Christ the royal Master*
> *Leads against the foe;*
> *Forward into battle,*
> *See, His banners go.*

Is this the song of peaceful people? Every Christmas believers proclaim, "Peace on Earth," ignoring Jesus's warning: "I came not to send peace, but a sword." Christians actually think they have a loving and peaceful religion! And if you complain about it, they will just tell you that you don't really understand. They will spout some mumbo-jumbo about a "just God," and that only those who are on His side will find true peace. It doesn't occur to them that this is the opposite of peace, the epitome of intolerance and unfairness. There is no way you can describe the Christian God other than as a blood-thirsty bully; and anyone who would *want* to be a friend to such a fiend is either filled with fear or "godly" arrogance. Jesus reportedly said, "And fear not them which kill the body, but are not able to kill the soul; but rather fear him which is able to destroy both soul and body in hell." *(Matthew 10:28) I John 5:12* says, "He that hath the Son hath life; and he that hath not the Son of God hath not life." How very unkind.

I was recently speaking with a Christian woman about my deconversion from minister to atheist. "What was it about God," she asked, "that turned you off?"

"Nothing really," I answered. "I simply learned that there is no evidence for a god. You can't be turned off by a person who does not exist. But if your biblical god *did* exist, I would be very much offended at his personality."

"But God is a God of love," she countered. "The whole plan of salvation is based on God's love for you. God is peaceful and kind. Can you find anything in the bible that proves otherwise?"

I opened the bible to *II Kings 2:23-24* and read these words to her: "[The prophet Elisha] went up from thence unto Bethel: and as he was going up by the way, there came forth little children out of the city, and mocked him, and said unto him, Go up, thou bald head; go up, thou bald head. And he turned back, and looked on them, and cursed them in the name of the Lord. And there came forth two she bears out of the wood, and tare forty and two children of them."

"Is that a very nice thing to do?" I asked.

"God is a God of justice," she said, "and He can't be mocked."

"But that is my point. He is not very nice, is he? Would you want to be a friend with someone like that?"

"God is a God of love," she repeated. "He is our Father, and we should accept His actions even though we don't always understand or agree with everything He does."

"But forty-two little kids were torn to pieces because they laughed at a preacher! Is that kindness?" I pressed.

"Yes, it is kindness, in a way, because sinful actions . . ."

"I'm sorry," I interrupted. "Anyone who thinks something like this is an act of kindness is a very dangerous person." I turned and walked away.

Christians also believe that the bible elevates the family, ignoring Jesus's admonitions, "For I am come to set a man at variance against his father, and the daughter against her mother, . . . and a man's foes shall be they of his own household" *(Matthew 10:35,36)*. "If any man come to me, and hate not his father, and mother, and wife, and children, and brethren, and sisters, yea, and his own life also, he cannot be my disciple" *(Luke 14:26)*.

Christians do not recognize the hatred and intolerance here. God's righteousness sometimes causes inconveniences (such as hell), they say, but the ultimate message is one of love. When the psalmist says, "Happy shall he be, that taketh and dasheth thy little ones against the stones," they say this is *mercy!*

I was on Boston's "People Are Talking" television show recently, and one of the other guests was a well-dressed woman from Beverly LaHaye's "Concerned Women of America." When I asked what will happen when I die, she gave me a "concerned" look and said I was going to hell. I looked her in the eyes and said that was not a very nice thing to say. It was unkind, unfriendly, and intolerant. She just smiled at me, as if hatred were the most normal thing in the world. She didn't care, and probably didn't know that she was saying ugly and offensive things: she was doing her Christian duty.

Another guest on that show was a minister, the head of Massachusetts' "Moral Majority." After the show I asked him why God would violate one of his own commandments and desecrate life by ordering pregnant women to be butchered by the invading Hebrews. "What crime did the fetus commit," I asked, "to deserve such punishment?" He told me that the Ten Commandments really say, "Thou shalt not *murder*," and that God was "killing," not murdering (as if that would make any difference to the woman with a Jewish sword in her body); and he said that those killings were "merciful" acts of a loving God who was saving the unborn babies from a life of immorality and inevitable hell. The Hiroshima argument: a few deaths today will save many deaths later. This great thinker apparently believes that salvation comes either through Jesus's blood or through abortion! Whichever comes first.

It was when I rejected Christianity and became a thinking human being that I truly began to care for life. I became un-numbed. The next time you try to impress Christians with the cruelty of their religion, don't be shocked when they are not shocked. How can you not be desensitized when you are "washed in the blood?"

Freethought Today, December, 1987

31

Christian Joy?

I USED TO PREACH that Christians are the only truly happy people in the world. And we sincerely believed that this was true.

"Humanity is groping in sin and darkness. Unbelievers are confused and lonely. Real joy comes through Jesus Christ. How can you be fulfilled if you reject the love of your heavenly Father? How can the human machine operate properly if you neglect the operator's manual, the Bible?" My congregation would smile and say "Amen," believing that our spiritual fellowship was a unique pocket of joy in an ugly, hurting world.

Did you know that the word JOY is an acronym for Jesus-Others-You? You can only be happy if you put Jesus first in your life, and if you put your own self last. At any rate, it makes a nice sermon outline. (I can just hear one of you heretics suggesting a different acronym: Jesus-Offends-You. But I would never stoop to such tactics myself.)

Several months after my deconversion I met with a group of fundamentalists to discuss the bible. I identified myself as an atheist and did not hesitate to examine critically the contradictions and errors in their "holy" book. After the meeting, one of the older men came up to my car window and said, "Dan, I think you're still a Christian."

"Why do you say that?" I asked.

227

"Because you seem so happy. You're a nice person; you enjoy life and love people. You appreciate God's beauty in music, art, and nature. How can an atheist have such peace? How can a nonChristian be so joyful?"

I looked at him and said, "No, I'm not a Christian—I no longer accept those myths. The reason I am happy is because I choose to be happy. For me, happiness is primarily a state of mind and since I now control my own mind, I also control my own happiness. I am no puppet of a higher mind, no slave to eternity. I never knew real joy before I regained possession of my own mind. You should try it!"

Are Christians the happiest people in the world? Can anyone else besides believers have joy in life? Are Christians even happy at all?

(Note I am treating joy and happiness synonymously here. A favorite sermon topic is the supposed distinction between the "fleeting happiness" of heathenism and the "deep abiding joy of Jesus." Splitting hairs like this is a religious tactic that allows Christians to pretend that their own particular feelings are more sublime or pure than the undeniable "worldly happiness" they see in the lives of unbelievers.)

The attractive feature of religion is that it offers an answer to the existential dilemma. Never mind that this "answer" is false. It is so woven into the fabric of human culture that most people feel naked without it. Since harmony, meaning, purpose, and love are relational ideas, they can only make sense contextually—none can exist in a vacuum. The cosmic question, "What is the meaning of life?"—if one insists on asking it—cannot be answered in a cosmic vacuum. Hence God, or something like God.

Christians feel that true harmony and meaning exist in the relationship between the Creator and the Created, between Parent and Child ("Our Father . . ."), or between Male and Female (the church is the "Bride of Christ."). Therefore, they say, the greatest love and the highest joy can only be attained within the relationship between "God and Man." Everything else is cheap love, worldly happiness, temporal thrills, worthless.

There are two sides to Christian joy. First there is the joy that comes when guilt and fear are removed: forgiveness of sin, redemption to eternal life, freedom from shame. The Christian is "washed in the blood of the Lamb." Since "the wages of sin is death," and since Christ died for sin, the penalty has been paid; we are free to leave the prison of guilt. You are a worthless bum, but Jesus has picked you up off the streets and has cleaned you up and erased your crimes. Aren't you just filled with thankfulness?

But let's think about this. The very concept of sin comes from the bible. Christianity offers to solve a problem of its own making! Would you be thankful to a person who cut you with a knife in order to sell you a bandage? Would you respect a doctor who makes you sick in order to stay in business? What is more joyful: "I am guilty but forgiven," or "I was innocent all along"? Sin is a vicious concept, an insulting lie. It keeps people subservient. Even Jesus was supposed to have said, "They who are not sick need no physician."

Even though believers are supposedly forgiven of all transgressions, they are never free from sin. Temptation lurks in every idle interlude. "Resist the Devil and he will flee from you," they must constantly rehearse. "Pray for strength." What kind of happiness is this? How happy can you be when you think every action and thought is being monitored by a judgmental ghost? (The heavenly father is a heavenly bother!)

How joyful can you feel when you believe that most of the world's billions, including many of your relatives and friends, are destined to eternal punishment? How enjoyable is lovemaking with the intrusive eye of divine appraisal peering over your shoulder? (The man's shoulder, presumably.) How healthy is it to accept the blame for the crimes of an ancestor? What joy is there in forced sacrifice, feigned humility and unnatural self-denial? What peace of mind can you have by donating money to a beautiful church building when your children need shoes? What pride is there in desiring someone else (Christ, or his representatives) to take responsibility for your own shortcomings?

I remember as a child being absolutely terrified listening to sermons about judgment day and hell. I was often panic-stricken with the thought that Jesus would return to the earth at any moment, descending from the clouds in a burst of light, and I would be left behind. I used to hope, "Oh, please let me grow up and get married and start a career before it all ends!" Those fire-and-brimstone sermons were effective—I clung to Jesus like a drowning kitten to an oar.

Christians will insist that all of this brings them joy. Well, sure. It's like the joy of a slave who makes it through the day without being beaten, or the joy of an abused child during a quiet moment alone, or the joy of a starving prisoner who is tossed a scrap of food. But is that real joy? Real joy would be to eliminate the oppression altogether.

As a teenage evangelist I worked with some Christian drug rehabilitation groups like Teen Challenge. I heard hundreds of testimonies of God's miraculous transforming power. Sure, religion can motivate people to astonishing feats. But that is rather like sinking a billiard ball with a cannon—it gets the job done but ruins the rest of the game. It is swapping one dependency for another. (Why not rather exchange dependency for self-control?)

So the first side of Christian joy is nothing more than the "joy" of being hammered into shape. The other side of Christian joy is that now that we are forgiven, and welcomed into God's family, we derive great pleasure from fellowship with our heavenly Father. Just like a Dad who is both stern and loving, God has a warm side. He supposedly imparts his superior strength, knowledge, comfort, and guidance to all who ask. Isn't it wonderful?

Sure, it's a great feeling. It's like a pleasant daydream, hitching your cart to a fantasy. Who doesn't like to feel special? Who wouldn't like to know that the universe is lavishing loving attention on their individual happiness? Many people make it through life like that. We would ordinarily call them neurotics, like Freud suggested, or in some cases, psychotics. One of my brothers, trained in psychology, likes to repeat the adage, "A neurotic builds castles in the sky; the psychotic moves in."

Of course, we know that many people make it through life just fine without religion. Most freethinkers are free of the fears and insecurities that drive people to hide under a superstitious blanket. Just as avoiding the number thirteen can make some people seem safer, I know that inner religious feelings can be quite strong, quite convincing. But of all the pleasant feelings Christianity may produce there is none that can compare with the pure ecstasy of atheistic self direction. I challenge any believer to demonstrate that his or her life is more joyful than mine. It is not. I should know: I went the whole Christian route and there is *nothing* there. Nothing but narrowness, fear, and confusion.

There is joy in rationality, happiness in clarity of mind. Freethought is thrilling and fulfilling—absolutely essential to mental health and happiness.

You cannot freely give or receive love until you first love yourself; and you cannot love yourself if your only claim to worth comes as an undeserved gift from a "merciful" dictator.

I have lived the Christian life. I prefer now to live my own life.
Freethought Today, August, 1985.

32

Trust Yourself

"**D**AN, IF I WERE an atheist like you, you would be dead," said a sixty-year-old Christian professor towards the end of an informal but grueling five-hour debate I was having with five fundamentalists in a San Dimas living room.

"Why would I be dead?" I asked, in a voice which was getting hoarse.

"Because I would kill you," he replied with a smiling gaze.

"Why would you kill me?" I asked, astounded.

"Because if it were not for the moral restraints of the Bible, I would be a wild animal, stealing, raping and murdering," he explained, his wife and daughter listening. "You had better thank Jesus for his love and protection." I was stunned to hear such talk from such a nice looking person.

"If you wish to be a murderous criminal," I said slowly, "you will soon find that it is not in your best self interest. There are many people like myself who respect life enough to protect ourselves from people like you. We have laws—and we have other methods of self defense."

I hope his threats were truly rhetorical. They do show how aggressively Christians tackle the question of morality, and how godlessness is still equated with evil.

One of the major reasons freethought is unpopular is that religionists do not perceive us to be saying anything positive. This is because redemptive religions hold a pessimistic view of self. My major theme as a traveling evangelist was the innate depravity of humanity and the opportunity for a "positive" solution through spiritual regeneration. Like all salespersons, the peddlers of propitiation thrive on their customers' needs, whether real or artificial. Salvation can only be sold to sinners, to the damned and depraved.

Freethought, on the other hand, holds an optimistic view of self. If salvation is defined as the removal of the problem of sin, then freethinkers are already saved! Jesus said, "They that be whole need not a physician, but they that are sick." Is this an admission that religion makes you sick!

We freethinkers don't need the Christians' positive solution. Although our actions may appear negative to them because we challenge the foundations on which their myth of depravity is built, freethought is inherently positive because of its affirmation of intelligence. Without intelligence, morality is impossible.

Morality is commonly defined as a code of ethical behavior. And ethics is nothing more than value. If A has more value than B, then choose A. The big question, of course, is why A should have more value than B. Value is relative. The price of gold fluctuates with numerous social factors. The value of a home, a loaf of bread, a rock star autograph, a green beret or an old book is determined by things like supply and demand, need, personality, taste, desire and sentimentality. But we all agree that ethical values are related to life itself and they are determined by intelligence.

The difference between the humanistic morality of most freethinkers and the spiritual morality of most religionists is that while humanists assert that ethical values are relative to human life and are determined by human intelligence, religionists claim that they are relative to God's life and are determined by God's intelligence. Both approaches are relative. However you look at it, some "mind" has to make the decision. The debate is not over how to be moral but over who makes the rules.

Many religionists feel that we humans are incapable of forming our own rules. This is largely due to their pessimistic view of self, and to the idea that a creator should know more about its creation than the creation itself. They point to history to illustrate the shortcomings of worldly morality, forgetting that our past was dominated by religion. And of course we freethinkers are convinced that the gods of the bible demonstrate a primitive concept of human ethics.

In short, born-again Christians don't trust themselves. They prefer an external code of behavior to be imposed on them. An absolute code of commandments engraved on stone tablets is comfortable to those who fear the dangers of human thought. In respect to human questioning, religion guarantees absolutes; but freethought is an absolute guarantee of respect for questioning humans. We are capable. Humanistic morality emphasizes not so much a code but a principle: that which contributes to human life is good. Consequently, that which threatens life is evil.

Of course, "good" and "evil" to the freethinker are not opposing forces in a cosmic battle. They are relative terms. Most ethical decisions are not clear-cut choices of right and wrong, which is what makes morality often difficult and intelligence always necessary.

Most moral choices involve a conflict of multiple values. To compare the relative values and determine an appropriate behavior requires thought. And intelligent thought requires an optimistic respect for the human mind. (There's a good question: If Christians distrust human thought, how can they respect their own decision to believe in God?)

Religious morality is dangerous. If we are not allowed to participate in the formulation of a moral code, even in principle, then the makers and enforcers of the code are in an authoritative position to control us. That is tyranny. It is the opposite of freedom. It is an insult to human capability and a threat to progress, intelligence, kindness and love. (Have you seen much love in the faces of Christian antiabortion demonstrators?)

I have something to say to the religionist who feels atheists never say anything positive: You are an intelligent human being. Your life is valuable for its own sake. You are not second-class in the universe, deriving meaning and purpose from some other mind. You are not inherently evil—you are inherently *human*, possessing the positive rational potential to help make this a world of morality, peace and joy. Trust yourself.

Freethought Today, September, 1986

33

Christian Designs

CHRISTIAN: IF YOU WILL just look at the mountains you will see the irrationality of atheism.

Freethinker: Why is that?

Christian: Just open your eyes. Aren't they beautiful?

Freethinker: Yes, they are very beautiful.

Christian: Well, there you go. How could something so elegantly designed as Nature just have happened by accident?

Freethinker: I don't think it "just happened by accident."

Christian: Then you agree it had to be created?

Freethinker: Of course. The mountains were "created" by forces like volcanic activity, erosion and the buckling of tectonic plates. They are very beautiful.

Christian: Since you use the word "beautiful" you must consider the mountains to be works of art. Works of art require an artist.

Freethinker: To suggest that Nature is a work of art betrays a theistic assumption, which makes your argument circular. Beauty is not limited to the products of conscious creativity.

Christian: But the very fact that you have an emotional aesthetic response to Nature proves there is more there than meets the eye.

Freethinker: Yes. In addition to the mountain, there is a human mind which perceives, evaluates and feels. You have changed the subject. Are you saying that some super being crafted the mountains for our enjoyment?

Christian: Whether or not they were created for our direct enjoyment, we still respond with a sense of awe to their design. And that sense of awe cannot be explained in purely naturalistic terms. It transcends the material world.

Freethinker: Your "sense of awe" is nothing more than amazement, or wonder at the unknown. It invented the gods of thunder and the goddesses of fertility before such forces were understood.

Christian: But you admit that you have the same feelings yourself?

Freethinker: Quite often. But the atheist stops short of fabricating a mythical explanation. It saves the embarrassment of having to dethrone a Zeus or Hera. Or Yahweh.

Christian: Yahweh is still on the throne.

Freethinker: And where is this "throne" of Yahweh? Where is it, exactly, that your sense of awe "transcends" you?

Christian: We're getting off the subject.

Freethinker: Yes, you are.

Christian: That type of question can only be answered in supernaturalistic terms like "spirit" and "faith," which you would doubtlessly consider to be irrational words in your present condition of spiritual blindness.

Freethinker: Doubtlessly.

Christian: How do you explain the beautiful orderly processes observed in Nature? Does not design require a designer?

Freethinker: Does it?

Christian: Of course it does. It is a valid scientific inference to note that there are numerous observable complex and orderly processes in Nature which act toward a specific purpose—like the human eye—and we have never observed such purposefulness outside the context of intelligent design.

Freethinker: And you therefore conclude that Nature was designed by a superior intelligence?

Christian: I knew you were capable of rational thought.

Freethinker: Then let me ask you this. Is the mind of this superior intelligence complex and orderly? Does it contain processes which act toward specific purposes?

Christian: The mind of God is perfect beauty.

Freethinker: And who designed this perfect beauty?

Christian: I know what you're aiming at. You're trying to get me into an infinite regress, but I won't fall into that trap. Perfect beauty is capable of designing itself.

Freethinker: Is that a "valid scientific inference" also?

Christian: No. But it is a logical necessity.

Freethinker: I see. You find it logically necessary to contradict your main premise.

Christian: Design does require a designer. But it is not contradictory for the designer to be the design itself.

Freethinker: Then the human eye could have designed itself?

Christian: You know that is absurd. A designed *object* requires an explanation outside of itself.

Freethinker: That is my point.

Christian: I can see this is getting us nowhere.

Freethinker: Exactly.

Christian: Then how do *you* explain the wonderful harmony and design of Nature?

Freethinker: There are many ways I could approach the subject, but they don't really matter. The point of atheism is that the theistic answer is unsatisfactory.

Christian: According to whom? Do you admit that if there *is* a God it would provide a purpose for existence and explain a lot of things?

Freethinker: Of course. The actual existence of your hypothetical Superbeing would probably be an adequate explanation for some of the as-yet unknown factors of the universe. But is it a true explanation? *Adequate* does not equal *actual*. Is it even a valid question to ask for the purpose of the universe?

Christian: My point is that if there exists only one adequate explanation, then it is logically justifiable to accept that explanation as the truth.

Freethinker: I never said there were no other possible explanations; and I think I proved that your reasoning from design is invalid. And even if it *were* valid, it would not demonstrate the existence of a single designer, or of a currently existing designer, or of a designer that has any dealings with human beings.

Christian: But you do at least admit that my explanation would be adequate?

Freethinker: It would be equally adequate to portray reality as the dream of a Hindu cow.

Christian: Well, a Hindu cow explanation is completely *ad hoc* and illogical. But, Hindu cow or biblical deity: they are both supernaturalistic explanations for design in the universe. If the naturalist is silent on this question, then some sort of transcendent Creator is most probable.

Freethinker: Most naturalists agree that there is much design, and much chaos, in the universe. If your god is to take credit for the beauty, does it not also take credit for the ugliness and cruelty, the cancers and tornadoes, the painful accidents of an indifferent universe?

Christian: You can't blame God for sin.

Freethinker: Your god supposedly created *everything*, including human nature, storm systems and amazingly adaptive cancer cells. Naturalists do see some design in the universe, but they do not see it as necessarily intelligent. We observe "design" by natural selection, which is the cruel opposite of purpose. We find design in geometric patterns, like ripples or snowflakes, by the limited number of ways atoms can combine. We observe design by natural laws.

Christian: Don't laws require a lawgiver?

Freethinker: For you to ask such a question shows that you misunderstand science. Laws which govern human conduct do require a lawgiver, but natural laws are a completely different thing. It is inaccurate to picture natural laws as somehow existing in or above nature. They are merely human conceptions about nature, ways for us to organize our thoughts about the way nature behaves or appears. What goes up must come down; there is no choice involved as with human laws. Natural laws are descriptions—they are not moral or legal prohibitions.

Christian: But if there is no lawgiver, then on what can we base our system of morality? Aren't you proving that atheists are immoral?

Freethinker: I think we are proving that Christians are confused.

Freethought Today, December, 1986

34

Blind Faith

CHRISTIAN: YOU CAN'T TELL me there is no God because I talk to Him every day.

Freethinker: Oh? You have a personal relationship with a supernatural being?

Christian: That's right. I know it's hard for you to understand, but God is very real to me in my spirit. We communicate with each other. He gives me a real peace, an indescribable joy, and a sense of His holy presence that can only be comprehended by fellow Christians who have had the same experience.

Freethinker: I see. You have this extra sense. Do you actually hear a voice?

Christian: No. But I have heard that some Christians do hear a voice. It's not an aural voice that I hear—not the sense of hearing. It's a spiritual sense, a "knowingness" that transcends the material world.

Freethinker: And where is this spiritual sense?

Christian: It's in the heart.

Freethinker: In the heart? You don't mean the physical organ that pumps blood?

Christian: Of course not. The "heart" of man is the seat of emotion and spiritual sensitivity. It's what brings love and compassion to men.

Freethinker: And to women also, I presume.

Christian: Of course.

Freethinker: Then this "heart" is actually just your mind. Your mind at the feeling level.

Christian: I suppose you would have to phrase it like that. But it's much deeper than that. It's a very real spiritual experience. If you have never felt it you will not know what I am talking about.

Freethinker: No, I don't think I have ever felt exactly what you feel, although I have had many emotional experiences, some of them very moving and powerful. You must understand that from my point of view it appears you are having nothing more than a psychological experience. It happens in all cultures and religions.

Christian: Of course you must say that. You lack the reality of the experience so you can do no better than attempt to explain it in natural terms. But believe me, I am really talking with God.

Freethinker: Why should I believe you?

Christian: Because since you lack the spiritual sense you are hardly in a position to make a judgment about it. It's like asking a blind man to evaluate a painting. You will just have to take my word for it.

Freethinker: Don't you see that this is a circular argument? The existence of "spirit" is the point in question, and you tell me that in order to determine whether it exists I must first have a "spiritual" sense. That would be like saying that the only people who are qualified to make a judgment about the existence of Santa Claus are those who have met Santa Claus personally. What if I were to insist that I have had experiences which prove that your experience is a psychological delusion? Would you take my word for it?

Christian: No, because my experience is spiritual, based on a higher sensitivity than your experiences. The fact that you question my claims is proof that you are limited to this natural world. If you are ever going to believe, you will first have to take someone's word for it. If not my word, then the Word of God.

Freethinker: I can't do that. It would be irresponsible for me to accept the truth of a statement without some means of verification. Until you give me a way to examine your claims I must insist that you are experiencing nothing outside of your mind.

Christian: Don't be absurd. Most of what you know comes through the testimony of others. Have you personally verified the existence of quarks or the historicity of Julius Caesar?

Freethinker: No, I haven't. But I could if I wanted to. Scientists and historians make their information and methods available to everyone. I could take the same paths and come to my own verification.

Christian: Could you really? What if you were blind? Could you repeat any experiment that requires light?

Freethinker: That would be difficult. I might decide to take the word of sighted investigators, provisionally. But I would be very careful to require a near-unanimous agreement among a large number of independent observers.

Christian: Now we are getting somewhere. That's exactly what I am saying. Millions of people through history have testified to the existence of a supernatural world. Since you are spiritually blind you can do no better than notice the universal agreement among Christians—a universal testimony of spiritual reality. Why should you object to such overwhelming evidence of God's existence?

Freethinker: Because there is no way to test your claims. I don't feel any spiritual sense myself. God is *not* real to me.

Christian: Does a blind man deny that the sky is blue? Millions testify to that fact. Does the sky cease to be blue because of a few blind doubters?

Freethinker: No. A blind person has good reasons for believing that there is such a color as blue, though he or she may not be able to picture it. The blind and the sighted are dealing with the same natural universe, which makes your analogy inapt. The physical eye can be examined as a sensory device. The path of light signals through the retina to the brain can be traced. The spectrum can be analyzed by frequency. A machine could be built that would respond with a tone to the color blue and the blind person would have solid indirect evidence for color. Can you give me a way to do that with God, even though I *am* spiritually blind?

Christian: Definitely. It's called faith.

Freethinker: And what is faith, if not wishful thinking?

Christian: The Bible says that "faith is the substance of things hoped for, the evidence of things not seen."

Freethinker: In other words, wishful thinking. How does a person receive this "evidence of things not seen?"

Christian: You examine the revelation that God has given in the Bible and in nature. You just believe it is true, accept God's presence, tell yourself He is real—and He will be real.

Freethinker: You mean I must lie to myself? Faith is a lie?

Christian: You obviously don't want to believe, so you never will. Selfishness and sin can block your willingness to accept the truth. Until you humble yourself and quit worshipping your own intelligence you will be blind to the truth which is so obvious to the rest of us, and you will be a fugitive from

God's grace.

Freethinker: That's fine with me. From what you say, faith seems more like fantasy than fact. I may as well tell myself that Santa Claus is real. After all, millions of children will testify to his existence.

Christian: How can you compare the faith of a mature Christian to the fantasy of a child?

Freethinker: With little difficulty.

Christian: It is you who are childish. Great scholars have studied God and have supported His existence. Are you smarter than all of them?

Freethinker: It doesn't take much intelligence to notice that these "great scholars" never agree with each other. How can the blind person agree that the sky is blue if some say it is usually orange, others say green, and still others say it is brown with lavender polka dots?

Christian: It is true that there are some minor disagreements among theologians. But they all agree, at least, that God exists.

Freethinker: Well, of course. Any theologian who ceases to believe in God ceases to be a real theologian, by your definition. There are probably more atheists in theological circles than you would imagine.

Christian: Theologians may all have differing subjective impressions or may be overemphasizing some doctrinal position, just as people may perceive the sky to be different colors at different times. But they all agree that there is, in fact, some kind of spiritual realm. You are certainly aware of that.

Freethinker: Yes, I am aware that there are many who do believe, but now I can't say what color the sky is, or if there is even a sky at all. It's too confusing to call. I begin to suspect that the problem is not with the nature of the perceived reality, but with the perceiving organ itself. You are certainly aware that millions of people believed in Zeus and Zoroaster, Marduk and Mithra. Why are you right and they wrong?

Christian: Because I know I'm right. It's that simple. I see the blue sky and I call it as I see it. Those ancient believers were deluding themselves, following culture and primitive fears. But I possess the reality of the Christian God in my heart. You can't tell me what I do or do not feel within myself. It is very real, and you would be arrogant to suggest that I am just making it all up.

Freethinker: Don't misunderstand me. I'm not denying that you have a real experience within yourself. I know it is strong. It has motivated people of all religions to build hospitals and fight wars. Christianity is no exception.

Christian: Thank you.

Freethinker: That wasn't a compliment. What I am saying is that I accept the reality of your religious experience, but since there is no objective

241

and independent evidence for the existence of a transcendent realm, I must reject the reality of the supernatural. Therefore, your very real experience must be rooted in our very real natural world. The only "evidences" you give me are statements which point to the existence of a psychological phenomenon and nothing more.

Christian: You are wrong.

Freethinker: Can you show my why? Jesus reportedly said you could move a mountain with faith? It would certainly be in God's best interest to keep His own word and produce a miracle to convince a skeptic. You seem to have a lot of faith. Let me see you move a mountain.

Christian: I can't do that. God doesn't do magic tricks on demand. Besides, not everything in the Bible was meant to be taken literally.

Freethinker: Somehow I knew that.

Christian: But I don't need a miracle to convince me that what I feel is real. Just because you are blind doesn't mean I can't enjoy a sunset.

Freethinker: A sunset in your mind.

Christian: Now you deny the existence of sunsets?

Freethinker: Not at all. Since I am not blind we can both agree that we have a mental picture of sunsets and that they actually exist outside of our minds. We can also agree that humans have mental religious experiences, but this is only a statement about the natural world. I am under no obligation to make your transcendent leap of faith and accept the existence of a supernatural realm. Have you ever been afraid?

Christian: Certainly. Many times.

Freethinker: Have you ever had a strong fear that turned out to be unfounded?

Christian: What do you mean?

Freethinker: I was once hiking in the mountains and I came upon a snake on the trail. It frightened me because I had heard that there were rattlers in that area. I jumped back and my pulse quickened. But on closer examination I saw that it was just a stick and I felt foolish for being afraid. Even then I cautiously stepped around it. You know how fear can sometimes grip the mind.

Christian: What does this have to do with the existence of God?

Freethinker: I had a *very real* psychological experience that convinced me, for a moment, that a stick was a snake. You can't deny the reality of my experience, can you?

Christian: Of course not. But you were wrong.

Freethinker: That's my point.

Christian: But I'm not wrong. God *does* exist. Just as you discovered on closer examination that the snake was not real, so I have discovered on closer examination that God is real.

Freethinker: Can you prove it?

Christian: Not to you.

Freethinker: Then you can't prove it. Suppose I told you there was a poisonous snake a few feet from here. Suppose I acted frightened and urged you to believe me. Would I be telling the truth?

Christian: Maybe.

Freethinker: But would you be convinced by the reality of my fear?

Christian: Well, if I knew that you couldn't tell the difference between a snake and a stick I might have my doubts. However, for safety's sake I might choose to believe you anyway. Provisionally, as you say.

Freethinker: But would you be correct? Is there in fact a snake here?

Christian: The only way to prove it is by looking.

Freethinker: No, I'm asking you to accept my fear as the only evidence.

Christian: That's absurd! We should be able to determine if your fear is justified.

Freethinker: And if it is not?

Christian: Then you should stop being afraid and we will have a good laugh about it.

Freethinker: And if I continue to be afraid?

Christian: Then you have problems. You might be suffering from a psychological instability, paranoia, delusions, or attention-seeking insecurities.

Freethinker: Then you agree with me that a feeling does not prove a fact.

Christian: Of course. I mean . . . except for spiritual things. In the spiritual arena the feeling is part of the fact.

Freethinker: Isn't that irrational?

Christian: I suppose it is. But faith transcends rationality.

Freethinker: My point, exactly.

Freethought Today, July, 1985.

35

Mere Assertions

ABOUT SIX MONTHS after my deconversion I had lunch with Hal Spencer, president of Manna Music. His company is a leading publisher of Christian music. In light of my deconversion to atheism I wanted to buy back the copyrights to my musicals which they continue to promote. "No way," he said. "Your musicals are very strong items in our catalog, among the few things that keep us in business." Talk about mixed feelings! I used to be excited to hear those glowing reports. Not any more.

Our conversation eventually drifted into one of those endless and usually fruitless discussions of design, first cause, morality, miracles, science, faith, and atheism. As we were paying the bill Hal turned to me with a grin and said, "I suppose this means you won't be writing us any more musicals?"

I laughed and said, "Sure I will! But I doubt you would publish anything I would want to say *now*."

Christian publishing is a huge industry. Have you ever been in a Christian bookstore? (They are sometimes euphemistically known as "Family Bookstores." I am tempted to go in and ask if they have any readings for atheistic families.) You should visit one sometime, just to see what we freethinkers are up against. You will see thousands of books by hundreds of presses, a plethora of albums by dozens of record companies, racks of bibles in every size, color, and version. You can read about child raising, gardening, abortion, psychology, worship, history, politics, romance, computers, humanism, and the women's movement—all from a Christian perspective. And science fiction, of course. You may also spot some of my material; but forgive me, for I knew not what I was doing.

On Christmas Eve I wandered into the Upland Christian Light Bookstore, for no particular reason, and was promptly accosted by a local minister who had heard that I had turned heretic and who thought I needed to learn a few things about the creation/evolution debate. (I do. So does he.) After our "friendly" chat, I took a nostalgic stroll down the hallowed aisles of religious reading. I was particularly interested in finding books that I had at one time considered to be great, books that I would like to reread in a new light. So I picked up C.S. Lewis's *Mere Christianity*.

C.S. Lewis is a very popular Christian writer. He was a professor at Oxford who claims to have converted from atheism to Christianity. Many people have been influenced by his work. He is known for his *Narnia* series for children, and for many books that popularize theology including *Screwtape Letters* (along the line of Twain's *Letters from the Earth*), *The Great Divorce* (a hell-to-heaven bus ride explaining that people are in hell because they choose to stay there), *Miracles, Pilgrim's Regress, The Problem of Pain,* and a science fiction trilogy. He writes in a convincing, readable style, is often humorous and usually thoughtful.

Mere Christianity, Lewis's most popular book, is really three books in one: 1. *Right and Wrong as a Clue to the Meaning of the Universe*, 2. *What Christians Believe*, and 3. *Christian Behavior*, all adapted from a series of radio lectures. The book's title comes from Lewis's attempt to strip Christianity of all that is nonessential, getting down to the "mere" basics of what it means to be a Christian. As a believer, I remember being impressed with the first book since it gives what many consider to be a compelling argument for the existence of a deity. I have an uncle who says that *Mere Christianity* was a major factor in his "conversion" to deeper commitment. So when I reread the book, I was anxious to reexamine its arguments.

Lewis goes to great anecdotal length to argue for the existence of a "Natural Law" of morality within each human. Unlike the law of gravity, though, this moral law can be disobeyed.

"This law was called the Law of Nature," he writes, "because people thought that every one knew it by nature and did not need to be taught it. They did not mean, of course, that you might not find an odd individual here and there who did not know it, just as you find a few people who are colourblind or have no ear for a tune. But taking the race as a whole, they thought that the hu-

245

man idea of decent behaviour was obvious to every one. And I believe they were right."

As an example, Lewis points to the opposition to the Nazis: "What was the sense in saying the enemy were in the wrong unless Right is a real thing which the Nazis at bottom knew as well as we did and ought to have practiced? If they had no notion of what we mean by right, then, though we might still have had to fight them, we could no more have blamed them for that than for the colour of their hair."

Lewis does not believe that differing civilizations have had differing moralities: " . . . these have never amounted to anything like a total difference." (Oh? What about culturally sanctioned polygamy, infanticide, cannibalism, wife beating, self mutilation, castration, incest and war?) He dismisses the critics who claim that morality is a result of the species' survival instinct by noting that we are free to obey or disobey this "instinct" and make our decision by a higher standard of Right and Wrong. "You might as well say the sheet music which tells you, at a given moment, to play one of the notes on the piano and not another, is itself one of the notes on the keyboard. The Moral Law tells us the tune we have to play: our instincts are merely the keys."

You can see that Lewis is fond of arguing by analogy. (His whole *Narnia* series is one huge metaphor.) This can sometimes be an effective way of communicating with uncritical readers; but it can be deviously misleading if used in place of disciplined reasoning. Mere assertions (a better title for his book) can be used in place of carefully defended statements, and can be made to "stick" in the mind with an analogy which, though perhaps apt, nevertheless skirts the question of the truthfulness of the basic idea.

For example, is it true that all persons in all cultures share a common knowledge of a Moral Law? Some would disagree. And his analogy about piano music completely misses the possibility of improvisation and composition, making robots of us all. Besides, the sheet music is external to the piano, and it can be replaced with another song if desired. And pianos don't grow and learn and hurt, like people . . . and so on. Analogies can be helpful to illustrate a point, but propping up a bald assertion with an analogy alone can backfire.

Even if it is true that all cultures share a common morality, why does this prove a supreme intelligence? After all, don't we humanists sometimes claim that there is a common thread of humanistic values running through history across cultural and religious lines? Lewis's attempt to leap from the shaky platform of a "Natural Moral Law" into the arms of a loving deity is even less convincing than his basic premise.

First, Lewis gets the *idea* of a deity from history, noting that there are two major world views: the materialistic and the religious. The materialistic world view asks questions that can only be addressed by science ("What is the structure of life?"); but the religious world view raises issues which assume a higher context ("What is the meaning of life?"). Science observes the material world, but religion sees the mental, nonmaterial. (Where does he put philosophy and psychology?) If there is a God, Lewis argues, then God is much more like mind than anything else, and if this God is to communicate with us it will be more likely that he will do so through our minds, not through the material world. (How does Lewis know any of this?) And this is exactly what this wise deity has done: he has placed within us this "law of morality" which connects us with the higher realm, which can never be verified with mere science.

So, according to Lewis, if you want to find God, look within yourself to discover this urging to morality and realize that you have broken this law, every day. *Mere Christianity* boils down to the same old sermon: you are a sinner and you know it, don't you feel bad? Then, when you are properly ashamed you will realize the beauty of the plan of salvation that this deity has revealed through the death and resurrection of Jesus Christ (which Lewis historically takes for granted).

Lewis does not address situational ethics in this book, though it would seem relevant. He assumes, I guess, that we would all agree what would be the "cosmic" right in every instance. In fact, Lewis is confident that his readers will be tacitly convinced of the correctness of this line of thinking. (God exists because we have morals and we wouldn't have morals if God didn't exist.) And Lewis can afford to relax, I think, because most of his readers are Christians who buy the book because they are looking for substantiation. They are not skeptical searchers of truth. Any writer can capture a sympathetic audience by capitalizing on those areas that everyone "knows" to be right.

Humanistic morality is a code of ethics based on the value and quality of human life. It is not derived from absolute engravings on a cosmic stone tablet. Morality is relative to human things like happiness, health, peace, beauty, love, joy, and justice. It is the preferring of those actions and ideas which enhance the human condition over those which threaten it. The Nazis, who were mostly Catholics and Lutherans, were wrong not because they broke an absolute law, but because they desecrated human life. Even though humanistic morality does assert some rights and wrongs relative to the human condition, it is flexible and free to improve. For example, on the one hand it is inconceivable that something like genocide would ever be considered moral, and on the other hand that something like genuine politeness could be considered immoral; but there will always be a middle ground between those extremes for things like birth control, divorce, diet, self defense, or patriotism, which will depend on the situation.

Any morality which is based on an unyielding structure above and beyond humanity is dangerous to human beings. History is filled with examples of what religious "morality" has done to worsen our lot. Whole cities can be gleefully exterminated in God's name. Society's "witches" can be eliminated. Free thought can be suppressed, squelching any hope for progress. (Why else were the Christian-dominated centuries called the "Dark" Ages?) Under Christian morality, anything goes if it furthers God's plan. In place of Lewis's Law of Morality, more enlightened people would champion reason and kindness: principles that are pliable and human, not rigid and cold.

So, now I have to ask myself why I once thought *Mere Christianity* was so special. Because it told me what I wanted to hear. As a freethinker I am now no longer satisfied with mere assertions, with creative rehashings of myth. Freethought demands evidence in place of analogy, data over dogma.

What do you think? Should I cash the royalty checks I continue to receive from my Christian musicals? Now there's a moral dilemma with which I struggle all the way to the bank.

Freethought Today, June, 1985. Originally "Mere Assumptions"

36

Without Reservation

MY GRANDFATHER TURNED ninety this summer [1985]. He is a Delaware Indian, a gentle person of few but well-chosen words. I often enjoy hearing stories of his childhood, of a past age, of hunting and fishing in the wild Indian Territory before Oklahoma became a state. His was the generation of transition. The tribe had been moved from New Jersey to Ohio, then to Indiana, and finally to what is now the Sooner state. The traumas of relocation and the realities of dealing with a modern America caused my great-grandparents to teach an important survival skill to their children: adaptation. They embraced the white man's religion, Christianity, and encouraged their sons and daughters to be educated in the new ways. Granddad's sister, Effie, was one of the first Indian women in those parts to graduate from college.

My grandmother has an entire room dedicated to the culture of the Lenni Lenape (Delaware) tribe. She is sometimes consulted by historians who want to know who married whom, where they moved, and how they lived.

[My grandfather died in 1986. In 1991 My grandmother and I published a book of his childhood memoirs, *Paradise Remembered*.]

Our tribe has an ancient custom of recording events on carved sticks called Walam Olum and can trace history back to the migration through Alaska across the continent to the east coast. They were named Delaware by Europeans who first discovered the culture on the banks of the Delaware River in New Jersey. The Lenni Lenape, nicknamed "Grandfather tribe" by other Indian groups, apparently was the first of the modern tribes to have reached the Atlantic Ocean in a general migration toward the source of the rising sun. They gained somewhat of a reputation as peacemakers among the Native American groups and became the first tribe to own a written treaty with the European settlers. We were also the first to have a written treaty with the newly formed United States government (for military reasons). This is no great honor since most treaties were quickly broken.

There is a story about how the Lenni Lenape were "made women" by the Iroquois. Many of the silly tribal wars would get completely out of hand as the warriors would be killed defending the group's honor. Our tribe was no exception. These conflicts would usually continue until the women started complaining and talking sense, convincing the remaining men that there was little honor in the death of their fathers, brothers, and sons. To be called a woman, then, was to be called a peacemaker, arbiter, reasoner.

During one conflict between the Lenni Lenape and their northern neighbors it was rationally agreed to dismiss the problem and "bury the hatchet" before the fighting began. The Iroquois thought it strange that the Delaware would act peaceably, and in later years bragged that they had won the war by "making women of the Lenni Lenape," incorrectly implying castration and submission. (The authenticity of this story is not universally accepted.)

In spite of this deliberate misinterpretation, the Lenni Lenape wore the indictment of "woman" with honor. And rightly so. Some of them apparently recognized the evils in patriarchal cultures and the benefits of common sense and peace.

In the same sense, my deconversion from Christianity to atheism has made a "woman" out of me. I was raised in a patriarchal religious culture based on an intolerant, sexist, irrational book. We boasted that our God was the Conqueror. The bible told us to "put on the whole armor of God." We pretended to be carrying the "sword of the Spirit," holding the "shield of faith" and wearing the "helmet of salvation." Christianity is a very macho religion. Look at the songs we sang:

Onward, Christian Soldiers
Onward, Christian soldiers,
Marching as to war,
With the cross of Jesus
Going on before:

Christ the royal Master
Leads against the foe;
Forward into battle,
See His banners go.

Stand Up, Stand Up for Jesus

Stand up, stand up for Jesus,
Ye soldiers of the cross;
Lift high His royal banner,
It must not suffer loss:
From victory unto victory
His army shall He lead,
Till every foe is vanquished,
And Christ is Lord indeed.

Stand up, stand up for Jesus,
The trumpet call obey;
Forth to the mighty conflict,
In this His glorious day:
"Ye that are men, now serve Him"
Against unnumbered foes;
Let courage rise with danger,
And strength to strength oppose.

Lead On, O King Eternal

Lead on, O King Eternal,
The day of march has come;
Henceforth in fields of conquest
Thy tents shall be our home.
Through days of preparation
Thy grace has made us strong,
And now, O King Eternal,
We lift our battle song.

Soldiers of Christ, Arise

Soldiers of Christ, arise,
And put your armor on,
Strong in the strength which God supplies
Through His eternal Son;
Strong in the Lord of hosts,

And in His mighty power,
Who in the strength of Jesus trusts
Is more than conqueror.

Sound the Battle Cry

Sound the battle cry!
See, the foe is nigh;
Raise the standard high
For the Lord;
Gird your armor on,
Stand firm, everyone;
Rest your cause upon
His holy Word.
Rouse, then soldiers, rally round the banner,
Ready, steady, pass the word along;
Onward, forward, shout aloud Hosanna!
Christ is Captain of the mighty throng.

Strong to meet the foe,
Marching on we go,
While our cause we know,
Must prevail;
Shield and banner bright,
Gleaming in the light;
Battling for the right
We ne'er can fail.

The Son of God Goes Forth to War

The Son of God goes forth to war,
A kingly crown to gain;
His blood-red banner streams afar:
Who follows in His train?

These are not obscure songs tucked into the back of the hymnal. In many churches these songs are sung regularly, Sunday after Sunday. I remember standing up during worship services, singing these melodies, proud to be conscripted into God's army. What an absolutely childish game! And what a dangerous mentality. Blood, militarism, sexism, power. Rather than signs of truth, these are the delusions of mental instability—like the guy who runs around saying, "I am Napoleon."

But I believed it all, I have to admit. I felt that I was called to be a soldier of the cross, a "man of God," and the spiritual leader of my family. Although it was never explicitly stated, I was glad to have been born male.

I viewed women as "weaker vessels" *(I Peter 3:7)*, as helpers in the masculine battle for the salvation of the world. Women were to stand by and support the more important work done by their husbands, fathers, brothers and pastors. God loved women, of course, as much as men; but he entrusted greater responsibility to the male. There was holy significance in the divinely instituted "chain of command." (God the Father: Jesus Christ: men: women: children: animals. It is not very clear precisely where angels fit in there.) After all, shouldn't children respect their parents? Shouldn't women respect their husbands? God's hierarchical authority flowed properly when we were all in our rightful place—like the military. I was glad to have been born male, blessed by God with a higher purpose.

We used to talk about "freedom in Jesus," but as a Christian I was not free. I had to fit in, to find my place. That isn't freedom. I wasn't allowed to be a full person. I had to "die to myself," based on the religious curiosity that without God we are slaves to ourselves. Now I am glad to be a true Lenni Lenape, a feminist and a freethinker, without reservation. For me freethought equals feminism.

I n my painful transition I have realized that relationships to society and friends are so often based not on true respect and love but on imposed role models. The relationships are predicated on the hierarchy: I am Husband, You are pastor, I am servant, You are wife, I am King, You are Child. When the authority imposing them dissolves, sometimes relationships do also. Any relationship not based on freedom cannot stand true freedom. How many masters could learn to accept their former slaves as true peers? And vice-versa?

As the Christian-imposed role models in my life broke down, so did my Christian marriage. The breakdown of my fourteen-year marriage was primarily philosophical ("for what communion hath light with darkness?" *2 Corinthians 6:14)*, but there were deeper reasons. My former wife had married a "good Christian man" (me) mainly in order to fulfill a role as supportive wife.

Long before I made the complete break with religion, even while an active evangelist, I had chafed under the discomforts of being responsible for "spiritual leadership" in our marriage. I could see no reason why I should be her superior; she is intelligent and capable. No woman needs a man's leadership to give her life direction.

At the point I became an atheist, I asked if she still considered me to be her spiritual leader. She said that yes, under God she was still committed to my direction. But when I jokingly asked her to follow me "spiritually" into atheism, she seriously declined. (I was her spiritual leader as long as I led her where she wanted to go.) It's just as well—she finds happiness in Jesus, her true captain, and should enjoy the freedom to live and worship as she chooses.

To throw out the religious structure and attempt to replace it with concepts of freethought and feminism was just too much strain on our relationship. You can imagine.

F rom my perspective as an active insider, I know how Christianity abuses women. I have worked in churches where most of the women were clearly superior to the men, yet they were denied access to any position of leadership. I have seen organizations virtually managed by capable beautiful women who were forced to submit to the puerile power plays of the male pastors. And I have seen the smiles disappear from their once eager faces, replaced by a disappointed but brave acceptance of "God's will." I was partly responsible for that, and I am sorry. Ignorance has no preference for gender, outside the bible.

Much has been said about the bible's impact on women, in freethought writings at least. But what about its impact on men?

It is clear that women have been victimized as religions attempt to put them in their place. It is less clear, though equally devastating, that men have also suffered from this artificial dichotomy between the sexes.

Patriarchal religions do a tremendous disservice to humanity by driving an unnatural wedge between the maleness and femaleness in each one of us, creating an unhealthy polarization that not only alienates women and men but also splits the individual personality. As a Christian man I was half a person. Sure, I managed to live with myself, but not without a nagging feeling that something was radically wrong with my self image.

The Christian imperative is to conform. Conform to the image of Christ. Conserve the old-time role models. Be all that you can be, in God's army. The pressure is tremendous, especially when you choose the ministry.

As a spiritual leader it is necessary to be an example, to seek perfection. *Matthew 5:48* says, "Be ye therefore perfect, even as your Father which is in heaven is perfect." I discovered that as I sought to conform to this external image of perfection, I lost sight of myself. That is supposed to be a high Christian virtue, to "die to self" in order that Christ might live through you. I denied many of my truly human emotions and thoughts in order to be *God's man.* I ignored, even despised the side of my character which contemporary culture would label as femaleness, professing "natural" male qualities like toughness and certainty even when I was weak or unsure.

There is much to be gained by rediscovering the whole person—the maleness and femaleness—in each one of us. A freethinker realizes that authoritarian models are usually attempts to control and tyrannize others. A freethinker can not be a racist, bigot, or sexist.

Christianity is responsible for fostering patriarchy and slavery, ideas which only serve to subjugate and control. A true Christian can not be a feminist, but must fight to preserve the traditional lines of demarcation. What true feminist would base life on the male authority of Jesus or Jehovah? As a male religion, Christianity is an enemy to humanity, and the antithesis of freedom.

Like my Lenni Lenape ancestors, I am glad that I have been "made a woman." Maybe, just maybe, I can help talk some sense into those silly tribal warriors.

Freethought Today, October, 1985.

37

Age of
Unaccountability

A T WHAT AGE is a child old enough to commit a sin? Will a toddler go
to hell for swiping cookies? Some churches teach that before the "age of
accountability" (around seven) children are not responsible for their actions.
This is contrary to the biblical doctrine that "all have sinned, and come short
of the glory of God" *(Romans 3:23),* but then theology is not supposed to make
sense.

My GrandDad was ninety-one when he died, in 1986. He and Grandma
had been married for more than sixty years. About ten months after his death
I went to visit Grandma in Oklahoma. She had not touched a thing since his
death, but she seemed grateful when I offered to help her remove GrandDad's
clothes from the house and go through his possessions.

My grandparents were not rich. They had lived a comfortable, middle-class
life, and they ended up with just enough savings to pay for the funeral. Since
that time Grandma has been managing fine, but not without struggling to
pay the bills.

Going through GrandDad's personal drawers I discovered a record of tax
information going back many years. I saw that they had given money to religious causes their entire lives. In 1964, for example, they had listed $996.27
in charitable contributions to their church and other religious groups, includ-

256

ing $90 to Oral Roberts and $140 to Billy Graham.

Later that night I mentioned to Grandma that I had heard that Billy Graham had a surplus of millions of dollars that was not being used for anything. She just stared at me for a moment.

I suppose it doesn't seem unfair that people like my grandparents are allowed to take a tax deduction for religious donations. In their minds the contributions are "charitable." But is church giving really charity?

Why do religions get a tax break? When I was a minister I took advantage of many tax exemptions, including my entire cost of housing, and I thought they were deserved. I believed that without the moral restraints and charitable imperatives demanded by religion, society would be wild: we would need more police, jails, hospitals, youth centers, counselors. I imagined that churches perform a valuable service to the world, feeding the hungry, throttling immorality, keeping potential criminals off the streets. (It does keep a lot of preachers busy.) Christianity saves society billions of dollars, I fantasized, and tax exemption is only fair.

Well, sure. A few churches feed the poor. But to what extent is religion truly "charitable?" After providing for rent, salaries, benefits, hymnbooks, choir robes, missionary and evangelistic outreach, how much does the average church actually contribute to the needy?

A syndicated Los Angeles Times article by George Gallup, Jr. and Jim Castelli noted the percentage of all congregations that have selected charity services. (The findings are from a study, identifying 294,271 congregations of all religious affiliations in the forty-eight contiguous states, issued in 1988 by Independent Sector. It was based on a yearlong Gallup study of religious congregations):

- **Homeless shelters**
    46% of liberal congregations
    36% of moderate congregations
    29% of conservative congregations
    26% of very conservative congregations

- **Meal Services**
    49% liberal
    41% moderate
    35% conservative
    33% very conservative

- **Environment**
  - 42% liberal
  - 30% moderate
  - 24% conservative
  - 16% very conservative

The study listed other things, such as family planning, day care, civil rights, and the arts, with similar results.

This shows that considerably less than half of all churches are involved in any kind of charity. And these figures represent only the number of congregations, not the amount of charity actually practiced by each church. Some churches (I remember) once or twice a year will pass a plastic "Bread for the Hungry" loaf-bank around Sunday-School classes, collecting pennies from the children which are supposedly sent to the denominational headquarters— and *this* allows them to tell Gallup that they are feeding the poor.

Certainly, there is a handful of truly charitable churches in America, but does their contribution make up for the tax dollars lost by granting a blanket exemption to religious donations? As the Freedom From Religion Foundation has repeatedly pointed out, so often when religion gets the credit for charity, taxpayers have paid the bill. Examples include publicly subsidized religious hospitals, shelters, social services, foster homes, and international relief organizations.

A large Baptist church in San Antonio needed more parking space, so they bought and demolished ten historic homes, after a long, bitter fight with the city, ignoring the protests of area residents. Those are ten homes lost to the tax rolls, and lost to history. Now the church is renting the parking space to local businesses during the week, and the pastor is outraged at the suggestion that they should pay taxes on this nonchurch-related income.

The March/April 1989 issue of "Consumer's Digest" contains a study of one hundred charities, which were asked to provide information about their groups. Among the religious groups that did not respond at all to the inquiry were: Southern Christian Leadership Conference, Atlanta; World Vision International; Larry Jones Ministries—Feed the Children; Operation PUSH; Morality in Media, Inc.; National Federation for Decency; and Billy Graham Evangelistic Association.

The report notes that Billy Graham took in $64 million in 1987, spending $48 million on "program services" and $7 million on "fund and administration." At the end of the year their fund balance was more than $32 million. Of course, we have to take Billy's word for it. Churches and religious organizations are not required to account for their money. And so they don't. In fact, more than a year after a financial-ethics code was adopted by the National Religious Broadcasters, at least half of the member organizations have yet to comply with the mandatory code.

Other tax-exempt groups, such as the Freedom From Religion Foundation, are forced to file an annual IRS form 990, specifying in torturously fine detail how funds are collected and used. We are accountable; Billy is not.

I had thought that perhaps the $32 million fund could be justified because an organization needs stability, and Billy Graham has such large expenses preaching all over the world. Then I read in the Syracuse New Times and Herald-Journal that Billy Graham does not pay his own expenses! He now only preaches by invitation. In April 1989 he had a huge, six-day crusade in Syracuse, and the entire $875,000 shindig was funded locally. A week before the event, local organizers were complaining that they were still $350,000 short. They had raised $148,857 from mailed appeals, $99,447 from offerings taken at rallies and events, $264 from the choir members, $22,194 from the executive committee, $121,886 from 115 churches, $35,000 from surplus gatherings at earlier crusades, and $91,043 from the crusade's finance committee. (All of this in a prominent newspaper story which they probably submitted.) Fundraisers were "praying for guidance" about how to raise the rest of the money.

Praying for guidance? Why not ask Billy for some help? He's got $32 million. He's got GrandDad's money.

If he's not going to spend it he should give it back. Grandma could really use it about now, what with the higher costs of prescription medicines and utilities.

I have a suggestion. Although I feel that churches should be directly taxed, the climate may not yet be ripe for such a reform. In the meantime, I think there is a way we can help reduce the federal deficit without raising taxes, and without taxing churches. We could increase tax revenues and at the same time honor state/church separation. Since only a tiny portion of church donations truly goes to charity, we should allow only a percentage of religious contributions to be deductible from personal income. To be generous, say fifty percent. Like now, churches would not pay taxes on receipts. Members could still give as much as they feel the church deserves. The result would be that more Americans would have a higher level of taxable income; and those of us who do not donate to religion would be subsidizing it less.

Oh, sure. Many churches would probably get around this by setting up a local charity. But at least they would have to be accountable, like other nonreligious charitable groups. And why shouldn't they be? Why would an honest organization object to accountability?

The national Council of Better Business Bureaus has issued a report saying that Pat Robertson's Christian Broadcasting Network does not meet the bureau's standards for public financial accountability. They cannot determine if funds solicited by CBN are being used as claimed. "Officials at the network did not answer repeated requests for audited statements or for a current board-approved budget."

Among broadcasters that the BBB said did not respond sufficiently about 1988 finances is the Billy Graham Evangelistic Association. Why not? What is Billy hiding? Hasn't he reached the "age of accountability?" What is he doing with my Grandma's money?

Freethought Today, June/July 1989

SPREADING
THE
BEST NEWS

Part 5

Losing Faith in Faith

38

In The Lion's Den

AN ATHEIST ON CHRISTIAN television? Christian Broadcasting Network (run by Pat Robertson) gave me the "privilege" of appearing on a CBN talkshow to defend atheism on July 27, 1989. I felt like Daniel in the lion's den!

The invitation was prompted by John P. Koster's book, *The Atheist Syndrome* (1989, Wolgemuth & Hyatt), that characterizes atheism as a form of "mental illness." I tried to check it out of the library before the show, but even in Madison, Wisconsin (which has at least thirty-five bookstores) I was unable to locate a copy. None of the three Christian bookstores had even heard of it!

However, the Freedom From Religion Foundation was familiar with the defamatory tome, thanks to a *New York Times* interview (February 5, 1989) and a syndicated column by Patrick Buchanan (April, 1989). We had sent a letter protesting the irresponsibility of the *Time's* biased piece to its executive editor (who never replied, much less provided equal time), and targeted Buchanan with letters of protest.

Koster's book is nothing more than a personal polemic. Invoking his armchair interpretation of the private lives of infidels such as Darwin, Huxley, Ingersoll, Nietzsche and Freud, Koster asserts that the "atheist syndrome"

263

has three phases: "One, in childhood there is suppression by the father. . . . Two, the escape phase in which they separate from fathers and home. . . . Three, the realization that they resemble their fathers. Depression sets in, relieved by antireligious activity, because by attacking their idea of God they were attacking their own fathers."

Asked where he got the idea for this "syndrome," Koster reveals his scientific sophistication: "With the origin of the plethysmograph . . . it seems clear that clinical testing for ESP turns up what could be called the footprints of the soul or spirit. I felt people refusing to look at this evidence were doing so on a purely subjective basis. I began to wonder, 'Was there a psychological conditioning for atheism?' "

Koster stated: "The turning point came when a friend urged me to read the biography of Robert Ingersoll, lawyer, philosopher and another atheist. He lost his mother at the age of two and hated his father, a depressed Calvinist clergyman, who used force to make his son read the Bible."

Patrick Buchanan wrote a glowing review of Koster's polemic, calling it a "withering assault on atheism's idols."

I was invited to CBN as a representative of the Foundation to appear opposite Koster on a talkshow called "Straight Talk," hosted by Scott Ross. The producers told me that even though CBN is a religious network, this particular show is an attempt to present a balanced treatment of issues—"sort of like Donahue, but better" (!), they said—which is why a heretic like myself was recruited. They confessed, however, to a built-in obstacle to objectivity since everyone involved is Christian: producers, host, audience, camera operators, make-up artists.

When I arrived in Virginia Beach I discovered that they *all* wanted to reconvert me on the spot. When the burly driver of the CBN van learned that he had just picked up an *atheist* at the airport, he flashed me a wide smile and started telling me about the love of Jesus. He said he had never met an atheist in his life. I told him that he has probably met many atheists, that on average at least every twentieth person he meets is an atheist, but they are not likely to advertise that fact. I mentioned that it is interesting that he can't tell the difference. "Maybe you're right," he replied, "I do know some alcoholics and drug addicts." He tried to quote scripture but quickly betrayed the depths of his biblical ignorance. Finally, dropping me off at the hotel, realizing he was losing his prey, he grinned and said, "Well, perhaps some arguments are better solved with a two-by-four." I hurried to the registration desk, forgetting to give him a tip.

With tears in her eyes, a make-up woman told me how a Jew had "found Jesus as his personal savior" the previous week, in the same make-up chair where I was sitting. A captive audience, I finally protested, "Hey, I used to preach these sermons myself!"

In the green room, before the show, I talked with Koster, pointing out that one of the most authoritative biographies of Ingersoll *(American Infidel: Robert G. Ingersoll,* Orvin Larson) quotes Ingersoll as saying, "I have a dim recollection of hating Jehovah when I was extremely small," yet nowhere is there any documentation that he hated his father. When I asked Koster which biography he had read, he cited Eva Ingersoll Wakefield's. This is actually a collection of letters edited by Ingersoll's granddaughter, with a brief biographical introduction. Wakefield's sketch, in fact, quotes Ingersoll saying that his father "was loving and generous in his nature, but his theology filled his sky with cloud and storm." Koster evidently can't understand how Ingersoll could distinguish between his father and his father's views.

According to Larson and other biographers, Ingersoll loved his father very much. He quit his job to help his father convalesce; and his father later died in his arms. "I never said to him an unkind word," Ingersoll wrote of his father, "and in my heart there never was of him an unkind thought." Ingersoll's celebrated love of family was one of the hallmarks of his personality, as anyone familiar with his life and writings would know. When I told Koster that Ingersoll never hated his father, and when I asked him to correct his error, he responded: "Well, any boy whose mother dies when he is two years old will end up hating his father." So much for historical credibility and objectivity! Why would anyone believe *anything* this man says?

The "Straight Talk" show itself was more balanced, timewise, than I had anticipated. Host Scott Ross was intrigued by my story of deconversion from a fundamentalist minister to an atheist, asking me to recount my experiences with faith healer Kathryn Kuhlman. I pointed out that my atheism has nothing to do with my psychological strengths or weaknesses; it is based simply on the fact that there is a lack of evidence for a deity.

Had time permitted, I would have testified to my always affectionate relationship with my father, both as a Christian and as an atheist. Dad was hard hit by my deconversion, and today is a freethinker. We have always been close. So much for Koster's theory.

On the show, Koster, tense and uptight, repeated his contention that atheism is a form of mental instability: "The stronger the atheism, the stronger the instability." (I didn't get a chance to point out that atheism does not admit of degrees. You either believe in a god, or you don't.)

When Koster humorlessly brought out the alleged mechanical proof for ESP, I asked how such evidence, whether it is reliable or not, indicates a deity. How can a physical machine in the natural universe point to something supernatural? Do radios prove that there is "something out there" transcending the material world? Koster's only answer was a *non sequitur,* mumbling that since psychology has failed to provide an origin for human thought, theism is the only rational alternative.

The program ended with an "objective" wrap-up sermonette by Ross, written *before* the show, quoting (surprise, surprise) *Psalm 14:1:* "The fool hath said in his heart, There is no God."

During lunch with the producers following the show, I said to Koster, "You believe in a book which has talking animals, wizards, witches, demons, sticks turning into snakes, food falling from the sky, people walking on water, and all sorts of magical, absurd, and primitive stories; and you say that *I* am the one who is mentally ill?" One of the producers who was listening stammered that I must have an "*a priori* bias" against the supernatural to be so close-minded.

Koster's book is nothing more than atheist-bashing. (So are most critiques of atheism.) Believers, failing to substantiate their assertions, often resort to *ad hominem* character assaults. If they are able to unearth a few "rotten atheists," or to smear the good name of such freethought dignitaries as Ingersoll or Huxley, they feel that this permits theism to win by default. (Rotten Christians, of course, do not count in this equation.) Koster's religious mindset distorts his grasp of freethought to such a degree that he imagines that freethinkers worship and deify intellectuals such as Freud, whom he fondly regards as an "atheist leader."

A century ago Robert Ingersoll confronted similar tactics directed at himself:

"And here, it may be proper for me to say, that arguments cannot be answered by personal abuse; that there is no logic in slander, and that falsehood, in the long run, defeats itself. People who love their enemies should, at least, tell the truth about their friends. Should it turn out that I am the worst man in the world, the story of the flood will remain just as improbable as before, and the contradictions of the Pentateuch will still demand an explanation."

Freethought Today, September, 1989

39

Good Morning, America

J UST WHEN WE thought it had been safely put to rest, the hotel-bible matter once again started our phones ringing, resulting in national television coverage for the Freedom From Religion Foundation on "Good Morning America" in August, 1989. The Foundation had sent letters to all the major hotel and motel chains back in February, requesting that some "bible-free" rooms be made available for nonChristian guests. Although not a state/church concern (except for the few cases where the hotel is state-owned, such as occurs in Indiana), the issue addressed freethought views of the bible, gaining many opportunities to promote freethinking through some forty radio talkshows and numerous articles.

In May, just as the issue appeared to be dying down, Foundation president Anne Gaylor received a letter from Jim Buick, president of the Zondervan Corporation, publishers of the *New International Version (NIV)* of the bible. Zondervan is big business, owning the so-called "Family" bookstores found in shopping malls around the country, and publishing books, music, and Christian products.

"In the event you may be waging a campaign against a book you haven't read recently," Buick stated, "please accept the enclosed copy of the [*NIV*] Bible . . . I hope there will always be room at the Inn for Bibles." Anne asked me to answer Buick's letter, and I replied that "many atheists credit bible reading as one of the reasons they no longer believe," highlighting some of the many inaccuracies of the *NIV* translation.

Meanwhile, Zondervan had hired big-time PR consultants to rev up some publicity, sending out hundreds of news releases to radio and TV, complaining about our complaint! This resulted in at least forty additional radio interviews by phone hookup, with a Foundation staff member on one line and Buick on the other. We agreed to do any shows that would announce or let us announce our address, thus making many new contacts with freethinkers around the country. Once I did seven shows in a two-day period. Anne averaged one a day for two weeks!

The silver lining in all this was that many stations chose not to book Buick at all, recognizing that our side of the issue is much more novel, guessing that Buick is just a bible salesman. Although polite, Buick was a rather boring guest, just wanting to talk about "God's love," and to promote the *NIV*. In one instance a station was not able to handle two phone-in guests and at the same time open up lines for calls from listeners, so about twenty minutes into the show the host asked Buick if he wouldn't mind hanging up so that Annie Laurie Gaylor could field the calls!

After a long stretch of acting in a gentlemanly manner, Buick finally showed his true colors. On a Boston radio show, for example, he tactlessly and comically admitted that the Jewish talkshow host, the great "unsaved masses" and atheists such as myself will wind up in hell, sent there by his loving god.

I was surprised to learn from a Gideon Society member who called in on one talkshow in Texas, that although the ubiquitous Gideon bibles are "free," they do solicit (and receive) donations from hotels carrying them. This means we are paying for them, to an extent, when we rent a room. (We should have known that religious "charity" comes with strings attached.)

Zondervan does not place bibles in hotels (although obviously that is their desire), but the *NIV* has been put in some New York inns by the International Bible Society. In fact, after being flown to New York City for "Good Morning America," I found *two NIV* Bibles (a New Testament and the entire bible) in my room at the Essex House. I had often heard Buick trivialize our complaint by claiming that he has never found an open bible in a hotel room, asserting that they are always inoffensively hidden in drawers—contrary to the experience of many of us. Yet the bibles at the Essex House are stamped: "Kindly leave this book in view. The next guest may need it."

Buick and I appeared on ABC's national "Good Morning America" television show August 9, 1989. Joan Lunden, who was very professional (she was told to end the segment by 8:22:50, and she did!), conducted the friendly but substantive interview, centering on the Foundation's consumer request. Many Americans, perhaps for the first time, heard why some of us consider the so-called "Good Book" to be offensive and dangerous. It was satisfying to have the chance to point out that there are millions of freethinkers who are infinitely more kind and reasonable than the god of the bible. I thought that was a nice way to start a "Good Morning, America."

Good Night, Zondervan!

When I mentioned some of the offensive passages of the bible on "Good Morning America," bible salesperson Jim Buick countered with his regular line that we atheists are guilty of "picking and choosing," taking things out of context in order to distort God's Word. Buick's accusation is amusing given the *NIV's* serious translation problems.

The *NIV* is not a reliable translation. While the *King James* and *Revised Standard Versions*, used by the Gideons, have their own problems, the *NIV*—a brand-new English translation that had allegedly sold more than forty-five million copies between 1987 and 1989—is a mine trap. (The *NIV*, by the way, is the version that was distributed to all Texas legislators in a bizarre "midnight Bible ceremony," for political consultation before all votes.)

The preface of the *NIV* admits that roughly one hundred translators "were united in their commitment to the authority and infallibility of the Bible as God's Word in written form . . . it contains the divine answer to the deepest needs of humanity . . . We pray that [this version] will lead many into a better understanding of the Holy Scriptures and a fuller knowledge of Jesus the incarnate Word, of whom the Scriptures so faithfully testify." This is hardly an objective agenda for a team of translators! Imagine if freethinkers published a new bible translation, prefacing it with a statement that we were "united in our commitment" to bash and disprove "God's Word." Buick admits that the translators were all evangelical Christians. This bias necessarily corrupts the process, although Buick says he can't understand why.

The *NIV* is a warm-fuzzy, twentieth-century Protestant version of the bible which Zondervan calls "user friendly." No wonder it is so popular with modern churchgoers! It dishonestly eliminates many contradictions, theologically reinterprets problem texts, and smooths over offensive passages. For instance, the sixth commandment is rendered, "You shall not murder," neatly sidestepping the ongoing theological controversy engendered by the correct translation, "kill," which is commanded, committed, or condoned by God throughout the rest of the bible. (See "Murder, He Wrote.")

Isaiah 3:17, describing the Lord smiting and uncovering women's "secret parts" [Hebrew: *poth* = "opening" or "hinged entrance"], is rendered by the *NIV* as, "The Lord will make their scalps bald." This is a ridiculous mistranslation.

But the following gaffe can't be topped. *Matthew 19:12,* in which Jesus advocates castration [*KJV*: "made themselves eunuchs"] is hilariously interpreted by the *NIV* as "Others have renounced marriage because of the kingdom of heaven . . ." (At least there is a footnote hinting at the dishonesty.)

Another example is the contradiction between *Acts 9:7* and *Acts 22:9.* (See "Confused: Bible Contradictions.") The discrepancy has been completely erased simply by changing the meaning of words.

Although it should be expected that a modern translation would correct the errors of the past, the *NIV*, like the *KJV*, perpetuates the mistranslation of the *Isaiah 7:14* "prophecy" simply because the writer of Matthew made the same mistake. (See "Prophecy.") However, without this verse there is absolutely no basis at all in the bible for the Christian myth of the virgin birth, so the *NIV*, and every believer, is stuck with the error.

Buick admitted on some talkshows that he was surprised to hear informed criticism of the bible. Zondervan apparently expected us to be pushovers, like most Christians, ignorant of the scriptures. This tactic backfired. Instead of promoting the *NIV*, Zondervan's news release gave millions an opportunity to hear the "other side" of bible criticism.

Freethought Today, September, 1989

40

Bible-Free Rooms

This op-ed column was printed in the Baton Rouge Sunday Advocate, *March 19, 1989, Palm Sunday. Baton Rouge is televangelist Jimmy Swaggart's home town.*

T he February 26, 1989 *Sunday Advocate* editorialized against the Freedom From Religion Foundation's request that hotels provide bible-free rooms for non-Christian guests. You said this is "one of the silliest concepts we have heard of" under the guise of separating church and state. Our group, a national organization of atheists and agnostics, has indeed tackled many First Amendment issues, but we have never claimed that this particular matter has constitutional or legal concerns. This is a consumer complaint.

Hotels are always seeking the opinion of their guests. They have every right to place bibles in their rooms, but as paying customers, we have every right to complain. We are expressing our dissatisfaction that innkeepers are

endorsing a book which offends many people. We are *not* asking them to remove all bibles. Just as some of the better establishments offer "smoke-free"
rooms, we are requesting some "bible-free" rooms in consideration of the feelings of millions of Americans who are not Christian.

Why would a business want to offend customers? The refusal of the Holiday Inn, among others, to even consider our opinion is quite inconsiderate. It
is just plain rude. Are hotels on record to state that this is a Christian nation,
that hotels are Christian establishments, and that unbelievers are second-
class guests in their rooms and in this country?

The editorial argues that "just as nobody forces readers to buy Playboy or
Penthouse, nobody forces anyone to open the Bible." True; but what if Penthouse were in every hotel room, sometimes open on the dresser (as we have
found some bibles), *free* for every guest? Wouldn't that be a strong message
that the hotel industry is actively endorsing the philosophy of the book it
places? Would that not offend many customers?

When the City of Berkeley proposed placing "safe sex" condoms in all hotel rooms, some Christians were outraged. How would believers feel if every
inn on the continent had a copy of the Koran, of Mein Kampf, or an Atheist
Manifesto (if there were such a thing)? It is true that no one is forced to read
the bible; but neither are hotels forced to carry them.

True, television sets can be left off, or the channel changed. But what if
there were only one channel which broadcast only white supremacist programs in all rooms? Leaving the set off would not change the strong signal
being sent by innkeepers that they approve of the content. Hotels are telling
customers that the bible is a good book, that it should be turned to for comfort
and for salvation.

There are at least twenty million atheists, millions of Jews, Moslems, and
Buddhists in America who are not convinced that the Christian bible is a
good book. In fact, the Gideon Bible is the Protestant *King James Version,*
which most Catholics do not support. And even the millions of believers who
do want the bible rarely read it! They don't know what is in it, else they might
join us in our complaint. For example, even though we are outraged at
Khomeini's recent death threat [against author Salman Rushdie for writing
"blasphemy"], we forget that the Koran is based largely on the Old Testament. *Leviticus 24:16* says, "He that blasphemeth the name of the Lord, he
shall surely be put to death, and all the congregation shall certainly stone
him." If you respect the bible, then the Ayatollah's actions are the "Christian"
thing to do. Believers who obey the bible are gleefully supposed to murder
Persian children: "Happy shall he be, that taketh and dasheth thy little ones
against the stones." *(Psalm 137:9)*

And Jesus, who upheld "every jot and tittle" of the Old Testament law, said we should beat our slaves, be castrated, handle snakes and drink poison, that unbelievers should burn in hell, that we should hate our parents, and reward thieves by giving them twice what they steal.

The so-called Prince of Peace said, "Think not that I am come to send peace on earth: I came not to send peace, but a sword." *(Matthew 10:34)* The biblical deity committed mass murders, denigrated women, created evil, punished children for their parents' crimes, ordered pregnant women and children ripped open, demanded animal (and human) sacrifice, discriminated against the handicapped, ordered virgins to be kept as spoils of war, spread dung on people's faces and sent two bears to devour forty-two children who teased a prophet. Is that nice? Is this the kind of bedtime reading material that should be in our hotel rooms?

Yet because we object to such horror, you call us a group of "thought monitors." Atheists have no creed, no bible, no eternal punishments, no weekly sermons nor collections. If anyone is a "thought monitor" it is the person who believes we should "bring into captivity every thought to the obedience of Christ" *(II Corinthians 10:5)*, or that we should all be "as obedient children." *(I Peter 1:14)* It is the Gideon Society that is trying to monitor thoughts, placing Christian propaganda not only in every hotel room, but pushing bibles on children in public schools. They are like those territorial animals who mark off their boundaries by spraying everything in sight. Some of us want to be free from such spray. Is that such a "silly concept?"

Is the *Sunday Advocate* on record that the bible is a "good book?" Jimmy Swaggart was immersed in the bible, and look what it did to him! It corrupted him. It fixated him at an adolescent stage of sexuality, with an unwholesome view of human nature, teaching him that women can be exploited, that people can be bought and sold (yes, this is all in the bible), and that we must continually fight against our lowly human passions of "original sin." Swaggart and most ministers teach that human beings are degenerate by nature, and it becomes a self-fulfilling prophecy. Even though Baton Rouge hotels have every legal right to carry the bible, I would think they should be ashamed to be identified with such perverseness, intolerance, and mythology.

The editorial says that "in the interest of freedom of expression, we would rather see the Freethinker's newsletter alongside the Gideon bible." Would you really? If we ask Baton Rouge hotels to place our newspaper, *Freethought Today*, in every room in the city, will the *Advocate* go to bat for us? And when they refuse, will the newspaper join us in accusing them, as well as the Gideons, of being "thought monitors?"

41

Freethought On Donahue

WHERE DO WE go when we die? Do heaven and hell exist? Will we someday be transported, transformed, reincarnated, or "assumed into the Oneness?" These are some of the questions "Donahue" producer José Pretlow asked when he called the Freedom From Religion Foundation in search of a guest who does not believe in life after death.

I flew to New York for the October 24, 1988 taping of the "Phil Donahue Show" about the "afterlife," which was broadcast live in about ten cities and aired the following day around the rest of the continent. The same show was later rerun during the summer of 1989. (This was my second visit to the "Donahue" show. The first time was in March, 1988 to tape a silly show about "Praying Dolls," on which I didn't have much time to say anything; the few freethought points I did make, such as comparing the postures of prayer and slavery, were dismissed by Phil as irrelevant.)

There were five panelists on the "afterlife" show: Rev. Smock, a frowning hell-fire street preacher who thinks most people are damned and only a select few will go to heaven; Rev. Berkich, a smiling Christian who believes we *all* go to heaven (universalism); Father Quinlan, an animated, loquacious priest ousted by the Church partly because he believes that heaven and hell are just useful metaphors (but God is real); Lady Sabrina, a friendly Wiccan priestess (witch) who preaches reincarnation; and myself, an ex-preacher who thinks all of the above is nonsense.

After the others had stated their cases, Phil introduced me, saying, "I've got a guest for you! Guess who's going to hell? We found him. Here he is. Dan Barker is an *atheist*. Danny, Danny, what's it going to take for you to believe?" (The other guests had their titles, but I was identified on the screen as "Dan Barker: Doesn't believe in an Afterlife.")

"I used to be an ordained fundamentalist minister, years ago," I answered.

"Really!" Phil said.

"I changed my mind," I continued. "In America there are at least twenty million atheists who agree with Albert Einstein that there is absolutely no evidence for an afterlife, a heaven or a hell. All of this [motioning to the other guests] is nonsense. We live in a natural world. We use our minds. We use reason. The desire for an afterlife is wishful thinking."

"You probably think it has a lot of real consequences in the world as well, belief does?" Phil asked.

"Well, because most people believe in an afterlife, and it's connected to judgment. Mr. Smock [I couldn't call him "Reverend"] believes that there's some kind of a damnation or salvation, which can be an intimidating tool to motivate people to do whatever you want them to do. That's an archaic, primitive belief. It is immoral to push that idea on children: the idea that they're guilty, they're going to hell."

"It makes them feel bad about themselves, too, I assume," Phil continued.

"Well, exactly. We should feel good about this life that we live now, and live it to the fullest."

During the rest of the show I received my fair share of time. I was able to point out that none of the believers agree with each other, and that the bible is mythology. I got a chance to define atheism, to address the design argument, to challenge the morality of the biblical deity, to counter the "evidence" of near-death experiences, and to promote the Freedom From Religion Foundation.

A woman in the audience asked, "Is this what you're teaching your children?"

"No," I answered, "I tell my kids to use their own minds, to look at all the facts, to question authority when necessary, to let no one tell them what to think, not even me, their mom, their teacher, their minister. They have a good mind." The audience broke into applause—a refreshing experience for an atheist on a talk show.

Near the end of the program a woman leaned into Phil's microphone and said, "The only person up here who makes any real sense is the atheist."

"Oh-oh, sit down," Phil said. "Don't let them see you."

Phil made the woman sit down, but hundreds of freethinking viewers refused to be put down. Mail from them came pouring in. We received almost two thousand positive responses from that one show, and surprisingly, there were only about fifty negative letters. Here are some excerpts from the many expressive, informative and entertaining letters:

North Carolina: I could not believe my eyes when Donahue actually put your address on the screen! You were the first I have ever seen or heard on the matter. I was raised by a Baptist minister, but after years in advertising and publishing I have formed my own version of the "nature of things." Thank heavens, or Jupiter, or whatever, that made me tune YOU in.

Missouri: Your address was flashed on the screen today. I was delighted. Perhaps now I'll meet someone who actually sees the harm of religion as I do. I have been an atheist for twenty years but have never met another. It's a bit lonely. I am moving to Key West in January. Is there a club of atheists down there? Or just one person even?

Washington: I was beginning to feel like the only enlightened person in a world of disgusting blindness and ignorance.

Georgia: Bravo! After teaching Sunday School for forty years I began to realize that religion is myth. Before they died each of my parents told me they were atheists—as if they couldn't die with a lie between us. I hear more people willing to say they are atheists. Humankind will be better off without the divisiveness of religion.

Florida: I am desperate for people I can relate to.

Wisconsin: I thought I was all alone in a world ravaged by religious insanity until I saw you on Donahue.

Nebraska: Being an atheist in small-town Nebraska is kind of lonely.

Florida: I believe we exist now and when I die, I die. No heaven or hell. Unfortunately, this is an unpopular view in this redneck county.

Kansas: I am an atheist myself, and being from a small town, I look uneasily over my shoulder as I write that statement. The churches are very influential here. However, I am also a twenty-seven-year-old free mind who would rather make decisions intellectually than have them rammed down my throat, and the minds of my three children, by hypocritical, bible-thumping preachers.

Arizona: I heartily agree with your views, even though I have never had any coaching or have read almost nothing about the subject.

Massachusetts: It was a relief to see you on Donahue. Having been brought up in a Catholic home it has been tough for me to speak out against the inconsistencies, and even tougher to admit my own disbelief. Even now, I can't admit to my parents that I don't believe, for fear of hurting them. I believe in nature, not in "God."

Alberta, Canada: I was impressed by your performance on Donahue. I was brought up in Scotland as a Presbyterian but have been a committed, if low-key, atheist for years.

Ohio: I am fifty-nine and have been an atheist for forty-seven years. It has always been a very isolated condition. I would appreciate any reading material.

Oklahoma: I am an atheist. While this may not amaze you, it amazes the God-fearing citizenry of my town. When I innocently mentioned this to a fellow employee, I was met with grief, pity, and loathing. I've been the target of odd looks, bad jokes, and comments like, "Do you worship the Devil?"

New Brunswick, Canada: It bothers me that most people think atheists are evil. My atheism began when I realized how many religions there are, and how they all believe everyone else is wrong. I've seen so much hatred. The "words of god" are just human words. Some people can't see it! I don't know why.

Georgia: I appreciate people like you. I used to be a Methodist. One day I woke up and realized, I'm myself, no more, no less. I now just live. All we have is ourselves.

Oklahoma: I am an atheist and feel very alone. I'm only fifteen and most people my age are blinded by the myth of God their parents taught them. I used to be a hard, strict follower of God so everyone is now disappointed in me because of my "realization."

Maine: More than once I have worked my way to nearly complete acceptance in a group only to have it fall apart because I don't believe in a "Supreme Being." Anything you can do to put me in touch with people of like mind would be greatly appreciated.

Texas: There is no one as lonely as an atheist in the Bible Belt.

Florida: I am sick to death of these bible-toting, illogical simpletons brainwashed from fear. I'm thirty-six, Italian, and need to know I'm not alone with my beliefs.

New York: Today was I able to get your address and, boy! am I glad I did. You say everything I have been feeling for years. I consider myself a Proud Atheist and would appreciate any information you have to try to get religion out of government and my life.

Ohio: I am a freethinker. I am sick of hearing about Jesus!

Colorado: We are atheists and very happy. It is amazing that believers cannot understand this.

Montana: I saw your representative on Donahue this week, and was impressed at how he took the words right out of my mouth!

South Carolina: What a wonderful feeling today knowing there are others with views that match my own.

Michigan: We were excited to learn that there are atheists who are organized. We think the support will be very nice.

Arizona: Living in a conservative, largely Mormon state, I am desperate for an opportunity to communicate with people who share my views. Please respond quickly!

California: Oh, I'm sitting here watching Donahue and can't believe what most everyone is saying. And they believe it! I've been through them all—Christian Science, Presbyterian, Mormon, Judaism, Assembly of God. I now believe in nature, and I'd like to be in contact with others who feel as I do.

Maine: I am an eighteen-year-old atheist and gradually, surely, becoming a crazy one. I recently tuned in the Donahue program and enjoyed one of the greatest exchanges of ideas I've ever seen on TV. It helped me to identify the conflicting beliefs held by theists and atheists. The hardest part is getting my ideas across.

California: You were the only one who didn't have to shout to get your point across. I have been an atheist for many years but I don't know anyone else who is.

Ohio: Frankly, I'm tired of being told most people believe in a God. As though it were a badge of normalcy. I'm quite normal, and I think religion is nonsense.

Kentucky: My employer is discriminating against me in response to my disbelief. Advice would be appreciated.

Ontario, Canada: You are reaching many people who have great doubts. We have been fed this pap for so long. This keeping a person dumb is too much for me to swallow.

California: I was brought up in Christian Science. Spent the first twenty-five years "putting it in" and the past twenty "pulling it out." There should be a law against these "mind molesters" which is a crime on a par with child molestation!

Texas: Please send information. I am a confirmed (by whom, you ask, ha ha) atheist. I respect what you are doing immensely.

California: Is there a retreat where I can find refuge from fanatics who think that thanking God is better than thanking fellow humans when something goes right, and blaming humans when it goes wrong?

South Dakota: Send info! I'm the only atheist in South Dakota.

California: I too would like "freedom from religion." It scares me that people are making decisions that affect our lives based on fairy tales.

California: You were the only sane person on the panel. I live in Orange County and the fundamentalists are so radical here, I feel I'm in Nazi Germany.

Utah: I am an on-again, off-again Catholic and very confused the more I think. I was a Mormon and a Southern Baptist before that. You have my interest. I would like to read as much as possible on atheism.

Massachusetts: Hurrah for your beliefs! I feel so much better knowing there are so many atheists out there. I have been leery about voicing my opinion. We are good people too!

Texas: I live in a small fundamentalist community and often feel I'm the only intelligent person left in this hostile, anti-atheist environment. I could desperately use some moral support in raising my children to be independent thinkers. I cannot bear the thought of them becoming Jerry Falwell clones.

Texas: Religion is a teddy bear/security blanket.

Texas: I served two years as a Mormon missionary in Texas. I am now back in Dallas years later as an atheist. I am anxious to hear the thoughts of others who are not clouded by an addiction to fantasy.

Arizona: I was never a believer. We are the result of evolution. If that, plus disbelief in a god, makes me an atheist, so be it.

Wisconsin: As open-minded college students, we agree with the gentleman (and he really socked it to those Christians). We have been searching for a group with our (atheist) views for some time.

West Virginia: Please! Hurry! I am having real religious (or nonreligious) problems. It wouldn't take much to convince me that I am (really) an atheist. Please Rush!

Georgia: I have been an atheist since I was seven. Only the tough survive.

Maryland: I come from Pakistan from a very liberal Muslim family. I agree one hundred percent with your arguments. I shall be pleased to be associated with you.

Wisconsin: I've been an atheist for thirty of my fifty-one years. My conception of "hell" would be to be condemned for eternity to the back seat of a tan Plymouth station wagon with seven Jehovah's Witnesses as they make their random rounds to every last dwelling in the universe, all the while being forced to join them in the chanting of "Rock of Ages" between stops.

Wisconsin: I am interested in information on helping my children make decisions about religion. I have a hard time answering questions about God when I no longer believe the myths I was brought up with.

Pennsylvania: For years I have called myself agnostic because I felt it presumptuous to say I was sure of anything. However, people have told me to stop sitting on the fence, so I now call myself an atheist. It's definitely preferable to the alternative.

Colorado: You say there are twenty million atheists in this country. I suspect there are many more than that. Nearly everyone would become atheists if they only did a little honest thinking.

British Columbia, Canada: I was happy to finally hear a voice representing us, the quiet atheists.

Florida: Please send info. For personal reasons I would prefer you send the reply to my brother's address.

California: I am eighteen and am at the point where I can now say with pride that I am an Atheist, at least on an intellectual level.

West Virginia: The idea of God cannot be proved, but I can't find the frame of mind to settle the question completely. I would appreciate any material you could recommend.

Missouri: I lost my parents to this idiot religion fifteen years ago. As soon as we realize there *ain't* no Jesus, *ain't* no Devil, heaven, or hell, we can enter the next century speaking the truth instead of speaking in tongues.

New York: My great-grandfather was a minister. When I was a little girl I spent summer with my grandparents. I had religion morning, noon, and night. And he didn't convince me.

California: I just watched Donahue and I no longer feel guilty admitting I am an atheist. I believe in doing right because of a moral obligation to society, not from any sense of retribution.

Louisiana: I am sick of all those hypocritical evangelists begging for money! There should be a national program telling the truth about religion.

Virginia: I am a twenty-year-old college student lucky enough to have watched Donahue yesterday. I need to know I'm not the only one that feels this way. The gentleman on TV was the one that I could associate with, so I guess that makes me an atheist too. Is there something I could read to console me that I'm not evil to feel the way I do?

Massachusetts: Thank god for your organization, sane people! (It could be the answer to my prayers.) It is refreshing to realize I am not alone. Until recently I believed that religion was mostly innocuous and its moral teachings generally good. I was very wrong.

Ohio: I am twenty-three and I have been distressed about religion since I was fifteen. I never knew what an atheist was. After I watched that show I felt great! Is there something I have to do to become an atheist? I would like to be one very much.

Just for fun, here are some excerpts from the religious letters:

Florida: I don't care what drugs you are on, Jesus can set you free.

North Carolina: Four thousand years of words spoken by faithful men allowed God to create the seed in the womb of a virgin to allow Christ's entry into the world in a legal human body. Join the team!

New Hampshire: This may be the reason you pulled away from Christ: Catholics are *not* Christians! Get back to the *King James Version*.

North Carolina: Homosexuals, you are dying in your sin! Many are paying millions to find a cure. I have the cure. God loves you, and so do I. Many hate me for telling the truth.

Ohio: I just watched Donahue and I was appalled! It's more proof that Satan abounds. You seem so intellectual and on top of everything. Well, I'm just a simple country girl, yet I feel so far above you. You'll find out in the very end, but I doubt if you'd listen to me.

Minnesota: The Word of God is too precious to waste on blind unbelievers that are going to burn in the everlasting hellfire that will be prepared for all that mock *God*. You were a clear picture of a stupid deviate. Prepare to Meet the God of All Creation. This is the *End* generation.

Wisconsin: It grieves my soul when I hear people Blasphemy [sic] my Savior. I'd be scared to death. Unless you except [sic] Jesus, your entire organization are going to *Hell* and will *Burn* forever and ever and ever. Love ya. You will be in my prayers.

I t is interesting to see the similarity of freethought views across the continent, even though there is no such thing as a "freethought church." Atheists and agnostics spring up on their own, as individual thinkers, not as a result of a preacher or mass movement. That is the point. It is impressive that without any deliberate cultivation, individual atheists and agnostics can be found growing like freethought wildflowers here and there, taking root in a hostile environment, decorating the landscape. We are definitely a movement, but a new kind of movement: one without followers. Every freethinker is a leader.

Freethought Today, January/February, 1989.
Originally, "Freethought Movement Alive And Well."

42

Immovable Wall

Whathappens when an irresistible force meets an immovable object? Isaac Asimov has been credited as the first to answer that question. It is impossible to imagine either of these items, since each would require infinite mass/energy. Even if we could mathematically describe one of these objects, it is inconceivable that they could coexist in the same hypothetical universe of infinite density. Therefore, Asimov quipped, if an irresistible force met an immovable object you would have . . . "an inconceivable event"!

Christianity is quite resistible, and the "wall of separation between church and state" has not always been immovable, but when the two clash they can produce some bizarre effects. I have been involved with one such inconceivable event.

The not-so-irresistible force is the Strode family of North Carolina, which I have encountered twice on national television, first on May 4, 1988 when I represented the Freedom From Religion Foundation on the "Sally Jessy Raphael Show," then June 14 on the "Oprah Winfrey Show." Both programs centered on the recent controversy involving three children from a fundamentalist family who have been suspended from school because they refuse to stop preaching on school property. The kids have been taught to preach not just hellfire and brimstone but to accuse bystanders of "sexual immorality," at an elementary school! I was invited because I used to be a street preacher myself.

[Later, I appeared on four more shows with the same family: the national "Morton Downey, Jr. Show" (more as a victim than a guest), the national "Maury Povich Show," the syndicated WWOR "People Are Talking" show, and Philadelphia's "People Are Talking."]

On Sally's show the children gave an example of their preaching techniques. First Duffey, the ten-year-old, stood leaning forward from the waist and screamed slowly at the top of his voice, "He that committeth sin is of the Devil!" Then his five-year-old brother, Matthew, put his bible beside his face and did the same thing. It was pathetic. They are little robots. I almost cried on camera when I saw this form of child abuse being proudly broadcast to America.

"Duffey, what does *whoremonger* mean?" Sally asked. The boy was silent. "Do you use that word when you preach?"

"Yes," he answered slowly, looking lost.

"Do you know what it means?" she asked again. After a painful silence the boy finally said he understood the word but couldn't think of a way to explain it.

On the "Oprah Winfrey Show," after a repeat performance of Duffey's preaching skills, he was asked to explain one of the bible verses in his own words, and the only response he could give was to remind Oprah that sometimes even the Old Testament prophets spoke the "word of the Lord" without understanding what they were saying! The children clearly do not know what they are preaching.

The six-year-old sister Pepper is not allowed to preach because "the bible says that women are to keep silent," her father explained.

"Pepper, how does that make you feel?" Sally asked.

"Happy," she said, grinning and squirming like a normal, nervous first-grader. That was the only word the little girl said during the show, and it brought the house down.

In the mind of the believer, Christianity is an irresistible force. During both shows David Strode, the father, displayed a smiling, gum-chewing smugness that enraged the audience. At one point he calmly pronounced, "Sally, you will have to go to hell."

"Sir," she responded slowly, "there are days when hell is having to do a show with guests like you!"

On both shows I identified myself as an atheist, but I was not perceived as the enemy! Sally's audience hated this family so much that my lack of belief seemed irrelevant. Although I was called a "Judas Iscariot" and an "adulterer" by Mr. Strode, and a "fool" by Mrs. Strode, quoting *Psalm 14:1* (I thought

283

she wasn't supposed to preach), I found myself in the odd position of being reluctantly appreciated by the mainly Christian audience. "These kids are like puppets," I said, "little clones, manipulated by their church and their family to do their religious dirty work. This borders on child abuse." This type of statement drew loud applause. However, the response was less enthusiastic when I said, "These Christians are like those animals who go around spraying their territory."

Well, what is the problem here? No one denies these people the legal right to preach their religious views. No one says they can't stand in a church and exercise their freedom of speech and religion, as long as they are not breaking any laws. In America, they can espouse any eccentric ideas they choose. This is a precious principle, especially to us freethinkers.

I used to preach on street corners myself. Although I got some funny looks, I was never asked to leave. Ignoring for a moment the moral issue of brainwashing, the Strode family has every right to stand on the public sidewalk and preach their little hearts out, as long as they are not violating any public ordinances, like obstructing traffic or disturbing the peace (you would think Christians would want to be law-abiding); but as soon as they step onto the school property, that is a different story.

The public school belongs to all of us. When we send our children to school we are trusting the state to take care of them. We expect that all children will be treated fairly with respect to race, sex, status, national origin and religion. We demand that the educational system be actively neutral in religious matters, keeping discussions of individual religious conscience out of the classroom, and keeping regular and/or organized religious meetings off the school grounds. Private religious views should be just that: private. That is why the Bill of Rights includes the First Amendment, which protects all the freedoms of conscience. There is ample opportunity for believers to practice their religion in churches, homes, and other public areas that do not give the appearance of state support or endorsement. (Of course, any child at school is free to pray individually, or to engage in spontaneous unorganized religious discussion during break, as long as there is no disruption to the regular school process and no support or encouragement from school officials or outsiders.)

The principal of Eastfield Elementary School in Marion, North Carolina was correct to suspend these kids: it is unconstitutional for a public school to allow a regular religious practice on its property. When the Strode children stand on the school grounds, yelling hellfire to students and teachers entering the building, their actions are not only rude, but just plain unAmerican.

What would you do if some preachers surprised you by entering your front door while you were eating dinner? Does anyone have the right to barge into anyone else's home uninvited and start moralizing? How would the Strode family feel if secular humanists stood on their front lawn singing freethought songs all day? You can bet they would call the police, at minimum.

The public school is the home of all Americans: Catholics, Protestants, Buddhists, Moslems, Jews, atheists—we all pay taxes. No one has the right to use our "home" in this manner. The public school is not a church. It is more "sacred" than a church. It is democratic, pluralistic America.

Christians are supposed to obey Jesus's advice to "render therefore unto Caesar the things that are Caesar's." *(Matthew 22:21)* In America, the public schools belong to Caesar.

The Strode family is always preaching against the "carnal sins." On the "Sally Jessy Raphael Show," the parents (in front of their children and the world) embarrassingly bragged about their own sins of "fornication, drunkenness and adultery." This mind-set is very much like a sexual fixation. As with Jimmy Swaggart, they are afraid of their own sensual urges, constantly fighting "the Devil" and suppressing the temptations of "original sin." They are morally stunted. Since there seems to be a human principle that makes you want what you can't have, the conflict expands, demanding greater resistance. No wonder these people go crazy! Christians have an unhealthy view of human nature, and they seem hell-bent on proving it. If they had a more natural view of self and sex, and if they were allowed to grow to a level of self confidence, they could become mature adults able to handle their own sexuality in a responsible and positive manner. As it is, they have to fight themselves all through their lives, denigrating their humanness, blaming their own shortcomings on "Satan," and visualizing the objects of their desires as "witches," "whores," and "harlots."

Of course, sexism and perversion are not the only fruits of Christianity. David Strode has admitted that he has beaten his wife and children, with pride. His children claim that their father is merely obeying God when he punishes them. (Duffey has complained that sometimes his father hits him too hard, and Mrs. Strode once filed criminal charges after being beaten, though she is now publicly supportive of her husband.)

Oprah Winfrey asked Mr. Strode if he believed that all humans were created equal. After his mushy answer, I interrupted and said, "Oprah, I read that this man teaches his children that blacks were born to be slaves." Her racially mixed audience was shocked at this revelation. Christians who were originally defending the Strodes suddenly and vehemently turned against them as they were forced to endure his torturous explanation from *Genesis 9:18-27* of how the descendants of Ham (black) were cursed in the Old Testament, condemned to be servants to Japheth (whites) and Shem (yellows).

"Is this the kind of thing your children are preaching in our public schools?" I asked. Imagine!

The Strode family can't get along with anyone. Duffey says he never really had any friends. Their Christian neighbors have almost come to violence in their demands that the kids stop harassing the other children with preaching. Their own pastor, who initially encouraged them to preach on the streets, is now criticizing their extreme behavior, claiming that David has a "persecution complex." (They consequently left that church and formed their own independent ministry.) The Strodes were unable to get along with the mainly Christian television audiences. And all of this is just Protestant vs. Protestant! Whenever religious issues are brought into the public arena, divisive fireworks follow.

People like this seem to thrive on persecution. If it weren't for the children, the best way to treat such attention-seekers is simply to ignore them. They love to be criticized because this validates their ministry. Jesus reportedly said, "Blessed are they which are persecuted for righteousness' sake . . . Rejoice, and be exceeding glad: for great is your reward in heaven: for so persecuted they the prophets which were before you." *(Matthew 5:10-12)* When you "persecute" someone like David Strode, you do him a favor.

But we can't ignore them, not completely. They are abusing their children. They are subjecting the kids to daily brainwashing. They are teaching the next generation that Catholicism is the religion of the Antichrist (Devil); that the world will end soon, probably by an Apocalypse (Mr. Strode told me in 1988 that it would all be over by 1992, but on the 1992 "Maury Povich Show" he changed it to the year 2000); that atheists are wicked; that the races should be kept pure; that we should hate the world we live in; that all nonChristian educational systems are evil; that evolution is a Satanic lie; and that women must be subservient. How can we hear of such tyranny and not feel compassion for those children?

Is this what we want in our schools? Shall the playground become a battlefield? This divisive controversy proves the need for an immovable "wall of separation between church and state."
Freethought Today, July, 1988

43

Ethnics Without God

IN AUGUST 1987 I flew to Baltimore to be a guest on Richard Sher's "People Are Talking" TV show. The topic was ministers-turned-atheists. I was joined by the articulate Delos McKown, Professor of Philosophy at Alabama's Auburn University, who is likewise a former clergy and member of the Freedom From Religion Foundation. As expected, the show was very lively and the audience was hostile, except for two of our Maryland members. I was told to "shut your mouth," Delos was labeled "wretched," Foundation member Carole (in the audience) was called "pathetic," Voltaire was accused of "burning bibles," and atheists were blamed for the flat-earth theory! Nobody converted, either way, but nonreligion was strongly presented.

The host acted genuinely surprised that people like us would want to air our views. Why are we so pushy? "Why do you go on these shows?" he asked.

"Well, you invited us," I answered.

"You just want to stir up trouble!" Delos quipped. We explained that atheists don't run into churches to drag believers out of their pews. We don't impose weekly tithes to erect gaudy churches inflicting our views on the world. Preachers daily drone from the pulpit, radio and TV, street corners, and in print. Would the host have asked a minister: "Why do you feel the need to publicize your views?"

Delos and I had agreed before the show that there was little chance we would win any arguments with such an audience, and that our primary aim was to reach freethinking viewers. Although there are about twenty million atheists in the United States, our organized numbers are tiny. Religionists, on the other hand, have had massive resources and vast opportunities to advertise. *They have had their say.* It is time the world heard another side. This can be better accomplished if nonbelievers pool talents and resources, and speak with organized clout. When the Freedom From Religion Foundation is publicized we usually attract members.

I can't resist telling what happened after the show, while I was at the airport waiting for my flight back to Madison. I was wearing my "I'm Your Friendly Neighborhood Atheist" shirt and reading Kai Nielsen's book, *Ethics Without God.* A young woman with an armful of literature approached me and said, "Excuse me, sir! I noticed you are reading a book about God."

I looked up and said, "Yes, this is Nielsen's classic on morality," holding it up so she could read the title.

"***Ethnics** Without God,*" she said. "Very interesting. Tell me, sir, have you ever heard about Pentecost?" She was canvassing the airport trying to get believers to believe in speaking-in-tongues! She asked if I were familiar with the bible. I told her I was, and that I was an atheist. We had a lively conversation, you can imagine.

After a while she said, "Well, you can deny anything you like, but you have no right to tell me that my personal experience with Jesus is false."

"Oh, I believe you," I answered. "I have had the same experience myself." I told her that when I was a Christian I had often felt inner strength, joy, peace and love. I had believed that I was in direct communication with an almighty deity. "But none of this points to anything outside of the mind. You are having a very real delusion."

When she handed me some literature, I took some Foundation brochures out of my pocket and offered to exchange. She quickly pulled her tracts back and retreated a step.

"What's the matter?" I asked. "If you expect me to read *your* stuff, don't you think you should also be open-minded?"

"No!" she said. "I mean—yes. We should be open-minded about the *Bible.*"

"And you think we should be close-minded to philosophies with which we differ?" I asked, holding my material out to her.

"Yes, I am close-minded," she confessed. "Well, I mean, we *should* be open-minded," she stammered. Finally noticing what my shirt said, she broke into a warm laugh. "That's terrible!" she said, teasingly, realizing the absurdity of the situation.

"What's so terrible about a friendly atheist?" I asked, as we exchanged material. "I'm on your side—I think we all need to seek as much truth as we can."

I know I didn't change this person's mind about religion, but perhaps I altered her opinion of atheists. Just as important, I think, is the fact that the people sitting around us heard every word of the incident. I'm sure they were happy I was the one she picked on. I like to think some of them were glad to see a religious nuisance challenged, to hear someone speak up for the other side.

Freethinkers have suffered from bad press, and it is time to correct that image. If we don't challenge the prevailing myths and stereotypes, superstition will win by default. If we hide freethought, we will fail to find others who are sympathetic to rationalism, who can lend the talents and resources necessary to confront religious nonsense.

Many Foundation members have suggested methods of advertising freethought: T-shirts, bumper stickers, letters to the editor, classified ads, radio and TV commercials, buttons, tracts, word of mouth, pickets, official protests, lawsuits, freethought literature in stores and libraries, films, awards, music, debates, talk shows, and more. But I would also like to risk dusting off one of my old motivational sermons and dare to apply it here: "Your best witness is your life."

If you are attracted to something, it is because it is attractive. Most freethinkers I have met are very likable people. They are friendly, thoughtful, articulate, productive, and caring individuals. Of course, this does not make atheism correct, but it can help make atheism attractive. Half our image problem would be solved if people would simply identify themselves as freethinkers.

I am amazed at how many opportunities there are to advertise freethought. When someone says, "God bless you" after I sneeze, I smile and say: "Thank you, but that's a funny thing to say to an atheist!" When making a purchase I sometimes comment, "Just because I use this currency doesn't mean I endorse the message on it. It's not easy being an atheist." And I almost always carry material with me, especially when traveling. I would hate to think that an interested person would not know how to join our group. They might be another Delos McKown, or Ruth Green (author of *The Born Again Skeptic's Guide to the Bible*).

Atheists and agnostics are notoriously individualistic. They are not all joiners. They are not all activists. I have even had a closet atheist criticize my openness as a replay of religious tactics. But what am I supposed to do? Some of us just can't keep our mouths shut. This world is too beautiful to be left to

Christians. Or Moslems. Or whatever.

Did you know that the word *ethnic* originally meant *heathen*? Since we all have cultural and national heritages of which we may be proud, I guess it could be said that freethinkers truly are "ethnics without god," of which we may also be proud.

Freethought Today, October, 1987

44

Popping Off

I'VE NEVER BEEN bounced from a meeting before. But I couldn't help it; I got myself thrown out of Peter Popoff's "miracle" rally.

Peter Popoff is the "faith-healer" who was exposed as a fraud by James Randi on the Johnny Carson Show. Roaming through an audience, Popoff would reveal suspiciously precise details about individuals that he could not possibly have known: names, addresses, exact illnesses. Randi's sleuthing uncovered the fact that Popoff's wife, from another room, was transmitting the data to a receiver in Popoff's hearing aid (why does a faith healer need a hearing aid?) as she viewed the meeting on a video monitor. She had slickly interviewed dozens of people before meetings, learning who could walk a little (whom Peter should select) and who was incurable (whom Peter should avoid), filling out a "prayer card" noting their appearance, address, and other details. With his wife piping information into his ear, Popoff appeared to have the God-given "gift of knowledge."

After public exposure, Popoff's ministry took a nose dive. Dozens of TV stations cancelled his show, fearing legal liability and a negative public image. Popoff's income dropped sharply from the $550,000 a month he admits he was receiving; his meetings shrank to a few dozen dupes.

When Foundation member Mike Miller learned that Popoff was coming to the Pfister Hotel in Milwaukee, he phoned our offices. For two weeks before the June 7, 1990 "Miracle Crusade," we tried to convince the Pfister to cancel the meeting. We sent them articles from *Freethought Today* and *Free Inquiry* documenting Popoff's antics. We asked the Pfister Hotel why it would want to jeopardize its charming reputation or risk liability by doing business with this con man. They said they would investigate; but they didn't cancel. We also called on the District Attorney to investigate Popoff's false advertising and fraudulent medical practice. Although this is a serious public health issue, Milwaukee's D.A. declined to follow through, citing "wide latitude" with religious groups. So we contacted the local media about our plans for a public protest.

On June 7, two carloads of Foundation members traveled from Madison to meet with members of the Wisconsin Committee for Rational Inquiry, directed by Mary Beth Emmerichs, also a Foundation member. Our strategy was to protest the Popoff meeting from various angles.

Helen and Mike Hakeem stood at one hotel entrance, and Ken Taubert and I stood at another, handing out fliers condemning "con artists" who prey on the gullible, detailing proof of Popoff's fraud. There were many activities at the Pfister that night (including a medical school graduation in the room next to Popoff!), but it was easy to spot those who were headed for healing: they were mostly poor, ill, and toting bibles. Ken and I did a double-take when we realized that the Governor of Wisconsin was standing between us! (Governor Tommy Thompson apparently had had dinner at the hotel after meeting with President Bush, who had been in town that afternoon. The Pfister does have a reputation.) We were glad to see that Tommy—a religionist who does not have the smartest reputation himself—was *leaving* the hotel.

One woman read our flier, tore it up and hollered, "Con artist! I don't wanna hear 'bout no con artist."

Ken and I helped a man get over the curb with his wheel chair. He looked like a Viet Nam veteran. As we directed him to the Popoff meeting in the seventh-floor Imperial Ballroom, we asked him to read our information. He did so carefully, giving us a backward glance as he headed for the elevator.

Meanwhile, Mike Miller and Jim Dew (both doctoral candidates in psychology) attended the hour-early warm-up session. This is the time when Popoff's assistant tries to identify candidates for "healing." Mike had written Popoff that he was dying (we're all dying), and was hoping to be singled out for a "healing." He tried to look sick and gullible as Popoff's assistant, Larry Skelton (Popoff's wife was not present), combed the early arrivals for information. Jim bravely distributed a flier that Mike had prepared which made reference to the biblical verse, "Beware of false prophets." Although Skelton was annoyed, none of the seventy or eighty people present objected.

As the crusade started, with Skelton's agonizing attempts to sing gospel songs, the Hakeems, Ken and I found chairs together in the center of the room, opposite the entrance on the other side. There was no pianist, just a poor quality pre-recorded sound track played through speakers placed on the platform, to which Skelton sang, obnoxiously off pitch. If you could draw a caricature of a snake con artist, it would look just like Skelton, complete with a Vaudevillian mustache. It was all pre-packaged and tacky. But the people had come to see miracles, and they were enraptured with the whole phony spectacle.

A reporter from the *Milwaukee Journal*, alerted by us, attended the meeting. When his photographer stood up, Skelton waved him off with "No pictures."

The first thirty minutes of Popoff's act was a sales pitch. He laboriously went through each of his books, cassettes, and videos, pointing to the table at the back of the room where they were all for sale. The actual "sermon" was about how an angel had helped Popoff's family escape from German prison camp, singling him out for the ministry. After this ridiculous story, Popoff launched into his faith-healing routine, which is the main reason the people had come.

Prowling about the room, he grabbed a woman's head, deliberately mussed up her hair, shook her and pronounced her healed. He told an old woman to get up and ordered her not just to walk, but to prance around the ballroom. The audience punctuated his "healings" by loudly speaking in tongues, raising their arms, shaking, crying, and hollering "Amen," "Thank you, Jesus!" and "Hallelujah!" It had the feel of one of those professional wrestling matches on TV.

Popoff's art of crowd manipulation involved working himself and the crowd up to a frantic pitch, then down to a whisper, or a few seconds of dramatic silence before he got another Message From God. He would stop, quickly turn and point, saying, "Back pain! Who has back pain? Is it you?" Usually more than one person would raise a hand. Looking down at his bible (he has abandoned his radio gimmick), Popoff would venture, "Roger. Does the name Roger mean anything?" Following a tremendous silence, Roger or someone who was praying for a Roger, would raise a hand.

Popoff approached one woman, saying, "Back pain." But she said her feet were hurting. "You have pain in your back *and* your legs," he improvised without missing a beat. He "cured" this woman, Praise Jesus!

It was comical; and it was sad. The man was practicing medicine without a license, raising false hopes and endangering lives. (Many of his believers have discarded medicine or cancelled doctors' appointments.) I remembered having participated in meetings just like this when I was a full-gospel evangelist, and I was ashamed. As I sat there watching the charade I started a slow burn. Ken said he looked over at me and thought that I was about to explode.

After about forty minutes into the sideshow, Popoff called out, "Pain behind the ear!" A heavy, balding man stood up. "Is it you?" Popoff asked. "I knew it, because I felt this burning behind my own ear," he said to the hushed crowd.

It was the perfect moment; I couldn't resist. "What a joke!" I projected strongly into the silence. "You're playing a game, Peter, but it's not working! Nobody is being healed tonight!"

Popoff gaped at me, mouth wide open. He looked like a kid who had got caught with his hand in the cookie jar. He said nothing. People in the audience, after a few silent seconds, started chanting at me: "We rebuke you, Satan! In the name of Jesus!"

Since I had the floor uncontested, I stood up and continued my sermon. People were praying in tongues, some standing and extending their arms toward me. I noticed the red-faced Skelton huffing around the room in my direction.

All the while, Popoff was frozen. The microphone hung at his side. It is difficult to describe his expression: slack-jawed, empty, afraid, timid, guilty. Knocked out of his routine, the man was helpless.

Skelton grabbed my arm and said, "We paid a lot of money for this ballroom. Why don't you rent your own auditorium? You're disrupting our meeting and I'll have to ask you to leave." (Notice the emphasis was financial, not spiritual. Why didn't he or Popoff do another miracle to give me lockjaw?)

I said I would be happy to leave, but that I could hardly be accused of "disrupting" a meeting like this. (All along, Popoff had been asking the audience to respond, and that's what I was doing.) As I walked in a deliberate pace through the audience on my way out, passing Popoff, who was still quietly trapped in the middle of the room, I turned to him and said, "*You* are the one who is sick tonight. You need professional help."

At this point, Ken, the Hakeems, and some of the other freethinkers joined the protest, standing, speaking, and leaving the room behind me. When a Christian woman yelled at me, "You are wrong," I reminded the group that Popoff is the one who was exposed as a fraud, that they were being tricked and robbed.

All of the skeptics left the room together, and right behind us came the man in the wheelchair whom Ken and I had originally helped over the curb.

He told us that Popoff had ignored him, stepping around his wheelchair *seven* times during the meeting. He still believed that God is real, but admitted that Popoff is a fake.

When the meeting ended about twenty minutes later, Beth and Jerome passed out fliers to the believers exiting the ballroom. The fliers repeated James Randi's offer of $10,000 to anyone who could prove an organic healing by faith alone. Many refused the fliers, apparently tipped off by Popoff that the Devil was waiting outside the door.

The *Milwaukee Journal* ran a story the next morning, alerting readers to the possibility of religious fraud, and reporting on the presence of skeptical, freethinking groups. The report unfortunately noted that Popoff's offering baskets were bulging with money, apparently unaffected by us "naysayers."

I'm not recommending that freethinkers disrupt religious meetings, but I have to admit that it was pretty satisfying to "pop off" at Popoff.
Freethought Today, August, 1990

45

Bible-Belt
Journalism

This letter was printed in the Arizona Daily Sun, Flagstaff, January 17, 1990, in response to a story that ran on New Year's Eve about a tragic multi-vehicle accident in the fog. Many lives were lost.

I read with dismay your front-page December 31 stories about the tragic pile-up on I-40. Who would not be saddened by such a horror?

I was surprised, however, by what appears to be an unnecessary intrusion of religious bias into the related story, "Family thankful to survive horror." It is not inappropriate for a reporter to quote the religious beliefs of interviewees, or to mention religion if it is relevant to the story, as long as it is objective and balanced. Sweitzer's piece, however, seems to cross the line from reporting to Christian cheerleading.

The Singletons prayed before leaving on their trip, and it is their belief that this prayer kept them alive. They are entitled to this belief, but Sweitzer says they "know who saved them." He gives the completely irrelevant report that "Singleton's wife talked earnestly to one young trucker and he became a born again Christian on the spot," assuming that this is a good thing, assuming that your readers would know what is a born again Christian, and doing nothing to move the story. If the trucker had converted to Islam during the tragedy, would that have been deemed relevant?

The praise and thanksgiving should go to the school districts that helped with buses, to the Flagstaff police and fire departments who saved lives, to the expert medical care of the Flagstaff Medical Center, and to the humanitarian efforts of the Red Cross. These are human, secular groups that put compassion into action. (The founder of the American Red Cross, Clara Barton, was a freethinker.) It is understandable that individuals will turn to their faith for comfort in times of distress, but using such an occasion to thank and recognize a deity is ludicrous.

Why would a deity allow such an accident? Were those who were killed and injured undeserving of protection? Did the victims not pray hard enough that day? When the accident first started to occur, when the first vehicle went out of control, did the watchful deity say, "Okay, here we go? Let's see, car #6 swerve this way because you haven't prayed all week. Truck #4 can totally flip out of control because the driver missed church last week. Oh look! Van #3 has occupants who prayed this morning; OK, smash the van but not too hard, they can probably scramble out and up the hill to observe how I punish the atheist in the station wagon and, let's see. Yes! I'll crush the mother, father, and sister, but let the one little girl live a few hours." And so on.

Who could love such a monster?

Did it occur to the Singletons, or the reporter, that if they had not spent the time praying that morning before leaving on their trip, their car might have been a mile or two farther up the road (depending on how long they prayed), avoiding the accident altogether?

Let's ask the injured (we can't ask the fatalities) if any of them prayed that morning. It was the Sabbath, after all. How many of them are (were) deeply religious people? What kind of message does this insensitive story send to those less fortunate?

One of the survivors of the crash of flight 232 in Iowa is an atheist and secular humanist, Peter Wernick. He credits his survival with the heroic human efforts of the pilots, and with luck. Many Christians died in that crash.

Let's hear the Singleton's story. But let's be careful to avoid "Bible-belt journalism" in the reporting.

Dan Barker

Freedom From Religion Foundation, Madison, Wisconsin

T here is a phenomenon among true believers which psychologists might call "projection." When some people hear criticism of their religious views, it makes them angry and they project that anger back on the messenger. They assume that the feelings they experience when they read the criticism are the same feelings the skeptic had when it was written. My letter was a rational, satirical criticism that I consider compassionate and helpful, not polemical. After all, when the Singletons said God spared them, exactly what do they think was happening?

My letter sparked a blast of protest. A flurry of angry responses was published in the paper. Rev. Spaulding of the Luthern Community Church wrote: "What a classic display of cruel, tasteless intolerance and 'Atheistic-belt' journalism! . . . I feel sorry for someone so ruled by the monster of hate within himself." See the projection here? It is not nice to criticize God. "If God were as he described," he continues candidly, "we would all wish to be free from such religion." That was my point exactly.

"[Barker's] tirade against a Higher Power . . . is offensive," wrote Rev. Cernek of the Evangelical Free Church. "Reconciling pain and suffering in our world with a loving God [is] a struggle to thoughtful believers. But the experience of many is that God's presence is felt even in pain. . . . [A]ccidents are never an expression of God's petty score-keeping as Dan Barker's satire suggests. I would hope the *Arizona Daily Sun* would show more prudence in the future than to give a platform to such flagrant and bombastic patter." These pastors want to protect their flocks from critical analysis of their faith by intimidating editors into censoring freethought views. His claim that God's presence is felt in pain is certainly not less "flagrant and bombastic" than my analysis.

"[Mr. Barker] went on to make a joke of a horrendous situation, for his own benefit," one woman wrote. "It seems clear to me," another woman added, "that Barker's letter is nothing more than a smear campaign against Judeo-Christian beliefs, utilizing tragedy and sensationalism to make his point." Who is guilty of utilizing tragedy? I simply gave credit where credit is due. The Singletons are the ones who used tragedy to make it appear that they are favored people.

Another man wrote paranoically: "Mr. Barker is attempting to have the media in each state submit to his irrational, narrow views and have any mention of religious belief driven from public view. . . . Driven by irrational thoughts, ignorance, and hatred, many people have targeted blacks, or Jews, or Christians, or women, etc. as being inferior and unworthy of equal rights." This is another example of projection. My letter did not say what he claims. It is as if criticism of religion touches a button, and then anything might come flying out. It is Christianity, not freethought, that has targeted blacks, Jews, and women.

There were many religious letters like these, and they were not short. It was as if the newspaper were apologizing to the community by allowing such a disproportionate number of Christian responses to my single letter. One of the members of the Freedom From Religion Foundation who kept track of the issue wrote me: "Your letter to the Sun has done this community a real service in focusing attention on the subject."

There is a positive ending to this story—a minor victory. Two years later there was another accident on the interstate outside of Flagstaff. It was not as bad as the first accident, but it was still a huge local tragedy. The same reporter, Paul Sweitzer, wrote the story for the *Arizona Daily Sun,* and this time there was not a single word about religion.

The Stay-Away Pope Polka
by Dan Barker

Chorus: Pope, Pope, stay away!
Don't come back some other day.
It's worse than a sin that we have to pay
To hear you preach against the American way.

How dare you show your face in the great USA,
Where dictators like you are out of place!
We believe in freedom and democracy here,
And fairness for the whole human race.
Now here you come parading in your pompous royal clatter,
Pretending that you govern the earth.
But a million mouths are hungry while the church is growing fatter.
That shows us just how much you are worth.

You always say that Woman is "God's holy flower,"
But you really cannot hide what you mean.
If you control her body and won't let her share the power,
She just becomes a breeding machine.
The world is overcrowded, and they're dying of starvation,
And you tell us what we need is a Prayer!
A simple word from you could help control the population,
But, No! You're too religious to care.

You think that we should cower to your great medieval power,
But who the Devil do you think you are?
Since we can't put up with you, why should we put you up?
This is really going much too far!
You say to "Pray for Peace," while your Inquisition rages,
And you push us to the end of our rope.
We will never get away from the bloody Dark Ages,
Till we've excommunicated the Pope.

Spanish: Papa, Papa, ya puedes ir!
Todos no te pedimos venir.
Si vas a predicar como debemos vivir,
No queremos oir lo que puedes decir.

© *Copyright 1987 by Dan Barker. Song lyrics. This was written as a
protest to the Pope's 1987 tax-supported visit to America. It was played on
the radio in all nine cities that the Pope visited, and sung by protest groups
outside his meetings, including the Gay Rights activists in San Francisco
(who changed "American way" to "American gay.").*

300

SEPARATING
STATE
AND
CHURCH

Part 6

Losing Faith in Faith

46

What's in a Phrase?

WHENEVER ONE OF the staff members of the Freedom From Religion Foundation does a call-in radio talkshow about the separation of church and state, there almost invariably will be a call from a Christian who says that the phrase "separation of church and state" cannot be found anywhere in the United States Constitution.

This is true.

It is also true that "separation of powers" appears nowhere in the Constitution. Neither do "Bill of Rights," "fair trial," "interstate commerce," "self-incrimination," "right to privacy," "freedom of association," or "religious liberty." Yet these phrases have come to represent well-established constitutional principles.

There is excellent historic and legal precedent for invoking "separation of church and state." President Thomas Jefferson coined the phrase in 1802 in a letter to the Danbury Baptist Association, commenting on the Establishment Clause:

"I contemplate with sovereign reverence that act of the whole American people which declared that their legislature should 'make no law respecting an establishment of religion, or prohibiting the free exercise thereof,' thus building a wall of separation between church and state."

This letter cannot be minimized. Jefferson gave it much thought, and before sending it, he cleared it with his attorney general, Levi Lincoln:

"The Baptist address, now enclosed, admits of a condemnation of the alliance between Church & State, under the authority of the Constitution. It furnishes an occasion, too, which I have long wished to find, of saying why I do not proclaim fastings and thanksgivings, as my predecessors did.

" . . . I forsee no opportunity of doing it more pertinently . . . Will you be so good as to examine the answer, and suggest any alterations which might prevent an ill effect, or promote a good one among the people?"

The Supreme Court has often used Jefferson's phrase "wall of separation between church and state." In 1947 *(Everson v. Board of Education),* they wrote:

"Neither a state nor the Federal Government can set up a church. Neither can pass laws which aid one religion, aid all religions, or prefer one religion over another. Neither can force or influence a person to go to or remain away from church against his will or force him to profess a belief or disbelief in any religion. No person can be punished for entertaining or professing religious beliefs or disbeliefs, for church attendance or nonattendance. No tax in any amount, large or small, can be levied to support any religious activities or institutions, whatever they may be called, or whatever form they may adopt to teach or practice religion. Neither a state nor the Federal Government can, openly or secretly, participate in the affairs of any religious organizations or groups, and vice versa. In the words of Thomas Jefferson, the clause against establishment of religion by law was intended to erect 'a wall of separation between Church and State.' "

In fact, an authoritative 1944 Catholic text said, "Our Federal and State constitutions forbid the legal establishment of religion thereby insuring the separation of Church and State . . ." (See *Catholic Principles of Politics,* Ryan and Boland, MacMillan, 1948). Most Protestant denominations officially support the principle, although the Catholic hierarchy is changing its tune now that Catholicism is not such a minority in America. Many religionists, during their sober moments, recognize that keeping religion and government separate is good for their church.

The next time believers tell you that "separation of church and state" does not appear in our founding document, tell them to stop using the word "trinity." The word "trinity" appears nowhere in the bible. Neither does Rapture, or Second Coming, or Original Sin. If they are still unfazed (or unphrased) by this, then add Omniscience, Omnipresence, Supernatural, Transcendence, Afterlife, Deity, Divinity, Theology, Monotheism, Missionary, Immaculate Conception, Christmas, Christianity, Evangelical, Fundamentalist, Methodist, Catholic, Pope, Cardinal, Catechism, Purgatory, Penance, Transubstantiation, Excommunication, Dogma, Chastity, Unpardonable Sin, Infallibility, Inerrancy, Incarnation, Epiphany, Sermon, Sermon on the Mount, Triumphal Entry, Palm Sunday, Last Supper, Eucharist, the Lord's Prayer, Good Friday, Doubting Thomas, Advent, Sunday School, Dead Sea, Golden Rule, Moral, Morality, Ethics, Patriotism, Education, Atheism, Apostasy, Conservative (Liberal *is* in), Capital Punishment, Monogamy, Abortion, Pornography, Homosexual, Lesbian, Fairness, Logic, Republic, Democracy, Capitalism, Funeral, Decalogue, or Bible.

Some of these words appear in some of the looser bible paraphrases, which are not translations. If believers argue that these words represent concepts that are derived from their founding document, then they have made your point. "Separation of church and state" is here to stay.

Freethought Today, September, 1990

47

Tradition

A FREETHINKER IS "a person who forms opinions about religion on the basis of reason, independently of tradition, authority, or established belief." This does not mean that freethinkers ignore tradition, authority, or established belief, or that these things are not important. The "humanistic tradition" can be meaningful, and the combined "authority" of scientists can help us laypersons form our opinions on evolution or miracles. But none of these things, *by themselves* constitutes proof.

Tradition can be useful, however, as a way to counter those who claim that America is a "Christian nation." We can play the "tradition" game as well as they can, if they insist.

One of the most common refrains is that the Colonists came here to escape religious persecution and to establish a Christian country. This is only partly true. The first European colony on the continent was Jamestown, not Plymouth Rock. Jamestown was not a religious experiment; it was simple colonization for settlement and trade.

Although the Mayflower passengers established the first *permanent* colony of Europeans, slightly less than half of them were Puritans in search of religious freedom. The majority were settlers along for the ride to opportunity.

In any event, the Colonists of the 1630's did not establish our country. The

United States of America was founded a century and a half later. If we are going to go back one hundred and fifty years before our founding, why stop there? Native Americans were on this continent at least twelve thousand years before the American Revolution. These were the true discoverers of our land, and if we must return to the tradition of our founders, then all "true Americans" should adopt the pantheistic, polytheistic, natural systems of Native American religions. The "Christian nation" argument is racist. (So is Columbus Day, for that matter.)

Christian-nation advocates like to point to the Declaration of Independence. But Jefferson was a Deist, and his phrase "Nature's God" is more in line with Native American views than with the middle eastern concept of a personal god who writes books and interferes with history. The words "Jesus," "Christ," or "Christian" appear nowhere in the Declaration. If this is a Christian nation, why doesn't it say so somewhere?

The Declaration of Independence had nothing to do with religious freedom, and many of its concepts are contrary to the bible. The purpose of the Revolutionary War was to "dissolve the political bands." The Declaration dealt with laws, representation, emigration, administration of justice, military, trade, taxation without consent, trial by jury, plunder and war—nothing about religious freedom or a "Christian nation." It recognizes that a group of people has a "separate and equal station," an idea that is contradicted by the bible. The concept that "governments are instituted among men, deriving their just powers from the consent of the governed," is entirely unbiblical. (The bible says that the power comes from God.) The idea that the people can organize "its powers in such form, as *to them* shall seem most likely to effect their safety and happiness" goes against the biblical warning that "There is a way that seemeth right unto a man; but the ends thereof are the ways of death." Instead of recognizing the authority of God, the Declaration of Independence bases itself on "the name and by authority of the good people of these Colonies." It is a humanistic document.

Even if the Declaration of Independence were religious, declaring everything that modern Christians wish it had said, we do not live under that document. We are governed by the Constitution, which is completely secular. Like the Declaration, the Constitution bases its authority on "We, The People," not on a deity. (Those who argue that the reference to "year of our Lord" points to a god are unaware that *anno domini* originally referred to Lord Caesar. The phrase appears outside the body of the Constitution, and was conventional usage for the Christian calendar. It no more acknowledges Jesus than the use of "Thursday" requires worship of Thor.)

Some believers will insist that it doesn't matter what the documents say explicitly. They claim that since the founders were religious people, they meant for this to be a religious nation. The religious views of most of the founders bear little resemblance to modern American theology; but it wouldn't matter if they were all born-again evangelicals: they wrote a godless Constitution. They included nothing in our founding documents to suggest that they wanted the rest of us to become carbon copies of their views.

But suppose the Christian nation advocates are right. Suppose we are all obligated to embrace the "traditional" views of our founding fathers. Many of them owned slaves; shall we return to *that* tradition? None of them gave women the right to vote or to own property. Shall we turn back the clock in deference to *those* traditions?

"One nation under God" was absent from the Pledge of Allegiance, and "In God We Trust" did not officially appear on all currency until the 1950's. Now there is a tradition that freethinkers would happily embrace!
Freethought Today, June/July, 1991

48

The Cost Of Freedom

IN THE UNITED STATES we freethinkers are fortunate to be living under a system which guarantees religious freedom for all individuals, believers and nonbelievers. If this were a "Christian nation," as some have insisted, our lack of belief would make us second-class citizens. But America is not a theocracy; it is a secular democratic state. No citizen is any more American than any other.

Some believers remind us that the colonizers originally came here to establish religious societies. They are right. In the early 1600's some of the European settlers did found Christian colonies, and most of them fought fiercely with each other. In the 1780's, more than a century and a half later, our Constitution was written in terms which guard us from such intolerances. There is no god in the document under which Americans live. If this is a Christian nation, then why doesn't our Constitution say so?

Why go back just to the Mayflower? Native religions were being practiced on this continent long before the Pilgrims got here. I am a Delaware Indian, from my Dad's line, and I could equally claim that "true Americans" should be polytheistic. It often amuses me when Christians say I should go back where I came from.

My mother's Dad was Swedish. (That makes me a Swede Indian.) If I were to "go back" to Sweden, I would find myself, in fact, in a Christian nation. The Lutheran Church is the constitutionally established state church in all of the Scandinavian countries (Denmark, Finland, Iceland, Norway and Sweden). But I don't think right-wing American Christians would want to "go back" to Sweden or any of the other Scandinavian countries. They might be very surprised to see what it is like living in nations that do have an established religion.

The Danish Constitution says: "The Evangelical Lutheran Church [ELC] shall be the Established Church of Denmark, and shall as such be supported by the State." *(Article 4)* The Constitution of Norway says: "The Evangelical Lutheran Church shall remain the public religion of the State. The inhabitants professing it shall be bound to bring up their children in the same. . . . The King shall always profess the Evangelical Lutheran religion, and maintain and protect the same . . . More than half the number of the members of the Counsel of State shall profess the public religion of the State." *(Articles 2, 4, 12)* Iceland has similar wording, and although the Swedish and Finnish constitutions are not as direct, they do make provisions for the administration of the ELC, making it the "established" religion. All of the Nordic countries allow for religious freedom, and some (especially Finland) bend over backwards to ensure fairness. But they *are* Christian nations. Roughly ninety percent of Scandinavians belong to the established Lutheran Church. All other denominations and beliefs play very minor roles by comparison.

In 1536 Christian III, who had met Martin Luther at the Diet of Worms, marched into Copenhagen and expelled the Catholics, appropriating the Roman wealth to pay off huge war debts, establishing Protestantism as the new faith of the area, not by any true religious revival, but by edict. (It is only fair that the Catholic wealth was confiscated for military purposes. After all, if the state and the church are allied, then can't religious donations be considered a governmental tax?) Since the middle of the sixteenth century, Scandinavia has been a stronghold of Lutheranism.

Perhaps since the Reformation "awakening" in Scandinavia was forced by military victory rather than a spontaneous religious movement, this is why, in part, modern Scandinavians have such an ambivalent attitude towards their faith. Church membership is very high, but attendance (at nonholiday services) is embarrassingly low: only one or two percent.

The established church is an arm of civil government. Generally, Scandinavians contribute one percent of their income to the church, through government taxation. The generous ministerial salaries are set and disbursed by the government. Local collections are not necessary, though churchgoers will sometimes donate to missionary or relief efforts.

310

The Church enjoys the benefits of state support, but it is not a free ride: it must submit to the responsibility for many civil functions—services which Americans might consider secular. In Sweden the Church arm of government is called the Department of Ecclesiastical Affairs. There are virtually no private cemeteries in all of Scandinavia: they are all managed by the Church. Other services rendered by the Church include public census records and vital statistics, education, daycare (for many of the new women entering the workplace), maintenance of historic monuments, construction and upkeep of church buildings, marriages, care of anti-social juveniles, religious services for the military, and the setting of ministerial pay scales.

Few atheists object to the arrangement. Most of them have learned to live with a system which does not bother them much, paying dues to a religious tradition which they neither want nor need to fight.

In Norway, for example, although eighty-nine percent of the people belong to the established church, only seventy-five percent believe in God. Since only twenty-four percent of Norwegians claim to be "personal Christians" (the rest are nominal members), this means that the Lutheran membership rolls include approximately equal numbers of believers and atheists! Like the monarchy, the Church has become a tolerated anachronism, long having outlived any meaningfulness outside of its civil or symbolic functions.

Another reason, I think, for the present apathy (besides the fact that there was no *earned* Reformation in Scandinavia), is the fact that popular movements tend to thrive on struggle. Religions grow when they are challenged. Since American ministers can't depend on public dollars for their paychecks, they must resort to persuasive tactics to attract a faithful following. They have to *work* at it. They compete with each other. Many emphasize motivations like the threats of hell or the rewards of eternal life. They must preach that church attendance, financial "stewardship," or some other kind of faithfulness really makes a difference to your cosmic well-being. They center on sin, guilt, and salvation. They offer social benefits of church community activities. They try *everything* to get you hooked!

In Scandinavia they don't have to try much at all. In fact, except for occasional political statements (especially in Finland, where Communism has been a stronger factor), Scandinavian ministers try *not* to attract much attention. Some of them are very sincere believers, but they all know that nothing they say or do will affect the size of next week's paycheck.

This does not mean there is no unrest in the Church or dissatisfaction among unbelievers. One of the primary questions in a state-church arrangement is, "which controls which?"

In Norway, for example, the liberal labor government has regularly angered Church officials by making controversial ministerial appointments against the wishes of the clergy. (One was a quasi-Marxist theologian.) In 1975 and 1978 the Church worked doggedly but failed to prevent the *Storting* from liberalizing the abortion law, which now allows termination of pregnancies on request. These and other actions have strained the church-state relationship almost to the breaking point. As a result, some of the bishops have advocated disestablishment.

The [former] prime minister of Norway is Ms. Gro Harlem Brundtland, a feminist activist who was one of the leaders in the pro-abortion fight in the 1970's. She thinks the Church should move into the twentieth century: "The Church should join in untraditional thinking . . . We need a new global system of ethics."

Religious dissent is growing in some areas. One of the largest and fastest-growing secular groups is the *Human-Etisk Forbund* (Humanists) in Norway. In a country of four million, they have forty thousand members! (Imagine if one of every hundred Americans belonged to the Freedom From Religion Foundation.) They are working for disestablishment, to reduce the amount of Christian influence in schools, and to provide secular alternatives to marriages, memorials, burials, and other public ceremonies.

The next time a believer throws the words "Christian nation" at you, point them to Scandinavia. Do they really want the federal government running their church? Do they want their religion to atrophy? It may be painful to admit this, but our First Amendment is one of the main reasons Christianity has flourished in America. One of the "rewards" of freedom (some might say "costs") is the tolerance of a wide diversity of religious views, and a plurality of voices clamoring for attention in the free market of ideas—voices like Falwell, Schuller, Swaggart, Bakker, Moon, Hubbard, Graham; and voices like the Freedom From Religion Foundation.

Officially, most Protestant denominations in the United States support state/church separation. They realize that disestablishment is not only fair, it is wise. All of us, especially Christians, benefit from the separation of church and state. Let's keep it that way.

Freethought Today, August, 1988

The Battle Of Church And State

by Dan Barker

(Can be sung to "De Battle Ob Jericho.")

Chorus: We got to fight the battle of church and state,
Church and state,
Church and state,
We got to fight the battle of church and state,
Or the wall'll come tumblin' down.

I've heard about your hero, Joshua—
But his accomplishments are not so great,
Because there's none like Thomas Jefferson
And the wall between church and state.

Some say that the wall between church and state
Is just a "bad metaphor,"
But if unbelievers can't be protected from the rest,
Then what is the Bill of Rights for?

"Congress shall make no law
Respecting an establishment
Of religion or prohibiting
The free exercise thereof."

49

What Is Christmas To An Unbeliever?

This column was printed in various daily newspapers across America during the Christmas season, 1990.

D EAR CHRISTIAN,

It's that time of year again: colored lights, carols, holly, reindeer, nativity scenes. We can't escape it. Whether we believe the story or not, we are all surrounded by your enormous birthday party for Jesus. It is as if December is a Christian "territory," and anyone who criticizes the myth or protests the public rituals is labelled an outsider.

Have you ever wondered how we "outsiders" might feel? *You* are observing Christmas, we are not. We atheists, agnostics, secular humanists, and other minorities are American citizens too. We pay our taxes, work hard, vote, sit on juries, serve in the military, do volunteer work, contribute to charity, and strive to improve life; yet during the holidays we are made to feel like second-class citizens. We realize that America is a nation of diversity, and we recognize your right to worship what is meaningful to you, and though we disagree philosophically, we support your freedom of religious expression.

But the line has to be drawn somewhere. The Constitution draws the line for us: "Congress shall make no law respecting an establishment of religion or prohibiting the free exercise thereof." Jefferson said that this builds "a wall of separation between church and state." In other words, you can celebrate Christmas, but don't force me to participate in your rituals by spending my tax dollars or using public buildings, public schools, or public endorsement to help you celebrate. If *you* love Jesus, then worship him with your own means. Keep it out of government.

How would you like it if one tenth of every year were set aside for the national proclamation of atheism? What if public officials happily announced the "Good News" that God is a myth and that Jesus is a fable? What if you were surrounded by anticlerical slogans and humanistic hymns from November to January, and made to feel like a Scrooge for not joining the party? Would you want your tax dollars supporting this discourtesy?

People have been making merry during December for many millennia without Jesus. The Winter Solstice is the shortest day of sunlight in the northern hemisphere, when all turns dark and cold and the promise of a new year is welcome. When most trees shed their leaves, the evergreen reminds us of our hope for continued life. Most cultures have celebrations with lights heralding the birth of the baby, the new year.

Hardly any scholars believe that Jesus was born in December, if he was born at all. Christians have simply stolen Christmas. During the first century the Romans feted the birth of Mithra, the Savior who was born in a cave on December 25. Christians, eager to make their new ideology palatable to the ancient world, simply imposed their new mythology on top of the old pagan practices, changing very little.

Most of us unbelievers today continue to join in this natural New Year tradition. My family decorates a solstice tree, exchanges gifts, enjoys festive meals and jubilant music. We even sing a few Christmas carols for their beauty and nostalgia, though we often giggle at the lyrics. Some of the melodies, such as "Greensleeves," were originally secular anyway. "It's that time of year," a wonderful opportunity to express family love and to mark the passing of another season of life. Christians do not have a corner on such values.

Everyone (except the shopkeeper) complains about the commercialization of Christmas. We freethinkers agree that turning personal beliefs into a public spectacle, a "civil religion," tends to cheapen them. What tolerance we might maintain for your holy festivals gets quickly smothered under the monotonous music, gaudy displays, and dime-store hoopla. Do you really expect that this overdose of tackiness is going to persuade us to jump on board?

Maybe you don't care. Maybe you enjoy rooting for your favorite religion, like your favorite football team. Or perhaps you feel that Christmas is so special that we are all going to celebrate it whether we like it or not.

Did it ever occur to you that many of us do not rejoice at the sight of the nativity? We are deeply and morally offended by the implication that we are all corrupt sinners deserving eternal torment, needing a savior. The baby in the manger suggests that we have wounded the unstable vanity of a megalomaniacal Creator and that our only hope is to submit to this vindictive Master. This is rudeness of the highest degree!

No American would tolerate an absolute Monarch. We would throw the bum out. Our Revolution was based on a disrespect for imposed authority. We are a great nation, in part, because of the values of rugged individualism, an open marketplace of ideas, and an uncompromising abhorrence of tyranny. It is a slave who rushes to kneel before a Lord, no matter how cute he may have been as a baby.

The so-called Prince of Peace said, "Think not that I am come to send peace on earth; I came not to send peace, but a sword." Those are fighting words! No wonder the world is not at peace after seventeen centuries of Christianity.

Those who notice that much of modern sexism stems from the patriarchal pages of the bible realize that there can be no peace on earth until there is goodwill toward women. We don't need a heavenly Father Figure; we need respect for one another, compassion for those who suffer, and fairness for everyone regardless of race, sex, age, nationality or religion.

In light of this plea for peace, you might ask why we unbelievers don't back off. Why do we complain about nativity scenes in public places and take legal action against religion in the schools?

But don't you see? We aren't trying to impose atheistic slogans on government. We simply want *you* to back off. No one is telling you that you can't worship. No one is dragging you out of your church pew. No one is legally protesting the creches in your front yards or church parking lots, or the Christmas symbols in privately owned shopping malls or banks. Our only constitutional complaints involve publicly owned facilities, such as the post office, public school, courthouse, city hall, and city park. Do you see the difference? Your religion and property belong to you; the government belongs to all of us.

Our government at all levels is supposed to be impartial towards religion. Some Christians, unable to distinguish between neutrality and hostility, feel personally offended when we succeed in removing a nativity scene from a state capitol building. (Jesus displayed the same paranoia when he said, "He that is not with me is against me.") But in a world of religious diversity and fervor, neutrality in government is the *only* way to have true peace on earth.

Christians, you don't own December. Why don't we all take advantage of this annual lip-service to "goodwill" and practice what we preach. Let's show some concern for the feelings of all people by keeping the state and church separate.

Freethought Today, December, 1990.

Solstice Tribute
by Dan Barker

(Can be sung to "O, Little Town of Bethlehem")

O, shining star of solstice time,
Your radiant hours are few.
You turn and strike the New Year's chime—
We owe our lives to you.
These darkest days of winter,
We miss your warming rays;
But every year this hemisphere
Returns to brighter days.

Since olden days the human race
Has feared your warmth would die.
The evergreen is ever seen
As hope that we will survive.
O, ancient drums, stop beating,
And superstitions fall!
It's time for Reason's Greetings,
For peace, goodwill to all.

EXPOSING CHRISTIAN MORALITY

Part 7

Losing Faith in Faith

50

Is The Bible A Good Moral Guide?

T HE WORD "moral" appears nowhere in the bible. Neither does "morality," "ethics," or "ethical." To inquire if the bible is a good moral guide is to ask a question that originates outside the bible.

This does not mean that the bible has nothing to say about behavior. The phrase, "to do right," appears throughout scripture, but this is usually followed by "in the sight of the Lord." To do right in one's "own eyes" is considered evil. There are a few passages that talk about doing that which is right or good without an explicit connection to deity, but taken in the entire context of Scripture, all behavior that Christians consider to be good is measured against the "righteousness" of God, not against moral or ethical principles of humanity. *Proverbs 16:25* says, "There is a way that seemeth right unto a man, but the end thereof are the ways of death."

Ironically, the first place the phrase "do right" is used in the bible is when Abraham questioned the morality of God. Abraham argued with God, and succeeded in getting him to change his mind about slaughtering innocent victims in Sodom: "That be far from thee to do after this manner, to slay the righteous with the wicked; and that the righteous should be as the wicked, that be far from thee; Shall not the Judge of all the earth do right?" *(Genesis 18:25)* God did change his mind about the minimum number of good people required to prevent the slaughter, but he went ahead and murdered all the inhabitants of Sodom anyway, including all of the "unrighteous" children, babies, and fetuses. It appears that Abraham was more moral than his god, a matter to be examined later; but his question is quite valid: "Shall not the Judge of all the earth do right?" If the basis for morality rests with a single entity, then what makes that entity accountable? What makes God moral?

True Christians should not ask if the bible is moral, or if God is moral. If God is the source of morality, then asking if God is moral is like asking if goodness is good. To ask seriously if God or the bible is moral (with a possible negative answer) is to assume that "moral" means something apart from God, and that we already know what it means independently of the bible. If the word "moral" has meaning by itself, then right-and-wrong can be understood apart from God, and judging the morality of God puts him under the jurisdiction of a higher level of criticism. This is true even if the judgment is favorable. To the believer, questioning the morality of God is blasphemy. It implies that the "supreme judge" can be judged.

But, of course, "Is God moral?" is a perfectly legitimate question. Not only does it make sense to freethinkers, who are outside the religious circle and therefore not required to reduce it to a simple ontological tautology describing the perfection of deity, but it has to make some kind of sense to Christians, if they are honest, in order for them to be able to worship. Can you worship someone who has not earned respect? In order for Christians to affirm that "God is good," aren't they judging God? Don't they think the character of God merits praise and adoration? Or are they simply giving blind obedience to whatever happens to be omnipotent? (I might "respect" the strength of a hurricane, but I would not call it good, nor would I worship it.) Most of us do not consider it an admirable moral quality to praise power alone, so if believers deem God to be good, then it must be because they have judged God to be morally worthy of respect. You can't praise what you don't admire.

The question turns out to be something of a trap for believers. If pressed they will have to back off from judging God, and will have to admit that God is moral by definition alone. It doesn't really matter how God acts: God is good because God said he is good, and we should worship him not because he has earned our admiration but because he has demanded it. Morality is not a question with which mere human minds should wrestle, believers insist; it is something that should be determined by the perfect, omniscient, omnipotent mind of God.

During my struggle to break free from the cocoon of Christianity, the most difficult issue with which I grappled was the idea of relativism. I used to preach that relativism leads to chaos: without absolutes, "anything goes." Like ships without rudders, or machines without operating instructions, human beings without absolutes simply wander through life, hit-or-miss, trying this or that, never knowing what is right or wrong. It makes a good sermon.

Christians feel that the basis for morality must be something absolute. This rock-solid foundation must be rooted outside humanity, they claim, providing an external and objective reference by which human behavior can be measured. Without this "cosmic code" for living, we would all choose or manufacture our own individual ethics relative to personal wants, whims and needs. An "inner directed" morality, they insist, leads to relativism, that is, to sin.

Additionally, believers claim that without an external absolute code, there is no ethical imperative. Why be good if there is no punishment, no reward, no all-knowing police officer to enforce the rules? They believe that if there is no god, then there is no accountability. Since human nature, they insist, is intrinsically corrupt (look at history, or current headlines), the tendency will be toward destruction and evil if not corrected by strict laws and absolute enforcement. The fear of punishment and the loss of divine approval provides the necessary moral imperative.

I have to confess that I used to find this logic persuasive and difficult to dislodge. For about a year after rejecting religion I felt uncomfortable flapping my own wings. It took some getting used to the idea that I can chart my own moral course through life, that I *must* chart my own moral course through life. Although there is no ultimate universal guide, I do have a mind, which I realized is the only rudder I will ever have or need. To use yet another metaphor, I felt as though I were on trial, and right in the middle of the proceedings my lawyer died and I was left to represent myself before the bench, which was scary enough until I looked up and saw that the bench was vacant! I was the plaintiff, the defendant, the attorney, and the judge! The responsibility was almost enough to drive me back to my cell, back to the cocoon of absolutes.

On the other hand, it did not take long to discover that there is no great mystery to morality. Although a few extreme ethical dilemmas might arise in one's lifetime, basic day-to-day morality is a simple matter of kindness, respect, and reason: don't deliberately cause harm. Once I shed the religio-psychological frame of mind, I learned that the Christian "struggle" with morality is overblown. I learned that relativism is all we've got. Human values are not absolutes—they are relative to human needs. The humanistic answer to morality, if the question is properly understood, is that the basis for values lies in nature. Since we are a part of nature, and since there is nothing "beyond" nature, it is necessary to assign value to actions in the context of nature itself. Since we were all born and raised in nature, most of us do this daily, as a matter of fact, without much thought or distress.

One simplified example of how nature provides the basis for value: human bodies happen to require water for survival. Since most humans want to survive, withholding water can be considered immoral. There is nothing cosmically "good" about water or cosmically "evil" about the lack of it. It is all relative to natural human needs, and if we had evolved to require arsenic, then offering arsenic would be appreciated while serving water might be a crime. It would miss the point to complain that "water versus arsenic" is irrelevant because it addresses nouns rather than verbs—that instead we should be discussing the relative morality of "withholding vs. not-withholding." The whole topic of morality implies preferring actions that are good. This is by definition. No matter how elaborate the philosophical arguments become, moral decisions in the daily world still boil down to assessing the value of things like water and arsenic—natural things—and their effects on other natural things, such as our bodies.

Since "value" is a concept of relative worth, and concepts, as far as we know, exist only in brains, which are material things, it is meaningless, even dangerous to talk of cosmic moral absolutes. The assessment of value requires the use of reason. In other words, morality comes from *within* humanity. If intelligent life had not appeared on this planet, morality would not exist.

Morality is in the mind, and reason is in the mind. No matter where you look for morality, it all comes down to the mind. Those believers who distrust the human mind are still required to look to some kind of mind for guidance, whether the mind of a god, prophet, preacher, or pope. If there were a god, then its moral decrees would originate from *its* mind. (I am using the word "mind" loosely, as a function of the brain, or body, just as digestion is a function of the stomach, or circulation is a function of the heart. I do not mean to concede that the natural brain/mind of a human is any way comparable to the intangible, "spiritual" mind of a deity—whatever that might mean—that believers imagine existing somewhere outside of nature.)

Why should the mind of a deity be better able to judge human actions than humans themselves? Has God ever been thirsty? The human mind and human actions are part of the natural world; the mind of a god is not. Human minds interact with each other in the real world. A human mind feels physical pain. The human mind can know sorrow, grief, regret, embarrassment; the mind of a perfect deity cannot. Can a god shed a tear, smell a flower or hug a child? Does a god perspire after a day of hard work under a burning sun, or shiver while trudging through a blizzard? Which mind is in a better position to make judgments about human actions and feelings? Which mind has more credibility? Which has more experience in the real world? Which mind has more of a right?

Those Christians who might argue that Jesus became human for just that purpose, that the "Word became flesh" to give the supernatural deity the opportunity to relate to natural human suffering, forget that the Ten Commandments were written long before the first century. The Man from Galilee said, "Think not that I am come to destroy the law, or the prophets: I am not come to destroy, but to fulfill. For verily I say unto you, Till heaven and earth pass, one jot or one tittle shall in no wise pass from the law, till all be fulfilled." *(Matthew 5:17-18)* The Law, according to the bible, originated in the mind of God long before he stuck his toe into our world.

In any event, how can the temporal sufferings of Jesus compare to the sufferings of the entire human race? Did Jesus ever experience the pain of childbirth? The billions of women going through labor are much more life-giving, much more nurturing of value than a few hours of self-imposed bleeding on a cross. The short life of Jesus can hardly compare with the suffering of brave heretics who have been persecuted for criticizing Christianity, or with the agony of the "witches" who were burned, drowned, and hanged by bible believers, or with the hard work, sacrifice, and discipline of intelligent individuals who have dedicated their lives to science and medicine. Just because Jesus was supposedly a "Higher Power" does not make his alleged suffering any higher than yours or mine.

Why do believers assume that a *higher* power is necessarily a *more moral* power? How do they know it is not the other way around? If you look at nature, you discover that there is very little crime in the plant kingdom. (Ignoring dandelions.) Is it a felony when an eagle kills a field mouse? Immorality, crime, malice and cruelty belong to the higher forms of life. Chimpanzees and other primates sometimes show behavior that appears malicious, but they are higher forms of animal life. If there is a "Higher Power," then shouldn't we be all the more suspicious of its motives and actions? Perhaps we would benefit from revering the "Lower Powers" of the universe, and would improve morality if we were to get back in touch with the fact that we are animals living in a natural environment, and that we are truly part of nature, not something separate and above.

J udaism, Christianity, and Islam, the "revealed" religions which directly or indirectly share the Jewish Law, pretend to find their answer to morality in a holy book that originates from a mind that exists outside the material world. Their way to be moral is simply stated: obey Scripture.

Regardless of whether humanism or other naturalistic ethical systems are successful, or even possible, and regardless of whether we truly need an external moral code, the question can still be raised about the adequacy of any particular religious solution. Is the bible a good book? Is the bible an acceptable guide for moral behavior?

The bible is indeed filled with very specific commandments for living. Let's look at one of them. The Fourth Commandment says, "Remember the sabbath day, to keep it holy." This is one of the Big Ten, so it can't be ignored. At face value it seems straightforward enough, but what exactly does it mean? How do you "remember" the Sabbath, and what happens if you fail? In the book of Numbers the "Lord" gives a specific example of how the Sabbath law is applied, but he first explains that there is a difference between sinning deliberately and sinning accidentally, comparable to the modern idea of "intent." Although this provides for varying degrees of sentencing, it does not mitigate the crime itself. A sin is still a sin:

"And if any soul sin through ignorance, then he shall bring a she goat of the first year for a sin offering . . . But the soul that doeth ought [sin] presumptuously, whether he be born in the land, or a stranger, the same reproacheth the Lord; and that soul shall be cut off from among his people. Because he hath despised the word of the Lord, and hath broken his commandment, that soul shall utterly be cut off; his iniquity shall be upon him." *(Numbers 15:27,30-31)*

Strong language. There is accidental sin and there is deliberate sin, though it seems that the former should hardly count as a "sin." In any event, the passage that immediately follows this clarification shows what happens to a person who *deliberately* breaks the Sabbath law:

"And while the children of Israel were in the wilderness, they found a man that gathered sticks upon the sabbath day. And they that found him brought him unto Moses and Aaron, and unto all the congregation. And they put him in ward, because it was not declared what should be done to him. And the Lord said unto Moses, The man shall be surely put to death: all the congregation shall stone him with stones without the camp. And all the congregation brought him without the camp, and stoned him with stones, and he died; as the Lord commanded Moses." *(Numbers 15:32-36)*

This is clear: don't pick up sticks on the sabbath. If you pick up sticks, God's followers will pick up stones. Is *this* a good guide for morality? When I was a child, each year my family would spend weeks camping in the mountains of California, and we kids often had the job of picking up kindling wood for the fire. This often happened on the weekend. Didn't my born-again parents read the bible? (Perhaps my sin was one of "ignorance." Where am I go-

326

ing to find a she goat?)

Some believers assert that these primitive Old Testament laws are no longer relevant and have been superseded by Jesus; but that is the point! If they use such an argument, they are admitting that at least part of the bible is not acceptable for today's society. How many of us stop and think what day of the week it is before we pick up sticks? However you interpret it, the fifteenth chapter of Numbers is still in the bible, and we see no condemnation of such barbarism, no moral outcry, no denunciation by Christians of these shameful practices in the Good Book. We see no pages being torn out of bibles with disgust. What if an Ayatollah were to command the execution of a person who picked up sticks on an Islamic holy day? What would we think of such bloodthirsty arrogance?

In dealing with such thorny scriptural issues as capital punishment for picking up sticks on Saturday (the Jewish sabbath) or Sunday (the Christian "sabbath"), some liberal Christians will agree that portions of the bible are now outmoded. The text should not be taken literally, they claim; we should seek instead the "spiritual lesson" that underlies the specific example. (That would be like saying, "I am going to teach you a lesson about obedience by telling you that I killed someone. It doesn't matter if it really happened. Don't worry about the violence, or that person's life, because I love you and want you to learn how righteous I am.") There is a subset of fundamentalists, called Dispensationalists, who claim that the Old Testament rules were in effect only for that period of history, and that we now have different rules because God's plan is unfolding in stages, or dispensations. (Though Jesus said he came to uphold the Old Testament law.) Other evangelical Christians will assert that tougher measures were required during the struggling infancy of the besieged Jewish religion, and that now that Christianity is on the scene such tactics are not needed. (Though they still preach that the world is more corrupt than ever, and that the forces of evil continue to attack believers.) All of these arguments, at minimum, admit that there are at least some parts of the current bible that are now no longer relevant to proper human behavior. All of us, believers and nonbelievers alike, whatever our reasoning, have to agree that the bible can be downright brutal.

Apologize, theologize, demythologize, and rationalize all you want—those barbaric scriptures are still being sold in bookstores. Many courts use the bible as the standard of truth-telling, and presidents place their hand upon it during inauguration—a practice, incidentally, not mandated by the Constitution. But any version of the bible that contains barbaric decrees cannot be *entirely* palatable to the modern world. Perhaps it could be argued that some parts are okay, but the bible as a whole is undeniably flawed.

Believers often accuse us skeptics of ignoring the good while picking out only the bad parts of the bible. Why don't we join them in emphasizing that which is good and beautiful in the bible? That might appear to be a fair question until you turn it around and ask them why they don't join us in denouncing the ugly parts. Let's first remove all the weeds and see what is left in the garden. It might surprise them to learn that there is precious little remaining that is worthy of admiration. Even if there are a few pretty flowers, would you call a garden beautiful that is overrun with weeds?

Those who can read the bible objectively, who are not handicapped with the requirement that it be worshiped or respected, notice that there are problems with using the bible as a guide for behavior: 1) The bible argues from authority, not from reason, claiming that "might makes right." 2) The bible nowhere states that every human being possesses an inherent right to be treated with respect and fairness—humans don't matter as much as God does. 3) The biblical role models, especially Jehovah and Jesus, are very poor examples, normally ignoring their own good teachings (what few there are), and ruthlessly pursuing their own tyrannical teachings. 4) Many moral precepts of the bible are just plain bad, even dangerous. 5) On closer inspection, most of the "positive" teachings are uninspired and inadequate.

Author Ruth Green calls the bible a "moral grab bag." Many pick and choose from its pages, most ignore it, and those few who do use it as a guide for behavior do so for religious rather than moral reasons. Those believers who are indeed good people and who credit the bible for their standards are giving credit where credit is not due. Christians, it turns out, don't have a corner on morality. On average they are no more moral than unbelievers. Some might argue that they are *less* moral. Those few shining examples from the Christian community shine no brighter than the caring unbelievers. But for all their talk about the need for moral guidance, they cannot substantiate the claim that the bible is a good guide for modern behavior.

Might Makes Right

> *"Vengeance belongeth unto me, I will recompense, saith the Lord. And again, The Lord shall judge his people. It is a fearful thing to fall into the hands of the living God." (Hebrews 10:30-31)*

> *"Be not afraid of them that kill the body, and after that have no more that they can do. But I will forewarn you whom ye shall*

fear: Fear him, which after he hath killed hath power to cast into hell; yea, I say unto you, Fear him." (Jesus, Luke 12:4-5)

"The fear of the Lord is the beginning of wisdom." (Solomon, Proverbs 1:7)

When someone tells you to do something, it is natural to ask "Why?" Why remember the sabbath? The bible tells us that we should remember the sabbath "to keep it holy." The word "holy" means "set apart," "sacred," or "clean," and has nothing to do with "good" or "right." In other words, this commandment does not deal with ethics; it deals with the superiority of God. When believers say that something is "wrong," they are saying it is wrong because it has been *decreed* wrong by a "holy" deity, not because there is a good reason. The child asks, "Daddy, why can't I do this?" and Daddy responds, "Because I said so!" If the commandment is violated, it becomes a crime of disobedience—the authority figure should not be offended.

The humanist, on the other hand, looks for some reason or principle independent of authority. The child asks, "Why can't I do this?" and Daddy or Mommy responds, "If you do it, you will get hurt. I love you and don't want you to get hurt." Or the parent says, "If you do this, someone else will get hurt." The crime is against humanity, not against Daddy. A deity might give reasons for its decrees, but they must be irrelevant. If God gives reasons, then he is appealing to a court outside himself—a court to which we could just as well appeal directly, circumventing his authority. If God needs reasons, then he is not God.

To the theist, punishment is administered by the offended Daddy. Whoever "reproacheth the Lord" shall be chastised. To the humanist, however, consequences, not punishment, happen as a natural effect of the behavior itself. This does not mean that a humanist parent will allow a child to run into a busy street; it means that the moral basis for restraint is found in the traffic, not in the "Word of Daddy." The humanist's child who disobeys and runs into the street is not committing a "sin" by offending the ego or "holiness" of the parents—the evil of the situation exists in the potential for getting run over by a moving vehicle, in other words, it exists in nature.

If there were something dangerous about picking up sticks on Saturday or Sunday, then humanity should know it by now. Since we all agree that such an act in itself is harmless, then whoever executes a person for committing such a "crime" is an immoral person. Even if there were something wrong about picking up sticks, it is not so terribly wrong that it deserves capital punishment. We don't send jaywalkers to the gas chamber, or hang children for stealing cookies.

Unless! Unless you argue from authority, and the authority figure decrees, for no good reason, that such an action offends *Him*. People who believe they are living under the thumb of such a vain and petty lord are not guided by ethics; they are guided by fear. The bible turns out to be not a moral code, but a whip.

Rather than asking believers the (to them) silly question, "Is God moral?", it might be more meaningful to ask: "What would the bible have to say in order to be immoral?" If the bible ordered killing, would that be immoral? If it encouraged rape? What if it commanded stealing, lying or adultery? What if its main characters called names, issued threats, and acted irrationally? Then would it be immoral? (The bible does all of these things, and more.) Exactly how bad would the bible have to get before it is discarded? Do Christians ever dare ask this question?

Such a thought is retrograde to the Christian agenda of faith in scripture and loyalty to Jesus. It is the nature of belief not to examine critically the object of that belief. Most believers have had it drummed into their heads, Sunday after Sunday, that the bible is a "Good Book." They are taught that thinking for oneself is, if not completely evil, at least woefully inadequate. *Proverbs 3:5* says, "Trust in the Lord with all thine heart; and lean not unto thine own understanding." *II Corinthians 10:5* says, "[bring] into captivity every thought to the obedience of Christ." This is a circular argument, of course: Don't question the bible—Why?—Because the bible says so.

Few Christians ask whether the bible is morally acceptable. (If they do, they are labeled "liberals.") Such questioning is heretical to most believers. Whether or not you assume or judge the bible to be morally acceptable, the important question to believers is whether or not you accept its authority. In their minds, authority equals morality. God is sovereign.

"Do this because I said so," is the kind of thing you say to a small child. A toddler may not be mature enough to follow a line of reasoning, so parents might have to exercise authority to prohibit something dangerous. But the "authority" in this case is not what actually determines what is right or wrong; it is simply an exercise of the minimum restraint necessary to enforce protective, rational guidelines until the child is old enough to reason independently. The parent who treats a toddler in such a manner, temporarily emphasizing authority over rationale, still should be able to explain to another adult why the child's action would be dangerous or undesirable. The child, in later years, should be able to obtain a reasonable explanation from the parent. If not, the parent is a petty tyrant.

Besides being childish, the morality-as-authority argument is dangerous.

330

People who do not question authority become easy prey to dictators. Cult leaders can manipulate followers who give them blind obedience. Many of the nine hundred followers of the Rev. Jim Jones drank the poisonous punch, *aware* of what was happening, because they were convinced that he was next to God. The Nazis wore "God is with us" on their belts, convinced that Hitler was doing the work of Jesus in exterminating the Jews, as he claimed in one of his speeches. Certain Christian fanatics, such as the Christian Scientists, pentecostals and other fundamentalists, allow their children to die of treatable illnesses because their church tells them that circumventing God's natural plan is a sin, or that Jesus will heal "all manner of diseases."

Another question for those who think God's authority is the basis for morality: If God told you to kill someone, would you do it? Some Christians will immediately answer, "Yes," arguing that some killing is justified (death penalty, war, self defense), or that the "giver of life" has the simple right to take life.

Then try this question on a male believer: If God told you to rape someone, would you do it? Some Christians, ignorant of biblical injunctions to rape, might answer, "God would never ask me to do that;" but this simply avoids the question. If God is the source of all morality, and if God asked you to do something that *you* considered immoral, would it matter what you thought? According to the bible, we should simply obey God, even when it is difficult. Abraham found it difficult to obey God's command to kill his son Isaac, but he was prepared to do it, and his obedience was considered praiseworthy! Jephthah found it hard to murder his daughter, but he was obligated by a vow to God to go through with it, and he did, without condemnation. Both of these men, if they were truly moral, would have defied God, regardless of the divine consequences. They should have said to God, "You may have the might, but you don't have the right."

Suppose a man were to say to his wife, "Prove how much you love me by helping me rob a bank; and if you don't help, I will beat you." We would call such a bully abusive and criminal. Yet this same bankrupt chain-of-command mentality is taught in the bible: God decides what is right and wrong, and if you don't play along you are punished in hell.

Speaking for myself, if the biblical heaven and hell exist, I would choose hell. Having to spend eternity pretending to worship tyranny would be more hellish than baking in eternal flames. There is no way a Bully will earn my worship.

Mark Twain said, "Heaven for climate; hell for companionship."

Humans have no intrinsic right to fairness or respect in the bible.

The bible nowhere states that every human being possesses an inherent right to be treated with respect or fairness. Generally, everything flows from God to humans, not the other way around. A true moral guide should have some principles. If humans are supposed to treat other humans in certain ways, or to avoid treating humans in other ways, then there should be some examination of the general value of human life and of human *rights*. Yet this is not to be found anywhere in the bible.

There are a few places where God appeared to respect certain key players, such as when the angel asked the Virgin Mary's permission to be impregnated by the Holy Ghost; but even then her response was submissive rather than egalitarian: "Behold the handmaid of the Lord." *(Luke 1:38)* It is all on God's side. If God can grant rights, then he can take them away, meaning that there actually are no human rights in God's scheme.

The biblical view of human nature is negative. Humans don't deserve respect; they deserve damnation. We are all tainted with Original Sin. *Romans 3:12* says, "There is none that doeth good, no, not one," and eleven verses later, "For all have sinned, and come short of the glory of God." Job (the sexist) said, "Man that is born of a woman is of few days, and full of trouble. . . . Who can bring a clean thing out of an unclean? not one." *(Job 14:1-4)* The view that humans are intrinsically evil is hardly commensurate with an ethical system based on mutual respect. On the contrary, it tends to produce a negative self image in those who were raised in bible-believing churches, and a cynicism toward other humans. It can become something of a self-fulfilling prophecy. Witness televangelist Jimmy Swaggart who preached that we are all corrupt and then proved it himself! If he had been raised with a healthier view of human nature, he may not have blown sexual temptation into such a demon in his mind, becoming obsessed with what he railed against. (Or was it the other way around? In either case, the bible fueled the problem.)

It is also historically clear that the true bible-believers have little respect for the human rights of anyone outside of their church. I know Christians who will do business only with other Christians, when possible. We all know about the way Christians and other religionists have treated outsiders: Native Americans, American Blacks and South-African natives, scores of pagan peoples around the world who had the misfortune of having been born and raised outside of the "true" faith. We all know about the Crusades in the name of Jesus, the Spanish Inquisition, the current Catholic-Protestant bloodshed in Northern Ireland, the militant Christian factions in the Middle East. Modern warm-fuzzy American Protestants who try to distance themselves from such intolerance and brutality should ask themselves: would I prefer my son or daughter to marry a Catholic, Jew, Moslem, or atheist? Paul advised Christians: "Be ye not unequally yoked together with unbelievers: for what fellowship hath righteousness with unrighteousness? and what communion hath light with darkness?" *(II Corinthians 6:14)* The intrinsic intolerance of Christianity cannot be denied or candy-coated.

Matthew 7:18-20 says, "A good tree cannot bring forth evil fruit, neither can a corrupt tree bring forth good fruit. . . . Wherefore by their fruits ye shall know them." Those of us outside the historically bloody religions have no restraints against denouncing the "fruit" that has been produced by such trees as Christianity. If the bible contains any seeds of respect or fairness toward other humans, it is sadly absent from a reading of the text, or from the institutions produced by it.

Good deeds, in the bible, are almost always connected with heavenly reward, "God's will," avoiding punishment, or with a missionary agenda. Most "Christian charity" is given to prove the superiority of Christianity, or to win converts, not because human life is good, valuable, and worthy of respect in its own right.

Truly good Christian individuals don't find their motivation in the bible. They do good because they are good people. Bertrand Russell said, "Men tend to have the beliefs that suit their passions. Cruel men believe in a cruel God and use their belief to excuse their cruelty. Only kindly men believe in a kindly God, and they would be kindly in any case."

The bible characters are poor role models.

We hear a lot of "God is love" sermons from the pulpit, but even a cursory glance at the bible reveals that God kills a lot of people. He drowned the entire population of the planet, saving one family. He sent a plague to kill all the first-born children in Egypt, human and animal. He rained fire and brimstone on Sodom, killing everyone—boys, girls, babies, pregnant women, animals. He sent his Israelite warriors to destroy the neighboring pagan tribes, man, woman, and child.

In *I Samuel 6,* the ark of the Lord was being transported across country and five farmers of Bethshemesh "rejoiced to see it." They opened the box and made a burnt offering to the Lord, and for this terrible sin, God "smote the men of Bethshemesh, because they had looked into the ark of the Lord, even he smote of the people fifty thousand and threescore and ten men: and the people lamented, because the Lord had smitten many of the people with a great slaughter." Is it moral to kill fifty thousand people for a petty offense?

In *I Samuel 25,* an industrious man named Nabal refused to hand his produce over to David. "Shall I then take my bread, and my water, and my flesh that I have killed for my shearers, and give it unto men, whom I know not whence they be?" In punishment for protecting what he rightfully owned, "the Lord smote Nabal, that he died."

In *Numbers 25:16-17,* "The Lord spake unto Moses, saying, Vex the Midianites, and smite them." Here is what happened six chapters later: "And they warred against the Midianites, as the Lord commanded Moses; and they slew all the males. . . . And the children of Israel took all the women of Midian captives, and their little ones, and took the spoil of all their cattle, and all their flocks, and all their goods. And they burnt all their cities wherein they dwelt, and all their goodly castles, with fire. And they took all the spoil, and all the prey, both of men and beasts." Well, this isn't so bad, is it? They slaughtered the men and burned the cities, but they saved the women and children, after all. Read on:

"And Moses was wroth with the officers . . . And Moses said unto them, Have ye saved all the women alive? . . . Now therefore kill every male among the little ones, and kill every woman that hath known man by lying with him. [How would they know this?] But all the women children, that have not known a man by lying with him, keep alive for yourselves."

It gets worse. As they were dividing up the "booty," they counted all the animals, gold, jewels, "and thirty and two thousand persons in all, of women that had not known man by lying with him," and "the Lord's tribute was thirty and two persons." It does not say exactly what happened to these thirty-two lucky girls, but after watching their fathers, sisters, brothers and mothers butchered by the Israelite marauders, they might have preferred to become burnt offerings rather than serve as "booty" for the priests of Jehovah.

Who will dare claim that this is moral?

Listen to these threats from the loving God: "If ye will not hearken unto me, and will not do all these commandments . . . I will appoint over you terror, consumption, and the burning ague, that shall consume the eyes, and cause sorrow of heart: and ye shall sow your seed in vain, for your enemies shall eat it . . . and ye shall be slain before your enemies . . . I will punish you seven times more . . . for your land shall not yield her increase, neither shall the trees of the land yield their fruits . . . I will also send wild beasts among you, which shall rob you of your children, and destroy your cattle . . . and I will bring a sword upon you, . . . I will send the pestilence among you . . . ten women shall bake your bread in one oven . . . and ye shall eat and not be satisfied . . . And ye shall eat the flesh of your sons, and the flesh of your daughters . . . and I will make your cities waste . . . and I will bring the land into desolation: . . . And I will scatter you among the heathen, and will draw out a sword after you . . . Then shall the land enjoy her sabbaths, as long as it lieth desolate . . . even then shall the land rest, and enjoy her sabbaths . . . and ye shall perish among the heathen." *(Leviticus 26:14-38)* So, the Sabbath will be observed, even if God has to kill everyone to make it happen. Does this litany of threats come from a stable or loving mind?

Deuteronomy repeats many of these threats, including the appetizing "And thou shalt eat the fruit of thine own body, the flesh of thy sons and of thy daughters, which the Lord thy God hath given thee, . . . so that the man that is tender among you, and very delicate, his eye shall be evil toward his brother, and toward the wife of his bosom, and toward the remnant of his children which he shall leave." You bet. All tender-meated people look over your shoulders!

The biblical God punishes children for things they did not do, and calls this "mercy." *Exodus 34:6-7:* "And the Lord passed by before him, and proclaimed, The Lord, The Lord God, merciful and gracious, longsuffering, and abundant in goodness and truth, Keeping mercy for thousands, forgiving iniquity and transgression and sin, and that will by no means clear the guilty; visiting the iniquity of the fathers upon the children, and upon the children's children, unto the third and to the fourth generation." Who thinks *this* is moral?

A moral and wise grown-up knows that children are sometimes ornery—kids will be kids. But God seems not to understand this. In *II Kings 2:23-24,* he massacred forty-two loud-mouthed children: "And he [Elisha] went up from thence unto Bethel: and as he was going up by the way, there came forth little children out of the city, and mocked him, and said unto him, Go up, thou bald head; go up, thou bald head. And he turned back, and looked on them, and cursed them in the name of the Lord. And there came forth two she bears out of the wood, and tare forty and two children of them." This sounds like an R-rated version of Little Red Riding Hood or the Three Little Pigs, but true bible believers are forced to pretend that this nonsense is historical as well as moral.

God's thirst for blood sacrifice is unparalleled, starting with Cain and Abel. Millions of animals were slaughtered to appease the anger and vanity of the Israelite deity. God even accepted a *human* sacrifice, Jephthah's daughter *(Judges 11:30-40).* In *II Samuel 21:1-14* the sacrifice of seven of Saul's sons, who were hanged, caused God to be appeased.

In *Leviticus 27:28-29,* God orders that "devoted" (sacrificed) humans must be put to death: "No devoted thing . . . both of man and beast . . . shall be sold or redeemed . . . but shall surely be put to death." This is human sacrifice, pure and simple.

God sold the Israelites to the king of Mesopotamia for eight years *(Judges 3:8)*. It doesn't say what God did with the money. He also sold them to the Moabites for eighteen years *(3:14),* to Canaan for twenty years *(4:2-3),* to the Midianites for seven years *(6:1),* to the Philistines for forty years *(13:1)* and to the Babylonians for seventy years. That's more than a century and a half of slavery—more than twice as long as slavery existed in the United States. Is *this* moral?

In *Exodus 21,* right after the Ten Commandments, God gives laws for dealing with slaves. "If thou buy an Hebrew servant, six years he shall serve . . . his master shall bore his ear through with an aul . . . and if a man sell his daughter to be a maidservant, she shall not go out as the manservants do . . ." and so on. Not only is this unabashed slavery, it is *sexist* slavery, treating women as less valuable property. God never denounces the institution of slavery, and in fact appears to encourage it.

God discriminated against the handicapped: "For whatsoever man he be that hath a blemish, he shall not approach: a blind man, or a lame, or he that hath a flat nose, or any thing superfluous. Or a man that is brokenfooted, or brokenhanded, Or crookbacked, or a dwarf, or that hath a blemish in his eye, or be scurvy, or scabbed, or hath his stones [testicles] broken . . . that he profane not my sanctuaries." *(Leviticus 21:18-23)*

God engages in deliberate deceit. *Ezekiel 14:9* says, "And if the prophet be deceived when he hath spoken a thing, I the Lord have deceived that prophet." *II Thessalonians 2:11* reports: "God shall send them strong delusion, that they should believe a lie."

God uses language that would never be allowed in church: "Behold, I will corrupt your seed, and spread dung upon your faces, even the dung of your solemn feasts." *(Malachi 2:3)* "The Lord commanded: And thou shalt eat it as barley cakes, and thou shalt bake it with dung that cometh out of man, in their sight." *(Ezekiel 4:12.* In other words, God said "Eat shit." Is this proper language for a moral example?) "I will cut off from Jeroboam him that pisseth against the wall." *(I Kings 14:10)* "I will discover thy skirts upon thy face, and I will show the nations thy nakedness and thy kingdoms thy shame." *(Nahum 3:5,6)* And the following misogynist verse celebrates sexual molestation: "Therefore the Lord will smite with a scab the crown of the head of the daughters of Zion, and the Lord will discover ("lay bare"—*NRSV)* their secret parts." *(Isaiah 3:17.* "Secret parts" is a euphemistic translation of the Hebrew word *poth,* which refers to the vagina, literally "hinged opening." Some pseudo-translations, such as the *NIV,* have tried to cover up this embarrassing image of a molesting deity by dishonestly translating *poth* as "scalp.")

God created evil *(Isaiah 45:7),* and hell. God blames everyone for Adam's sin. God is partial to one race of people, which is racism. He gets jealous *(Exodus 20:5),* in fact, he says that his *name* is Jealousy: "for the Lord, whose name is Jealous, is a jealous God." *(Exodus 34:14)*

There is not enough space to mention all of the places in the bible where God committed, commanded, or condoned murder. In Ruth Green's *Born Again Skeptic's Guide to the Bible,* it takes ten tightly typeset pages just to list briefly the killings of Jehovah. Is this the kind of character we would let our kids spend the day with? This sounds more like the stuff of a violent, X-rated movie than a guide for moral behavior.

Hearing these indictments, some Christians might ask, "Why are you attacking God?" I would respond, "Why are you looking the other way?" Christian apologists can dig up bible verses that say or demonstrate that "God is love," but how does this help? The most that can be proved with oppositional verses is that the bible is contradictory. Hitler's love for his wife, dog, and close followers did not excuse the Holocaust.

Some Christians will complain that we should not be concerned with the Old Testament deity because Jesus has superseded all of that. The words and actions of Jesus Christ are the perfect role model, they claim. Let's see if that is true.

In *Luke 12:47,48,* Jesus said: "And that servant [Greek *doulos* = slave] which knew his Lord's will, and prepared not himself, neither did according to his will, shall be beaten with many stripes. But he that knew not, and did commit things worthy of stripes, shall be beaten with few stripes." Jesus encouraged the beating of slaves! Is this an example of moral superiority? Some Christians will argue that this is just a parable based on the culture of the day, and that Jesus did not mean it to be taken literally. But an examination of the context proves otherwise. Jesus had just given a parable about servants a few verses earlier, and Peter had asked for an elaboration *(12:41).* The quote about beating slaves is in the explanation, not the parable. Besides, what an ugly thing to say! Even if it were a metaphor, it is a poor choice of words. It would be like a politician making an antisemitic or black joke, and then saying "I was just kidding." Why did Jesus, the unrivaled moral example, never once speak out against slavery? Why did the loving, wise Son of God forget to mention that slavery is a brutal institution? Why did he incorporate it into his teachings, as if it were the most natural thing in the world? I'll tell you why: because he supported it. The Old Testament endorses and encourages slavery, and Jesus, being equal to God, supposedly wrote the old laws, so he *had* to support slavery. This is not to concede that a man named Jesus actually uttered these words in history. It merely demonstrates that the Gospels were written by human beings who were locked into their culture. Not only did they refuse to denounce slavery, they could not conceive that there was anything wrong with it.

Jesus never spoke out against poverty, or did anything to eliminate it. In fact, he taught that the poor should accept their lot in life. In *Mark 14:3-9,* some of Christ's disciples objected to the waste of a costly ointment used to anoint Jesus's head, "for it might have been sold for more than three hundred pence, and have been given to the poor." Jesus responded, "Ye have the poor with you always, and whensoever ye will ye may do them good: but me ye have not always." This is selfish and callous. Where were the wise words of Jesus regarding waste and inequality? Where were the social programs that would eliminate poverty?

Jesus indicated that he and his followers were a special class, above the rest, free to take liberally from the property and work of others. In *Mark 2:23* he and his disciples roamed through cornfields, taking what they wanted, which was doubly unlawful since it was the sabbath. In *Matthew 21,* Jesus instructed his disciples to take a horse without first asking the owner. This is the kind of attitude that a landlord or king might have adopted toward the peasants.

Jesus upheld the Old Testament view of women. Not a single woman was chosen to be among the twelve disciples or to sit at the Last Supper. This is cited as one of the reasons the pope does not approve of ordaining women. But does he forget that the disciples, besides being male, were also all Jews? How can there be an Italian or Polish pope, Irish bishop or Mexican priest?

Jesus was violent. He cast some devils into swine, and "the whole herd of swine ran violently down a steep place into the sea, and perished in the waters." *(Matthew 8:32)* Why not show a little more respect for life?

His violence was tempered with irrationality. "Now in the morning as he returned into the city, he hungered. And when he saw a fig tree in the way, he came to it, and found nothing thereon, but leaves only, and said unto it, Let no fruit grow on thee henceforward for ever. And presently the fig tree withered away." *(Matthew 21:18-19,* repeated in *Mark 11:13-14,* which adds that it was not even fig season.) Is it kind or rational to destroy a plant that happens to be out of season when you are hungry? Is such behavior indicative of mental health?

In *Luke 19* Jesus told a parable which includes these ruthless words: "But those mine enemies, which would not that I should reign over them, bring them hither, and slay them before me." He is clearly comparing the "Lord" in the parable to himself. In *Matthew 10:34* Jesus said, "I came not to send peace, but a sword," and in *Luke 22:36* he told his disciples that "he that hath no

338

sword, let him sell his garment, and buy one." He made a whip and drove people out of the temple. *(John 2:15)*

In *Matthew 15:22-28*, Jesus refused to heal a sick child until he was pressured by the mother. What if the mother had not been persistent? Would he have withheld his magical favors and let the child die?

In *Matthew 19:12* Jesus encourages castration: "There be eunuchs, which have made themselves eunuchs for the kingdom of heaven's sake. He that is able to receive it, let him receive it." Modern believers are eager to interpret this verse figuratively. The *New International Version* loosely (and hopefully) translates it as "renounced marriage." But the literal meaning is "castrate," and many devout Christian men in history have done it to themselves, including the early church father Origen and entire monastic orders. Jesus gives no indication that he is speaking in a parable, or that his words mean anything other than what he said. This is no moral precept—this is sick.

We hear a lot of talk about the humble Jesus, but his words reveal something different. He looked at his disciples "with anger." *(Mark 3:5)* He said that he was "greater than the temple," *(Matthew 12:6)*, "greater than Jonas [Jonah]," *(Matthew 12:41)* and "greater than Solomon." He also appeared to suffer from the paranoia that afflicts dictators: "He that is not with me is against me." *(Matthew 12:30)*

But probably the worst of all of Jesus's ideas is the teaching of hell. In fact, the Christian doctrine of hell originated with Jesus. In the Old Testament, hell is just death, or the grave. With Jesus, hell became a place of everlasting torment. In *Mark 9:43,* Jesus said that hell is "the fire that never shall be quenched." *In Matthew 13:41-42,* Jesus gives us a graphic (and almost gleeful) description of the place he created: "The Son of man shall send forth his angels, and they shall gather out of his kingdom all things that offend, and them which do iniquity; and shall cast them into a furnace of fire: there shall be wailing and gnashing of teeth." Hitler's gas ovens were horrendous, but they did not burn forever.

I don't believe in Jesus or in God, so I qualify as one of those "things that offend" in the above verse. Anyone who thinks that it is moral for me to be eternally punished for my views hasn't the faintest concept of morality. Who could possibly believe that the Jesus who preached hell is a kind man?

And who could possibly think he was wise? The moral teachings of Jesus include these pearls of wisdom: don't make any plans for the future *(Matthew 6:34);* don't save any money *(Matthew 6:19-20);* don't become wealthy *(Mark 10:21,25);* sell everything you have and give it to the poor *(Luke 12:33);* don't work to obtain food, such as meat, because it doesn't last forever *(John 6:27);* don't have sexual urges *(Matthew 5:28);* marrying a divorced woman is committing adultery *(Matthew 5:32);* act in such a way that people will want to persecute you *(Matthew 5:11);* let everyone know that you are special and better than the rest *(Matthew 5:13-14);* hate your family *(Luke 14:26);* take money from those who have no savings and give it to the rich investors *(Luke 19:23-26);* if someone steals from you, don't try to get it back *(Luke 6:30);* if someone hits you, invite them to do it again *(Matthew 5:39);* if you lose a lawsuit, give more than the judgment *(Matthew 5:40);* if someone forces you to walk a mile, walk two miles *(Matthew 5:41);* if anyone asks you for anything, give it to them without question *(Matthew 5:42);* if you do something wrong with your hand, cut it off, and if you do something wrong with your eye, pluck it out *(Matthew 5:29,30*—said in a sexual context); if you are a man, then a good way to make points with "the kingdom" is to avoid women *(Matthew 19:12.* Literally or figuratively, this amounts to the same thing).

Much could be said about the moral character of other biblical personages, such as Noah (drunkard), Abraham (who lied about his wife), Lot (incestuous father), Moses (a murderer), David (adulterer and murderer), Solomon (polygamist), Peter (who swung swords and lied like a coward), Paul (who told women to keep silent), and many others. Believers could argue that these are mere mortals, and that we should expect them sometimes to act according to their corrupt human nature, and that this actually proves the need for a Savior who can love evil creatures in spite of our humanity. Only in a theological context might this be a plausible, if unsatisfactory, response. The fact remains that it is difficult to find consistent examples of moral behavior in the bible. We might grant the benefit of the doubt to the human characters in the bible, but why should we expect any better when the deities themselves, our examples, God and Jesus, act like thugs or lunatics who ought to be locked up?

Many moral precepts of the bible are unacceptable.

We have already noticed how the bible encourages slavery. It took a Civil War to rid ourselves of the fruits of such brutality in the United States, a task that was made more difficult due to the preachers who used the bible to defend their position. Not all churches were actively pro-slavery, but those that were found little difficulty supporting slavery with scripture.

Even though the phrase "original sin" does not appear in the bible, the scriptural concept that human nature is intrinsically evil has been an insidious doctrine. Jesus admits that mere humans can do good things, but we are nevertheless evil by nature: "If ye then, being evil, know how to give good gifts unto your children . . . " *(Matthew 7:11, Luke 11:3)* What worse psychological damage could be done to children than to tell them that they basically are no good? What does this do to self image? How many children go to sleep at night afraid of hell?

Jesus said, "If a man abide not in me, he is cast forth as a branch, and is withered; and men gather them, and cast them into the fire, and they are burned." *(John 15:6)* All through history, the church has interpreted this verse literally, using it to execute heretics with fire and other forms of capital punishment. Somebody tell Bruno, or the other victims of the Inquisition, that the bible is a morally superior book.

Exodus 22:18 says, "Thou shalt not suffer a witch to live." This one verse was responsible for the murder of thousands, perhaps millions, of women who were believed to be witches. Anyone who thinks this is a good moral teaching ought to join the Nazi Party. It is manifestly *immoral* to deal with enemies, real or perceived, by genocide.

One of the most damaging ideas in the bible is the concept of a Lord and Master. The loftiest biblical principles are obedience, submission, and faith, rather than reason, intelligence, and human values. Worshippers become humble servants of a dictator, expected to kneel before this king, lord, master, god, giving adoring praise and taking orders. According to the bible, we all eventually will be *forced* to bow before Jesus: "every knee shall bow to me, and every tongue shall confess to God." *(Romans 14:11)* The master/slave relationship has become so ingrained in the Jewish/Christian/Moslem world that independent thinkers are considered heretical, evil rebels. Prophets, popes, and ayatollahs have capitalized on this dichotomy of abasement in order to manipulate gullible followers. And even if they hadn't—even if the church had had a blameless history—why is there merit in submission?

We are proud of the American Revolution. It was a good and moral act to rebel against the tyranny of the king. It seems incongruous that so many Americans, who would never tolerate a dictator in government, are so eager to pay tribute to a universal dictator. Jesus said, "Render therefore unto Caesar the things which are Caesar's; and unto God the things that are God's." But what about the individual? Jesus considered that human beings are cogs in someone else's machine, be it God's or Caesar's. This goes against the grain of a modern democratic society. It is not moral.

Most Christians talk a lot about the bible, but don't know what it says. They *think* it is filled with wonderful advice. Many of them act shocked or incredulous when skeptics quote horrible scriptures. During many TV and radio shows on which I have quoted unsavory bible verses, biblically illiterate callers or audience members have asked me, "What bible are you reading?"

341

Most "positive" teachings in the bible are uninspired, inadequate, or dangerous.

I participated in a debate in Atlanta in 1988, "Is the Bible an acceptable guide for moral behavior?" My opponent was Dr. Walter Lowe, professor of systematic theology at Candler School of Theology at Emory University. During his entire prepared statement, he never once used the bible to support his position! He spent his time debunking the critical mindset of skeptics, presenting a "framework" for certain liberal understandings of Christianity, as if the mere discounting of skepticism could stand in place of evidence that the bible is a good book. My presentation was filled with specific quotes demonstrating that there is much immorality in the bible. His rebuttal was simply to label my interpretation of scripture as "fundamentalist." I was unwilling to give the bible the benefit of the doubt, he claimed, or to understand that the moral principles are contained over and above what the text actually says.

I hear this criticism a lot. If we freethinkers were mature and sophisticated enough to study the scriptures as they *should* be studied (higher criticism, context, metaphor, cultural elements, and so on), then we would have fewer problems with the bible. But this is nothing more than saying, "If you held my point of view, then you would hold my point of view." *Everyone* thinks their interpretation of the bible is the correct one. I agree that taking the bible at face value is simplistic; but liberal scholars should admit that skepticism regarding scriptural integrity is greater among liberal experts. They cannot deny that there is a storm of disagreement among scholars, theologians, and ordinary believers about the "true" meaning of the text. If a god is trying to get his message across to the masses of humanity, why did he do it in such a way that the only people qualified to grasp its true significance are those with doctorates in biblical studies? And then, how do we know which authorities to believe? What the bible means *in plain English* is what most people read, and if it embarrasses itself in plain English, then it is discrepant. In any event, Dr. Lowe did not explain how his sophisticated liberal understanding makes the brutal scriptures less brutal. No matter how you interpret it, administering the death penalty for picking up sticks is cruel and barbaric.

Toward the end of the debate I asked Dr. Lowe to give an example of a good moral teaching in the bible. He was unable to cite a single verse. Curiously, he did not mention the Ten Commandments, the Beatitudes, "turn the other cheek," "love thy neighbor as thyself," or the Golden Rule, passages that historically have stood as shining examples in the "Good Book." Yet a close look at even these "good" teachings shows that they shine rather dully.

The Ten Commandments

After a speech in which I mentioned a lawsuit by the Freedom From Religion Foundation seeking to move the Ten Commandments from the Colorado capitol grounds to an appropriate private location, such as a church, a woman asked me, "How can you object to the Ten Commandments? They are the most perfect set of laws ever given to humans! Our country is based on those laws." People who make such statements apparently have never studied the Ten Commandments.

Only three of the Ten Commandments have any relevance to American law: homicide, theft, and perjury. (Adultery and Sabbath laws are still on the books in some states, but they are anachronisms.) It is a good thing there is no law based on the Tenth Commandment against coveting or else our entire system of free enterprise would collapse!

The first four commandments have nothing at all to do with ethics or moral behavior:

First Commandment: "Thou shalt have no other gods before me." This was spoken by *Elohim* (ironically, a plural name for the god *El*), who is the "Lord" (*Jehovah,* the Jewish national name for God) and is the equivalent of establishing the nation of Israel, not the United States of America. It can be taken as either monotheistic (only one god) or henotheistic (only one supreme god), and in any case is contrary to the American constitutional guarantees of freedom of conscience and against an establishment of religion.

Second Commandment: "Thou shalt not make unto thee any graven image." This statement, ironically, appears on a graven image monolith of the Ten Commandments in many locations. As law, it would violate free speech.

Third Commandment: "Thou shalt not take the name of the Lord thy God in vain." This would be like prohibiting criticism of the president or other public officials. It is contrary to free speech.

Fourth Commandment: "Remember the sabbath day." The Jewish sabbath is Saturday, not Sunday. According to the biblical application of this law *(Numbers 15),* millions of Americans deserve capital punishment.

The first four commandments are religious orders, not moral guidelines. They certainly have no official place in a country that "shall make no law respecting an establishment of religion."

Fifth Commandment: "Honor thy father and thy mother: that thy days may be long upon the land," is the first statement in the Decalogue that approaches morality, although there are no details here explaining exactly how to honor parents. Do we obey them in everything? How long do we obey them? Until they die? There is obviously some merit in the idea expressed by this commandment, but there is precious little guidance here beyond a general

343

principle that parents should be respected. Isn't this just another variation of the bible's "respect authority" message? Wouldn't a moral principle suggest that you should not do anything to hurt your parents, that you should not take advantage of them, and that you should treat them with the basic respect deserved by all human beings? What if your parents are uneducated and poor advisors? What if they are evil? We all know that some parents do not deserve to be honored or obeyed. How do you "honor" a father who commits incest? Notice also that the rationale, "that thy days may be long," is an appeal to self interest, not to the value of parents as human beings.

Sixth Commandment: "Thou shalt not kill" is the first genuine moral statement in the decalogue, although it is unqualified. Does this mean that capital punishment is wrong? What about self defense? What about war? What about euthanasia requested by the terminally ill? The drawback of this law is its absoluteness—good laws make distinctions. Since the actions and commands of God burst with bloodthirstiness, this commandment seems to lose its import. Besides, prohibitions of murder existed long before the Ten Commandments or the Israelites appeared on the scene. It is not as if the human race never would have figured out that it is wrong to kill without some tablets coming down from a mountain. Laws against murder and manslaughter, based on self preservation and social stability, have found their way into almost every culture, before and after Moses, and it would be odd if the Israelites did not have a similar principle. (See "Murder, He Wrote" for an examination of the Hebrew word "kill" in this commandment.)

Seventh Commandment: "Thou shalt not commit adultery" is also a good idea, though it hardly merits the death penalty: "And the man that committeth adultery with another man's wife, even he that committeth adultery with his neighbor's wife, the adulterer and the adulteress shall surely be put to death." *(Leviticus 20:10)* Adultery involves a broken promise between two individuals and has nothing to do with a government. In many, if not most, cases it is destructive to a relationship and affects children if the marriage falls apart as a result. (Other things, such as fundamentalism, can cause the same problem.) But adultery by consenting adults does not fall into the category of malicious or harmful felonies. It is a legitimate concern of ethics; but it is no crime. Why don't the Ten Commandments mention rape? What about incest? Why don't they tell husbands that it is immoral to force an unwilling wife to have intercourse? Why doesn't the bible say that it is wrong for you to have sex, even with your spouse, if you knowingly have a sexually transmitted disease? Although adultery is important, does it rate the Big Ten?

Eighth Commandment: "Thou shalt not steal" is generally good advice, and makes good law. Except in wartime, most cultures, before and after the bible, have observed statutes that respect the property of others. But what about exceptions? The Ten Commandments, couched in absolute terms, admit no exceptions. Would it be immoral to steal bread to feed your starving child? Robin Hood is a folk hero. Nevertheless, most cultures recognize that taking someone's rightful property without permission, in principle, is generally wrong. Do Christians claim that without the Tablets from Mount Sinai, it never would have dawned on the human race that stealing is wrong?

Ninth Commandment: "Thou shalt not bear false witness" is also a generally good principle, but there is no universal law in America against telling lies. We have adequate laws against perjury and false advertising, and they are needed. But we all know that it is sometimes necessary to tell a lie in order to protect someone from harm. Lies in wartime are considered virtuous. If I knew the whereabouts of a woman who was being hunted by her abusive husband, I would consider it a moral act to lie to the man. True morality is able to weigh one principle against another and to judge their merits rationally. The bible, on the other hand, makes absolute statements without admitting the possibility of ethical dilemmas. As with killing and stealing, most cultures through history have made honesty a high ideal, with or without the Ten Commandments.

Tenth Commandment: "Thou shalt not covet thy neighbor's house . . . wife . . . manservant . . . maidservant . . . ox . . . ass . . . nor any thing that is thy neighbor's." Notice that this treats a wife like property. It does not say, "Thou shalt not covet thy neighbor's husband," because it is assumed that everything, including law, is directed at males. This is a plainly silly commandment. How can you command someone not to covet? Why? If stealing is wrong, then there is no need for this commandment. If I tell you that you have a beautiful house and that I wish I had it for myself, is that immoral? (Some claim that "covet" in this verse more properly means "to cast an evil eye" or spell upon something, and should be viewed as a prohibition of sorcery. But the Hebrew word *châmad*, according to *Strong's Concordance,* means "to delight in: beauty, greatly beloved, covet, delectable thing, delight, desire, goodly, lust, pleasant, precious thing.")

So the Ten Commandments are composed of four religious edicts that have nothing to do with ethics, three prohibitions that are irrelevant to modern law, and three shallow absolutes that are useful but certainly not unique to the Judeo-Christian system. Any one of us could easily come up with a more sensible and more thorough code for human behavior.

There is a more serious problem with the traditional Ten Commandments, from a biblical perspective: it is the wrong batch of commandments! The common listing (such as the one at the Denver capitol) is from *Exodus 20,* although it is not identified as the "Ten Commandments" in that passage. The title "Ten Commandments" is found in *Exodus 34:28* and *Deuteronomy 4:13* (a retelling of *Exodus 34*). The first set of commandments in *Exodus 20* was later smashed to pieces by Moses when he came down from the mountain and saw the people dancing before the golden calf. Moses had to go back up Mount Sinai to get them again. It is quite revealing to read *Exodus 34:* "And the Lord said unto Moses, Hew thee two tables of stone like unto the first: and I will write upon these tables the words that were in the first tables, which thou brakest. And be ready in the morning, and come up in the morning unto mount Sinai . . ." So Moses obeyed, "And he was there with the Lord forty days and forty nights; he did neither eat bread, nor drink water. And he wrote upon the tables the words of the covenant, the ten commandments." Here is the list Moses got the second time around:

1. Thou shalt worship no other god.
2. Thou shalt make thee no molten gods.
3. The feast of unleavened bread shalt thou keep.
4. Six days thou shalt work, but on the seventh day thou shalt rest.
5. Thou shalt observe the feast of weeks.
6. Thrice in the year shall all your menchildren appear before the Lord God.
7. Thou shalt not offer the blood of my sacrifice with leaven.
8. Neither shall the sacrifice of the feast of the passover be left until the morning.
9. The first of the firstfruits of thy land thou shalt bring unto the house of the Lord thy God.
10. Thou shalt not seethe a kid in his mother's milk.

What is this? The first, second, and fourth commandments are the same, except that "molten" rather than "graven" images are verboten; but the others are totally different! Did the rules change between visits? Did God lose his memory? What happened to homicide, theft and perjury? What might have happened with a third visit, or a fourth? Notice that these are not additional commandments: they are "the words that were in the first tables, which thou brakest." If you have ever been tempted to boil a goat in the milk of its mother, now you know better. This silly, confusing list has been presented to the world as the highest code of moral conduct ever created.

Other religions have lists of laws. The "Ten Precepts" of Buddhism (at least 500 BC) include 1) abstinence from destroying life, 2) abstinence from stealing, 3) abstinence from impurity, 4) abstinence from lying, 5) abstinence from strong drinks and intoxicating liquor, and five more rules for monks only. Notice that these are "precepts," not commandments, and that they also contain prohibitions against killing, stealing, and lying, which did not originate on Mount Sinai. This shows that the human race has a tendency to make behavior lists, and that the biblical Ten Commandments are not unique.

The Golden Rule

The phrase "Golden Rule" does not appear in the bible. Neither does the famous "do unto others" wording. What Jesus was actually reported to have said is this: "Therefore all things whatsoever ye would that men should do to you, do ye even so to them: for this is the law and the prophets." *(Matthew 7:12)* The author of Luke relates it this way: "And as ye would that men should do to you, do ye also to them likewise." *(Luke 6:31)*

Matthew's version is interesting. It appears to parallel an earlier wording of the same idea by Rabbi Hillel in 10 AD: "What is hateful to you, do not to your fellowmen. That is the entire Law; all the rest is commentary." *(Talmud, Shabbat, 31a)* The Golden Rule is not unique to Jesus, nor did it start with Christianity.

In Hinduism (Brahmanism), around 300 BC: "This is the sum of duty: Do naught unto others which would cause you pain if done to you." *(Mahabharata, 5, 1517.* The Vedic period of Hinduism goes back to 1500 BC.)

In Buddhism we read: "Hurt not others in ways that you yourself would find hurtful." *(Udana-Varga, 5, 18)*

In Confucianism, which started around 500 BC: "Surely it is the maxim of loving-kindness: Do not unto others that you would not have them do unto you." *(Analects, 15,23)*

In Taoism we have, "Regard your neighbor's gain as your own gain, and your neighbor's loss as your own loss." *(T'ai Shang Kan Ying P'ien.* The date of this writing is uncertain, but it was probably between 900-1200 C.E. Taoism came into its own around the fourth century BC.)

Zoroastrianism: "That nature alone is good which refrains from doing unto another whatsoever is not good for itself." *(Dadistan-i-dinik, 94, 5.* This particular quote came after Christianity, but the religion goes back to about 1500 BC.)

Some theologians claim that the Christian version of the Golden Rule is superior because it is phrased as a positive statement ("Do . . .") rather than the negative ("Do not . . ."). But the positive version is ambiguous; the negative version is useful. What if you are a masochist? Should you "do unto others" what you would like to have done unto yourself? What if you enjoy being preached at? Should you pester those who might not enjoy it? What if you have bad taste in food or clothes? Should you prepare meals or buy gifts for others based on what *you* like? What if you are an ascetic? Would you withhold a comfortable life from others? What if you have bizarre sexual preferences? Should you do unto others as you would have them do unto you?

This rule does not deserve a gold medal. It would be better named the "Bronze Guideline."

While the positive version tells you to "do unto others," there are many people who don't want anything done to them at all. Although phrased positively, the Golden Rule does not give any positive guidance. It does not say, "Do kind things, peaceful things, compassionate things to others." The negative version, on the other hand, allows people to be left alone. It rightly recognizes the essence of morality: don't cause harm. I like the Hindu and Buddhist versions because they identify pain as the real culprit in moral decisions.

Whether phrased positively or negatively, what do you do with a wife who hates back rubs and a husband who loves them? The positive expression of the rule would tell the husband to give his wife a back rub, which she doesn't want. The negative version would tell the wife not to give her husband a back rub, which he would love to have! Either way they lose.

Jesus's Bronze Guideline has sometimes been called the Law of Reciprocity, and the general idea, of course, is to consider how your actions affect others. But since it is not unique to Jesus, and since the Christian version is poorly phrased, it hardly supports the claim that the bible is a superior guide for moral behavior.

"Love thy neighbor"

Closely related to the Golden Rule is "Love thy neighbor." In *Leviticus 19:18* we find the commandment: "Thou shalt not avenge, nor bear any grudge against the children of thy people, but thou shalt love thy neighbor as thyself." Although this is not found in any version of the Ten Commandments, Jesus and Paul treat it as if it were on the main list.

In *Matthew 19:16* a man asked Jesus how to achieve eternal life, and Jesus replied, "Keep the commandments." When the man asked, "Which? Jesus said, Thou shalt do no murder, Thou shalt not commit adultery, Thou shalt not steal, Thou shalt not bear false witness, honour thy father and thy mother: and, Thou shalt love thy neighbor as thyself." If God had known that "love thy neighbor" was to be one of the biggies, why did he not include it in his Big Ten? Why not put it in place of boiling a goat in its mother's milk?

This section presents an additional problem for most Protestants who are taught that salvation comes by faith alone, not by keeping the commandments.

When the man asked Jesus how to achieve eternal life, why didn't Jesus say, "Believe on me."? The bible is contradictory.

In *Romans 13:8-9* Paul lists some important commandments: "for he that loveth another hath fulfilled the law. For this, Thou shalt not commit adultery, Thou shalt not kill, Thou shalt not steal, Thou shalt not bear false witness, Thou shalt not covet; and if there be any other commandment, it is briefly comprehended in this saying, namely, Thou shalt love thy neighbour as thyself." In *Galatians 5* Paul wrote: "For all the law is fulfilled in one word, even in this; Thou shalt love thy neighbour as thyself." *James 2:8* said it also.

Again, while we all agree that love is good, this rule is not specific. It does not give any advice about how to treat others. What about people who do not love themselves—how can they love others "as themselves?" What if you were raised in a dysfunctional and abusive family and have a very low self image? What if you are suicidal?

It is important to understand that "love thy neighbor" in the Old Testament meant something less than in the New Testament. In the Leviticus wording it deals with "the children of thy people," not with the entire earth. The word "neighbor" simply meant fellow Israelite. This is obvious when we observe how God's people treated other nations. In the context of the Old Testament, "love thy neighbor" is actually discriminatory. It would be like Ku Klux Klan leaders advising their followers to "love your white neighbors." It was perfectly allowable for God's people to hate the heathen. King David said that he hated them "with perfect hatred." *(Psalm 139:22)*

Jesus enhanced the concept by making it universal: "Ye have heard that it hath been said, Thou shalt love thy neighbour, and hate thine enemy. But I say unto you, Love your enemies, bless them that curse you, do good to them that hate you, and pray for them which despitefully use you, and persecute you." This is an improvement over Israelite imperialism, but the fact that it is nondiscriminatory does not necessarily make it an exceptional moral guide.

Love can't be commanded. No one has the right to tell me to love someone else. I can treat people with fairness, I can give respect where respect is due, but I can't just turn on love. Love, if it has any special meaning at all, is something that is reserved for those who are dear to me, for those who have earned my admiration, for those whom I find attractive or lovable. It is contrary to human nature to expect that I can have equal feelings for all people; and it cheapens love to bring everyone to the same level. When you say "I love you" to your spouse or lover, try adding, "but it could have been anyone else, because I love all my neighbors the same."

What if my neighbor is a jerk? What if after all my sincere attempts to be friendly and fair, my neighbor continues to act destructively? Is it healthy for me to pretend to love this person? I might be concerned for this person's lifestyle (or I might not), wishing to see an improvement for his or her sake as well as mine, but I certainly am not going to feign love. The biblical Jesus should have known better than to command believers to fake an emotion that is often inappropriate, unnatural, irrelevant, or phony.

As with most other biblical rules, Jesus makes "love thy neighbour" a condition for reward: "For if ye love them which love you, what reward have ye? Do not even the publicans do the same? . . . Be ye therefore perfect, even as your Father which is in heaven is perfect." *(Matthew 5:46-48.* The biblical god didn't love everyone, so he isn't perfect either.) Try saying to someone you love: "The reason I love you is because I am trying to attain perfection, and hope to be rewarded someday." These sayings are based on self interest, and are out of touch with reality. A better guide for human behavior would take into account the physical conditions, the individual cases, the nature of human feelings and the results of certain actions before making a blanket commandment. "Love thy neighbor" might make a lofty sentiment, but it is an impractical moral guideline.

The Beatitudes

The word "Beatitude" does not appear in the bible. The Beatitudes describe the first eight sayings of the "Sermon on the Mount" (also a phrase absent from the bible) spoken by Jesus in the fifth chapter of Matthew, all beginning with "Blessed are . . ."

Five of the eight beatitudes have nothing to do with morality. At face value the entire group is more of a pep talk than a code of ethical behavior. None of them are truly ethical in themselves since they are all conditions for a future reward. A true ethical code might mention the benefits ("Blessed are") of certain actions, but should stress the inherent value of the behavior on its own merits before detailing the gain or loss for the individual.

(1) "Blessed are the poor in spirit: for theirs is the kingdom of heaven." This praises a condition which is not admirable. Are we all supposed to become "poor-spirited?" What does "poor in spirit" mean? This verse does not advocate any specific, positive ethical action. It only says that if you happen to be "poor in spirit," then be happy because you are going to heaven. Verses such as these have been cited to keep slaves and women in their place with promises of "pie in the sky."

(2) "Blessed are they that mourn: for they shall be comforted." As with the first one, this does not advocate any behavior, unless it is interpreted as a command to go into mourning. Instead, why not encourage people to comfort those who are in mourning?

(3) "Blessed are the meek: for they shall inherit the earth." This might have some value if meekness is equated with gentleness, but even then it is valued only as a condition for a major pay-off in the future. This is like saying, "Be nice to Grandma because she might put you in her will." Incidentally, meekness is one attribute which is rarely seen in Christian history, current or past. How meek is the popular hymn, "Onward, Christian Soldiers?" How much meekness is found in the face of televangelist Jimmy Swaggart? How meek is the pope? Are the faces of the anti-abortionists filled with gentleness as they scream threats and physically block access to clinics, all in the name of God? How meek was Jesus when he cursed the fig tree, drove out the money changers, murdered a herd of swine, or looked at his disciples "with anger"? Meekness might be a useful attribute of those who are supposed to be in submission, such as slaves or Christian wives; but since much of life calls for firm, decisive, sometimes forceful action in order to correct inequalities and abuses, "meekness" seems like a rather weak and useless order.

(4) "Blessed are they which do hunger and thirst after righteousness: for they shall be filled." This merely encourages religious rituals, such as prayer. It offers no advice about how to treat other human beings. If "righteousness" is interpreted politically, then this is a dangerous verse. Righteousness breeds censorship, segregation, persecution, civil inequality, and intolerance. Millions of people have been killed and persecuted by the righteousness of others.

(5) "Blessed are the merciful: for they shall obtain mercy." This might be admirable, but how many of us are ever in a position to bestow mercy? The ability to grant mercy implies an authoritative rule over others: slavery, kingship, military. Christian parents ought to observe this mandate when they are about to follow the biblical command to spank their children. However, the motivation for this Beatitude is wrong: "for they shall obtain mercy." This beatitude is actually a threat, implying that God will not be merciful to those who are not merciful. Why would God not want to be merciful? Wouldn't the "crime" of a lack of mercy be one of the situations producing a need for God's mercy? A better moral principle might say, "Blessed are the merciful, because no human being has the right to harm another."

There is a potential dark side to this verse. Many believers are eager to forgive the sins of their pastors, priests, and other church leaders, unwilling to denounce them or to seek criminal or civil justice when they commit crimes. This is painfully evident in the many cases of pedophilia and child abuse in the ministry. Blaming or ignoring the victims, many church members rally to the support of the minister, consoling him with "mercy" in his time of need. If this beatitude produces such a lack of accountability, then it is truly an evil verse.

351

(6) "Blessed are the pure in heart: for they shall see God." What does "pure" mean, in real terms? If it means "the lack of desire to hurt others," then it is not bad. If it means "being spiritual, separate from worldly concerns," then it is bigoted and potentially dangerous. No ethical benefits arise from anti-social or self-denying attitudes. The Apostle Paul talked about having a "pure conscience," and this might be considered an admirable attitude in certain groups, but if there is no elaboration about how this affects conduct, then it is useless as a moral guide.

(7) "Blessed are the peacemakers: for they shall be called the children of God." This is the best of the bunch. We all want peace. But how do we obtain peace? Was the bomb at Hiroshima peaceful because it ended the war? Are nuclear warheads "blessed?" The United States is currently "at peace" with the Native Americans; was United States policy therefore peaceful and blessed toward the Indians? Besides, Jesus contradicted his own advice, warning, "Think not that I am come to send peace on earth: I came not to send peace, but a sword."

(8) "Blessed are they which are persecuted for righteousness' sake: for theirs is the kingdom of heaven. Blessed are ye when men shall revile you, and persecute you, and shall say all manner of evil against you falsely, for my sake. Rejoice, and be exceeding glad: for great is your reward in heaven: for so persecuted they the prophets which were before you." This Beatitude is potentially dangerous. Besides being in the passive voice and not advocating any specific moral behavior, "Blessed are they which are persecuted" appears to invite, encourage, and praise confrontation and dispute among human beings. Some have even interpreted this verse as a command to go out and "get persecuted." (See "Immovable Wall.") This persecution complex, admittedly not shared by all Christians, contradicts the seventh beatitude! If you stir up trouble for Jesus, you are blessed, and will receive a great "reward in heaven." You are supposed to "rejoice, and be exceeding glad" when your actions incite others to treat you badly. Persecution is something that could happen to anyone, whether that person has integrity or not, in the course of supporting a cause—freethinkers have garnered their share of undeserved abuse while working for separation of church and state—but to seek it and to "rejoice" about it is perverse.

The Beatitudes are immature: "If you kids will stop fighting, I'll give you dessert." Since they give little behavioral advice, stressing inner attitudes of being, they have been sometimes called the "Be–attitudes" by preachers. They are fluff. Offering skimpy moral guidance, they turn out to be mere platitudes to keep the poor and disenfranchised content to stay in their place. They are not good guides for behavior.

"Turn the other cheek"

I have heard Christians say that "turning the other cheek" is what makes Christianity unique, comparing it to Martin Luther King's nonviolent resistance. Here is how Jesus phrased it in the Sermon on the Mount: "Ye have heard that it hath been said, An eye for an eye, and a tooth for a tooth: but I say unto you, That ye resist not evil: but whosoever shall smite thee on thy right cheek, turn to him the other also." *(Matthew 5:38-39)*

At face value (no pun intended) this appears to be a plea for pacifism, and if it is interpreted as such, then it is acceptable. Most of us agree that it is usually more moral to avoid violence. But the way Jesus put it, this is not nonviolent resistance—it is violent nonresistance! To invite an abusive person to engage in further abuse is not pacifism. It is reckless.

Some might argue that the phrase "turn the other cheek" is just a figure of speech and that Jesus did not actually mean we should encourage maltreatment. But reading the context in the following verses *(Matthew 5:40-42)* reveals that this is indeed what he meant, ordering believers to reward doubly those who steal or kidnap.

A more sensible rule would say, "If someone smites thee on thy right cheek, then get away from that person! Defend yourself to avoid further harm. Ask for help, file charges, try to stop the abuse from happening to someone else. Let the person know that this kind of behavior is unacceptable. Never invite abuse."

How can we have morals without the bible?

The bible contains a smattering of potentially useful advice, such as the admonition against laziness in *Proverbs 6:6-11;* but even this admirable attempt to improve character fails to point out that there is nothing immoral about laziness itself. Ethical considerations are situational, and laziness would be wrong only if it caused harm to someone. On the whole, the bible does not have a grasp of ethics.

Even if we all agreed that an absolute moral code were necessary, we would have a serious practical problem. How do we know what that code is? Who decides how the bible is interpreted? Millions of devout, bible-believing Christians and Jews who study scripture carefully cannot agree on many important moral issues. They come down on different sides of the debate about capital punishment, abortion, physician-assisted suicide, death with dignity, ordination of women, women's rights, gay rights, birth control, war, and many other issues. What good does it do to have a divine code of ethics if no one knows what it is?

If morality means anything, it means that we are accountable to others. Christians believe that we are accountable not to people, but to God. Since God is nonexistent, then they are accountable to no one; and even if a god does exist, they are in practice not directly accountable to anyone in the real world, which amounts to the same thing. Since bible believers are accountable to God and not to humanity, they can ask for forgiveness from God for any crimes they commit against humanity. In other words, they can act with impunity. And they often do.

It does no good to say that Jesus died on the cross to pay for our sins. What self-respecting person would allow or want someone else to take responsibility for his or her actions? If I commit a crime, Jesus can die a million deaths and still not change the fact that the guilt lies with me. If I am convicted of a felony, does the law allow someone else to go to prison in my place? What good would that do? It would make a mockery of law and justice, and would turn me into an even more reprehensible character, fobbing responsibility off on another. To sing "Jesus died for my sin" is to admit that wrongful actions have nothing at all to do with consequences in the real world against flesh-and-blood individuals who hurt; they have to do with buying off an imaginary authority figure.

Humanists are accountable to real, breathing human beings, and to enforceable human laws, not to an unprovable, pie-in-the-sky deity. This makes humanism superior as a guide for moral behavior. Humanism is not just better than the bible, it is the only way we can be moral.

The May 27, 1992 issue of the Wisconsin State Journal ran this story:

Scriptures silenced in death penalty push

WASHINGTON (AP)—The Supreme Court on Tuesday refused to let Pennsylvania prosecutors invoke the Bible when attempting to get convicted murderers sentenced to death.

The justices, without comment, left intact a Pennsylvania Supreme Court ruling that banned prosecutors from referring to the Bible or any other religious writing when trying to persuade a jury to impose a death sentence.

The state court said such references always are impermissible, and may subject prosecutors to disciplinary action. York District Attorney H. Stanley Rebert had contended that the state court's ban violates prosecutors' free-speech rights and is too hostile to religion. The state Supreme Court last November threw out Karl Chambers' death sentence for a murder in York, ruling that he was entitled to a new sentencing trial.

The state court upheld Chambers' conviction for the Feb. 1, 1986 killing of Anna Mae Morris. Police said Morris was beaten to death with an ax handle and robbed.

At the sentencing trial, a prosecutor concluded his remarks to jurors by stating: "Karl Chambers has taken a life. As the Bible says, 'And the murderer shall be put to death.' Thank you."

The state Supreme Court said the prosecutor's remark told the jury "that an independent source of law exists for the conclusion that the death penalty is the appropriate punishment for (Chambers)."

Higher Mind

by Dan Barker

Every now and then
Comes that lonely interlude.
I find myself again
In a melancholy mood.
It seems that life is wrong
And no one cares for me.
I can only sing a song
In a minor key.
But I will not despair—
I've come to comprehend
The answer's always there:
I've found the perfect friend.

Chorus   There's a Higher Mind,
Yes, there's a Higher Mind.
That mind is my own.
I'm never alone.
There's a Higher Mind,
Yes, a much Higher Mind.
It rises above.
It rises to love.

Love is not a thing
I can make myself believe.
Love is not a thing
I can give or receive
Until I find the pride
To love myself first—
To drink from deep inside,
And satisfy this thirst.
It seems that peace of mind
Is precious and rare.
It's not a thing I find
Rushing here and there,
Acting out a part
In someone else's play.
I will listen to my heart,
And do it my own way.

HISTORY
OR
MYTH?

Part 8

Losing Faith in Faith

51

Jesus:
History or Myth?

IN ALL THE years I was a Christian minister, I never preached a sermon about the evidence for a historic Jesus. There was no need for such a sermon. I stood before many congregations and associated with many ministers, evangelists and pastors, and not one of us ever spoke about the possibility that Jesus was a fable, or that his story is more myth than history. We had heard, of course, that there were academic skeptics, but we dismissed them as a tiny minority of quacks and atheists.

In my four years of religious study at Azusa Pacific College, I took many bible classes—an entire course about the book of Romans, another class about Hebrew wisdom literature, and so on—but I was offered only one course in Christian apologetics. It was called "Christian Evidences," and I found it to be the least useful of all my studies. Since I preferred evangelism to academics, I found the information interesting, but irrelevant. The class did not delve deeply into the documents or arguments. We recited the roster of early historians and church fathers, and then promptly forgot them all. I figured that Christian scholars had already done the homework and that our faith rested on a firm historical foundation, and that if I ever needed to look it up I could turn to some book somewhere for the facts. I never needed to look it up.

As a freethinker, I decided to "look it up." I am now convinced that the

Jesus story is just a myth. Here's why:

1) There is no external historical confirmation for the New Testament stories.

2) The New Testament stories are internally contradictory.

3) There are natural explanations for the origin of the Jesus legend.

4) The miracle reports make the story unhistorical.

Can Jesus be confirmed historically?

At face value the Christian evidences appear to be overwhelming. Looking outside of the New Testament, many texts in apologetics will include a long list of names and documents that claim to confirm historically the existence of Jesus: Josephus, Suetonius, Pliny, Tacitus, Thallus, Mara Bar-Serapion, Lucian, Phlegon, Tertullian, Justin Martyr, Clement of Rome, Ignatius, Polycarp, Clement of Alexandria, Hippolytus, Origen, Cyprian, and others. Some of these names are church fathers writing in the second to fourth centuries and are therefore too late to be considered reliable first-century confirmation. Being church leaders, their objectivity is also questionable. These facts were not important to us evangelists nor would they cause any red flags to raise in the minds of the average believer reading the average book of Christian "proofs."

However, the list does include some nonbelievers—Jewish and Roman writers who were likely not biased towards Christianity—so it would appear that there can be no question about the historical existence of Jesus. Who could possibly doubt it?

It is rarely if ever pointed out that none of these evidences date from the time of Jesus. Jesus supposedly lived sometime between 4 BC and 30 AD, but there is not a single contemporary historical mention of Jesus, not by Romans or by Jews, not by believers or by unbelievers, not during his entire lifetime. This does not disprove his existence, but it certainly casts great doubt on the historicity of a man who was supposedly widely known to have made a great impact on the world. Someone should have noticed.

One of the writers who was alive during the time of Jesus was Philo-Judaeus. John E. Remsburg, in *The Christ,* writes:

"Philo was born before the beginning of the Christian era, and lived until long after the reputed death of Christ. He wrote an account of the Jews covering the entire time that Christ is said to have existed on earth. He was living in or near Jerusalem when Christ's miraculous birth and the Herodian massacre occurred. He was there when Christ made his triumphal entry into Jerusalem. He was there when the crucifixion with its attendant earthquake, supernatural darkness, and resurrection of the dead took place—when Christ himself rose from the dead, and in the presence of many witnesses ascended into heaven. These marvelous events which must have filled the world with amazement, had they really occurred, were unknown to him. It was Philo who developed the doctrine of the Logos, or Word, and although this Word incarnate dwelt in that very land and in the presence of multitudes revealed himself and demonstrated his divine powers, Philo saw it not."

There was a historian named Justus of Tiberius who was a native of Galilee, the homeland of Jesus. He wrote a history covering the time when Christ supposedly lived. This history is now lost, but a ninth-century Christian scholar named Photius had read it and wrote: "He [Justus] makes not the least mention of the appearance of Christ, of what things happened to him, or of the wonderful works that he did." (Photius' *Bibliotheca,* code 33)

Josephus

My Dad's birthday present to me when I turned nineteen was a copy of the complete works of Flavius Josephus. When it comes to hard evidence from outside the bible, this is the most common piece of historical documentation offered by Christian apologists. Outside of the New Testament, Josephus presents the only possible confirmation of the Jesus story from the first century.

At face value, Josephus appears to be the answer to the Christian apologist's dreams. He was a messianic Jew, not a Christian, so he could not be accused of bias. He did not spend a lot of time or space on his report of Jesus, showing that he was merely reporting facts, not spouting propaganda like the Gospel writers. Although he was born in 37 AD and could not have been a contemporary of Jesus, he lived close enough to the time to be considered a valuable second-hand source. Josephus was a highly respected and much-quoted Roman historian. He died sometime after the year 100. His two major tomes were *The Antiquities of the Jews* and *The Wars of the Jews.*

Antiquities was written sometime around the year 90 AD. It begins, "In the beginning God created the heaven and the earth," and arduously parallels the Old Testament up to the time when Josephus is able to add equally arduous historical details of Jewish life during the early Roman period. In Book 18, Chapter 3, this paragraph is encountered (Whiston's translation):

"Now, there was about this time, Jesus, a wise man, if it be lawful to call him a man, for he was a doer of wonderful works,—a teacher of such men as receive the truth with pleasure. He drew over to him both many of the Jews, and many of the Gentiles. He was [the] Christ; and when Pilate, at the suggestion of the principal men amongst us, had condemned him to the cross, those that loved him at the first did not forsake him, for he appeared to them alive again the third day, as the divine prophets had foretold these and ten thousand other wonderful things concerning him; and the tribe of Christians, so named from him, are not extinct at this day."

This truly appears to give historical confirmation for the existence of Jesus. But is it authentic? Most scholars, including most fundamentalist scholars, admit that at least some parts of this paragraph cannot be authentic. Many are convinced that the entire paragraph is a forgery, an interpolation inserted by Christians at a later time. There are many reasons for this:

1) The paragraph is absent from early copies of the works of Josephus. For example, it does not appear in Origen's second-century version of Josephus, contained in *Origen Contra Celsum* where Origen fiercely defended Christianity against the heretical views of Celsus. Origen quoted freely from Josephus to prove his points, but never once used this paragraph, which would have been the ultimate ace up his sleeve.

In fact, the Josephus paragraph about Jesus does not appear until the beginning of the fourth century, at the time of Constantine. Bishop Eusebius, a close ally of emperor Constantine, was instrumental in crystallizing and defining the version of Christianity which was to become orthodox, and he is the first person known to have quoted this paragraph of Josephus. Eusebius said that it was permissible for Christians to tell lies if it furthered the kingdom of God. The fact that the Josephus-Jesus paragraph shows up at this time of history, at a time when interpolations and revisions were quite common, makes the passage quite dubious. Many scholars believe that Eusebius was the forger.

2) The passage is out of context. In Book 18, which contains the paragraph about Jesus, Josephus starts with the Roman taxation under Cyrenius in 6 AD, talks about various Jewish sects at the time, including the Essenes, and a sect of Judas the Galilean. He discusses Herod's building of various cities, the succession of priests and procurators, and so on. Chapter 3 starts with a sedition against Pilate who planned to slaughter all the Jews but changed his mind. Pilate then used sacred money to supply water to Jerusalem, and the Jews protested. Pilate sent spies into the Jewish ranks with concealed weapons, and there was a great massacre.

Then comes the paragraph about Jesus, and immediately after it, Josephus continues: "And about the same time another terrible misfortune confounded the Jews . . ." Josephus, an orthodox Jew, would not have thought the Christian story to be "another terrible misfortune." It is only a Christian (someone like Eusebius) who would have considered this to be a Jewish tragedy. Paragraph 3 can be lifted out of the text with no damage to the chapter. It flows better without it.

3) Josephus would not have called Jesus "the Christ" or "the truth." Whoever wrote these phrases was a Christian. Josephus was a messianic Jew and never converted to Christianity. Origen reported that Josephus was "not believing in Jesus as the Christ."

4) The phrase "to this day" shows that this is a later interpolation. There was no "tribe of Christians" during Josephus's time. Christianity did not get off the ground until the second century.

5) Josephus appears not to know anything else about Jesus outside of this tiny paragraph and a reference to James, the "brother of Jesus" (see below). He is silent about the miracles of Jesus, although he reports the antics of other prophets in great detail. He adds nothing to the Gospel narratives, and says nothing that would not have been known by Christians already, whether in the first or fourth century. In all of Josephus's voluminous works, there is not a single reference to Christianity anywhere outside of this tiny paragraph. He relates much more about John the Baptist than about Jesus. He lists the activities of many other self-proclaimed Messiahs, including Judas of Galilee, Theudas the magician, and the Egyptian Jew Messiah, but is mute about the life of one whom he claims is the answer to his messianic hopes.

6) The paragraph mentions that the life of Jesus was foretold by the divine prophets, but Josephus neglects to mention who these prophets were or what they said. In no other place does Josephus connect any Hebrew prediction with the life of Jesus. If Jesus truly had been the fulfillment of divine prophecy, Josephus would have been the one learned enough to confirm it. The hyperbolic language is uncharacteristic of a careful historian: " . . . as the divine prophets had foretold these and ten thousand other wonderful things concerning him . . ." This sounds more like the stuff of sectarian propaganda.

Christians should be careful when they refer to Josephus as historical confirmation for Jesus. It turns around and bites them. If we remove the forged paragraph, the works of Josephus become evidence *against* historicity. If the life of Jesus was historical, why did Josephus know nothing of it?

There is one other passage in the *Antiquities* that mentions Jesus. It is in Book XX, Chapter 9:

"Festus was now dead, and Albinus was put upon the road; so he assembled the sanhedrin of judges, and brought before them the brother of Jesus, who was called Christ, whose name was James, and some others, (or some of his companions). And when he had formed an accusation against them as breakers of the law, he delivered them to be stoned . . ." (Whiston's translation)

This is flimsy, and even Christian scholars widely consider this to be a doctored text. The stoning of James is not mentioned in Acts. Hegesippus, a

Jewish Christian, in 170 AD wrote a history of the church saying that James the brother of Jesus was killed in a riot, not by sentence of a court, and Clement confirms this (quoted by Eusebius). Most scholars agree that Josephus is referring to another James here, possibly the same one that Paul mentions in Acts, who led a sect in Jerusalem. Instead of strengthening Christianity, this "brother of Jesus" interpolation contradicts history. Again, if Josephus truly thought Jesus was "the Christ," he would have added more about him than a casual aside in someone else's story.

So it turns out that Josephus is silent about Jesus. If Jesus had truly lived and had accomplished all of the deeds and miracles reported in the Gospels, Josephus should have noticed. Josephus was a native of Judea, a contemporary of the Apostles. He was Governor of Galilee for a time, the province in which Jesus allegedly lived and taught. "He traversed every part of this province," writes Remsburg, "and visited the places where but a generation before Christ had performed his prodigies. He resided in Cana, the very city in which Christ is said to have wrought his first miracle. He mentions every noted personage of Palestine and describes every important event which occurred there during the first seventy years of the Christian era. But Christ was of too little consequence and his deeds too trivial to merit a line from this historian's pen."

The second century and later

After Josephus, there are other writers who mention Christianity, but even if they are reliable, they are too late to claim the confirming impact of a first-century witness. Suetonius wrote a biography called *Twelve Caesars* around the year 112 AD, mentioning that Claudius "banished the Jews from Rome, since they had made a commotion because of Chrestus," and that during the time of Nero "punishments were also inflicted on the Christians, a sect professing a new and mischievous religious belief . . ." Notice that there is no mention of Jesus by name. It is unlikely that Christianity had spread as far as Rome during the reign of Claudius, or that it was large enough to have caused a revolt. "Chrestus" does not mean "Christ." It was a common name meaning "good," used by both slaves and free people, and occurring more than eighty times in Latin inscriptions. Even if Suetonius truly meant "Christus" (Christ), he may have been referring only to the Jews in Rome who were expecting a Messiah, not to Jesus of Nazareth. It could have been anybody, maybe a Roman Jew who stepped forward. It is only eager believers who will to jump to the conclusion that this provides evidence for Jesus. Nowhere in any of Suetonius's writings did he mention Jesus of Nazareth. Even if he had, his history would not necessarily have been reliable. He reported, for example, that Caesar Augustus bodily rose to heaven when he died, an event that few modern scholars consider historical.

In 112 AD, Pliny (the younger) said that "Christians were singing a hymn to Christ as to a god . . ." Again, notice the absence of the name Jesus. This could have referred to any of the other "Christs" who were being followed by Jews who thought they had found a Messiah. Pliny's report hardly counts as history since he is only relaying what other people believed. Even if this sentence referred to a group of followers of Jesus, no one denies that Christianity was in existence at that time. Pliny, at the very most, might be useful in documenting the religion, but not the historic Jesus.

Sometime after 117 AD, the Roman historian Tacitus wrote in his *Annals* (Book 15, chapter 44): "Nero looked around for a scapegoat, and inflicted the most fiendish tortures on a group of persons already hated for their crimes. This was the sect known as Christians. Their founder, one Christus, had been put to death by the procurator, Pontius Pilate in the reign of Tiberius. This checked the abominable superstition for a while, but it broke out again and spread, not merely through Judea, where it originated, but even to Rome itself, the great reservoir and collecting ground for every kind of depravity and filth. Those who confessed to being Christians were at once arrested, but on their testimony a great crowd of people were convicted, not so much on the charge of arson, but of hatred of the entire human race."

In this passage, Tacitus depicts early Christians as "hated for their crimes" and associated with "depravity and filth," not a flattering picture. But even if it is valid, it tells us nothing about Jesus of Nazareth. Tacitus claims no first-hand knowledge of Christianity. He is merely repeating the then common ideas about Christians. (A modern parallel would be someone reporting that Mormons believe that Joseph Smith was visited by the angel Moroni, which would hardly make it historical proof, even though it is as close as a century away.) There is no other historical confirmation that Nero persecuted Christians. Nero did persecute Jews, and perhaps Tacitus was confused about this. There certainly was not a "great crowd" of Christians in Rome around 60 AD, and the term "Christian" was not in use in the first century. Tacitus is either doctoring history from a distance or repeating a myth without checking his facts. Historians generally agree that Nero did not burn Rome, so Tacitus is in error to suggest that he would have needed a scapegoat in the first place. No one in the second century ever quoted this passage of Tacitus, and in fact it appears almost word-for-word in the writings of someone else, Sulpicius Severus, in the fourth century, where it is mixed in with other myths. The passage is therefore highly suspect and adds virtually no evidence for a historic Jesus.

In the ninth century a Byzantine writer named George Syncellus quoted a third-century Christian historian named Julius Africanus who quoted an unknown writer named Thallus who referred to the darkness at the crucifixion: "Thallus in the third book of his history calls this darkness an eclipse of the sun, but in my opinion he is wrong." All of the works of Africanus are lost, so there is no way to confirm the quote or to examine its context. We have no idea who Thallus was, or when he wrote. Eusebius (fourth century) mentions a history of Thallus in three books ending about 112 BC, so the suggestion is that Thallus might have been a near contemporary of Jesus. (Actually, the manuscript is damaged, and "Thallus" is merely a guess from "_allos Samaritanos.") There is no evidence of an eclipse during the time Jesus was supposedly crucified. The reason Africanus doubted the eclipse is because Easter happens near the full moon, and a solar eclipse would have been impossible at that time.

There is a fragment of a personal letter from a Syrian named Mara Bar-Serapion to his son in prison, of uncertain date, probably second or third century, that mentions that the Jews of that time had killed their "wise king." However, the New Testament reports that Jesus was killed by the Romans, not the Jews. The Jews had killed other leaders, for example, the Essene Teacher of Righteousness. If this truly is a report of a historical event rather than the passing on of folklore, it could have been a reference to someone else. It is worthless as evidence for Jesus of Nazareth, yet it can be found on the lists of some Christian scholars as proof that Jesus existed.

A second-century satiricist named Lucian wrote that the basis for the Christian sect was a "man who was crucified in Palestine," but this is equally worthless as historical evidence. He is merely repeating what Christians believed in the second century. Lucian does not mention Jesus by name. This reference is too late to be considered historical evidence, and since Lucian did not consider himself a historian, neither should we.

Bottom of the Barrel

In addition to Josephus, Suetonius, Tacitus, and the others, there is a handful of other so-called evidences and arguments that some Christians put forward. One very silly attempt is the *Archko Volume* containing supposedly authentic first-hand accounts of Jesus from the early first century, including letters from Pilate to Rome, glowing eye-witness testimony from the shepherds outside Bethlehem who visited the baby Jesus at the manger after being awakened by angels, and so on. Its flowery King-James prose makes entertaining reading, but it is not considered authentic by any scholar, although an occasional Christian has been duped into swallowing it. It was written in the nineteenth century by a traveling salesman who said he translated it from original documents found in the basement of the Vatican, although no such documents have ever been found.

Some of the other highly questionable confirmation attempts include Tertullian (197 AD), Phlegon (unknown date), Justin Martyr (about 150 AD), and portions of the Jewish Talmud (second through fifth centuries) that mention Jesus in an attempt to discredit Christianity, supposedly showing that even the enemies of Jesus did not doubt his existence. Though all of these so-called evidences are flimsy, some Christians make a showy point of listing them with little elaboration in their books of apologetics. Ministers can rattle off these "historical confirmations" with little fear that their congregations will take the time to investigate their authenticity.

In *Evidence That Demands a Verdict,* Josh McDowell makes an argument that is common among apologists: "There are now more than 5,300 known Greek manuscripts of the New Testament. Add over 10,000 Latin Vulgate and at least 9,300 other early versions (MSS) and we have more than 24,000 manuscript copies of portions of the New Testament in existence today. No other document of antiquity even begins to approach such numbers and attestation. In comparison, the *Iliad* by Homer is second with only 643 manuscripts that still survive." This information might cause believers to applaud with smugness, but it misses the point. What does the number of copies have to do with authenticity? If a million copies of this book you are reading are printed, does it make it any more truthful? Are the "historical" facts reported in the *Iliad* considered reliable? There are currently hundreds of millions of copies of the Koran in existence, in many forms and scores of translations. Does the sheer number of copies make it more reliable than, say, a single inscription on an Egyptian sarcophagus? This argument is a smokescreen. There are no original manuscripts (autographs) of the bible in existence, so we all agree that we are working from copies. Critics might agree that the current translations of the bible are based on a reasonably accurate transcription of an early form of the New Testament, but what does this have to do with authenticity, reliability, or truthfulness?

Another argument made by McDowell and others is the close interval of time between the events or original writing and the earliest copies in our possession. Homer wrote the *Iliad* in 900 BC, but the our earliest copy is from 400 BC—a span of five hundred years. Aristotle wrote in 384-322 BC and the earliest copy dates from 1100 AD—a gap of fourteen hundred years. In contrast, the New Testament was written (McDowell says) between 40 and 100 AD, and the earliest copy dates from 125 AD, a time span of twenty-five years.

This is important when considering the reliability of the *text* itself. A shorter interval of time allows for fewer corruptions and variants. But it has no relevance to the reliability of the *content*. If the New Testament should be considered reliable on this basis, then so should the Book of Mormon, which was supposedly written (copied by Joseph Smith) in 1823 and first published in 1830, a gap of only seven years. In addition to Joseph Smith, there are signed testimonies of eleven witness who claimed to have seen the gold tablets on which the angel Moroni wrote the Book of Mormon. We are much closer in history to the origin of Mormonism than to the origin of Christianity. There are millions of copies of the Book of Mormon and a thriving Church of Jesus Christ of Latter Day Saints (with millions of members and billions of dollars in assets) to prove its veracity. Though most scholars (pro and con) agree that the current edition of the Book of Mormon is a reliable copy of the 1830 version, few Christian scholars consider it to be reliable history.

Not The Gospel Truth

If we stick to the New Testament (we have no choice) how much can we know about the Jesus of history? Although the four Gospels (Matthew, Mark, Luke, and John) have been placed first in the current New Testament, they were not the first books written. The earliest writings about Jesus are those of Paul, who produced his epistles no earlier than the mid 50s. Strangely, Paul mentions very little about the life of the historical Jesus. The Jesus of whom Paul writes is a disembodied, spiritual Christ, speaking from the sky. He never talks about Jesus's parents or the virgin birth or Bethlehem. He never mentions Nazareth, never refers to Jesus as the "Son of man" (as commonly used in the Gospels), avoids recounting a single miracle committed by Jesus, does not fix any historical activities of Jesus in any time or place, makes no reference to any of the twelve apostles by name, omits the trial, and fails to place the crucifixion in a physical location (Jerusalem). Paul rarely quotes Jesus, and this is odd since he used many other devices of persuasion to make his points. There are many places in the teachings of Paul where he could have and should have invoked the teachings of Jesus, but he ignores them. He contradicts Jesus's teachings on divorce *(I Corinthians 7:10)* allowing for none while the Gospel Jesus permitted exceptions. Jesus taught a trinitarian baptism ("in the name of the Father, Son, and Holy Ghost"), but Paul and his disciples baptized in Jesus's name only, which makes perfect sense if the concept of the trinity was developed later.

Paul never claims to have met the pre-resurrected Jesus. In fact, one of the most glaring contradictions of the bible appears in two different accounts of how Paul supposedly met the disembodied Christ for the first time. When Paul was traveling to Damascus one day in order to continue persecuting Christians, he was knocked to the ground and blinded by a great light (struck by lightning?). In both versions of this story, Paul heard the voice of Jesus, but in one account the men who were with Paul heard the voice *(Acts 9:7)*, and in the other his men specifically "heard not the voice" *(Acts 22:9)*. Did Paul's men hear the voice, or didn't they? There have been many *ad hoc* attempts by apologists to reconcile this contradiction (for example, pretending that the different declensions of φονη imply "voice" vs. "sound," or that "hear" means "understand" in one passage—a dishonest tactic employed by some modern translations, such as the popular *New International Version*), but they are defensive and unsatisfactory.

The "silence of Paul" is one of the thorny problems confronting defenders of a historical Jesus. The Christ in Paul's writings is a different character from the Jesus of the Gospels. Paul adds not a speck of historical documentation for the story. Even Paul's supposed confirmation of the resurrection in *I Corinthians 15:3-8* contradicts the Gospels when it says that Jesus first was seen of "Cephas [Peter], then of the twelve." (See "Leave No Stone Unturned.")

The Gospels were written no earlier than 70 AD, most likely during the 90s and later. They all pretend to be biographies of Jesus. No one knows who wrote these books, the names having been added later as a matter of convenience. The writer of Matthew, for example, refers to "Matthew" in the third person. Neither Mark nor Luke appear in any list of the disciples of Jesus, and we have no way of knowing where they got their information. The general scholarly consensus is that Mark was written first (based on an earlier "proto-Mark" now lost) and that the writers of Matthew and Luke borrowed from Mark, adapting and adding to it. Matthew, Mark, and Luke are commonly known as the "synoptic Gospels" since they share much common material. The writer of John appears to have written in isolation, and the Jesus portrayed in his story is a different character. John contains little in common with the other three, and where it does overlap, it is often contradictory. (See "Leave No Stone Unturned.")

There is very little that can be ascertained from the four Gospels about the historic Jesus. His birthday is unknown. In fact, the year of Jesus's birth *cannot* be known. The writer of Matthew says Jesus was born "in the days of Herod the king." Herod died in 4 BC. Luke reports that Jesus was born "when Cyrenius [Quirinius] was governor of Syria." Cyrenius became governor of Syria in 6 AD. That is a discrepancy of at least nine years.

Luke says Jesus was born during a Roman census, and it is true that there was a census in 6 AD. This would have been when Jesus was at least nine years old, according to Matthew. There is no evidence of any earlier census during the reign of Augustus; Palestine was not part of the Roman Empire until 6 AD. Perhaps Matthew was right, or perhaps Luke was right, but both could not have been right.

Matthew reports that Herod slaughtered all the first-born in the land in order to execute Jesus. No historian, contemporary or later, mentions this supposed genocide, an event which should have caught someone's attention. None of the other biblical writers mention it.

The genealogies of Jesus present a particularly embarrassing example of why the Gospel writers are not reliable historians. Matthew gives a genealogy of Jesus consisting of twenty-eight names from David down to Joseph. Luke gives a reverse genealogy of Jesus consisting of forty-three names from Joseph back to David. They each purport to prove that Jesus is of royal blood, though neither of them explains why Joseph's genealogy is relevant if he was not Jesus's father: Jesus was born of the Virgin Mary and the Holy Ghost. Matthew's line goes from David's son Solomon, while Luke's goes from David's son Nathan. The two genealogies could not have been for the same person.

Matthew's line is like this: David, Solomon, eleven other names, Josiah, Jechoniah, Shealtiel, Zerubbabel, Abiud, six other names, Matthan, Jacob, and Joseph. Luke's line is like this: David, Nathan, seventeen other names (none identical to Matthew's list), Melchi, Neri, Shealtiel, Zerubbabel, Rhesa, fifteen other names (none identical to Matthew's list), Matthat, Heli, and Joseph.

Some defenders of Christianity assert that this is not contradictory at all because Matthew's line is through Joseph and Luke's line is through Mary, even though a simple glance at the text shows that they both name Joseph. No problem, say the apologists: Luke named Joseph, but he really meant Mary. Since Joseph was the legal parent of Jesus, and since Jewish genealogies are patrilineal, it makes perfect sense to say that Heli (their choice for Mary's father) had a son named Joseph who had a son named Jesus. Believe it or not, many Christians can make these statements with a straight face. In any event, they will not find a shred of evidence to support such a notion.

However, there is a more serious problem to this argument: the two genealogies intersect. Notice that besides starting with David and ending with Joseph, the lines share two names in common: Shealtiel and Zerubbabel, both commonly known from the period of the Babylonian captivity. If Matthew and Luke present two distinct parental genealogies, as the apologists assert, there should be no intersection. In a last-ditch defense, some very creative apologists have hypothesized that Shealtiel's grandmother could have had two husbands and that her sons Jechoniah and Neri represent two distinct paternal lines, but this is painfully speculative.

The two genealogies are widely different in length. One would have to suppose that something in Nathan's genes caused the men to sire sons fifty percent faster than the men in Solomon's line.

Matthew's line omits four names from the genealogy given in the Old Testament (between Joram and Jotham), and this makes sense when you notice that Matthew is trying to force his list into three neat groups of fourteen names each. (Seven is the Hebrew's most sacred number.) He leaves out exactly the right number of names to make it fit. Some have argued that it was common to skip generations and that this does not make it incorrect. A great-great grandfather is just as much an ancestor as a grandfather. This might be true, except that Matthew explicitly reports that it was exactly *fourteen* generations: "So all the generations from Abraham to David are fourteen generations; and from David until the carrying away into Babylon are fourteen generations; and from the carrying away into Babylon unto Christ are fourteen generations." *(Matthew 1:17)* Matthew is caught tinkering with the facts. His reliability as a historian is severely crippled.

Another problem is that Luke's genealogy of Jesus goes through Nathan, which was not the royal line. Nor could Matthew's line be royal after Jeconiah because the divine prophecy says of Jeconiah that "no man of his seed shall prosper sitting upon the throne of David, and ruling any more in Judah." *(Jeremiah 22:30)* Even if Luke's line is truly through Mary, Luke reports that Mary was a cousin to Elizabeth, who was of the tribe of Levi, not the royal line. (Some Christians desperately suggest that the word "cousin" might allowably be translated "countrywoman," just as believers might call each other "brother" or "sister," but this is *ad hoc*.)

Since Jesus was not the son of Joseph, and since Jesus himself appears to deny his Davidic ancestry *(Matthew 22:41-46),* the whole genealogy is pointless. Instead of rooting Jesus in history, it provides critics with an open window on the myth-making process. The Gospel writers wanted to make of their hero nothing less than what was claimed of saviors of other religions: a king born of a virgin.

The earliest Gospel written was Mark. Matthew and Luke based their stories on Mark, editing according to their own purposes. All scholars agree that the last twelve verses of Mark, in modern translations, are highly dubious. Most agree that they do not belong in the bible. The earliest ancient documents of Mark end right after the women find the empty tomb. This means that in the first biography, on which the others based their reports, there is no post-resurrection appearance or ascension of Jesus. Noticing the problem, a Christian scribe at a much later time inserted verses 9-20. The Gospel ac-

371

counts cannot be considered historical, but even if they were, they tell us that the earliest biography of Jesus contains no resurrection! They tell us that the Gospels were edited, adapted, altered, and appended at later times in order to make them fit the particular sectarian theology of the writers.

The Gospels themselves are admittedly propagandistic: "And many other signs truly did Jesus in the presence of his disciples, which are not written in this book: But these are written that ye might believe that Jesus is the Christ, the Son of God; and that believing ye might have life through his name." *(John 20:30-31)* This hardly sounds like the stuff of objective historical reporting. This verse sends up a red flag that what we are reading should be taken with a very large grain of salt.

How did the myth originate?

If Jesus is a fable, how did the story originate? How did there come to be a worldwide following of billions of Christians spanning two millennia if the story is not true? An idea does not need to be true in order to be believed, and the same could be asked about any other myth: Santa Claus, William Tell, or Zeus. Nevertheless, it is not an unfair challenge to ask skeptics to suggest an alternative to historicity.

There are a number of plausible explanations for a natural origin of the Jesus myth, none of which can be proved with certainty. Unbelievers are not in agreement, nor need they be. Some skeptics think that Jesus never existed at all and that the myth came into being through a literary process. Other skeptics deny that the Jesus character portrayed in the New Testament existed, but feel that there could have been a first-century personality after whom the exaggerated myth was patterned. Others believe that Jesus did exist, and that some parts of the New Testament are accurate, although the miracles and the claim to deity are due to later editing of the original story. Still others claim that the New Testament is basically true in all of its accounts except that there are natural explanations for the miracle stories. (It is not just atheists who possess these views. Many liberal Christians, such as Paul Tillich, have "de-mythologized" the New Testament.)

None of these views can be proved, any more than the orthodox position can be proved. What they demonstrate is that since there do exist plausible natural alternatives, it is irrational to jump to a supernatural conclusion.

1) One of the views, held by J. M. Robertson and others, is that the Jesus myth was patterned after a story found in the Jewish Talmudic literature about the illegitimate son of a woman named Miriam (Mary) and a Roman soldier named Pandera, sometimes called Joseph Pandera. In *Christianity*

and Mythology, Robertson writes: ". . . we see cause to suspect that the movement really originated with the Talmudic Jesus Ben Pandera, who was stoned to death and hanged on a tree, for blasphemy or heresy, on the eve of a Passover in the reign of Alexander Jannaeus (B.C. 106-79). Dr. Low, an accomplished Hebraist, is satisfied that this Jesus was the founder of the Essene sect, whose resemblances to the legendary early Christians have so greatly exercised Christian speculation."

2) Another view is that the Jesus myth grew out of a pre-Christian cult of Joshua. Some suggest that the New Testament story about swapping Jesus for Barabbas (meaning "son of the father") arose from the tension between two different Joshua factions. Origen mentioned a "Jesus Barabbas." The name "Jesus" is the Greek for Joshua ("Yeshua" in Hebrew). In *Mark 9:38* the disciples of Jesus saw another man who was casting out devils in the name of Jesus (Joshua). The Sibyllene Oracles identify Jesus with Joshua, regarding the sun standing still.

3) Other scholars suggest that the Jesus story is simply a fanciful patchwork of pieces borrowed from other religions. Pagan mythical parallels can be found for almost every item in the New Testament: the Last Supper, Peter's denial, Pilate's wife's dream, the crown of thorns, the vinegar and gall at the crucifixion, the mocking inscription over the cross, the Passion, the trial, Pilate's washing of hands, the carrying of the cross, the talk between the two thieves hanging beside Jesus, and so on. There were many crucified sun gods before Jesus. There was the crucifixion of Antigonus, the "King of the Jews," and Cyrus, a Messianic figure. Prometheus and Heracles wear mock crowns, and in some versions of the story, Prometheus is executed by crucifixion. Babylonian prisoners dressed as kings for five days, then they were stripped, scourged, and crucified.

Attis was a self-castrated god-man who was born of a virgin, worshipped between March 22 and 27 (vernal equinox), and hanged on a cut pine tree. He escaped, fled, descended into a cave, died, rose again, and was later called "Father God." Dionysus was a savior sacrifice who descended into hell. There is the story about Simon the Cyrenian sun God who carried pillars to his death. (Compare with Simon the Cyrene who carried the cross of Jesus in the New Testament.) Before Jesus there were many ascension myths: Enoch, Elijah, Krishna, Adonis, Heracles, Dionysus, and later Mary.

Mithra was a virgin-born Persian god. In 307 A.D. (just before Constantine institutionalized Christianity), the Roman emperor officially designated that Mithra was to be the "Protector of the Empire." Historian Barbara Walker records this about Mithra:

"Mithra was born on the 25th of December . . . which was finally taken over by Christians in the 4th century as the birthday of Christ. Some say Mithra sprang from an incestuous union between the sun god and his own mother . . . . Some claimed Mithra's mother was a mortal virgin. Others said Mithra had no mother, but was miraculously born of a female Rock, the *petra genetrix,* fertilized by the Heavenly Father's phallic lightning.

"Mithra's birth was witnessed by shepherds and by Magi who brought gifts to his sacred birth-cave of the Rock. Mithra performed the usual assortment of miracles: raising the dead, healing the sick, making the blind see and the lame walk, casting out devils. As a Peter, son of the *petra,* he carried the keys of the kingdom of heaven . . . . His triumph and ascension to heaven were celebrated at the spring equinox (Easter) . . . .

"Before returning to heaven, Mithra celebrated a Last Supper with his twelve disciples, who represented the twelve signs of the zodiac. In memory of this, his worshippers partook of a sacramental meal of bread marked with a cross. This was one of seven Mithraic sacraments, the models for the Christians' seven sacraments. It was called *mizd,* Latin *missa,* English *mass.* Mithra's image was buried in a rock tomb . . . . He was withdrawn from it and said to live again.

"Like early Christianity, Mithraism was an ascetic, anti-female religion. Its priesthood consisted of celebate men only. . . .

"What began in water would end in fire, according to Mithraic eschatology. The great battle between the forces of light and darkness in the Last Days would destroy the earth with its upheavals and burnings. Virtuous ones . . . would be saved. Sinful ones . . . would be cast into hell . . . . The Christian notion of salvation was almost wholly a product of this Persian eschatology, adopted by Semitic eremites and sun-cultists like the Essenes, and by Roman military men who thought the rigid discipline and vivid battle-imagery of Mithraism appropriate for warriors.

"After extensive contact with Mithraism, Christians also began to describe themselves as soldiers for Christ; . . . to celebrate their feasts on Sun-day rather than the Jewish sabbath; . . . . Like Mithraists, Christians practiced baptism to ascend after death through the planetary spheres to the highest heaven, while the wicked (unbaptized) would be dragged down to darkness." (*The Woman's Encyclopedia Of Myths And Secrets,* pages 663-665)

The name "Mary" is common to names given to mothers of other gods: the Syrian Myrrha, the Greek Maia, and the Hindu Maya, all derived from the familiar "Ma" for mother. The phrases "Word of God" and "Lamb of God" are probably connected, due to a misunderstanding of words that are similar in different languages. The Greek word "logos," which means "word" and was used originally by the gnostics, is translated "imerah" in Hebrew; but the word "immera" in Aramaic means "lamb." It is easy to see how some Jews, living at the intersection of so many cultures and languages, could be confused and influenced by so many competing religious ideas.

In the fourth century a Christian scholar named Fermicus attempted to establish the uniqueness of Christianity, but he was met at every turn by pagan precedents to the story of Jesus. He is reported to have said: *"Habet Diabolus Christos sous!"* ("The Devil has *his* Christs!")

4) W. B. Smith thinks there was a pre-Christian Jesus cult of gnosticism. There is an ancient papyrus which has these words: "I adjure thee by the God of the Hebrews, Jesus."

5) G. A. Wells is one scholar who believes Jesus never existed as a historical person. He, and others, see Jesus as the personification of Old Testament "wisdom." The Dead Sea Scrolls have Essene commentary on the Old Testament wisdom literature, and Wells has found many parallels with the life of Jesus. The book of Proverbs depicts "Wisdom" as having been created by God first, before heaven and earth. Wisdom mediates in creation and leads humans into truth. Wisdom is the governor and sustainer of the universe. Wisdom comes to dwell among men and bestows gifts. Most people reject wisdom and it returns to heaven. Solomon's idea of a just man is one who is persecuted and condemned to a shameful death, but then God gives him eternal life, counting him as one of the "sons of God," giving him a crown, calling him the "servant of the Lord." He is despised and rejected. In *The Jesus of History and Myth,* R. J. Hoffman writes: "In sum, musing on the Wisdom and on other Jewish literature could have prompted the earliest Christians to suppose that a preexistent redeemer had suffered crucifixion, the most shameful death of all, before being exalted to God's right hand."

6) Another view is presented by Randall Helms in an article, "Fiction in the Gospels" in *Jesus in History and Myth.* Helms notices that there are many literary parallels between Old Testament and New Testament stories. He calls this "self-reflexive fiction." It is as if there are some skeletal templates into which the Jews placed their stories. One example is the comparison between the raising of the son of the widow of Nain in *Luke 7:11-16* and the raising of the son of a widow of Zarephath in *I Kings 17.* Not only is the content similar, but the structure of the tale is almost identical. Other examples are the storm stories in Psalms and Jonah compared with the New Testament storm story in *Mark 4:37-41*, and the story of Elijah's food multiplication with that of Jesus. The first-century Jews were simply rewriting old stories, like a movie remake. This view, in and of itself, does not completely account for the entire Jesus myth, but it does show how literary parallels can play a part in the elaboration of a fable.

7) John Allegro suggested that the Jesus character was patterned after the Essene Teacher of Righteousness, who was crucified in 88 BC. He wrote that the Dead Sea Scrolls prove that the Essenes interpreted the Old Testament in a way to make them fit their own Messiah. Allegro writes: "When Josephus speaks of the Essene's reverence for their 'Lawgiver' . . . we may assume reasonably that he speaks of their Teacher, the 'Joshua/Jesus' of the Last Days. By the first century, therefore, it seems that he was being accorded semi-divine status, and that his role of Messiah, or Christ, was fully appreciated." *(The Dead Sea Scrolls and the Christian Myth)*

8) An example of one of the many naturalistic attempts to explain the miracles is the "swoon theory," found in *The Passover Plot* by Dr. Hugh J. Schonfield. This is the idea that the resurrection story is basically historically accurate but that Jesus merely fainted, and was presumed to be dead, coming back to consciousness later. Some of these explanations turn out to be just as difficult to believe as the miracle reports themselves, in my opinion; but they are, nevertheless, viable hypotheses that show that even if the documents are entirely reliable, the story itself can be explained in other ways. If it is possible for part of a story to be misunderstood or exaggerated, then why not the whole thing?

Prudent history demands that until all natural explanations for the origin of an outrageous tale are completely ruled out, it is irresponsible to hold to the literal, historical truth of what appears to be just another myth.

Are the miracles historical?

During a debate at the University of Northern Iowa, I asked my opponent, "Do you believe that a donkey spoke human language?"

"Yes, I do," he responded.

"Yesterday, I visited the zoo," I continued, "and a donkey spoke to me in perfect Spanish, saying, '*Alá es el único Dios verdadero.*' Do you believe that?"

"No, I don't," he answered without hesitation.

"How can you be so quick to doubt my story and yet criticize me for being skeptical of yours?"

"Because I believe what Jesus tells me, not what you tell me."

In other words, miracles are true if the bible says so, but they are not true if they appear in any other source. When questioning the miracle reports of the New Testament, this become circular reasoning.

The presence of miracle stories in the New Testament makes the legend highly suspect. But it is important to understand what skeptics are saying about miracles. Skeptics do not say that the miracle reports should be automatically dismissed, *a priori*. After all, there might be future explanations for the stories, perhaps something that we yet do not understand about nature.

What skeptics say is that if a miracle is defined as some kind of violation, suspension, overriding, or punctuation of natural law, then miracles cannot be *historical*. Of all of the legitimate sciences, history is the weakest. History, at best, produces only an approximation of truth. In order for history to have any strength at all, it must adhere to a very strict assumption: that natural law is regular over time.

Without the assumption of natural regularity, no history can be done. There would be no criteria for discarding fantastic stories. Everything that has ever been recorded would have to be taken as literal truth.

Therefore, if a miracle did happen, it would pull the rug out from history. The very basis of the historical method would have to be discarded. You can have miracles, or you can have history, but you can't have both.

However, if a miracle is defined as a "highly unlikely" or "wonderful," event, then it is fair game for history, but with an important caveat: outrageous claims require outrageous proof. A skeptic who does allow for the remote possibility of accurate miracle reporting in the Gospels nevertheless must relegate it to a very low probability.

Since the New Testament contains numerous stories of events that are either outrageous (such as the resurrection of thousands of dead bodies on Good Friday) or impossible, the story must be considered more mythical than historical.

Conclusion

Either in ignorance or in defiance of scholarship, preachers such as televangelist Pat Robertson continue to rattle off the list of Christian "evidences," but most bible scholars, including most non-fundamentalist Christians, admit that the documentation is very weak. In *The Quest of the Historical Jesus,* Albert Schweitzer, wrote: "There is nothing more negative than the result of the critical study of the life of Jesus. . . . The historical Jesus will be to our time a stranger and an enigma . . ."

To sum up: 1) There is no external historical confirmation for the Jesus story outside of the New Testament. 2) The New Testament accounts are internally contradictory. 3) There are many other plausible explanations for the origin of the myth which do not require us to distort or destroy the natural world view. 4) The miracle reports make the story highly suspect.

The Gospel stories are no more historic than the Genesis creation accounts are scientific. They are filled with exaggerations, miracles, and admitted propaganda. They were written during a context of time when myths were being born, exchanged, elaborated, and corrupted, and they were written to an audience susceptible to such fables. They are cut from the same cloth as other religions and fables of the time. Taking all of this into account, it is rational to conclude that the New Testament Jesus is a myth.

For documentation and additional study from a critical perspective:

Allegro, J. M., *The Dead Sea Scrolls and the Christian Myth,* Prometheus Books, New York, 1984.

Arnheim, M. A., *Is Christianity True?,* Prometheus Books, New York, 1984.

Baigent, Michael and Leigh, Richard, *The Dead Sea Scrolls Deception,* Summit Books, New York, 1991.

Brandon, S. G. F., *The Trial of Jesus of Nazareth,* Scarborough, 1979.

Carmichael, J., *The Death of Jesus,* Horizon, 1982.

Flew, Antony (a debate with Gary Habermas), *Did Jesus Rise From the Dead?,* Harper & Row, 1987.

Frazer, Sir James G., *The Golden Bough,* MacMillan, 1956.

Gratus, J., *The False Messiahs,* Taplinger, 1975.

Hoffman, R. Joseph, *Jesus Outside the Gospels,* Prometheus Books, 1984.

Hoffman, R. Joseph, ed, *The Origins of Christianity,* Prometheus Books, 1985.

Hoffman, R. Joseph, and Larue, G. A., editors, *Jesus in History and Myth,* Prometheus Books, 1986.

Martin, Michael, *Is Christianity True?*

McCabe, Joseph, *The Sources of the Morality of the Gospels,* Watts, London, 1914.

McKinsey, Dennis, "Jesus, The Imperfect Beacon," Biblical Errancy (periodical) Issues 24, 25, 27, 28, 1984-1985.

Paine, Thomas, *The Age of Reason,* (first published 1794), Citadel Press, 1974.

Remsburg, John E., *The Christ,* The Truth Seeker Company, New York, circa 1909.

Robertson, A., *Jesus: Myth or History?,* Watts, London, 1949.

Robertson, J. M., *Pagan Christs,* London, 1911.

Robertson, J. M., *Christianity and Mythology,* London, 1910.

Smith, Morton, *Jesus the Magician,* Harper & Row, 1978.

Schweitzer, Albert, *The Mysticism of Paul the Apostle,* MacMillan, 1955.

Schweitzer, Albert, *The Quest of the Historical Jesus,* MacMillan

Stein, Gordon, "The Jesus of History: A Reply to Josh McDowell," The American Rationalist (periodical), 7/82.

Talbert, Charles H., editor, *Reimarus: Fragments,* (Lives of Jesus series), Fortress Press, Philadelphia, 1970.

Till, Farrell, "The Skeptical Review" (periodical), PO Box 617, Canton IL 61520-0617

Walker, Barbara G., *The Woman's Encyclopedia Of Myths And Secrets,* Harper & Row, San Francisco, 1983.

Wells, G. A., *Did Jesus Exist?,* Elek, Pemberton, London, 1975.

Wells, G. A., *The Historical Evidence for Jesus,* Prometheus Books, 1982.

Wells, G. A., *The Jesus of the Early Christians,* Pemberton Books, 1971.

A MATCH NOT MADE IN HEAVEN

Part 9

52

A Match Not Made In Heaven

The following is the text of the wedding ceremony read by Judge Moria Krueger when Annie Laurie Gaylor and I were married. The wedding took place at Freethought Hall in Sauk City, Wisconsin, May 30, 1987.

ANNIE LAURIE AND DAN met in September, 1984, in Chicago. They both had flown there to be guests on Oprah Winfrey's television show, "A.M. Chicago." The topic was freethought.

Dan, who lived in California, had read Annie Laurie's book, *Woe to the Women,* and was very much interested in her activities as owner and editor of the Madison-based newspaper, *The Feminist Connection.* Annie Laurie, who is a native Madisonian and a third generation freethinker active in the Freedom From Religion Foundation headed by her mother, was very much interested in Dan's story of deconversion after seventeen years as a fundamentalist minister.

They met a second time in Milwaukee the following month at the seventh annual Freedom From Religion Foundation convention where Dan was the Saturday evening banquet speaker. At this time they started a correspondence, a lively exchange of ideas, books, clippings and anecdotes which could fill volumes.

In February of 1985 they met again in Nashville during a three-day media blitz and freethought debate. It was there in Nashville, working for a common cause, admiring of each other's work, where their romance began.

Since that time Dan has moved from California to Wisconsin, to be with Annie Laurie and to share a common interest in writing, freethought, feminism, and cats.

More than a century ago Lucy Stone, a leading feminist, and Henry Blackwell took a revolutionary step by remolding marriage into their own ideal of love and equality. They composed a protest which was read aloud at their wedding:

"This act on our part implies no sanction of, nor promise of, voluntary obedience to such of the present laws of marriage as refuse to recognize the wife as an independent, rational being, while they confer upon the husband an injurious and unnatural superiority."

Likewise, Annie Laurie and Dan announce at this time that their wedding today and their continuing marriage shall not be construed as an endorsement of matrimony as an historically unjust institution, nor as a sanction of any remaining marital laws, in Wisconsin or any other state, which may still be unfair.

Annie Laurie and Dan will each retain their respective birth names, and prefer to avoid the labels "husband" and "wife" as much as possible and practical. Annie Laurie and Dan are peers, friends and lovers; and neither of them wishes to be a *manager* of the other, as the term "husband" implies, or the *property* of the other, as the term "wife" has been used.

Annie Laurie and Dan wish it to be known that they are appreciative of your presence here today. A *wedding* is a public testimony for the sake of family and friends, society and legality. But a *marriage* is a very personal thing.

To Annie Laurie and Dan, a *marriage* is an affectionate agreement between equals, a loving contract between peers that requires no blessing above or beyond the mutual respect, admiration and trust of two individuals who cannot imagine not spending the rest of their lives together.

Two notes on the piano, if they are the right two notes, when played together will produce a pleasing sound called *harmony,* which is dependent on the character of each tone, but which is somehow more beautiful than the individuals apart. Anyone who knows Annie Laurie and Dan as individuals knows that neither of them is apt to sacrifice their individuality for *any* reason; but you also know that as a couple united in love and common goals, they most often find themselves thinking and acting "as one," in harmony.

Both of them know that you cannot give or receive love unless you love yourself first. Marriage is not an institution in which the self is *lost:* it is a place where the self is *found.* Annie Laurie and Dan have found themselves, with each other, "at home."

Vows: Do you, (Annie Laurie Gaylor, Dan Barker), take (Dan Barker, Annie Laurie Gaylor) to be your lawfully wedded partner? Do you intend to live the rest of your life with (him/her) in mutual love, respect, and fidelity?

Pronouncement: (Since Dan and Annie Laurie have witnessed, pledged . . . and by the power of the state of Wisconsin, . . .) I now pronounce you a Lovely Married Couple. You may now kiss the groom.

Presentation: It gives me great pleasure to be the first to present to you as a married couple, truly a match *not* made in heaven: Annie Laurie Gaylor and Dan Barker.

Losing Faith in Faith

Index

385